FV

791.43 W747s
WILSON
 SHOW BUSINESS LAID BARE
                        7.95

SHOW BUSINESS LAID BARE

By the author of

I AM GAZING INTO MY 8 BALL

PIKE'S PEAK OR BUST

LET 'EM EAT CHEESE-CAKE

LOOK WHO'S ABROAD NOW

EARL WILSON'S NEW YORK

THE SHOW BUSINESS NOBODY KNOWS

EARL WILSON

SHOW BUSINESS LAID BARE

G. P. PUTNAM'S SONS, New York

Contents

8 CONTENTS

SHOW BUSINESS LAID BARE

Introduction

PORNOGRAPHY must go and should go.

Only a few of us know how far the peddlers of obscenity have gone in this wild era called the New Permissiveness, which the United States Supreme Court now has undertaken to check.

Show business took the lead in extending liberalism into permissiveness into eroticism into pornography. Now show business is taking the lead in protesting that the Supreme Court is injuring the entertainment industry by giving local communities greater authority in cracking down on pornographic movies and publications. The spokesmen for the moviemakers complain that there'll be widespread unemployment because producers are confused about how far they can go in turning out the popular "realistic" films which almost always involve sex.

But the pages of this book will prove to the most liberal-minded that some control is needed.

As a working newspaperman for half a century, I rebel at censorship. Yet as a close observer of all sections of show business, I know that show business and "the media" will not properly police themselves. They have brought censorship down on their own heads.

Here we have a great motion-picture industry which seems to fascinate itself by glorifying fellatio, cunnilingus, and sodomy. Who could have believed that there would one day be a series of successful films devoted almost entirely to a girl performing oral sex on a man?

Yet in this "liberal" age, the so-called Best People, the thinkers, the scholars, the celebrities, are rushing to see *The Devil in Miss Jones*, *High Rise*, *It Happened in Hollywood*, and *Deep Throat*. The more fastidious will go to see *Last Tango in Paris*, which, despite Marlon Brando, I also consider a dirty picture. This film is a favorite of the sodomists.

On my desk are samples of the sex publications which go hand in hand with show business' leadership.

Swing Magazine, published in California and sold for 50 cents, is dedicated to sex. Its lead article is "Can You Get Too Much?" The conclusion is based on an opinion given by a professor of psychology at the University of Pennsylvania. He says that it is better to avoid being a record breaker and to try for quality rather than for quantity—to aspire to become a sexual gourmet.

Here's a red-backed magazine *Select*, also published in California, sold for $3, which boasts: "6000 Personal Ads of Gals, Guys and Couples Who Want to Meet You. Largest Swingers Contact Magazine. New Jersey Members."

Every state in the Union is represented, with ads, pretty pictures of bare guys and gals: "Studio attorney and wife seek other couples . . . everything goes except pain . . . she lovely, he safe . . . wide range of discreetly uninhibited erotic interests including lingerie and photography . . . available either sex or threesome . . . will travel 200 miles . . . liberal, with good stamina . . . You'll love it . . . I do!"

One page has an additional message: "Oral sex is not fattening."

Then came *Playgirl, The Magazine for Women*, showing pelvic photographs of George Maharis, pubis on display. This would surely lead to more magazines each showing more and more of the private property of the male celebrities. Soon the girls would be hoarding them as the boys once hoarded the *Playboy* center spreads of the girls.

Isn't all this contributing to the outbreak of sadomasochism such as we saw in the mass murders of homosexuals in Houston? Show Business was not responsible there. And its producers of sex-and-violence pictures could justifiably maintain that the movies they made were simply reflecting life (and death) as they occur today. Show Business was, however, on the edge of the Sharon Tate murders in California, "master-minded" by one who thought he was a sex king.

In this book, I have gone into the life of Marilyn Monroe in some detail because I had access to privileged material about the actress who still must be regarded as the most alluring, fascinating and, yes, "glamorous," actress of our time.

Marilyn seemed almost sinful in the late 1950's and early 1960's, when she was the sex symbol, for admitting that she wore no underwear. She outraged certain areas of public decency when she confessed that she secretly posed for a nude calendar picture. Yet that scandalous picture showed no pubic hair. Marilyn was topless just as girls are topless nowadays on some of the beaches in France and England and in America, too. . . . just as topless and no more. Marilyn is almost nun-like in that calendar picture compared to the American girl next door . . . compared even to your sister or daughter . . . today. And all this happened in only about a dozen years.

The country's attitude has changed so much that the old place is hard to recognize.

Marilyn Chambers, one of the oral sex *artistes* who became famous in "explicit sex" pictures after she'd done a soap commercial holding a baby, told me that she was personally outraged by the Supreme Court obscenity guidelines.

"What right has the Supreme Court to try to run my sex life?" she demanded, and she echoed the protests of many of her age and thinking.

It was pointed out that the Supreme Court was only trying to allow local communities to decide exactly what constituted obscenity in films, books and plays.

"It all comes down to sex," she said. "Why should Chief Justice Burger tell me what to do in bed either on the screen or in bed with my husband or anybody else for that matter? It's an individual's right to decide on his sex life, and it's very disheartening to find President Nixon's Court guiding our morals especially after Watergate taught us a lot of things about morals and honesty in Washington! I don't think the public will stand for these restrictions." She added, "It's more dirty tricks."

Miss Chambers, with a zealot's fire, said she stood for more sex ("in a controlled way") both in films and in real life. And that in films it could not be simulated. "It's got to be real sex. The public won't buy the simulated sex any more."

"It doesn't make bad people out of you," she said. "My husband and I experimented with wife-swapping. It didn't work. I'd rather do it with my husband. I do it on screen with other men but I don't do it off screen except with him because I love him."

The Supreme Court did not end the fight. It only started it. My own conviction is that Pornography must and should go. I don't say it will. There are many other reasons that it should go, cited in the following pages.

EARL WILSON

New York
Sept. 1, 1973

Very Free Speech

⚑ ANYTHING can be said now in America—almost anywhere. Vulgarity has taken over, even in the best places and the high places. Comedian Buddy Hackett pioneered in the field of risqué language by using the word "ass" in nightclubs and on the Palace Theater stage—and progressed to the word "fuck" in 1973.* Comedian Don Rickles, another advanced thinker in ribaldry, who got laughs with a sodomy routine, moved into the toilet for some jokes about the same time Buddy Hackett was saying, "What's wrong with saying fuck, lady? Everybody does it." The popularity of these two comedians with what the late comedian B. S. Pulley used to call "venereal material" may have influenced leaders in government to lighten up their speeches with some dirty jokes. U.S. Senators were very free in their free speech, and so was then Mayor John V. Lindsay.

A few nights before the Nixon landslide of November, 1972, I had a revelatory experience. At a dinner of the Police Honor Legion of New York, attended by the police brass and their wives, I heard Comedian Jackie Clark monologize about Zsa Zsa Gabor.

"She went to see her doctor," Jackie Clark recounted, "and he asked whether she'd recently had a checkup.

"She answered, 'No, only Hungarians.' "

I didn't recoil from that joke, but rather liked it. Thinking over that fact, I realized that despite my proclaimed revulsion against dirty-mouth comedians in my column, I was beginning to like comedy that was—well—"in poor taste." I began rationalizing. Why had I changed? I finally worked out a face-saving answer. It wasn't a change in me. It was a change in the times.

"We're having so much vulgarity now that we're accustomed to

* Morris Ernst, the distinguished lawyer and libertarian, claims the distinction of "liberating the word 'fuck' " in 1933, when he won the censorship case against Joyce's *Ulysses*. The late Jake Ehrlich, San Francisco lawyer, also "liberated" the four-letter word in 1960, when he freed Allen Ginsberg's poem, *Howl*, which was temporarily stopped in San Francisco.

it and it doesn't seem vulgar anymore. . . ." That was my thinking.

It reminded me of the time I visited a nudist camp at Sunshine Park, Egg Harbor, New Jersey, and took my clothes off, traipsing around completely naked. For the first half hour, it all seemed horrible. The sights I beheld were very repulsive, and I believed that I must look more repulsive than anybody. But the longer I was naked, the less revolting it seemed, and in about three hours it all became normal. Not only that—I began to see advantages to it and arguments for it. By the sixth hour I was thinking of becoming a full-time year-round nudist. I could envisage nude people riding the buses and subways. It would certainly be more comfortable than wearing clothes, especially in the summer.

My more tolerant attitude toward very free speech was part of the New Permissiveness, the disappearance of morality, to which show business made a major contribution.

Don Rickles' closing night at the Copacabana on Wednesday, April 11, 1973 (and the morning of April 12), was the dirtiest I'd seen, and perhaps the best received. When he started his insult technique several years before, he needed celebrities at the ringside he could heckle. But there weren't always celebrities present. He began to speak of "an Italian guy, a Polish guy, a Jewish guy, or a colored guy" in the audience who were making remarks and observations (which were fictitious, as they were usually dumb lines that he made up). Thus he ridiculed average or "little" people, rather than celebrities, and got laughs from these lines. Whether they were actually funny lines is something else again. Several of my friends declared they weren't humorous; they were just stupid and dirty, and we laughed because they made us feel superior to the people he quoted (and misquoted).

Don's act was almost stream of consciousness. It had no pattern that I could see. "There's a *schmuck* from Pittsburgh! You ever go to Pittsburgh? You see smoke comin' from a broad's *tochis.* I'm a proctologist. The Italian guy says, 'What's a proctologist?' His wife says, 'That's what you're supposed to do to me. Jam it to me.' Jesus, warm up the car, put skates on my ass, and wheel me outa here. . . . Hey, Italian guy, is that the wife? Jesus Christ! What are you laughing about? You married her. Your wife's the type she lays on the bed on her wedding night and says, 'Is that it, Al?' "

He followed his custom of bringing a couple of men to the mike with him and pretending to fall in love with them on the spot. To one, a tall, young, clean-looking, attractive fellow, whom he called Jimmy, Don said as they stood very close, "May I ask you, Jimmy, as a friend, are you taking a leak on me? Take a leak on this fat Greek bastard. . . ."

"Son of a bitch," he said once, "I'm funny! . . . German guy over there. I hope you get the runs and lose your helmet. . . . As Moses said as he stood on top of Mount Sinai, 'Is this where we put the hospital?' . . .

When the comedy team of Bernie Allen and Steve Rossi opened at the Rainbow Grill a few nights later, I was one of the loudest laughers—at some material that a *Variety* reviewer berated for its "tastelessness."

"Hey, do you know that Mayor Lindsay is driving the prostitutes off of Broadway?" was one feed line. . . . "Yeah, I saw him driving two of them down Broadway this afternoon."

"Do you know the answer to birth control?" . . . "No." . . . "That's right!"

"Do you know there's a sex crime committed in New York every sixty seconds?" . . . "Why do you bring that up?" . . . "Got a minute?"

"What do you call a Polack with a thirty-eight IQ?" . . . "An Italian."

Bernie Allen happily discovered a woman at the ringside with an exposed bosom. "Do you have a chest cold, honey?" he asked. "You're all swollen!" Snatching a pack of cigarettes from her table, he threw them into a corner. "Do you know what this is? Cancer! Don't you know that eighty percent of breast cancer is caused by men who smoke?"

"A wife," Bernie insisted, "is an ice cube with a hole in it. I've been married to one for twenty years."

They had one about a nude woman lion tamer who said she could handle the lion better than a man with just her bare body. "But you have to get that lion tamer out of there," she said. Inside the cage, naked, she made friends with the lion who began kissing her all over and getting sexually excited. "Can you do that?" the boss of the circus challenged the male lion tamer. "Yeah! Get that lion out of there!" he shouted.

The spectacle of Senator George McGovern telling a woman and a man to kiss his ass, during tense moments in his Presidential campaign, and his defense of his words prove that speech has become exceedingly free. People even said that George, the firm religionist and man of God, was finally showing some "color." He was becoming humanized.

One incident that I couldn't print in full in my column made a similarly colorful figure out of Mayor John Lindsay of New York. After seeing a TV special about New York City, which had some sketches about crime, mugging, and rape, the mayor went to a party at Sardi's for playwright Neil "Doc" Simon who had written it.

The mayor and his wife were in a convivial mood. The mayor, very sensitive about New York City's reputation, was right in the midst of a campaign to get the TV comedians (like Johnny Carson) to desist from telling mugging jokes.

A friend of mine overheard the mayor tell Simon that he liked three of the five sketches but that two were "shitty."

"How can we get tourists to come to New York when you put that kind of shit on television?" the mayor demanded.

Simon, an extremely sensitive soul, who is uptight even when things are going smashingly with one of his hit shows, managed to say good night and go home. He was "destroyed," his friends said, and he left for the country next day to try to recover from the shock at his home away from New York City. The mayor read of the effect of his remarks on Simon in my column and phoned an apology and explanation to Simon. The playwright told me that "the mayor had had a bad day" and that their friendship was strong as ever. Simon may have been "undone"; but he was again whole and invited the mayor to his next play opening, and the mayor accepted.

The curious part was the mayor's taking a famous four-letter noun and making a six-letter adjective of it.

But Simon got the message.

The Broadway stage maintained its right to free speech with a dreadful "new English version" of Aristophanes' *Lysistrata* by the gifted Cypriot director Michael Cacoyannis. It was his 1955 movie, *Stella,* that made Melina Mercouri an international star. That unfortunate and fearless lady was also the star of *Lysistrata* which had to be seen to be hated. The play program said of Cacoyannis, the winner of many awards, "Not only did he adapt the Aristophanes comedy, but he is also responsible for the lyrics."

And what lyrics! Weeks before the show finally opened, I heard that Miss Mercouri rebelled at some of the language. And

Broadway was reviving an old gag: that girls in the cast were saying, "Who do I have to lay to get out of this show?"

"There are Greek soldiers running around with erections showing in their tunics," I was told. "They're using sticks or rods or something artificial—because these erections are about a foot long!"

Early in the show, Lysistrata appealed to the women of Greece to unite and bring lasting peace.

"If you want to impose lasting peace," she says, "we must agree, unanimously agree, to give up—"

"Give up what?" the women cry. "We'll give up our lives for it. Say the word. What is it?"

"Fucking, that's the word," sings out Lysistrata.

The first night Broadway audience had been prepared for the fact that the Grecian women would be going on a sex strike but hadn't expected it to be stated so bluntly. There was a nervous murmur and some shocked laughter around me.

The Grecian women on stage in front of us didn't answer Lysistrata's proposal.

"What's the matter?" demands Lysistrata. "Will you or will you not do it?"

The women reply in anguished panic. "I would if I could but I can't. . . . Ask anything else, Lysistrata. But not that! Never! . . . But Lysistrata, even if—heaven forbid—we give that up, how do you know there will be peace?"

Lysistrata has the answer. "Next time our men come home, we'll receive them in our sexiest negligees, perfumed and beautifully groomed, and lead them on till they burst their seams. Then we'll say no and they'll be on their knees ready for anything—including peace. Believe me, I know!"

"And what if our husbands should get up and go?"

"God in his infinite mercy has given us hands!" thunders Lysistrata.

The audiences don't like these shows, and the critics detest them. *Lysistrata* ran the same length of time that *The Engagement Baby* lasted back in 1970. That show, by Stanley Shapiro and starring Barry Nelson and Constance Towers, was perhaps a little more shocking because many of us knew Barry Nelson and Constance Towers personally and couldn't quite believe what we heard them saying up there onstage.

It's 7 A.M. They're in bed. Connie's asleep, but Barry's wide awake and restless. He's waked up with an erection.

"What's wrong with you?" Connie asks sleepily.

"I have a hard-on," he says. "I want to fuck you."

She's not in the mood. Barry keeps saying he wants to fuck her. She suggests he do what other husbands do—jog. He refuses to consider it. He wants to fuck. Connie is now sitting up in bed with her head down over her knees trying to keep away from him. He is standing up on the bed, trying to figure out how he can take her despite her coolness. She certainly is not cooperating with his copulating.

"Turn over, or, so help me, I'll do it to you the way you are," he warns her.

"That's impossible," she says.

"Not when you're desperate," he says. "Like the Man of La Mancha, I shall screw the impossible screw."

Barry Nelson told me, when I spoke to him after the show's fast closing, "You should have seen it before we cleaned it up."

But perhaps new depths were reached with the opening in December, 1972, at the Astor Place Theater of *The Bar That Never Closes*, which was described as a "unisex musical." Its advertisements showed a man looking down at his own bare chest on which there is quite clearly, as though it has grown there, a woman's breast. He seems surprised to see it there. That, I take it, is the "unisex" angle.

It was such hard core pornography that some of the first-night critics left after, if not during, the first act. Saul Richman, the publicist, went around trying to find more critics who had the stomach to see the entire show.

Its producers, Albert Poland and Bruce Mailman, had given us *The Dirtiest Show in Town* two years earlier. One critic said that *The Bar That Never Closes* made *The Dirtiest Show in Town* seem like *Rebecca of Sunnybrook Farm* by comparison. In its defense, Clive Barnes of the New York *Times* and Kevin Saunders of ABC-TV spoke well of its Rabelaisian and pornographic aspects.

Again I turn to the script. It tells us of a girl of seventeen losing her virginity and then having so many sex experiences that she wearies of all that and finds perfect bliss in masturbation.

"As she lay writhing on a hooked rug before a roaring fireplace, her fingers grappling her cunt, she opened her eyes to wonder why she was expending so much energy on what had come to seem a senseless melodrama.

"Why involve others at all?

"She went into seclusion to ponder the answer.

" 'Orgasm is the quintessentially private experience,' she reasoned, 'and the notion that we must share it with others is the final corruption of what's left of civilization. The only time that people should fuck is to make babies.'

"Accordingly, she locked herself in . . . had her food delivered and her phone taken out . . . removed all the furniture except for a single mattress which she covered with a black satin sheet. When she gave herself to masturbation, unfathomable worlds opened to her."

On her thirtieth birthday, "as she took herself to her room to masturbate, she was so filled with herself that it seemed no external force could ever impinge upon her again. . . ."

"But, as she reached down to cover her cunt with her hand, the space was slowly suffused with a golden light."

(The stage directions state that taped "ethereal space sounds" are heard.)

"A tall naked man with green skin and long curly violent hair appeared, his red eyes piercing her gaze, his succulent cock throbbing gently." This seems to be a vision, for immediately a man (bare-chested) enters wearing a gilded hat, and pinned to his trousers is a golden phallus. He has interfered with her masturbation plans.

This is God.

"But what are you doing here?" she asks God. . . . He has come to see her, God says. . . . What for? . . . "Why to fuck you, of course," God said and laughed a deep baritone rumble. "To fuck what you have created? That doesn't make sense."

God sank to the floor and sat on the edge of her mattress. "Oh, I haven't created everything." . . . "But if all this is true, why should you want something as limited as fucking?" the girl asks. . . . God unbuttoned the girl's shirt and began to fondle her breast. He made her extremely uneasy.

"The other day," God said, "I thought, 'I haven't been to earth for a while. Let me go see if there's anybody there worth fucking these days. 'I saw nothing but a plethora of such shallow sexuality that it made my cock shrivel. But on second look around, I saw you."

"And you want *me?*" she asked. "I must look a mess."

"When you fuck me, you can have everything you have when you are alone," God said. "Everything." He told her, "you can enter new dimensions of being altogether."

"And what do you get out of it?"

"Just a piece of ass," God said. "My tastes are simple."

"I'm not sure I want to, even if you are God. Why should I give you pussy? How good a fuck can you be? You're still in the form of a man. That thing between your legs is only a cock."

"I can offer you Heaven," God said. As the girl shifted her weight around, God said, "You really do have a nice ass."

Then God said he could make her immortal.

"Earth is the only place in all of creation that has fucking. Its rarity makes it highly prized. I've granted this boon to several others in the course of your history, and if you accept my offer, I will remove you to a planet that you will share with them. Once there, you can have privacy, or the company of the greatest fuckers the world has ever seen. And when I'm in the area, I'll drop by."

"All right," the girl said, as the lights dimmed, soft music played, and God stroked her ankles. "You win. Let's fuck."

God moved forward until he was between her legs, and her hips began to rotate. She put her hands on his shoulders. "Just don't get me pregnant," she said.

That was in the first act; some of the critics felt that was all they needed to see.

Curiously, this was the second time in a couple of weeks that the Supreme Being emerged as sexy in the Broadway and Off-Broadway neighborhood. At a tribute dinner to Frank Yablans, the then thirty-seven-year-old president of Paramount Pictures, one of the speakers related that St. Peter came down to earth and proposed a colossal film project to director Billy Wilder.

"We're going to give you an all-star cast we'll bring down from heaven," promised St. Peter. "Humphrey Bogart, Gary Cooper, John Barrymore, Lionel Barrymore, Alan Ladd, Fatty Arbuckle, Lou Costello, Buster Keaton, Al Jolson, Douglas Fairbanks, Will Rogers, Eddie Cantor, Ed Wynn. . . .

"For writers," St. Peter continued, "we'll give you Hemingway,

George S. Kaufman, William Faulkner, Jim Tully, even Shake-speare if you want him. . . ."

"Sounds good," Billy Wilder had to agree.

"To help you as producer, we can get you Walt Disney, L. B. Mayer, David O. Selznick, Spyros Skouras, Harry Cohen. You name 'em and we'll get 'em," St. Peter said. "Of course God will be the executive producer."

"Naturally." Wilder nodded. "You've mentioned everybody but the leading lady. Hell, you could get Marilyn Monroe, Sarah Bernhardt, Jean Harlow. Say, Jean Harlow'd be terrific. What a comeback!"

St. Peter stammered and got nervous. "Well, you see," he stuttered, "G-God happens to have a girlfriend. . . ."

The most vulgar comedy spoken today is heard at the Friars Club stag luncheons in New York and Hollywood. They are held to "honor" some show business celebrity who always turns out to love cunnilingus, though he does not put down fellatio, and these terms are translated into modern lockerroomese. He of course has had and still may have gonorrhea and once gave his little sister that disease. He is no stranger to syphilis and in a pinch he will do it to a nanny goat. The great men who have received this honor include Johnny Carson, Ed McMahon, Milton Berle, George Jessel, Jack Benny, George Burns, and, I must confess, myself.

But these of course are "closed" to the public and to women, although Milton Berle tape-recorded the horrendous vulgarities spoken about him and hurried to a restaurant to play it back for his mother, Sandra, who was brought up in show business and was broad-minded. Maurice Chevalier was one of the club's pet guests of honor. His lower lip was already famous in the singing world. The comedians made much of this in their discourses on his fondness for cunnilingus.

Most of this is much too raw for the daily newspapers. At the luncheon for Ed McMahon, the MC was young David Steinberg, who was getting married. All I was able to print was the sanitized line, by Steinberg, that Johnny Carson had been a friend of Ed's for eighteen years.

"Which shows that Johnny finds announcers easier to get along with and keep than wives."

"In your marriage," Carson told Steinberg, "I wish you all the luck that I have had." That was the innocent beginning and then. . . .

Some of the material was more than Rabelaisian and had been carefully written before the luncheon. Comedian Fred Roman said McMahon "was born in Boston, lived in Philadelphia, and died at the St. Regis Maisonette." (McMahon had opened a café act there the night before.)

On came Carson. "Ed has always had a great love for children . . . according to the Philadelphia Police Department. He was arrested once for sodomy. It was an unusual case—because he was alone at the time."

There were references to Ed's affection for the Clydesdales (horses) that pull the Anheuser-Busch beer wagons for which he did commercials. There were numerous jocular mentions of alleged sycophancy. "From the beginning," Carson said, "I always wanted Hugh Downs for the job. But Ed auditioned for it and got the job after they completed the operation—which was removing Ed's tongue from my ass."

The luncheon was held on a November day when rain swept the neighborhood of the Americana Hotel in sheets driven by the wind. It was difficult for the guests to buck the wind and rain to get there. Therefore, there was appreciation for another Carson remark: "It's a shitty day and a shitty luncheon for a shitty guest of honor."

Always the speakers refer to others than the guest of honor, and they never fail to emphasize the preoccupation of the celebrities with their penises. "He," they once said of one big name, "has his cock in his hand more than Portnoy." David Steinberg, introducing popular and good-looking William B. Williams, the disc jockey, said, "A lot of people wondered why he never made the transition from radio to TV. When you see him, you'll know."

The Friars out-Friarsed themselves with their luncheon for Henny Youngman on February 16, 1973, when Milton Berle, who'd come from Beverly Hills to be roastmaster, opened the cannonading by saying "This is the Friars' answer to *Deep Throat* because we are honoring a big prick!"

Leading the laughing for that one was the guest of honor, who later admitted that his small grandson was in the audience. "He's got to get used to these things," Henny said.

Berle was at his obscene best. "I have been looking forward to

this event with all the anticipation of getting a blow job by
————," he said, naming a middle-aged English actress not noted
for her sex appeal. "I think fondly of Henny Youngman every
night just before I apply my Preparation H," he continued. Berle
stopped to pay his respects to the luncheon food served by the
Hilton Hotel.

"The chicken tasted like it was fucked to death," he said. He
resumed about Youngman. "This man who was sworn at,
maligned and spit on—and rightly so—this man who to me is the
funniest man since Troy Donahue . . . he was born of poor but
stupid parents . . . he had an uncle who used to put chocolate on
his schlong and then call Henny and say 'Wanta popsicle?' . . .
and even to this day Henny can't eat fudge unless it has nuts on it
. . . this man who, when he played the 'Star-Spangled Banner,'
the audience sat down. . . . He fought sex for twenty years and he
finally licked it. . . . He took on anything with hair. . . . He once
humped Mitch Miller's beard. . . .

"In the 1930's," Berle said, "Henny Youngman met Milton
Berle and said, 'You're my idol.' He stole my act, and then I was
idle. He was a young up-and-going-down-on comedian. He was
king of the one-liners because the *shmuck* can't remember two
lines. He's very witty. If a broad bit his lob, he couldn't ad-lib an
'Ouch!' . . . He wanted to get into a very private club of which I
was a member. To try to put him in his place, I said, 'But, Henny,
they don't need you. They've already got one cocksucker in the
club.' He said, 'But suppose you get sick?' Everybody is saying
Henny Youngman is sexy. Why, he hasn't had a blow job in so
long he forgot what it tastes like."

One of the slickest performers at Friars' roasts is Red Buttons,
who always comes prepared with new and special material. It was
well after 2:30 P.M. when Berle got to him, saying, "This next guy
is known as the comedians' comedian, which means that there are
about eight guys that like him."

"I'm thrilled to be here," Red Buttons said, "for a guy who still
jerks off in the movies, and if you don't believe it, ask any of the
stewardesses on TWA. He had an acupuncture operation—it
wasn't exactly acupuncture—he tried to fuck a porcupine in
Fallsburgh . . . in Holland he stuck his finger in a dike and she
kicked him in the balls. . . ."

Milton Berle snatched the mike back into his hands. "And now
our guest of honor—the piss de resistance . . . he's never been

honored like this before, and after you hear his stupid speech, you'll understand why. . . .

"Getting one of these awards," Berle said, "is like getting hemorrhoids. Eventually every asshole gets one."

I find in quickly reviewing my notes that I omitted an imaginative story from Norm Crosby that, though a piece of fiction, fitted nicely into the horrible picture they'd drawn of Youngman.

Youngman had gone to a druggist for a quart of Spanish fly. The druggist protested loudly, saying a few drops were enough to arouse and prolong the sexual excitement of anybody. Youngman insisted upon a quart, declaring that the druggist might as well give him a quart, because he would only get it somewhere else. The druggist gave him a quart.

"Next day Youngman dragged himself into the drugstore, his clothes almost ripped off, exposing himself, his sexual instrument a torn and bloody mess frightening to look upon. Youngman was calling, "Help, help, help!" He gasped, "Liniment, liniment!"

The druggist rushed for liniment to apply to his torn sexual apparatus.

"No, no, not there!" Youngman said. "Here . . . my arm . . . it's for my arm. The broads never showed up!"

When Milton Berle finally brought Youngman to the mike, each and every star on the dais arose from his seat and walked out, leaving him there on an empty platform. It was not a new trick; Youngman had seen it happen before, and when somebody said, "Please, please, don't walk out on the guest of honor," he wasn't disturbed. He began making his acceptance speech and the guests returned to their seats.

The free speech reached the point that the New York *Times*' modest little house organ, "Winners and Sinners," chastised an unnamed somebody on March 8, 1973, for permitting a headline in the February 25 theatrical section that read "Why Is the Co-Eatus Always Interruptus?"

It sounded like a dirty joke, and it was undoubtedly intended to be one by John Simon, critic for *New York* magazine, in an article about Luis Buñuel's *The Discreet Charm of the Bourgeoisie*. The film was about some decadent bourgeois always having their dinner plans interrupted. Thus the headline "Why Is the Co-Eatus Always Interruptus?" had nothing to do with having one's sex act, or coitus, interrupted, as one might have expected at first glance.

The *Times'* rebuke said, "You can picture the critic giggling when the idea hit him, and then he giggled three times more in the course of the article. At best it's a less-than-fair pun, and it's pure vulgarity. The world has moved, and once-verboten words are now printable. In a story about 'Deep Throat' it is permissible to speak factually of 'seven acts of fellatio, four of cunnilingus and a half-dozen other sex acts' though only a few years ago it wouldn't have been. The demarcation line of vulgarity has certainly moved but we would be well-advised to stay a fair distance behind it. In that area we are not in competition with the underground press."

Probably the most monumental advancement in free speech in our time was the admittance into polite conversation of the word "fuck."

Maybe it's wrong to characterize it as "polite" conversation. But certainly no man or woman is expelled now for blurting out the word that aroused a whole nation when Kenneth Tynan dropped it into an interview on the BBC back in 1965. Questioned about the propriety of showing intercourse on the stage, he said, "I think there are very few rational people to whom the word 'fuck' is particularly revolting or totally forbidden. . . ."

He very soon found out that there were millions who objected, but he had them at a disadvantage, because the word they objected to was so objectionable they couldn't print it.

"He used the four-letter word for fornication. . . ."

"He used the four-letter word for act of love. . . ."

More and more I heard the word used by women, and strangely, women used it without shame or hesitation while men apologized. I heard men say, "I have to use a word here that you may find objectionable," but I never heard a woman apologize for it. To women, it was out with it, and no apologies or regrets.

Then one day somebody slipped into my mail a treatise on the word "fuck" entitled "The Intellectual Fuck."

Somebody had finally given a lot of thought to that word.

The late comedian Lenny Bruce, a leader in the use of obscenities, might have been a great hero of free speech had he lived. Narcotics cut him down when he was on the threshold of martyrdom. Buddy Hackett has been more clever, and never bitter, in his handling of the risqué. When Buddy and Eddie Fisher were appearing together at the Palace Theater in New York, Buddy repeatedly attempted to get Eddie to repeat some of his shocking words. Eddie would look down at the floor as though embarrassed and never repeated them.

"Go ahead, Eddie, it's easy," Buddy would say. "Say it once and you'll always say it."

One night the late famous hotelkeeper Jennie Grossinger was in Buddy's audience at the Palace. "Hi, Jennie," Buddy said. "Remember when you paid me thirty-five dollars a week and told me not to talk dirty? Well, if I'd listened to you, I'd still be talkin' clean and gettin' thirty-five dollars a week."

Something should be said, though, for the clean-talking comedians. Bob Hope has probably the world's greatest collection of risqué stories, which he preserves only in his memory, but he never uses them on stage. His material is at times a little bit blue but never dirty. Yet he is the best paid of all the comedians, proving that you don't have to be dirty. Bob admires other comedians and has the ability to laugh uproariously at a joke of theirs which he first used a quarter of a century ago. The comedienne that Bob seems to appreciate most is Phyllis Diller whose "dirty" jokes mostly concern her dirty kitchen. Pearl Bailey, Carol Channing and Kay Ballard also "work clean" and are in the top money brackets with such clean workers as Marty Allen and Mort Sahl. Phyllis Diller's jokes mostly spoof Phyllis Diller. She said that she was arrested for singing topless "but they dropped the charges—for insufficient evidence."

The Genitalia Generation

WE are members of the Genitalia Generation.

Not the Age of Aquarius, but the Age of Genitals! Forgive my explicitness. But the whole so-called civilized world is exposing itself. A few years ago much of it could have been arrested for indecent exposure.

Its privates are no longer kept private. They're pubic, public, and published as well.

I have hesitated to write this, fearing that I would appear to be crude or lewd. But on looking about and listening, I see that virtually all restrictions have disappeared. Crudity and lewdness scarcely exist among the Genitalia Generation. "Anything goes" in the New Permissiveness which preceded the Age of Genitals.

I keep pulling back from the typewriter as I peck out the word "genitalia" as though it were dirty, and I suppose it was, a decade ago. It was a word we hardly ever spoke aloud, and we mispronounced it as often as we pronounced it. We didn't come right out in conversation and say "genitals" either.

Now one not only openly discusses genitals, but often shows them as well. "Shows" them, reveals them, displays them, exhibits them. And from the polite "genitalia" has come the vulgar but complimentary adjective "ballsy." One of the grandest compliments that can be paid a woman in one part of our society is to call her "a ballsy broad." What a sorry but memorable age this is—the Age of Genitals.

To blame for much of this are the exhibitionistic free souls of show business, the producers, the writers, entrepreneurs, as well as the actors.

Swinging show business has led the way in this wild hedonistic adventure. Its front runners are the flamboyant, freakish friends of yours and mine, whose conduct we sometimes deplore. But remembering that history frequently finds conservatism has been wrong, we do not say they are not right in their advanced views. If they want to worship the genitalia in the Age of Genitals, maybe they are right. If the leading female movie stars are to be girls with educated tongues most gifted at the art of fellatio, we show business buffs must be prepared to accept it. We must grant that there is a place for films depicting hard-core pornography in which we are supposed to be viewing actual penetration of a vagina by a penis or a reasonable facsimile thereof. It must not be "simulated" or it is not "art." Do you have that fairly clear now? That is important.

Are we beginning to get bored with genitalia? One would hope not, of course. However, an actress notorious for her sexuality walked out of a porno film the other night, remarking with a shrug, "After all, there are just so many ways to fuck."

She hadn't seen any new ways, so the picture was "no good." We find ourselves more fascinated with trifles such as "transvestite boutiques."

"Let Your Dreams Come Alive at Michael Salem's Miss Julia's TV Boutique," said an ad in *Penthouse* magazine. "Sensations in lingerie, sportswear, foundations, wigs and shoes in regular and larger sizes—in finest fabrics, FOR MEN."

Operating legally and openly, at 135 East Forty-ninth Street, in the expensive Madison Avenue section, Michael Salem caters to heterosexuals who happen to derive sexual gratification from wearing women's attire. "We have accumulated about ten thousand names of transvestites which we keep in a bank vault to save them from possible embarrassment," he says.

Known as TV's, an abbreviation for transvestites, they thrill to the feel and touch of clingy, lacy, satiny garments. Their wives frequently know, understand, and sympathize. They pay about $50 for a pair of silicone-filled bosom pads that fit into brassieres made just for men.

"The bosom pads bounce up and down just like a woman's when they walk," Salem says. "And that is what they want and what they like."

Sometimes they come bravely, sometimes they come furtively, into the "TV boutique" for the cross-dressing attire, as it is also called. They let their hands lovingly touch such specialties as padded girdles curved around the hips and derriere. There's also a Merry Widow, which is a corselet that includes a waist cincher, a strapless brassiere, and a panty girdle, "all for $18.50."

Men's cosmetics are heavier than women's. They cover the hair and beard and remove the deep lines, making the man's face look softer and more girlish.

The prize package, however, is the gaff, which is a man's G-string. It's also called the basket. It holds the gentleman's penis and testicles. Sometimes Kotex, Tampax, or other sanitary napkins are inserted in the basket, and this is all smoothed and flattened so that the front of the gaff resembles the front of a vagina. Price: $6.

Within the show business neighborhood of Times Square, there developed another manifestation of the Genital Generation—the procuring of boys as young as ten or twelve by pimps who peddle them to middle-aged males willing to pay $50 to $100 to sodomize a tender youngster.

Revolting as it was, the traffic in chicken, as the boys were called, was there to be seen by anybody who had the stomach to look for it. I saw the customers, usually well dressed and prosperous in appearance, with an air of supersophistication, lingering watchfully around the juice bars patronized by homosexuals. They were waiting to be brought a fresh youthful tidbit by one of the pimps working the boy market. The black procurers bringing in "tender chicken" for these perverts with a specialized taste considered themselves a cut above the procurers who had a stable of ordinary girl whores.

Old as history, this practice that had been kept secret or at least under cover, suddenly burst into the open with the New Permissiveness, and the purveyors of boy flesh boldly discussed it with a defiant attitude, saying, "You're not going to stop boy prostitution any more than you're going to stop girl prostitution."

The chicken-hawks, as the middle-aged customers were called, were so satiated that an eighteen-year-old was considered "tough," or old. Much more desirable was real young stuff about twelve or thirteen suitable for raping. The kids who served them, often Puerto Ricans and blacks, weren't genuine homosexuals. They were just peddling their buttocks for the money they could get.

Almost always the gay sophisticates on the buying end were white men with money. They drew no color line, though they preferred, as they said, white meat, but black meat was acceptable. As for the black boys, they often thought of themselves as getting back at the white race for past wrongs by taking a sucker's money again and again and making him like the treatment so much that he would suffer emotionally when the black boy ended it by leaving him and taking along his wallet and his best clothes. And probably his TV set.

Intriguing things like this—plus *Deep Throat, High Rise, It Happened in Hollywood, The Devil in Miss Jones* and of course *Last Tango in Paris*—were happening which made a member of the Genitalia Generation laugh out loud at the stories in the newspapers that the permissiveness pendulum was swinging back toward nonpermissiveness.

That prophecy in early 1973 was just preposterous. There were more genitals on display than ever. In its excessiveness, the Age of Genitals had just about made sex meaningless.

I will cite an actual conversation. An ordinary-looking actor of about thirty-five leaned his elbows on the bar at Sardi's, the famous show business restaurant. He said to the pretty girl with him, "You girls have just about ruined sex for me."

"I thought we'd improved it," she said.

"I don't mean you and I don't mean this place," he said. "But in nearly any place where there are girls, especially in the singles places, I can have almost any girl in the place, and I don't have to ask her, I don't even have to buy her a drink."

"Girls in show business do hop into bed pretty freely," she said.

"Not just in show business," he said. "But especially in show business. You've made your commodity too available."

"But," the girl argued, "I get turned on by porno movies and talking about fellatio and cunnilingus and new positions to try and group sex. That made sex better for me."

"Not for me," the man said. "You girls have taken the chase out of it. When there's no resistance, who wants it? You've made a fuck too easy to come by!"

"You're just making a speech." The girl lit a cigarette. "If you really mean you don't want it, I'd better make other plans for tonight."

"I don't mean you've ruined it *completely*," he said. "But when it's so easy to get, some of the thrill is missing. You know, for a while, I thought something was happening to me." As he paid the check, he asked, "Your place or mine?"

"Yours," she said. "My roommate's got a visitor tonight."

"Anybody she knows?" he said as they got into a cab.

As a spectator at the ringside of show business, I've seen the Sex Revolution grow into a Sex Riot. Since *Deep Throat* and *Last Tango*, it's become wilder. At the beginning of 1973, I was naïve enough to believe that the pendulum was swinging back. The New York *Times* headlined a London story EUROPEANS ACT TO CURB SEX MARKET saying that "free-wheeling Copenhagen closed clubs featuring live sex shows," driving some of the entertainers to do their live-sexing over in Stockholm, Sweden.

And *Variety*, the show business paper, had a headline:

NEW MORAL WAVE SWEEPS ARMY—NOW
IT'S PASTIES FOR GI CLUBS' GO-GO GALS.

But that was from Worms, Germany. There was no moral wave in the United States. The whole country was salivating with happiness at the opportunity of paying $5 a ticket to see Marlon Brando sodomizing Maria Schneider in *Last Tango in Paris*. It was making jokes about his using butter, and wouldn't margarine do just as well?

Women's Wear Daily solemnly reported that Mr. Brando had his pants off showing his bare back side and some of his front side when he had anal intercourse with Miss Schneider in the first version. But he thought better of it; perhaps he was moved by "the moral wave." In a later filming, he appeared to be penetrating her with his pants on, but only open. Such was the thinking in the upper echelons of our major art form in the year of Our Lord 1973. This was the film that some of the most respected movie critics believed to be the greatest film ever made. Columnist Hank Grant in the Hollywood *Reporter* wondered, however, what would be the final fate of the frontal nudity pictures of Marlon Brando that were scissored from the film. Shouldn't the precious pictures of Mr. Brando's instrument be stored in some great Pubis Preserve? Mr. Brando was surely the Mr. Big of the Genitalia Generation up to then.

Correction! He would have been if he hadn't been scissored out. The prize went to Burt Reynolds for his center spread in *Cosmopolitan* magazine, a photograph which led to many jokes such as "What big hands he has!" Then came George Maharis completely and fully on display in *Playgirl* magazine, everything showing, and girls at cocktail parties saying, "Did you see so-and-so's cock in that center spread?"

Besides showing George Maharis' genitals ("Four Page Center-fold Bold and Beautiful George Maharis"), *Playgirl* had a full color-page picture of a vagina with an article by Gwen Gibson, "Radical Breakthrough in Sex Therapy." It told how a sensuous woman could achieve greater fulfillment by strengthening her sexual muscles with the use of Vagitone, a small, cylindrical device that provides electrical stimulation when inserted in the vagina. Its successful use would improve "the squeeze and grip" for both parties in the sex act, according to Gwen Gibson.

Genitals were everywhere and on display everywhere. "Let it all hang out" was a literate statement.

Deep Throat, the first dirty movie I ever saw, was so vulgar, so inexcusable, so lacking in merit of any kind—and yet so successful commercially—that it proved beyond doubt that the pendulum, instead of swinging back, was swinging farther ahead into eroticism.

I went to see it partly from duty, but largely, I confess, from curiosity. Thousands of others saw it, I'm sure, not because their morals were eroded, not because they were degraded, but because they'd heard it was the ultimate example of pornography on film and *had* to find out for themselves.

Suppose I were to try to explain this phenomenon of the Age of Genitals to a future generation. . . .

"You see, back in the years 1972 and 1973, when Richard Nixon was trying to end the war in Vietnam . . . and get reelected President . . . and inaugurated . . . and bring the prisoners of war home . . . and just before Watergate . . . there was a movie actress called Linda Lovelace . . . and she wasn't especially beautiful . . . but she had something . . . not a talent . . . really a kind of a trick . . . she had a large mouth . . . and a deep throat . . . and she could take a man's very large erect penis and hold it in her mouth and throat until he ejaculated . . . and because of the way she kissed it and sucked it and made him come to a climax, Linda Lovelace became a motion-picture star."

"Jesus Christ!" I can hear the future generation exploding. "Is that how one became a movie star in 1972 and '73?"

"That was one of the ways."

When you looked at it that way, Linda Lovelace was really one of the most remarkable women of our time, signing autographs, posing for pictures, giving interviews; she was a genuine celebrity. Linda and *Deep Throat* inspired many a joke and contributed to the frivolity of the year. Inasmuch as the plot of *Deep Throat* involved Linda Lovelace's having her clitoris somehow mislocated in her throat, making it impossible for her to have an orgasm until she had nine inches of penis in her mouth, Linda was the subject of more or less serious discussions in many of the better, cultivated homes.

"Poor Linda Lovelace," I heard one girl say. "When I hear her story, I get all choked up."

In one Park Avenue penthouse, Linda Lovelace's clitoris was discussed across the dinner table by a seventy-year-old hostess, who confessed to her guests that she learned something every day.

"I never knew anything about the importance of the clitoris," this lady admitted. "To me it was always my husband jumping on and off. *Now* they tell me!"

I thought back to the 1940's when I first wrote the word "falsies" in a newspaper and shocked many of the sedate. Here was a woman candidly seeking advice at a dinner table about manipulating her clit! What a moralistic leap in thirty years. Linda Lovelace's performance of fellatio on the oversized gentlemen in *Deep Throat* led to other types of jokes. At a luncheon of the Dutch Treat Club in mid-1973, I heard a most scholarly speaker say, "The three most dangerous things in the world are an Irishman with a quart of whiskey, a Jew with a law degree, and an Italian with an erection."

Cheap, dirty *Deep Throat* made a much bigger mark on show business than it should have. I will have much more to say about it and its companion pictures in a later chapter. It brought into the open some sex practices not generally understood by some people. It may have contributed to more candid language—and I don't say that was good.

Bette Midler, the protégée of Johnny Carson, was the new pet comedienne in Las Vegas. Appearing at the Sahara, Miss Midler was, as they say, campy and a little crazy and a little shocking.

"You'll like this song," she announced as she was beginning one number. The Hollywood *Reporter* quoted her as explaining, "I shake my tits a lot."

Tits!

We hadn't quite got accustomed to Buddy Hackett saying "ass." (In 1973, Buddy also started saying "fuck" in his act.) But there it was, from a presumed lady, the word "tits." It was, until this Genitalia Generation, a word you just didn't say. There were two schools of thought about the propriety of such a remark among the show business specialists I know.

"What do you want her to say—teats? You talk about a cow's tits, don't you? Nobody gets uptight about that." That was one opinion.

The other was: "Oh, maybe she should have said boobs. That might have been nicer. That's what Jacqueline Susann calls hers on the talk shows."

Nobody thought it was wrong of her to talk about shaking them to start with, which would have been my opinion, until I thought it over when I started asking myself, "What *is* wrong about it?"

Everywhere I looked, I found sex breaking through the old boundaries. There were occasional forays of righteousness that were forgotten. An editor told me he had worked on a book with an actress whose confessions were racy. Talking to a well-known woman interviewer in TV, he mentioned that the actress wrote well.

"How was she in bed?" the TV woman interviewer asked instantly.

The editor swore to me that he hadn't even considered seducing her or vice versa. "I didn't know you were supposed to do that to your lady writers," he said. "Where did I go wrong?"

The slice of show business that most graphically typifies the Age of Genitals is what is now called burlesk. In these few theaters on Broadway and in other parts of America, these stripteasers actually show the customers the inside of their sexual apparatus and manipulate themselves. They are, of course, completely nude, "frontally," as they say, their pubic hair being about all they have on. They squat open-legged in what they call beaver and spread beaver positions. In one of these open positions, with everything exposed that can be exposed, they say in the language of burlesk that they are "taking a picture."

Meeting and interviewing one of these ladies, who had "a star-spangled vagina," made up and coiffured especially for patriotic occasions, was one of my greatest journalistic achievements and will be described in a later chapter in detail. It was an amazing revelation to this farm boy who hadn't seen burlesque since a "flash" and a peek at a suddenly bared nipple was "goin' about as fur as a girl could go."

Sex (Movies) Can Be Fun

 ON the crowded terrace of the Hotel Carlton in Cannes, down on the rainy Riviera, the film distributors of the world sip their drinks, appraise the buttocks and breasts of the ambitious starlets, and haggle with producers for their "product." After attending several of the Cannes Film Festivals, I've had to recognize the truth of an observation by an Englishman who declared, "Americans were slow getting into making dirty pictures, but once they started, they soon made the dirtiest dirty pictures of anybody." A British woman star lamented to me, "You know, we don't have the privilege of seeing as many pornographic pictures as you Americans do!"

At the 1973 Festival, I met a friend in the Carlton lobby who said, "Jesus Christ, did you see that ad in that French trade paper for a picture they're showing here? It's got a guy's head and long tongue right in a dame's vagina!"

I looked for it, and sure enough, there was the outline of a woman's midsection, and in the crotch area was Satan, with horns, and his long tongue stuck out in licking position.

"CE SOIR à 22:00," the ad said, "at Star II Theater.

"Excellent, divertissant, sophistiqué . . . Un grand film . . . Peut et doît être presenté dans presque tous les pays du monde."—Cine-Interworld.

Yes, sophisticated, diverting, should be seen in nearly every country . . . in color from "Saliva Films. . . ."

"Saliva Films!" That had to be a joke, I thought.

And the picture?

"THE BEST OF THE NEW YORK EROTIC FILM FESTI-VAL . . . A collection of prize-winning and specially selected films presented at the annual New York Erotic Film Festival. The Official Judges included Andy Warhol, Sylvia Miles, Terry Southern, Milos Forman, Xaviera Hollander, Holly Woodlawn, Gore Vidal, Executive Director of the Festival: Ken Gaul."

Right from my own backyard! Not wishing to be associated with such a project when it was in New York, I'd avoided seeing it. But now that it was one of the lures of the Cannes Festival, although not a part of it, I felt I must attend, even on a Saturday night when there were several so-called major events scheduled. Knowing something of the popularity of such material in this Era of Eroticism, I went early to the Star Theater over on Rue d'Antibes but not any too early. For I was literally pushed, shoved, and crushed till it hurt.

Ropes had been stretched from the theater door out into the street to form aisles, and in the crowd, I was pushed against one of the ropes which was cutting the back of my neck. My yells—in English—didn't especially deter the French mob, but I escaped injury.

Pushing my way in, I found I was in a nest of a couple dozen Italians who in their passionate interest in this eroticism, were literally breathing down my neck.

There was an effort to keep it light and amusing. Ken Gaul, the executive director, said it involved "some men, some women, and some who aren't sure yet," and that there was "some balling" and "good head" (fellatio and cunnilingus) and that in three and a half hours of porno film, "a lot of sperm was being spilled." We soon saw a short whose title was "Sexual Schtick or the Perils of Doing It Quick."

One memorable scene was sadly Chaplinesque or Marx Brothersian. Two not very attractive young people meet in a lonely uninviting room under a boardwalk reached by a subway. It's an ugly rainy day, and there are a couple of clandestine phone calls first to confirm "The Appointment" (which is also the name of the short). Then they're together, and they tear at each other ferociously to get each other's clothes off. The speed is raced up to make it ridiculous. To me there was little of interest in it except the pace which made it absurd. At the end of the affair, they get dressed at the same high speed, and the young man says, "Next week, same time?"

A girl goes supermarket shopping—for vegetables—in another short. She carefully chooses bananas, tomatoes, large pickles, and cucumbers. And there's no doubt that she's thinking of using the big pickle or cucumber as a substitute for a penis later. And indeed we do see her inserting it in her vagina later, first, however, putting a condom on it and lubricating the tip with Vaseline.

The Italian contingent back of me hooted at that.

There was a girl in another short with athletic leanings. She seemed to be turned on by her brother, who was observed (through the window) playing baseball. She kissed his jockstrap which she brought from a closet, and then she sat down on some kind of a ball that seemed to be part of his athletic equipment. She appeared to be caressing it with her sex instrument.

Everybody was entitled to his or her fantasy. A black stripteaser titillated herself by looking at her own body, feeling herself, and finally masturbating.

While I received no thrill from the black stripper's autoeroticism (it used to be known as jerking off before we discovered such terms as "the sexual subculture"), it set me to wondering about narcissism. I may have written about it a thousand times without understanding it. When a gal is described as narcissistic, does that mean she's the kind that slinks around her room naked, admiring her face and breasts and falling in love with her derriere and pubic area and finally falling down on the bed playing with herself? Marilyn Monroe used to get described as narcissistic almost every day when she was keeping reporters waiting for her to come out of her bedroom for interviews. But I would have been willing to fight anybody who said she was in there making love to herself in the manner that I have not quite fully described.

"Judge" Sylvia Miles later told me that she didn't assist with the judging in the Second Erotic Film Festival because she considered herself more an actress than a critic—but that she thought the maiden effort was worthwhile.

"There was that wonderful short with a great musical score where a girl's eating an orange," Sylvia Miles said. "Do you remember where you just see her tongue and her teeth and she's eating and sucking an orange? Do you remember it?" I didn't remember it, which must make me very unpopular with the citrus fruit world!

In Cannes, especially at the Carlton, you receive a day's program in the mailbox in your room door every morning, which serves to hustle you out of bed and off to the screenings beginning at ten or even earlier. Try to picture yourself having the continental breakfast at nine and stepping out to see *The Diary of a Nymphomaniac* at ten. That was part of the schedule for Wednesday, May 16, 1973. But you could see another film if you preferred, for example: *Fleshpot on 42d St.* Or at ten thirty: *La Maman et la Putain* (The Mother and the Whore).

It was difficult not to have sex on your mind when you read *Cinema TV Today*, an entertainment industry paper, often left in your mailbox. Perusing this with your orange juice and eggs, you might have read this:

> CANNES: Director David Greene is to make a comedy film in Chicago which will be based on the play "The Little Boxes."
>
> The light-hearted story is about two girls who live together as a couple and have to rent a boy to show off whenever either set of parents turns up for a visit.
>
> Greene, whose film "Godspell" opened the Cannes Festival, is fascinated by the question of bi-sexuality, and though his new project will be essentially a situation comedy, he believes that more and more films will take up the subject seriously.

What a title—*The Little Boxes*! With all these offerings to select from, I hankered to see a supposed documentary: *Massage Parlor*.

Two naked masseuses were massaging a smiling young man who seemed, in an illustrated pamphlet about the movie, to be enjoying the rubbing he was getting.

I thought, "What a fitting opening!" A bed, with several pillows on it. That was all. But how eloquent.

There's this young journalist Per, flying to Munich, who meets Sonya, and they have a wild night together in Istanbul. Sonya gives him an unforgettable massage; she's as good a masseuse as she is a lover. She sort of took over the seducing. The next morning Sonya has disappeared, leaving no forwarding address or clues to her address. Now Per has to find her—for more massages.

Fortunately for Per, his editors decide he is their massage parlor expert, and they are going to do a series on massage parlors. He is assigned to investigate all the massage parlors which gives him the opportunity to get massages everywhere while looking for the talented fingers of Sonya.

In one massage parlor, a beautiful young masseuse loosens him up.

"My mother's my competition," she confesses, as Mama comes in to finish him off. . . . "Can I play with both of them?" he says. . . . "Forget it . . . it's too late."

Per gets into a big-time VIP massage therapy operation where politicians scream at each other while naked at lunchtime. Where else would Sonya be but right here with all the bare-assed VIP's? Per and Sonya are reunited in the massage parlor; then she disappears. She is reported taking over as boss of the massage parlor in Rome. Will Per and Sonya get together for another massage in a massage parlor in Rome? Watch tomorrow's installment at the same time, same station.

The Swedes came up with a comedy, *Troll,* directed by Vilgot Sjoman, who directed *I Am Curious (Yellow)*, and starring Borje Ahlstedt, who also had the leading part in *Curious*. But here was a picture with a plot and what a plot!

Forget all the tired old plots of all the tired old sex films. For five years, Maja and Richard have been happily married. But they've never made love to each other. Maja has a wild obsession: Maja thinks you die when you do it.

Friends try to tell Maja you don't die when you do it, so Maja and Richard see a marriage counselor, a minister, who tells them they had better consummate their marriage, or they'll break it.

They're happy as they are, without lovemaking. And anyway, who in hell got them to see a marriage counselor? Their good friends Lillemor and Sture!

They decide to invite Lillemor and Sture to dinner and to get them into bed making love, and they will die, and it'll serve them right! But Richard begins to doubt Maja's obsession a little. Crushed, she heaves him out, dresses up as a prostitute, snags a John, and is ready to go to bed with him. She is not only going to lose her virginity, but according to her understanding, she's also going to die. . . .

Well, as though you hadn't guessed, there's lonely Richard walking the lonely streets of lonely Stockholm, and he finds a brothel which isn't lonely, because the truth is that there's a small orgy in progress. And you'll never believe me but among the arms and legs mixed up in all the arms and legs and buttocks and busts are the buttocks and busts of one who looks up and chimes: *"Richard!"*

Hurling himself upon the bed with this horde, Richard discovers he can't get physically inspired by anyone save *the* one, Maja.

Whereupon they conclude there is only one solution. They must commit double suicide. They must make love and die together.

A "love meal" is prepared. Maja is still sure they're going to die afterward. To their mutual astonishment, they have a lot of fun and . . . it's more like a wedding . . . and, again, watch for tomorrow's installment. . . .

One must not discount these funny porno films because they may be regarded as masterpieces instead of masturbation in tomorrow's cinema world.

The Cannes Film Festival is unrealistic to start with.

You have flown to Nice and limousined or taxied over to Cannes. On the highway, a large rambling beige villa called L'Horizon has been pointed out to you.

This is where the handsome prince once lived with the beautiful movie star. Here in the good days the late Prince Aly Khan drove his fast cars and wooed Rita Hayworth who became known as Princess Margarita. Aly was famous for sneaking out for some sex between courses at a dinner party. In this villa also reigned Aly's late father, the fat old Aga Khan, and his bejeweled Begum.

It is picture postcard stuff, but it is true. Down there along that coastline and among some of those rooftops is where Cary Grant made a picture called *To Catch a Thief.* And at that very time and not far from here, Grace Kelly, his co-star, met and bagged Prince Rainier, acquiring for herself a title and a realm. Of small dimensions, true (the newspapers like to sneer "not as big as Central Park"), but what girl of your acquaintance did better? In those years, Aristotle Onassis had not yet been made world famous by Jacqueline Kennedy and got such publicity as he could by being part owner of the Monte Carlo gambling casino. He used to sit in the casino's Club Privée gambling listlessly and lonesomely, not knowing that one day his picture and innermost secrets would be on the fan magazines of every land.

It's fifteen years later now. All the heroes and heroines have lost their looks, except Grace Kelly. The Cannes Film Festival has aged somewhat. Like a middle-aged movie sex queen, the festival has grown baggy-chinned and baggy-bottomed. She endeavors to retain her seductiveness with innumerable face, bust, and buttlifts. She tries to renew her allure by submitting to new and wilder injections of youthfulness administered by the young revolutionaries of the motion-picture industry.

A kid with long hair and a beard in Levi's may be the hottest new producer.

But in the lobby of the Carlton and on the terrace, there is excitement as the men in black ties and women in long dresses move toward the Palais des Festivals. The showing of the cinema is just a block away, and they can promenade.

Parading through the lobby in the year '73, more than in previous years, are the outrageously garbed drag queens.

They are putting on their own festival. They swish through the lobby with vast courage. They are the boldest of the transvestites, heavily made up, with false breasts, gold lamé dresses, wigs that give them great height, high heels, and of course they float past in a cloud of heavy perfume.

They giggle, and they flirt. And they enjoy the buzz-buzz of comment that wins them more attention than that received by Ingrid Bergman, the president of the jury, when she goes modestly off to the theater.

But that's part of the Age of the Genitals. These drag queens were expressing their own independence and getting their own releases.

The Swedes were among the first to show sexual emancipation in movies. But the country was like that. A Stockholm newspaper of repute printed a column of questions from readers about sex.

The questions were cited as proof that the general public wanted to know more and more about sex.

"Is my penis too small?" was one question.

"My husband wants me to pee on him," was another from a wife, who asked, "should I?"

These were the learned topics of discussion among some of us at the Cannes Festival in '73. Harold Robbins gave a cocktail party on his yacht. I asked him whether one could compare *Last Tango in Paris* and *Deep Throat*.

He took me very seriously. "No," he said. "One is a comic strip, one is a novel."

Marlon Brando's sodomizing of Maria Schneider after first reminding her to bring some butter for lubrication was part of every discussion. Terrence Young, the director, said, "I hate to think of Marlon Brando sharing billing with a pound of butter." One famous producer told me that he would never again hear the expression "Pass the butter" without thinking of "Brando buggering the broad."

"I took my wife to see that picture," the producer said. "Afterward, she said, 'I hope that picture didn't turn you on; I think it's turned me off for about a month.'"

Troll, the Swedish film about the wife who thought you died if you had sex, was publicized at the Cannes Festival as a parody of Swedish sex films.

"One magnificent prank after another," one Swedish critic wrote, "climaxing in the group sex-scene where our best opera soloists frolic on a giant bed, singing the quartet from Verdi's 'Rigoletto.'"

One lesson learned from the Cannes Festival is that the picture we smirk and leer about now may be the artsy-fartsy gem of next year. A couple of years ago I wrote about a topless super-groupie girl named Gerri Miller who boasted of being a "celebrity fucker." I was fascinated by her speech and her admissions of hunting down well-known rock singing stars to go to bed with. There were girls who did that in groups, called groupies, but big-breasted Gerri claimed to be the super-groupie. She had a small part in an Andy Warhol film *Trash* in which she performed fellatio on an impotent homosexual.

This wasn't work for Gerri. It was fun.

"If I see a cute guy, I want to ball him the same as a guy wants to ball a chick," she said. "If I like them, I ball them. The ones I don't like, I just blow. I got a special trick they all like. I rim their ass."

Gerri had gone to a party where a photographer kept following her around. "To get rid of him, I blew him in front of everybody. But he took it wrong. He thought I liked him. I was just blowing him for a laugh."

I dismissed Gerri's movie effort at the time, categorizing Gerri rather as a "personality" than an actress. To my considerable surprise, at subsequent gatherings of "filmmakers" at Cannes and elsewhere, I learned that *Trash* was one of the greatest pictures ever made and that Gerri's blow job of the impotent homosexual was sensational and brilliant.

But that's how stars emerge, I suppose.

In the 1950's, there was a cute little teen-age cigarette girl named Juanita Slusher from a small Texas town working in the Theater Lounge, a stripteasery, on Forest Avenue in Dallas.

She envied the slightly older girls working as strippers and wanted to become one. She had no act, no experience. She did have a sexy figure. One of the strip stars, Bonnie Bell, encouraged her, and lent her the first pasties the girl ever put on her nipples.

"But that name—ugh—you can't call yourself Juanita Slusher. What can we call you? You look like a piece of candy. You're so pretty," Bonnie Bell said. "You're like a candy bar. How's that for a name? Candy Barr?"

And that was the birth of the stripteaser Candy Barr, who later got jailed for possession of marijuana and was one of the girlfriends of mobster Mickey Cohen. But what we learn today from historians of the Age of Eroticism and Genitalia is that Candy Barr was one of the great sex actresses—on stag films.

I wouldn't have known of her artistry but for an article in *Sun Dance*, by George Csicsery, which said that for many years, the Hollywood films were so laundered that "only bad people fucked." Stag films were something different. They "showed fucking in the grubbiest forbidden fruit sense. Actors performed the ghastly deed without so much as a word or expression of joy. Motel rooms and dark sunglasses were *de rigueur*.

"There was one exception to that generation of sex actors— Candy Barr.

"Candy brought a joy to her performance . . . it was her grace and beauty, that—resembling Marilyn Monroe—underlay her persecution. She had the courage to openly enjoy sex when others were performing without feeling. A recent camp revival of her films has allowed her to survive the tons of scrap reels that lie dormant in private collections."

To talk about the progress of the cinema in the Generation of Genitals is to indulge in perhaps excessive references to fucking and sucking. Andy Warhol and his underground superstars produced *Blow-Job* with Warhol holding a camera on a man's face while another actor sucked his penis. . . . Ingmar Bergman showed a woman fingering herself to the musical accompaniment of Johann Sebastian Bach in his picture *The Silence*. . . . In Leo Productions' film *Guess Who's Coming at Dinner*, in 1971, there was quite a laugh at the expense of the myopic priest at the dinner table. He couldn't see that three couples were getting well laid at a well-laid dinner table right in front of him.

Thinking back over this, we realize that it's a long, long way from the comparatively innocent days (and nights) of Brigitte Bardot, and her towel, to the total frontal nudity of today.

In 1959, I flew over to St.-Tropez from Cannes to see B.B. ("the unattainable dream of all men") because she didn't want to attend that year's festival. B.B. was so unpopular with most women because of her habit of throwing in the towel that you seldom heard a good word for her from another female.

"B.B. didn't want to come to the festival this year because she would spoil it for Kim Novak, Sophia Loren, Rhonda Fleming and Zsa Zsa Gabor," declared her good friend and producer the late Raoul Levy, who later killed himself. "She didn't think she should show up here especially because she doesn't have a picture entered in the festival."

The fact that she assumed she would steal the festival from the other ladies may have seemed a bit conceited, but it was undoubtedly true. Her fans and the curious tourists came right up to her villa in boats, and the poor girl couldn't go swimming in the nude or even with a swimsuit on.

Bardot was the creation of Roger Vadim, who later went on to Jane Fonda. He taught her how to lie in bed for the photographers and cameramen so that she seemed to be inviting men to hop in with her. Poor B.B.! The Great Sex Kitten was deprived. She never knew true fame as it is today. She's around forty now. She was too old even to get buttered up by Marlon Brando.

Cheri Caffaro, a Strange Interlewd

✍ THE showing of pubic hair in the respectable magazines was to me a shocking development of 1971 and 1972.

My Bible Belt background told me that it was wrong. Why, I could remember back to 1925, when my home town, Rockford, Ohio, was torn into two camps over the prospect of "mixed dancing" in the high school auditorium. Two ministers protested that a boy and a girl dancing together "was almost as bad as adultery."

Card playing was also a sin to these church people. Because I made a brave stand for mixed dancing as editor of the high school paper (*Hi-Life*), they thought I must be a pervert. I was seventeen at the time.

Flashes of pubic hair began appearing in *Playboy, Penthouse,* and other magazines after *Screw* pioneered in exposing that area. Suddenly there were acres of pubic hair being shown. The author Tom Tryon and I were discussing it one day and decided that it was a far cry from the Public Library to the Pubic Library.

For the nameless girls in *Screw* to bare their pubis was one thing. But when the girl was a formidable actress of movies and TV, Angel Tompkins, it was quite astounding. So we thought back in those innocent days.

"Did you have any hesitation about doing pictures showing your pubic hair?" I asked Miss Tompkins one day at lunch. She was the first one I'd interviewed who'd "gone the whole way."

"Two years' hesitation," she said, adding that she got to know the photographer who put her at her ease. "I had no qualms about showing it unless it wasn't trimmed. Anything I can't stand is a wooly bush. I never saw even a straggly cat that doesn't preen itself."

And then the dream—the impossible dream—that I should interview a Hollywood "lovely" while she was naked, formed in my mind. It was now 1973.

I was sitting in one of the window seats in the promenade of the

45

New York Hilton Hotel interviewing the upcoming blond sex symbol Cheri Caffaro, who was to get quite well known later for a picture, *Girls Are for Loving.* Her husband, writer-producer Dan Schain, had previously boasted to me that she was more voluptuous than Raquel Welch.

"This," I decided, "is the girl!"

Cheri had posed for magazine photographers naked. They'd shoot for days, take maybe a thousand pictures, and use five.

"All right," I said. "I'm a reporter for newspapers writing about you posing nude. Why shouldn't you be naked when I interview you?"

"Oh, but that's different!" moaned Cheri, who had some of the blond softness of Brigitte Bardot. She was getting known for her film roles as *Ginger*, a private eye. Cheri was bright, adventurous, and daring.

"What's the matter?" I asked her. "How can I honestly write about a nude girl unless I see her nude?"

I was joking when I posed the question, but the more I thought about it, the more convinced I became that I was right.

"What's different about it?" echoed Cheri. "A photographer you get used to."

"You could get used to me," I volunteered.

"But this photographer has his cameras," Cheri argued.

"I could bring my new Polaroid and my Instamatic if that would make you less nervous."

"And that makes it the same?" Cheri asked.

"Oh, no! I would also have my notebooks and pencils."

Cheri kept looking at me in a strange way. "I just couldn't do it," she said.

"All right, then," I said, "but I may as well tell you that several other girls also said no."

Cheri and I parted friends, me thinking, "What might have been." I returned to my desk and wrote what I hoped would prove an amusing column about Cheri trying to muzzle the press. I claimed jocularly, I trusted, that it was an issue of freedom of the press. Why should photographers see beautiful women naked when reporters couldn't? Arise, all reporters, all newspaper editors, publishers, and newsdealers, too, and stand up for your rights! Why should magazines report on areas that were forbidden to newspapers?

That, I assumed, would be the end of it. But a few days later, Cheri's New York publicist, Sheldon Roskin, phoned.

"Cheri liked your column," he said.

"Good," I said.

"And she's changed her mind. She'll do it."

"*No!*" I said.

"*Yes!*" he said. "She'll be here April 10 to be naked for you."

Bold and unafraid as I was when I was sure she wouldn't do it, I was positively scared now that she said she would. I hadn't really meant it at all. It was some kind of reportorial bravado talking.

"Well . . ." I hemmed and hawed. "Are you sure she wants to?"

"Certainly! She's got guts," Roskin said.

"I would think," I said, still looking for an escape hatch, "that her husband would object. He's such a nice guy. I wouldn't want to hurt his feelings."

"He's sold," Roskin said. "Your arguments convinced him. He says you were very logical. Now Cheri'll be staying at the Sherry-Netherland and she'll be naked for you in her suite promptly at four P.M. You'll be in town, I hope?"

There was my chance! I scanned my calendar. "Uh, yes," I said.

"You don't sound very enthusiastic. You're not afraid, are you?" he asked.

"Who, *me!*" My bravado returned. "She probably won't go through with it."

"Maybe your wife won't let you," Sheldon said. "Maybe she won't give her consent."

I only wished at that moment that she would object, but I knew that she wouldn't. It would be the same as several years before when I told her I was going to go nude at a nudist camp. She said, "Thank God, one trip you're going on, I won't have to pack a bag for you."

Now that Cheri had accepted my challenge, I actually worried about another angle—some of my readers, with families, might object. They might think I was setting a bad example for their children. A columnist becomes quite conscious of his so-called image when he reads his mail.

Accordingly, I wrote another column about Cheri, asking my readers, "Should I interview a beautiful and shapely movie star in the nude?"

Unfortunately, some readers didn't understand and thought *I* was to be in the nude. A reader in Dallas even wrote to me, "Don't you think Cheri should be naked, too?" Of course it was never my thought that I would be naked, but Cindy Adams, among others, was convinced that I had planned to strip for the interview. Cindy threatened to picket me, naked, if I didn't go nude. Her husband, Joey Adams, argued against her point of view for an hour. It was one of the most controversial subjects I ever dealt with in my years of columning, and some people really were serious about it. That made me more apprehensive about doing it.

During my indecision about it, I was giving an interview by phone to Charles Ashman of KMOX, St. Louis, and casually suggested that his listeners tell me whether I should go through with it.

"I got eleven hundred answers in the mail," he reported a few days later. "I'd say it's running about three to two against."

A possibility of a reprieve came a few days later. Cheri had set April 10 for N (for Nude) Day. Now she wanted to make it a day later. I couldn't find a proper alibi to reject the change of date. Besides, I felt that a bit of gallantry was required here. The lovely girl was offering to bare all, her all anyway, and I couldn't just casually wave her aside to make up for my own rashness, could I?

"So April 11, then. At four P.M. OK?" Sheldon Roskin said.

"Oh, sure," I said (nervously).

Certain ground rules had to be established so that there would be no misunderstandings and no accidents. I would go to Cheri's suite and wait for her with Roskin and a photographer who would take pictures of Cheri nude and me clothed, just as proof that it really happened. But first, room service would bring hors d'oeuvres and a bottle of wine. "It would be a little awkward if room service brought the hors d'oeuvres while Cheri was sitting there naked with you interviewing her, wouldn't it?" Sheldon said. Then after the picture taking, the photographer and Sheldon would withdraw, leaving Cheri and me alone at last.

Riding upstairs in the elevator at five minutes before the zero hour, I saw a woman I knew, who smiled at me. I had a strange feeling that it was a smile of accusation—*that she knew I was going to interview a movie beauty naked!*

When I got to the suite and entered the room where I was to wait for Cheri, I found Sheldon in a frivolous mood.

"What a good-looking shirt you're wearing!" he said. "Too bad you have to take it off."

"Wait a minute," I said. "I'm not stripping, it's Cheri who's going to be naked."

"I keep forgetting," he said. "You know Paul Schumach, don't you?" He was the photographer. The interview had been well orchestrated, and the room service waiter arrived immediately with the olives, the ice, and a bottle of wine.

"Why don't we just take some pictures of Earl waiting like the man in the death house about to go to the chair?" Sheldon said. "Are you nervous?"

"What have I got to be nervous about?" I shot back (still nervously).

"Yeah, what have you got to be nervous about?" Sheldon said mockingly.

While the photographer was taking my picture (being nervous), I was keeping my eye on the door to the other room, from which Cheri would shortly emerge in just her skin. And then there was a tap-tap-tap on the door. It opened . . . and the naked lady swung in wearing little silver sandals and a Gucci necklace with a Taurus sign dangling around her breasts. Her strawberry blond hair fell to her shoulders. From there down she was completely naked—astonishingly so, I thought, as I arose from my seat on the couch to greet her.

"Oh, well, here you are," I said, or something as banal as that.

"Yes, here I am, all of me," Cheri smiled, completely at ease. She walked toward me and in the Hollywood manner, gave me a kiss (which is different, somehow, when the lady's naked). "Oh, now you've got lipstick on you!"

"Well, now," I said, still not in control of myself, "how have you been lately?"

"I was just sitting in there reading a book," Cheri said. The photographer began shooting pictures of her kissing me and I'm afraid I tried to squirm out of the shot.

"You were reading naked?" I said. "Isn't that a funny way to read a book? I usually wear something."

"But I had to be naked to meet you." Cheri smiled again. "You insisted upon it."

"Yes, I did," I replied. "What were you reading naked?"

"I was reading the autobiography of Lana Turner, honest to God," Cheri said.

"I think it's the biography of Lana Turner, not the autobiography," I said, in the least important contribution to conversation in the history of the world.

"Yes, I think it is the biography, not the autobiography," Cheri said. At this moment I was desperately trying to keep my eyes off of Cheri's pelvic zone, but I'm afraid there's something in the nature of man that makes his eyes wander there against his will.

As Sheldon Roskin was to say later, "Well, at least you and I know that Cheri is a real blonde!"

"You don't mind posing for these pictures?" I asked Cheri. The photographer was maneuvering her about so he could get complete full-length frontal-nudity pictures.

"Oh, no, I'm used to it. Do you mind?"

"Not if you don't mind, I don't mind," I said, another brilliant riposte. "By the way, is it too warm in here?"

"There *is* a draft. At least I feel one," Cheri said.

"Don't you think you ought to take something off, Earl?" Sheldon said in jest.

"I think the reason I feel a draft is that I don't have any clothes on," Cheri said.

"That very likely could be the explanation," I said. The photographer had now shot Cheri from almost every possible beautiful angle, including a couple of poses which should capture the pubic area without Cheri raising any objection.

"By the way, Cheri," I said, "you are more at ease than I am."

"Aren't you at ease, Earl?"

"I'm afraid I'm not at all at ease, Cheri," I said, trembling.

"Maybe you should have a drink." Cheri wandered over to the table with the hors d'oeuvres and the wine and poured me a glass of wine. She walked back across the room in all her nakedness and handed me the glass.

"I'm not drinking, but today I'll make an exception," I said. "It's a rather special day."

Sheldon Roskin interrupted with a cough. "I guess we had better go now," he said. "We'll leave you two to your own devices."

To that remark I had always wanted to reply, "Of which we have several," but this didn't seem the moment. As they left, Cheri swung nudely back across the room to the table and returned with a glass of wine for herself.

She sat down beside me on the couch. In my nervousness, I moved myself back from her a few inches.

"Well," I said, searching for an appropriate toast and lifting my glass, "here's looking at you?" My eyes were on her chin or higher. I kept trying again—and it was hard—to keep them away from the areas that are forbidden to stare at.

"Now I should tell you," Cheri began, "why I did this."

"I would like to know."

"You dared me," she said. "You bet me in effect that I wouldn't do this. I'm a type that takes dares, and I thought you might back out of it. I wouldn't do this with just anybody."

Cheri reached over and picked out an olive, which she nibbled.

"Thank you," I murmured.

"And my husband trusts you, Earl. He knows it's just going to be you and me and fifty million readers."

"In time, you mean." I nodded. I had begun to settle down now and started to appreciate the way that God had "structured" Cheri. She was long-limbed and lean, and while she was not bovine, she was ample-breasted. She was definitely a sunbathing type of girl. I could tell that from the white around her bosom and her buttocks where she wore the bikini. When Cheri leaned forward to nibble another olive, she made me nervous all over again because she was so close to me.

"It's been a pretty dull interview so far," Cheri said. "Have you got some racy questions to ask me?"

"Have I!" And I consulted my notebook into which I had entered the rough questions. "Here's one. How do you stand on ecology? Do you think it should be an issue in the next election?"

Cheri shifted her weight around toward me, making me still more nervous. "Let's face it," she said. "With all that pollution, how can we sunbathe when we can't find any sun to lie in because of all that brown stuff hanging in the air?"

"Very nicely, succinctly put." As I entered her answer in my book, I kept wondering how her derriere felt on that hard leather couch, and should she have a pillow for it, but how does one bring that up without sounding fresh, and anyway, I'm not the host here—I'm just a guest, right?

"Have you done many nude pictures, Cheri?" I asked.

"The only nudes I did was while playing *Ginger*," Cheri said.

"Were you embarrassed?"

"Well, I was a little nervous when I did a love scene with a nice young man when the camera crew was there and the lights were on and I was trying to remember my lines at the same time."

Cheri leaned forward again, with her hand on her knee, never trying to cover any part of herself as I'm sure I would have done if I'd been naked, which thank God, I wasn't.

"After the love scene, after we'd been in bed, I said to him, 'Hi, glad to meet you.'

"Yes," Cheri continued, "here we'd been in bed together supposedly making love, and now we were getting dressed afterward, and *we closed the doors* of our dressing rooms. When we both came back to reality, we began to laugh. And I think he said, 'Haven't I seen you somewhere before.' "

"I think I'll have another wine since this is sort of a special occasion," I said, carelessly. "Did you have any guilt feelings afterward?"

With a toss of her head, which turned out to be a toss of her torso always, Cheri retorted, "But I wasn't guilty of anything! I don't do pornographic films. Those were love scenes. If Walter Matthau can show off his bare fanny with Carol Burnett in a movie, why can't I?"

"You can, Cheri, you can!" I said. "I was just asking what you felt about it?"

"When we can't talk about our bodies without thinking there's something obscene about it, we're getting a little sick," Cheri said indignantly. "Anyway, I think it's a good thing to have some of these pornographic films, and there should be places to see them!"

"You do? You really do?"

"Yes!" Cheri reached for a cigarette and I lit it for her. I had to lean forward, and she had to lean forward, and now I noticed that I was not so self-conscious about her nudity being near me.

"There should be legalized pornography. It should be shown in certain sections," Cheri said. "It would be a release sexually for some people. I'd rather have somebody go watch a porno movie than wait in a park and rape and murder a sixteen-year-old girl."

Cheri couldn't have been more serious. "Everything should have its place," she said.

Endeavoring to get the interview into a lighter vein, I asked Cheri, "Now, when you sat there waiting to come out naked and be interviewed, did you primp?"

"Sure!"

"How?"

"Well, just the way that all girls do." She laughed. "Except that I had no clothes to wear out here."

"So what did you have left to primp with? Just your finger-nails."

"Well." She giggled.

"I wondered if you had any hesitation about—" I found it hard to finish the sentence.

"You mean, to show or not to show?" Cheri supplied the thought for me.

"That's what I meant," I said.

"Well, I don't see why you shouldn't show it. Everybody knows you have it! I don't think there's anything wrong with showing it. We're supposed to be adults. Children know about their bodies. What's wrong with it?"

Therefore, Cheri said, still making no effort to cover up anything of a controversial nature, she appeared before me without so much as a G-string. "It's better for children to see this," she said, "than those monster films they used to show, of them chopping up their arms and legs!"

It was time for me to explore and examine Cheri's background. "I'm five seven and a half," she said, "My measurements are—"

Cheri smiled at me, and I was afraid she was going to ask me to guess—after all, I had a firsthand, close-up view. I was glad she didn't ask me, for I certainly would have been off an inch or two here or there.

"—36-24-36," Cheri continued. "That's what it was about two years ago."

"You wouldn't have a tape measure, I suppose?" I said. "I used to take one on all my interviews. . . ."

To my practiced eye, the two 36's looked about right. Cheri was not overendowed, not underendowed. Just endowed! She was born in Miami, but her mother wanted to go to California, so Cheri was brought up in Pasadena. She swims, works out in a gym, goes in for modern jazz dancing, and is interested in the autobiographies of Hollywood figures, including the late David O. Selznick.

"My favorite male actor is Burt Lancaster, my favorite actress Sophia Loren. I find both of these people very earthy. Burt is a very sensuous, sexy man without being a pretty boy. I don't care for pretty boys that much."

I was now able to look directly at my naked interviewee without flinching, and I asked her, "What do you think of the Watergate affair?"

"Whose affair?" Cheri said.

"I guess I must have been mumbling," I said. "The Watergate case?"

"Oh, Earl." Cheri laughed. "I think if you ever get to the bottom of this—but we're only going to find out what they want us to know. . . ."

Cheri was like that about everything. Thoughtful. What about Marlon Brando and the Oscar? "There are no rules that you have to accept the Oscar," she said. "Where is it written in the Ten Commandments? He didn't hurt anyone. Maybe himself. This," Cheri added, realistically, "is a flesh-peddling business. That agent peddles you. He takes the highest he can get for you. All the people come out to grab what they can. It takes ten to fifteen years of hard work before you're of any value. I used to think, how can people do the things they do?"

She was so serious that for the moment I was so busy scratching her words into my notebook that I didn't remember I was talking to or listening to a naked lady. It was when she rose in front of me and turned with her derriere toward me and poured some more wine that I remembered where I was.

"Are you at ease now, Earl?" Cheri was kind enough to ask.

"I'm afraid not," I said.

"What can I do to put you at your ease?" She was standing full-length and full-bosomed, looking down at me.

"Just be yourself," I said.

"I thought I *was* being," Cheri replied.

"Now don't take that the wrong way!" I put my hand out to pat her comfortingly on the, uh, shoulder. That didn't seem the right thing to do, either. One must watch where one puts one's hand; he must be careful about any extravagant gestures, in a situation like this. One wrong move and. . . .

"The reason I'm doing this"—Cheri indicated that she meant walking around in front of me nude—"is that I'm afraid of the least little bit of censorship. When we founded this country, naturally we had to fill half the boats with convicts, half of our forefathers came over here to get out of prison. . . .

"And that's what's great about the country now. Freedom of speech. We need the Jane Fondas, because somewhere between the two extreme points of view we'll find the middle of the road. How dull it would be if we all agreed!"

"And a free press, too," I reminded Cheri. "That's why you're naked here now, don't forget. Because I pointed out to you that you were trying to muzzle the press by not taking your clothes off for me when you would for a photographer."

"And a very sneaky thing it was, too, Earl," Cheri said. "Don't think I didn't see through it!"

"How old are you, and what do you want to do now?" I asked. "I will put it another way. How old do you say you are?"

"Twenty-six."

"And how old are you?"

"Twenty-six. As for what I'd like to do, I'd like to do some dramatic roles. I have a couple of properties."

This would have been a great time to say, "I can see them," but I refrained. I felt I was getting to know Cheri well enough now that I could tell her about Monica Kennedy, the girl who made up her pubic hair in a special coiffure. In cautious language, I detailed the idea to Cheri, who was very impressed.

"I want to show you something, Earl," Cheri suddenly said.

"Uh, but I think you already have," I said.

Cheri went bouncing off into the other room of the suite and bounced back carrying a calendar promoting her film *Girls Are for Loving*. This calendar was definitely different. The first month in this calendar wasn't January—but May. That was the first month when they were going to be exploiting the film. Cheri had posed for some nude pictures for the calendar, which I was now allowed to see.

"What do you think of it? What do you think of when you look at it?" Cheri asked me.

"I'm not going to tell you," I replied very primly.

"Seriously," Cheri said, "you'll notice it doesn't specifically zero into the pubic area."

"No, but you know it's there," I said.

"That's just the point," cried Cheri. "You know I've got one. . . ."

"You've definitely got one," I retorted, getting as brave as hell.

"And you know it's there and where it is, so why hide it? Why make a big mystery of it?"

Cheri bent over me again as she turned the pages of the calendar and the sweet aroma of femininity or whatever the hell it is rose from her naked breasts. There was this nude beauty with the bare pubis and the bare back cheeks tantalizingly close. I was getting scared.

"Well, Cheri," I said, "I think that about does it. . . ."

"You going?" She acted positively disappointed.

"It's been a milestone," I said. And was I glad to get away from there! I can't remember if I kissed her so-long, but I was a damned fool if I didn't!

The Blonde and the President

🖋 NOW that it's out in the open, now that it's in the public domain with the whole world having been misinformed about it, I have chosen to tell the true story of Marilyn Monroe's liaison with the Brothers Kennedy.

It is a story I have withheld for several years. Until Norman Mailer wrote a book repeating the gossip that the sexiest of the sex symbols was having a great love affair at the end of her life with the late Attorney General Robert F. Kennedy, I was not moved to put it on paper. I didn't really want to tell it.

But the time has come to set the record straight. I am telling what I know, I am taking nothing from other men's books. I'm not snatching at dreams. I knew Marilyn Monroe for 13 years and through many, many interviews and meetings and cocktails. I photographed Marilyn Monroe scores of times and, preposterous as it was, Marilyn Monroe photographed me. I knew, nearly intimately, all her close friends.

The man whose clandestine companionship she enjoyed most in her last tortured year was not Bobby Kennedy, but his brother, the young President of the United States, John F. Kennedy.

I have writhed in embarrassment reading and hearing stories of "Marilyn and Bobby" from so-called experts on Marilyn Monroe who never knew her. That is why I am trying to tell in the proper perspective and with proper respect, the straight story. Much of it came from Marilyn herself, because she looked upon sex lightly, did not regard her bedroom adventures as sacred secrets, and, under proper conditions, discussed them.

Marilyn Monroe *was* fascinated by the dynamic Bobby Kennedy and had a continuing flirtation with him. But Marilyn's first choice was the President whom she usually called "Mr. President," even in the boudoir, although in gossipy confessionals with intimates, she sometimes called him "him," or "he." Marilyn turned to his younger brother Bobby when the President was inaccessible or when their relationship got too "sensitive."

My respect for John F. Kennedy as a President and person was enormous. Most of all, I admired his sense of humor. I recall as probably every contemporary of mine does, the moment I heard he had been shot. I wept over his funeral.

Yet Presidents, as other men, are all things. John F. Kennedy was a great man and a fine man, but he was also a man in the manly sense, one of the manliest of the masculine. And this adds a new dimension to the humanness of JFK. For what is more human than Sex? And now that I have decided to go into it, I will go the whole way and say that as John F. Kennedy was a giant in politics and statesmanship, he was also a giant in sex. He was a little bit ahead of his time in believing that a President should set aside some time for sex. Most of our country's leaders in previous administrations had been too old to enjoy love-making. But John F. Kennedy was young, healthy and virile. I truly believe he would have approved my contention that he was the sexiest, swingingest President of the century, and not have thought it disrespectful.

Usually, President Kennedy indulged in his adventures with such dignity and elegance that other men envied his finesse. Charismatic, handsome, wealthy, athletic, flattering in the clever way that he dispensed compliments and other forms of blarney, he was irresistible to most women. Not that many thought of resisting him. He reveled in his successes and gained a reputation for the busy life he led in that secret world. In fact, there were many who wondered how he kept up the pace. One gentleman declared that the F in JFK certainly could have stood for Fornicate.

Marilyn Monroe was his happy collaborator in this distinctly non-political area of his life after many girls had preceded her, and just as many men had preceded him.

For of course there were other actresses, practicing the eternal lure of Show Business on great men, who slid secretly into JFK's sex life. There was one starlet of whom it was said that he had been her sponsor for a dozen years. But she did not become famous, her name is little known today. The chemistry of the charismatic Kennedy and the equally charismatic Marilyn was bound to be a mixture that the pharmacists of love would exclaim over, however. All the other sex symbols faded away and the bosomy blonde from the foster home who got famous posing nude for a calendar won the man in the White House . . . at least she had him, and vice versa, occasionally. It wasn't of vast importance to the President who had his feet on the ground. It was, however, the President's most secretive relationship, and rightfully, because when these two got together . . . well, it was the World Series, the Superbowl, the breakfast of champions.

Marilyn Monroe was an actress, and actresses—those sex-obsessed creatures from sex-obsessed Show Business—have always excited and enchanted men of great power and great wealth: Howard Hughes, to cite just one. Marilyn Monroe's stud list included Howard Hughes. She once explained that her cheeks were red because Howard Hughes hadn't shaved for several days. In his own short lifetime, John F. Kennedy was perhaps even more active amorously or amorously active than Howard Hughes.

Norman Mailer's confusing compendium of other authors' research about Marilyn Monroe did her many an injustice, some of which I will correct. Mailer never knew Marilyn; he became an authority on her life 10 years after it ended. He published the thinnest hint about her relations with JFK, and then passed along the worst-kept non-secret of the day, the story about Marilyn and Bobby, which he then seemed to take back. You pay your money and you take your choice.

I am wading out of that sea of confusion hoping to get to dry land with some facts. I am positive that Marilyn Monroe's sexual pyrotechnics excited the President of the United States, and that Marilyn and JFK had a liaison which was only of about a year's duration. The President carried out his side of it with his usual imperturbable self-assurance. Marilyn wasn't as discreet. The President never talked about it, or boasted; he was a gentleman. Marilyn, in that giggly, gasping, whispering voice, *did* talk about it. She did boast. After all, he was The President of the United States.

My sources for these statements are people with excellent credentials. They include people who were of near-Cabinet status when Kennedy was President. They include film stars, theatrical managers, theatrical agents, and film stars' secretaries. They include plane pilots and plane stewardesses and hotel employees.

Their lips have come unsealed since the deaths of the President, Bobby Kennedy and Marilyn. I have spoken to three people who were "beards" for JFK and Marilyn. One, whose position is such that he was ideally situated to be a "beard," pretended that he was Marilyn's escort or date, so that the world would not know that Marilyn was seeing the President. As he "bearded" for the President at 1600 Pennsylvania Avenue, this was another kind of "White House cover-up."

One day soon there will step forward a witness who will tell in detail of Marilyn Monroe's private confessions of "the difficulties of being made love to by the President of the United States." Marilyn did not use expressions like "being made love to," she used a shorter, stronger word.

Marilyn also declared that those damned Secret Service men were always hovering around trying to prevent a little Presidential fun—and that they got to be a real pain in the ass! That is practically a direct quote from the Sex Symbol of the age.

"Can you document that, Mr. Wilson?" people are going to ask.

Yes. I have the word of New York businessman Henry Rosenfeld, one of Marilyn's dearest, most trusted friends, and his permission to quote him. Two days before she died, she was conspiring through him to see the President.

And there is ready documentation from another newspaperman: the one who knew more about this affair than any living journalist, syndicated Hollywood columnist Sidney Skolsky, my good friend and colleague.

In Hollywood, when anybody says, "Sidney Skolsky says so," that ends the argument. He is respected for his veracity and his nonsensationalism.

Only a few of us knew of Marilyn's secret intimacy with President Kennedy. Sidney Skolsky knew Marilyn through sixteen or seventeen years, through many love affairs. He knew her through husbands and lovers and husbands and back to lovers. It was in the summer of 1962 that Marilyn broke the news to him that she was having secret dates with "the Prez," as she sometimes called President Kennedy.

"Are you surprised?" Marilyn asked Skolsky. She asked the question like a little girl telling her daddy she'd been naughty, and would she be punished?

"No, nothing you do surprises me," he said. But he added, thinking back to how unknown she'd once been, *"The Prez?"*

When I reconfirmed all this with Skolsky, putting my facts with his in the summer of 1973, we agreed that their affair lasted about a year. Skolsky said Mailer, "writing about Bobby, put together purple prose to make greenbacks."

But wait! The rumors about Marilyn and Bobby (rather than about Marilyn and the President) stemmed from reports from guests at a dinner party. Purportedly, the two of them, somewhat inebriated, were early departers from the party and were later observed having knowledge of each other in the back seat of a parked car. This purported misconduct was seen by many more people than were there—as always happens after some famous event—and it may have happened. But the anguished romance that Marilyn was suffering through when she died was with "Mr. President," as she liked to call him, even in the boudoir. She called him "Mr. President" in a song she sang to him in Madison Square Garden, and he smiled . . . "reminiscently," some people thought.

"You say President Kennedy has a stable?" remarked a somewhat older woman at a Washington party in the summer of 1961 to a younger man who'd been speaking to a friend beside him. "I didn't know the President was interested in horses."

"Horses?" the young man replied. "Did I say anything about horses?" He turned to the friend beside him.

"You definitely referred to 'Jack's stable,' " the older woman said.

"Oh, God, I did!" The young man went through the motions of clapping his own mouth shut. "I really did. I said, 'There goes one of the new fillies in Jack's stable.' "

To some puritans, the picture was repellent. This slick, lean, laughing, good-looking leader of the free world found it hard to escape the many impassioned girl—and woman—recruits in the Sexual Rebellion who desired his body. He was as a rock star before a groupie.

The President had always been a lover. The fellows in "Jack's

Pack," as it was sometimes called, were in the habit—before he attained high office—of greeting him with "Hi, lover."

He had come by it naturally from his father, Joseph P. Kennedy, ambassador to the Court of St. James's, one of the legendary lovers of New York and Washington. "Old Joe" was frequently seen at the office of one doctor who boasted that he had exclusive rights to treat any of the ambassador's sexual situations.

It would be a while, though, before Marilyn Monroe would meet John Fitzgerald Kennedy. Jack was floating around Sherman Billingsley's Stork Club and John Perona's El Morocco in his college years. I saw him frequently and remember his politeness; but he was such a boy! He seemed much too boyish-looking at thirty to be elected a Congressman, and much, much too boyish-looking to be elected a Senator six years later.

The young Senator during his Stork Club visits formed a lasting attachment with a girl with eloquently snapping eyes which continued through many years—including the years he was President.

"Jack's getting to be a little bit of a problem," old Joe is reputed to have said. Always dreaming of the Presidency for some member of his family, old Joe tried to get young Jack married off to a nice respectable society-type Catholic girl. In the Stork Club, old Joe actually made the approach (on his son's behalf, he said) to a young beauty of the day who fit that description.

"No, thanks," she said with a fine smile, "I'm going to marry a newspaperman."

When John F. Kennedy married Jacqueline Bouvier in 1953 (the year that he also became Senator), it did not cause vast excitement, nor did he give up all his old feminine friends in deference to his bride. He continued the friendship with the girl with the snapping eyes, for example, and he was, according to the singer and actress Monique Van Vooren, then known because of her bustiness as "The Belgian Bulge," something of a stage door Johnny—a stage door Johnny Kennedy.

"I was in John Murray Anderson's *Almanac*," she has told me, "and he sent me a note backstage, and flowers, and asked to meet me. He wasn't so well known then. He was a Senator—but from Massachusetts! I had a girlfriend from France who told me she'd been going out with him. I didn't ask him whether he was married, but I guess he was."

It wasn't any big secret. Monique was a close friend of statuesque actress Tina Louise, and a couple of years later in an interview in Rome, Monique said, "I know Tina Louise well. She used to take care of my dog when I went out with Kennedy."

To Tina Louise, it read as though Monique were casting her as baby-sitter for a dog. "Our friendship came to an abrupt end," says Monique, sadly.

The brilliant, promising young Senator was really beginning to move in the field of amour. Though representing Massachusetts, he seemed more like a swinging New Yorker. Adlai Stevenson and Eleanor Roosevelt patted him on the head, but he had his eye on the target. He didn't lose his interest in girls in 1960 when he was nominated for President in Los Angeles. There were members of "the stable" on the periphery of the politicking, and I recall a few rumors about this one and that one at a big party given at Dave Chasen's restaurant by David McDonald of the United Steelworkers Union. "Senator Jack," as they were calling him, was becoming the new hope of the Democrats. His sister Patricia, the wife of Peter Lawford, was becoming potentially "the sister of the President." Peter Lawford would be, if all went well, "the President's brother-in-law." Frank Sinatra and Judy Garland glamorized a $100-a-plate dinner so big that it required two ballrooms and two toastmasters. Show business was on its way to the White House with sex riding shotgun.

Within a couple of months after Senator Jack's ascendancy to the White House in January, 1961, the members of Jack's Pack had more candidates for the President's attention than they could field. The President seemed to accept his fate willingly.

They said—and I heard it many times at the Inauguration— that he would go down in history as the White House lover because he was the youngest man ever to be President. He was so charming; you had to love his manner. I was walking through a hotel lobby with Gene Barry, the Bat Masterson TV star, when the President-elect, coming from a reception, strode up to Barry and shot out his hand to both of us.

"I watch your program all the time," John F. Kennedy said. "But I guess they all tell you that, don't they?" To me he said, "I still have to go to New York tonight."

On the night before his inauguration as President, this swingers' swinger arranged for one of his several "beards" to assist him in carrying out a rendezvous with a divorcée who had a child.

Jacqueline Kennedy was a bit neglected during this wild take-over of Washington by the incoming Democrats. When Jackie stepped off a plane at the Washington airport, there wasn't a single Kennedy there to meet her. They were all with Frank Sinatra or Peter Lawford. A society editor complained she had to get her news from Sinatra! On the night of the Inaugural Gala produced by Sinatra and Lawford, Jackie left at 1 A.M., half an hour before it ended. I remember her husband thanking Sinatra, declaring "You have seen excellence tonight. . . . It is now Inauguration Day. . . ."

Then they all went to a steak and lobster supper at Paul Young's restaurant, given by Joseph P. Kennedy, where, at 3:30 A.M., the President-to-be danced with a girl and kissed her ear.

About nine hours later he would be posing with First Lady Jacqueline, the happy family man who had become President.

The new President enjoyed the show business personalities brought to him by Sinatra and Peter Lawford. They called him "that Old Jack Magic." Marilyn Monroe hadn't appeared on the Kennedy scene yet. She would have to await her turn with JFK. Marilyn was in Juárez, Mexico, divorcing Arthur Miller at the precise time that he was being inaugurated. A couple of weeks later, Marilyn was discovered to be a patient at the Payne-Whitney Psychiatric Clinic in New York Hospital, suffering from a mental disorder. When she emerged from there, she would become one of the "stable."

But in the interchange between Washington and Hollywood, the President developed an intimate relationship with another actress, a beautiful blond star who was then single. As she is now the wife of a quite famous man, her name will not be printed. I once interviewed her in Cannes and wondered how it happened that she was flying to one of our embassies in Africa in a State Department or ambassadorial plane. That is how pretty girls are pampered by an adoring President.

The President was thought to be a one-nighter; but this was unfair. Besides the blond actress, there was still the girl with the snapping eyes, who was a brunette who was later married to a diplomat, and eventually there would be Marilyn.

His manner was open. One night at a small White House dinner party, not attended by Jackie, he suddenly arose after the coffee and dessert and said, "See you a little later."

One of the girl secretaries left at the same time.

"Where did they go?" inquired one of the guests.

The answer from the President's closest friend there was: "Are you kidding?"

The President was so casual about his affair with the blond actress that she danced around quite openly in a negligee in front of guests of the press during one of his visits to Palm Springs.

"Isn't that a dangerous thing for her to do?" I asked.

"Why is it dangerous? Why shouldn't she show herself off to be the girlfriend of the President?" replied a man who must be considered an authority on Hollywood morals, or the lack of. "It proved to her bosses at the studio that she's sexy."

"But he was married to Jackie."

The authority on Hollywood morals looked at me strangely. "So?"

The President was probably the first White House nudist, loving to sit around naked there or at Camp David or in visits to California. Once he asked one of his "beards" to come into the bedroom where he and a girl were nude. The girl was angry at being exposed and endeavored to cover up her vulnerable points by spreading her hands over them.

JFK chuckled softly.

The girl was so enraged that the next time she saw the man who'd seen her naked, she pretended not to know him.

"If I didn't recognize her—when I saw her with her clothes on—that would have been understandable!" the beard said to me.

President Kennedy favored the Hotel Carlyle on East Seventy-sixth Street in New York, and many was the young beauty who met him there. Not all celebrities, either. Stewardesses, secretaries, models, and those strange creatures who like to offer their bodies to Big Names. The President's "score" card, if he'd kept one, would probably have run into dozens, even possibly hundreds. There was always a male friend to provide an apartment if there was some complication—such as his wife!—at the hotel.

Marilyn Monroe was needle-sharp.

She was smarter than they knew. Until they put the pieces together after her death, they didn't know she was capable of cunning, bitchiness, and meanness that sometimes outweighed her little-girl naïveté, which at times was an act she put on and at times was sincere. Marilyn was selling sex, packaged differently for each customer, every day of her life.

Marilyn knew hundreds of men and used them. The little

orphan waif who became the new sex goddess knew how to maneuver and operate. It had been apparent to her since the boys began noticing her largish breasts and cute behind, when she was about fourteen, that she had something valuable there.

In 1953, when she was making one of her early films, *River of No Return*, in Niagara Falls and Canada, she phoned Sam Chapman, whose wife, Ceil Chapman, was operating a successful New York dress house, with a familiar problem: "Can you help me get some clothes? I'm going to try to sneak into New York," she explained to Chapman. "I've got a date, but I don't have anything to wear."

Chapman had been asked by Marilyn to supply her clothes before. She was a child of nature and didn't care for underwear. Some of the Ceil Chapman models objected to her trying on dresses there because they didn't want to wear them later after she'd worn them just against her skin.

"She came in by plane from Niagara Falls, wearing dungarees and sneakers," Sam Chapman remembered. "She really had no clothes.

"I picked her out a black jersey dress and a white jersey dress. She had no accessories. She wasn't wearing stockings. I got her a black fox to wear with the white jersey and a white fox to wear with the black jersey. I got these from an apartment we had at the Hotel Algonquin where we kept some fur pieces. She wore the tight clinging jerseys without underwear, and she looked sensational.

"Since she had no accessories, I took her to Saks Fifth Avenue to get shoes and so on. A saleswoman there bawled me out for bringing in a girl who was trying on things without underwear or stockings.

"Marilyn kept telling me, 'No one must know I'm here,' because she'd sneaked away from the picture company for her date. I was amazed a day later to see pictures of her in the paper, wearing the jersey dress and fur piece, having a date with Joe DiMaggio.

"But a strange thing was that, though she had no clothes, she wasn't poor. In all the changing dresses she was doing, I discovered at the end that she had a roll of hundred-dollar bills!"

It wasn't long after this that Marilyn became a sex legend. She was rumored being kept by this banker and that real estate tycoon. Movie mogul Joe Schenck allowed her to stay at his big house in Beverly Hills and referred to her as "my No. 2 girl." One of her friends said, "Marilyn is promiscuous but only with one man at a time." George Jessel was not one of the many Hollywood personalities who boasted of having had Marilyn. (It was the fashionable thing to do, the in thing.) George told me that he had held out to her the lure of fine clothes and good contacts if she would.

"She said no," confessed George.

Everybody was talking about Marilyn Monroe's sex life. I investigated a story that she'd been a New York call girl. I satisfied myself that it wasn't true. One afternoon, I heard a famous film actor discussing Marilyn's vagina.

He spoke knowledgeably of its peculiar construction. He explained that it wasn't just like any vagina; it had a unique kind of structure that made her suffering more intense when she was menstruating. She had explained all this to him when she was frequently too sick to work while they were filming together. Marilyn had told him about it in detail without hesitation. They had known each other since she was a nobody married to her first husband. He and the actor were working side by side in the Lockheed plant during World War II. James Dougherty one day brought in a picture of the woman he called "my old lady." It was Marilyn Monroe, then a teen-age wife, naked.

Miss Monroe was alleged by those who claimed to have shared her to not have been a true disciple of love. They claimed she wished to have the thing over and done.

I found a reason for this. There was a legend that her great lover of her early days, the late Johnny Hyde, of the William Morris agency, had persuaded her to have her Fallopian tubes tied when she was still a starlet, so that she would not get pregnant.

Johnny Hyde was dead, and so was Marilyn, when I heard this story but I confirmed it from Peter di Leonardi, who had been her hairdresser, confidant, and friend. It took me until 1965—three years after she was gone—to nail down a part of her secret.

He was a man who had loved her in his way, and he still had some of her shoes and dresses and wigs. Marilyn had a great fondness for her hairdressers and masseurs and confided details of her sex life to them that she seemed not to have disclosed to anybody else.

"It's the story of why she couldn't have children, and it is one of her tragedies," Peter di Leonardi told me.

He sketched in the story of Johnny Hyde, a short-statured,

dynamic talent agent, married and father of grown children, much older than Marilyn, who was so smitten by her that he gave up all the important things of his life to help her. He begged her to marry him even when he was sick, and though she could have been a rich widow, she would not because, she said, she just didn't love him.

"Johnny Hyde knew that in Hollywood the girls have to go to bed a lot," said Peter di Leonardi.

"He told her she'd have to do it. Can you imagine a man loving her so much, he'd tell her, 'Go ahead, it's your career'? So she got her tubes tied, and after that sex meant nothing to her. It was before the Pill, and Johnny Hyde just didn't want her to be encumbered with children."

Marilyn had four miscarriages, one when she was married to Arthur Miller. "That helped kill Marilyn Monroe," di Leonardi said. "If she could have had a child, she could have been saved."

Nobody worked harder at projecting sex than Marilyn, and Peter di Leonardi's theory that sex meant nothing to her after the tubes were tied probably isn't correct. Or maybe she just worked harder at it outwardly. Both in New York and Hollywood, Marilyn would frequently say to a man after a fairly brief acquaintance, "Why haven't you made a pass at me?" It was her insecurity speaking. She seemed to have been insulted by not being invited to sex.

I should feel let down that in the years I knew her she never said that to me. She regarded me, with my notebook always open, too conscientious a reporter to have such thoughts. Others saw her naked, but I never did, nor did we really ever discuss sex.

Marilyn practiced nudity around the house. "I'm only comfortable when I'm naked," she would say. Once when she was sitting in her apartment giving telephone interviews, she stripped in the presence of the publicist Joe Wohlander and proceeded to give "naked interviews." She enjoyed that. It seemed naughty.

Bouncing around in front of Wohlander naked, she said, "Now when they say it's plastic surgery, you can say you know better." And to him she also addressed the question, "Why have you never made a pass at me?"

Talking to Arthur Miller on the phone one day when they were still married, she said, "I'm waiting for you in my room with my clothes off." There were other exhibitionistic examples. One summer day she walked down Fifth Avenue in a new mink coat she loved. Her friend Mrs. Ben Bodne, wife of the proprietor of the Hotel Algonquin, who was walking with her, said, "That's a beautiful coat. What are you wearing with it?"

"Nothing," replied Marilyn, and flashed the coat open to prove it.

Marilyn promenaded nude around the house when she was married to DiMaggio. A woman friend of Marilyn's was there, and Marilyn's nakedness disturbed Joe. She was just showing off, he felt. The woman friend placed a different interpretation on it. She thought Marilyn was extending Joe an invitation. "I think she's trying to tell you something," the woman told Joe. He just looked grim.

Nakedness, sex, child of nature had always been her platform. In one of my early interviews with her, she came out against wearing underwear—to the vast annoyance of the underwear industry. She didn't wear panties when she didn't have to. "Pants gag me!" she said. She burned her bra before the bra burners burned theirs. (Marilyn kept some around, though.) She wore bras to bed to keep her bosom from flopping around too much. She worked out with weights which she had on the end of a broomstick she held over her back and shoulders, performing exercises which kept the breasts firm. She was always demanding more and more nudity which she knew was good for her. When she was filming *The Seven-Year Itch* with Tom Ewell in 1954, around twenty years ago, she wanted to do a nude love scene, which in those years was unthinkable. "But it would be true to the story," she said to director Billy Wilder and producer Charles Feldman, who overruled her.

Marilyn would have been far ahead of the pack if she'd shown herself in the flesh on screen. She was also ahead of the mob in her attitude about sexual freedom.

They will be debating for years to come around the swimming pools of Hollywood whether the Sex Goddess was with Jack or Bobby.

Were a vote taken of those who had heard the rumors and "the inside story," the decision would go to Bobby.

But those who knew "the inside *inside* story" would say that Jack was the prevailing favorite and the winner all the way, although Bobby was by no means kept off the track.

It was fleeting . . . it was a flash act . . . a short but happy interlude in the too-short lives of each that they carried off rather well without any vulgar public display.

It would have begun in the summer of 1961, a few months after John F. Kennedy was inaugurated, and it would have ended the next August.

"The inside insiders" who speak quietly of it were those who helped and who participated in the maneuvering in the Jack and Marilyn friendship. I go with them. They were there.

Only about a year; brevity was the soul of it. It offered very little time. The President, now one of the most powerful men in the world, was making no secret of his friendship with the other blond actress.

"Jack's promised to marry me," she supposedly told some of the other girls.

They didn't believe it. Jack was very married to Jacqueline.

"After he leaves the White House, he says he'll divorce her and marry me," she came back.

"A famous Catholic like the President would never get a divorce!" they said. "And anyway, *after* he leaves the White House—eight years?"

Marilyn was just coming onto the Kennedy scene. The plan had just worked out perfectly for the Lawfords. Peter was the President's brother-in-law, his wife, Pat, was the President's sister. They were flying around in Kennedy planes, and Marilyn, seemingly recovered from the sleeping pill problem that sent her to the Payne-Whitney Psychiatric Clinic, was taken into the pack and became its most prominent member.

On June 7, 1961, I wired my papers a story from Las Vegas that Marilyn stole Frank Sinatra's show at the Sands by leaning on the railing at the ringside table and applauding every one of his songs while she drank champagne.

Crowded into the same showroom were President Kennedy's sisters Mrs. Lawford and Mrs. Stephen Smith, and Elizabeth Taylor, who was with her fourth husband, Eddie Fisher. Marilyn was on time for the show, a surprise to everybody, and she was vibrant. She said she hadn't been to Las Vegas since she obtained her first divorce there eleven years before.

"The now close friendship of America's two sex symbols—Marilyn Monroe and Frank Sinatra—exploded into the open," I wrote.

As Frank took Marilyn to Dean Martin's forty-fourth birthday party, Frank dismissed such talk. "I just took Marilyn out a few times so she wouldn't be cooped up in her hotel," he said.

The President flew to California—and he was seen at the Beverly Hills Hotel, as well as the Peter Lawfords' house in Santa Monica. Sinatra was building a guest house at Palm Springs for the President's scheduled visit to his home. It was to accommodate the Secret Service. Bobby Kennedy was a visitor at the Lawfords, too, and so was Marilyn Monroe. The rumors began.

That other blonde kept the President well occupied, and Marilyn was still future tense.

The scene shifted back East. The President was occasionally at Camp David or at the Kennedy compound, and tales came to me of his continuing fondness for nudity. At Camp David, the men and the girls went nude swimming, long before it was called skinny-dipping, and sat around naked afterward. The President in the same civilized, dignified, and elegant manner as always, would ask to be pardoned for yawning along about the middle of the afternoon.

"I'm going to take a nap," he would say as he left the group.

One of the girls would also leave later.

The President and Marilyn began to take a bedroom interest in each other in New York. She was frank in talking about it to one of her confidants. She tossed the thing off with her customary frivolity. "He may be a good President, but he doesn't grab me sexually," she reported—this was only after the first experience, however. Asked by this confidant to rate the Presidential performance, she giggled and answered, "He's very democratic." And she added: "Very penetrating."

His lofty position in the universe, his incandescent charm which was winning the applause of the whole world overawed most of the retinue of John F. Kennedy. But not all. A certain member of the Presidential pack was asked one night to pick up Marilyn Monroe at her New York apartment and escort her to a dinner party. It had been arranged by the President and the Kennedy acolytes. It was to be a little bit special, and at the Carlyle. The man to whom this request was made knew that these were his "bearding orders" for the evening. He did not object. The JFK warmth was infectious. There was a flavor of the clandestine to the party. With Marilyn Monroe there, and secretly set to frolic with the President after the dinner party, it would undoubtedly be a night to remember. The man who was commanded to be Marilyn's escort was actually flattered. A few weeks before, in

Washington, the President had tapped him gently on the face and said, "Hiya, baby!"

A Cabinet officer observing this familiarity with a man he hadn't seen before, said, "Who is *that?*"

The man who heard the remark about himself thought of saying "Oh, just one of Jack's beards," but thought better of it.

Because the President wanted to sneak off with Marilyn, the sit-down dinner was scheduled for 9 P.M. The President's "personal beard," as he was calling himself, was urged to fetch the Love Goddess on time. Some of the guests were already down on her for her famous lack of punctuality, as well as her sex reputation.

Arriving at her apartment on East Fifty-seventh Street at 8:45, the "personal beard" found Marilyn trying to wake herself up.

She was sitting in her bedroom, nude, looking into the mirror, studying her curves as though they were something new to her.

He knew her well enough from other boyfriends to be basic and imperative. Standing over her in her bedroom, he said, "Get dressed, for God's sake. We've got a date with the President of the United States!"

"I don't know what to wear," mumbled Marilyn, sleepily, going into her narcissistic trance, staring at herself in the mirror.

Angrily, her escort-to-be pulled a dress from a hanger and thrust it at her. "The way you go around, this is all you wear anyway. So get into this and you're dressed."

"No," said Marilyn, "I want to wear a disguise."

"A disguise!" shrieked her escort. "What for?"

"So anybody seeing me going to meet President Kennedy won't know I'm Marilyn Monroe!"

"You're keeping the President of the United States waiting, for Christ's sake. Does that mean anything to you?" he demanded.

"I'll go as a brunette. Where are my black wigs?" Marilyn rummaged through her wig collection. The phone rang.

It was somebody calling for the President. "Where the hell is Marilyn?"

Marilyn tried on three black wigs, chose one, tried on and rejected three dresses, finally accepted the fourth, and was ready to go one and one-half hours late.

"I swear this is the last time!" her escort told her. "This is too much. Jack will kill me."

Busily looking at herself in the mirrors along the way and enjoying her wig, Marilyn, now awake, made a forecast. "Five minutes after I'm there, they'll forget I was late."

The President was uncharming. "I can't believe this really happened," he blazed at her. "You ruined this whole dinner party. The food's spoiled. Everything's cold."

"I'm not," cooed Marilyn, putting a wiggle in her voice.

The President pouted about two or three minutes about her affront. "Then," the escort remembered, "the President looked down at her beautiful ass in that white dress that didn't have anything under it, and he melted. Five minutes later Marilyn twisted past me and winked. She was right. Everybody had forgotten that she'd been late. Including the President of the United States."

Thus began her *deliriums Kennedy*—John F. Kennedy. If Bobby had been in the picture, he seemed to be out by now. That was the view of "the inside insiders," at least. Marilyn, who would have loved to be a lady private eye, practiced her secrecy on her few confidants. She was airily mysterious about what was going on with "Mr. President," but at the same time she wanted them to know that something was.

Ebulliently, she told her masseur Ralph Roberts, one of the mornings after a visit to the Carlyle, the identity of the man she'd entertained.

The President had suffered back pains which had been so well reported in the press that everybody knew about them.

"And how was it?" asked Ralph Roberts.

"I think I made his back feel better!"

Marilyn became more open about it to other people. And she became possessive. To one of her dearest friends, in Hollywood, she said, "I've been telling Jack about you." (That was how he knew it was Jack and not Bobby.) "He wants us all to have dinner at the White House."

Then she voiced a complaint. "I wish we didn't have to have a beard all the time!"

Jacqueline Kennedy was really a barrier to Marilyn's happiness, the way Marilyn looked at it. Actually, Jackie Kennedy was spending a lot of time with her own friends in Europe and proving very enchanting to Rome and Paris. Marilyn was spending hours every day with her analysts trying to unhook herself from sleeping pills and continuing her close friendship with Joe DiMaggio, who loved her in his stubborn, stolid way although they were divorced two marriages back.

I saw Marilyn twice, all alone . . . well, alone except for her girlfriend, press agent Pat Newcomb. When Marilyn was alone, that meant to me that she was really hiding somebody or something because a sex symbol had to have sex the way a ball team had to have a ball.

Marilyn, it turned out, told more about it to Ralph Roberts, the masseur. "Jack and I have only done it twice so far," she said being very prim about it, as this was quite early in their intimacy. She would later recount to others how they had eluded the Secret Service at the Beverly Hills Hotel in Beverly Hills, at the White House, at the Carlyle, and how even on the President's family's plane they had hoped that the Secret Service agents had turned their eyes away and allowed the President a smidgeon of privacy.

Having been converted to the literati by ex-husband Arthur Miller, Marilyn frequently visited Martindale's bookstore in Beverly Hills. She bought books quite inconsistent with the Marilyn Monroe image.

She bounced out carrying books by obscure poets, some people thought just to cause comment. She selected a dictionary of terms used in analysis and pondered over "eroticism" and especially "anal eroticism." She purchased *The Thinking Body* by Mabel Ellsworth Todd which said that life seems to stem from the pelvic girdle area and that it isn't true that the thighbone's connected with the hipbone.

Fascinated by this revelation, she discussed it with her friend Ralph Roberts, the masseur. Then, while on a date one night, she phoned him.

"I'm with someone, Ralph," she said mysteriously. "Well, we're having an argument about the thighbone and the hipbone. And I told him. . . ." She had remembered it correctly. "Do I have it right?"

"Exactly," he said.

"I'll tell you all about it later," Marilyn said.

It wasn't until weeks later that she mentioned it. Not until after she'd made a cross-country trip. Paula Strasberg was giving a party for her daughter, Susan.

"Ralph," Marilyn said across a drink, "you remember that night I called you about the thighbone and the hipbone. . . .

"Well," she went on, "it was *he*."

Ralph knew she referred to Mr. President.

"And," she went on, like a proud little first-grade pupil, "I remembered what you'd taught me. And that's what I meant when I said I thought I had made his back feel better."

Mr. President was rapturously contented with the way most things were going. He didn't have as much time as he would have liked for his hobby (touch football). But that other blonde was still in the neighborhood from time to time. The girl with the snapping eyes was in trouble. Jackie Kennedy had found out about her. She was barred from the White House. There was the Bay of Pigs. A famous man who knew of this complexity commented, "Here's this man with his head full of the Bay of Pigs, and he's got all these little suckling pigs running around after him!"

His charm never left him. He was the hosts' host. He kept in good condition, having become a physical culture freak. One morning when all the rest of the pack had hangovers, he began summoning them to join him in a drink at 9 A.M.

One friend of his who told me about it said that he was unable to stir from the activities of the previous evening and that morning.

The President phoned personally.

"I warn you. The Secret Service is coming for you and has orders to bring your ass over here whether you're dressed or not!"

The friend reported, "Jack was there with a big bowl of Bloody Marys, and we started all over again."

More and more, Marilyn moved into the pack, into Jack's Pack. Cleverly, the Swinging President's surrogates placed her on some of the private jets shooting from Hollywood to Las Vegas to Reno to Palm Springs. She was welcome on her own; she was about the biggest show business celebrity in the world. She looked a Hollywood friend of mine right in the eye and told him, "It's Jack, not Bobby."

"You're kidding!" He thought he knew what was going on.

She nodded, and her chin looked very determined. (And well that chin should; it had once been repaired by a New York plastic surgeon.)

"Damn it, I'm telling you it's Jack!"

Her friend laughed at how she'd fooled him. "Not Bobby?"

"Oh, *no!*" She shrugged her shoulders, so violently that the tops of her breasts shook all the way up to her chin.

"Jack! The President of the United States!" Her friend shook his head. He could have believed Bobby, but the President! "I've never been to the White House."

"You'll go," Marilyn said. "I've talked to Jack about you. He wants us to come down."

It was getting into the spring of 1962, the last year of Marilyn's life. Marilyn saw the President at the Beverly Hills Hotel, but the Peter Lawfords' house in Santa Monica was a preferred rendezvous. Marilyn and Pat—complete opposites socially and ancestrally—had become close friends. They were both easy to like. They both enjoyed a drink. They were both privileged characters. If Pat wanted to take Marilyn on a trip on President Kennedy's plane, *The Caroline*, Marilyn would slip on one of her black wigs and smuggle herself aboard.

"Who's she kiddin'? I'd recognize that can anywhere!" remarked one of the witnesses to her fun. To help her carry out her disguise, her friends pretended not to recognize her.

On one of her trips with the pack to the Cal-Neva Lodge at Lake Tahoe, Marilyn, drinking more and more, got too much booze and too many pills, and her beautiful body was found nude and inert in one of the rooms. The phone was off the hook. The telephone operator, screaming for help, said she'd tried to kill herself.

Revived by doctors later, Marilyn came back fast, ran out into the corridor—nude—and hollered, "Look, gang, I'm off the pills!"

She explained, "I've got a new kind." The new kind appeared to be little less dangerous than the other.

President Kennedy was doubtless too busy to be informed of such incidents, but Marilyn's close friends were deeply concerned. She was literally gulping sleeping pills while drinking, and they believed her mental state to be precarious. This they said while recognizing that she was one of the leading women of the world, beautiful, sexy, desirable, and "box office."

A call came to me one day from a man who claimed to be an intermediary for Joe DiMaggio. He was asking me to warn Marilyn in my column that she would find herself in trouble if she didn't give up her associates.

I never found whether it was truly from Joe DiMaggio, but it could have been a roundabout request from him. He was strongly opposed to her new social life with the Kennedys and the Lawfords on their new plateau of power.

"Marilyn Monroe has lost her mind!" That was the alarming rumor I heard around the Beverly Hills Polo Lounge and Dave Chasen's restaurant in Hollywood. "She's taking thirty, forty pills a day, and boozing. It's just a matter of time."

One felt such sadness for the troubled creature who could be so sweet and loving that you forgave her all her tardiness. She made you wait because she literally was afraid to come out and face you.

I never saw her any way but soft and lovable. Maybe it was different working with her. Tony Curtis, who made a famous and odd remark, "It's like kissing Hitler," never retracted that statement concerning his experiences with her making *Some Like It Hot*. Tony Curtis said to me, "Billy Wilder once said, 'Marilyn Monroe is a mean seven-year-old girl.' I think he missed it by about a year and a half."

Dementia praecox, they were privately calling it. Her lawyers, doctors, analysts knew that she was almost around the bend and on the edge. Marilyn was pestering her lawyer Milton "Mickey" Rudin about changing her will. He stalled, afraid that he could not concede that she was "of sound mind."

Of course she did not know. That was their fear. If she knew that it had come as she always feared it would, she would kill herself. If she were placed in an institution, she would know and would kill herself. Better, perhaps, for her to work . . . still, if she really couldn't work, didn't show up at the studio, went on more sleeping pill blackouts, wouldn't she also one day kill herself?

The happy paranoiac Marilyn had decided on another important rendezvous with John F. Kennedy. The idea sprang from the brains of Broadway Producer Richard Adler and Peter Lawford.

Marilyn would sing "Happy Birthday" to President Kennedy at a party for 20,000 people at Madison Square Garden on Saturday night May 19 . . . and they would be together later.

Marilyn was already in serious trouble with Twentieth Century-Fox for falling into sleeping pill comas and failing to report for work in a picture with Dean Martin—*Something's Got to Give*. But she was determined about that chance to be with "Mr. President."

Marilyn cunningly plotted the trip weeks ahead, tricking producer Henry Weinstein into a promise to let her off the picture for a few days.

He was worried about her mental condition because she'd phoned from home one day when she couldn't come to work and invited him to her house. He found her naked and incoherent. But he had a picture to make.

Before starting the picture, Marilyn asked to be free from work on May 18–19.

"Why?" he asked.

She dissolved him with her innocence. "Because it's my period."

"OK," he said.

Marilyn's illnesses, whatever they were, delayed the beginning of shooting for two weeks. They finally began about May 15. The producer, a little panicky over being two weeks behind before they started, suddenly read in the papers that Marilyn Monroe was going to glamorize President Kennedy's birthday party in New York.

"I don't want you to go," he said.

"Why not?" she said. "We're not going to shoot those days."

"But we're not shooting because you said it's your period! You can go to the President's birthday party with your period—but you can't work with your period? What kind of period is that?"

"It's not really my period," confessed Marilyn. "I just told you that to get off to go to the birthday party!"

Weinstein shook his head. "You make me so mad I may vote Republican." He had been dirty-tricked not only by feminine wiles but by feminine hygiene.

When the company heads learned of her deception, they ordered Marilyn not to go to New York. But with a couple of her favorite four-letter Marilynisms, she flew off to the birthday party and one of her greatest personal triumphs.

Producer Richard Adler, "the President's favorite producer," was staging the party. Weeks before, discussing it, he told her "You have to be there on time—and you have to sing the song. I'll write a few lines of special lyrics. Now what will you wear?"

"Oooh, I think I'll wear a black, high-necked, full-length. . . ."

Peter Lawford was pressing him on. Adler got enthusiastic. Adler told me at the time, "Marilyn is the only girl in the world who should sing 'Happy Birthday' to the President . . . she's America's Sweetheart, a Sweet All-American Girl."

Not surprisingly, some VIP's objected. Some Cabinet members, some brass at the Pentagon, protested that it was wrong to have "a girl like that." Some objections came from within the White House itself, but nobody ever said that Jacqueline Kennedy dissented, although it was known that she would not attend.

In view of all the protests, Richard Adler checked with the President personally. He had been informed of the plan already by Peter Lawford, and there was the prospect of meeting Marilyn afterward.

"Why, I think it's a fine idea," the President said.

For Marilyn, singing this song to the President, who would be sitting right there enjoying it all, would be like a special kiss between them. And she kept saying, "Oh, I'm thrilled."

The President was kept in touch with all the "Happy Birthday" developments by Peter Lawford. To prove she'd learned the song and the special lyrics, she invited Richard Adler, Peter Lawford, and her coach Paula Strasberg to her East Fifty-seventh Street apartment to hear her rehearse.

It was a disaster.

"Can you imagine anybody not being able to remember the lyrics to 'Happy Birthday'?" Adler said later.

Nor did she remember the special lyrics. It took her six or seven minutes to stumble through a song that should have taken less than half that. Although he pretended that everything would be all right, Adler phoned the President who was already at the Carlyle.

The President had already heard from Marilyn, evidently.

"Mr. President," Adler began.

"Dick," said the President, "I hear you're having troubles."

"I'm a little afraid of Marilyn Monroe's singing 'Happy Birthday,' " he admitted.

The President laughed. "What can be wrong with Marilyn Monroe singing 'Happy Birthday'?"

On the phone, Adler gave an impersonation of Marilyn's singing of the anthem. The President laughed again, for the idea of such a triviality occupying a Presidential mind even for a couple of minutes struck him as hilarious.

"Oh, I think she'll be very good," the President said.

What Adler didn't know—and the President and Peter Lawford did—was that Marilyn purposely bungled the song in rehearsal just to upset Adler. It was her conception of a good joke to play on the President's favorite producer.

When Marilyn was introduced by Peter Lawford, she did not come out on the stage . . . not the first time . . . not the second time . . . and there was a great groan from the crowd that had heard a rumor that she had failed to show up.

Had she stood up the President of the United States?

Peter Lawford began again . . . a third time—it was his contribution of humor to the evening. "Mr. President, this lovely lady . . . this one lovely lady who has done so much . . . . who has meant so much . . . here she is, Mr. President . . . the late Marilyn Monroe. . . ."

Out she swung, stomach in, breasts and buttocks out, in a dress that Adlai Stevenson later said "looked like flesh with sequins sewn onto it."

Marilyn gasped. She worked her lips. She wound up her hips. She opened her mouth wide and round . . . she slithered and oozed and twisted and undulated . . . she gyrated, she hugged herself . . . with a hoarse whisper, she sang, "Dear President . . . Happy Birth-d-ay to-o-o you-oo-oo:

> For all the things you do
> The way you deal
> With U.S. Steel. . . .

Marilyn sang it so breathily, so gaspily, and with such a sexy interpretation that the coldest people were moved. The stagehands were wheeling out an enormous birthday cake while excitable fans of the President were actually jumping up and down. Marilyn had stolen the evening from the President, just she and her little bust and back side.

It showed unmistakably that Marilyn Monroe, thought by many to be a mental case, who should have been in an institution, was probably the most exciting woman in the world.

A year later, plus a few months, Jackie Kennedy would capture the sympathy of the whole world when she buried her assassinated husband. But that night Marilyn was queen of the May evening, and in due time, the President registered his great appreciation for the photographers. It was extraordinarily difficult for Jack to sneak away with Marilyn that night. But for a man who was able to leap fences in the cause of love or at least sexual gratification, Marilyn Monroe was worth an extraspecial effort.

Producer Richard Adler was vastly impressed.

"It showed," he said, "that the President was a better showman than I was. When Marilyn sang, she handled the lyrics well enough. But you couldn't hear them anyway. For the crowd was yelling and screaming for her. It was all like a mass seduction, with Marilyn whispering 'Happy Birthday, Dear President,' and the crowd drowning her out with its yells and cheers."

One thing that escaped most people was that to Jack Kennedy it was all a big joke, a send-up. He went along with Peter Lawford's elaborate description of Marilyn. He said, "I can now retire from politics after having had 'Happy Birthday' sung to me by such a sweet wholesome girl as Marilyn Monroe."

Sweet? Yes, at times. Wholesome? . . . Not quite the word. As JFK well knew.

Marilyn's flesh-colored dress was such a sexy success that President Kennedy picked up a copy of *Time* magazine, which showed her wearing it, and pointed it out to a few visitors at his desk in the White House the next week. He laughingly called particular attention to the way it caressed her posterior. One visitor, seeing the magazine on his desk, commented, "This is the kind of an administration I like. It's a big improvement over Eisenhower's!"

The big party that Saturday night was not at the Garden, but one immediately afterward at the home of movie executive and leading Democrat Arthur Krim (later on President Nixon's "enemy" list). Jimmy Durante got at the piano; Marilyn's ostensible escort was Arthur Miller's father. Marilyn's praises were sung, and her success was toasted. And she drank champagne as she made a spectacular swing across the room and introduced her former father-in-law to the President. Bobby Kennedy and the Kennedy sisters were there, too. But Jacqueline Kennedy wasn't—and not many people asked where she was.

The First Lady avoided political affairs. This was really a fund-raising event. She'd been sick with a cold the previous week—"from christening a submarine," the President had said earlier in Washington.

She'd canceled most of her weekend schedule, but the schedule, as she'd announced it at the beginning of the month, hadn't included her husband's party.

Her friends said she'd gone to the "horse country" or the "hunt country" where the Kennedys had leased a house at Middleburg, Virginia. The First Lady spent the weekend riding.

Two weeks after the birthday party, Marilyn looked extraordinary. She was working, "she seemed happy . . . it looked like we were really going . . . ," Producer Weinstein said.

Paula Strasberg, Marilyn's drama coach, getting $2,000 a week and expenses, was on the sidelines, murmuring that one must be careful. "This is the way it is with a Marilyn Monroe picture. You have to learn to live with it."

She referred to the days when Marilyn couldn't work owing to her "anxieties."

Suddenly something happened. Marilyn couldn't make it to work. She went into a deep depression from which psychiatrists and analysts couldn't extricate her. The studio knew that when she didn't work she cost them thousands of dollars. They had experienced more than they could bear. Paula Strasberg urged caution.

"I can't get the New York office to understand," Weinstein said. "They're looking at that damned payroll every week and how little we're getting done."

Later he believed that if he could have persuaded them to give her more time, they might have had a masterpiece and a financial winner, but the New York office had decided to fire her. Weinstein who understood schizophrenia, knew that Marilyn was in deep trouble mentally. Marilyn had come to the crossroads that her more thoughtful friends had feared. They had known of her constant dread that she was sure to go insane.

Troubles were coming fast for Marilyn. On June 6 the studio formally fired her; then Dean Martin announced he was quitting because he didn't intend to work with anybody else. The studio announced it was abandoning the picture. But on June 7 Marilyn gave me a story claiming she hadn't been fired and that she would leave her sickbed Monday and return to work. Marilyn maintained that she hadn't been able to work because she got an ear infection after doing a nude swimming scene. She had really been sick, she said.

"She is not physically ill," producer Weinstein said; he knew that Marilyn's returning to the studio Monday would do no good. The picture was over.

But Marilyn was making news all over the world. An Italian magazine was banned for publishing her nude swimming scenes. The Vatican paper *L'Osservatore Romano* in an amusing editorial wondered why no director would have suspected Marilyn might catch a cold in her ear from going swimming naked . . . "without an ounce of clothing on her."

It mentioned also that the dress she wore at the President's birthday party "weighed about an ounce."

The nude swimming that she'd done voluntarily—it was her own idea—produced such thrilling results that she began to fight back. For one reason, she was determined to see President Kennedy again following their last get-together after the birthday party.

She was at the telephone as she'd never been before. She was giddily gadding from Los Angeles to Lake Tahoe, and from the Lawfords she heard about the big midsummer social event of the year in Washington, the opening of Irving Berlin's new musical, *Mr. President*, starring Nanette Fabray and Robert Ryan. It was scheduled for September 25. Her taste of politics through the Lawfords and the Kennedys was heady wine for a girl of such background. Her previous contact with Washington had been with Arthur Miller, when he testified in some Congressional investigations.

"I'm going to that opening," she promised the Lawfords, who imagined that the President would be happy to see her.

But Marilyn was also trying to charm Peter Levathes and other studio heads of Twentieth Century-Fox to take her back and start the picture over.

"Marilyn invited me to her house," Levathes told me. "She wanted me to see some pictures she'd taken for *Vogue*. She spread the pictures out on the floor of the patio, and we picked some we liked.

"We were going to start the picture over and take her back. The announcement was to be made after we'd put all the elements together. She felt bad about not working. It was the first time she'd been fired like this. I was delighted to get her back and sympathetic. We would get out a statement that she had re-affirmed her determination to do the picture, and by God, we and she would go through with it this time."

Her lawyer, who knew her condition better, did not want to hurry into it. He had his secret doubts about her ability to do it. "When she feels better," he said.

And now it was the week before her death.

The many, many plans and appointments she made for the next week reveal the conflict in her disturbed mind. She was gaily talking to old friend Sidney Skolsky, the columnist, about the possibility of doing a picture about Jean Harlow. He was going to show her some film. She was going to meet with attorney Rudin Monday to talk about the new contract with the studio and about making changes in the will. But she was also going to New York, and she told the Strasbergs and others that she'd be staying for a while. But how could she when she had several appointments in Hollywood . . . and was planning to resume the picture?

Ostensibly she was happy and clear-headed talking to producer Arthur Jacobs about doing another film, *What a Way to Go*, which he eventually did with Shirley MacLaine.

"She wanted very much to do it, so she said," Jacobs (who died in 1973) recalled when I talked to him after her death. "I wanted Lee Thompson to direct it, and Marilyn wanted to see some pictures he'd directed.

"She came over to our office on Sunset, and we ran three of them, on Monday, Wednesday and Friday. She brought her physician [Dr. Hyman Engelberg] along one day. After seeing the pictures, Marilyn said, 'That's the right guy. What about meeting him?' "

"What about five o'clock Saturday?" Jacobs said.

Marilyn approved. But Jacobs phoned her about seven Friday that Thompson would be available at five o'clock Monday instead. (This is significant because at five on Monday Marilyn was dead.) Marilyn responded, "Monday at five, then," and was enthusiastic about the project—at least Jacobs, who'd known her for several years, including a period when he'd been her press agent, thought she was.

On that same Friday, producer-composer Jule Styne phoned her from New York, offering to throw a life belt to a drowning woman, figuratively. Having read of Marilyn's troubles at Twentieth Century-Fox, he inquired whether she'd like to attempt a musical version of *A Tree Grows in Brooklyn*. He would want to use some of the score of *Pink Tights*, which she knew and liked. He hoped to get Frank Sinatra.

"OoooOOh, I'd love to work with Frank! I'll be in New York Thursday, and we'll talk about it."

She'd be in New York Thursday? Well, she said she would. Styne noted on his desk pad an appointment with Marilyn Monroe for two thirty Thursday—which, as it turned out, would be after her funeral.

After the tragic end, Styne remembered he had been answered personally by Marilyn when he called, not by a secretary. Marilyn was also on the phone with the poet Norman Rosten, an enchanting little gentleman who likes berets, and his wife, who had become close, understanding friends. They were in Brooklyn, and they remembered Marilyn asking, "When are you coming out to see me? Let's go to the theater. Let's have some fun."

They couldn't be sure that she'd said she was coming back to New York immediately.

And Norman Rosten later contributed the wise observation: "When some people make the rosiest plans, they may really be planning something else entirely."

Their impression was that she wanted to get away from the Hollywood scene—some time.

But as she dialed long distance to call a close friend, Henry Rosenfeld, the New York textile manufacturer, she revealed the other side of Marilyn. This had to do with meeting with the President.

Good-looking, slim-waisted Henry Rosenfeld was one of the friends she called upon from time to time. To her, he stood for success and security—which she felt she didn't have.

"I hate the idea of growing old," she would tell him. "I'm afraid I'll wind up poor like my mother . . . or some old washerwoman." How could she be certain she'd never be like that? Once she suggested that she give him proceeds of *Some Like It Hot*—and he'd guarantee her $1,000 a week for life.

Henry Rosenfeld, a kindly man, married and father of grown children, respected her sincerity and need for help. He calmly told her that she never need worry.

He knew about the President. He knew about a lot of things, including Marilyn's "false pregnancies," when she got the symptoms of approaching motherhood and gained ten or twelve pounds: a psychological thing. He told me about Marilyn and the President in 1965 when we had lunch at the old Toots Shor's on Fifty-second Street. He told me again about Marilyn and the President in September, 1973, when we had lunch at Gallagher's on the same street.

"There was no doubt it was Jack and not Bobby," Henry Rosenfeld assured me, and I cite him and Sidney Skolsky as the unquestioned authorities on this subject. Henry Rosenfeld was such a close personal friend that he lent her thousands of dollars when she wasn't working, without a suggestion of collateral. He went back with her a dozen or more years when she was in El Morocco "sitting on the wrong side of the room," in the remote unfashionable section they called Siberia.

"We invited Marilyn and her escort to sit with us. She was thrilled, and we were friends till the day she died," Henry Rosenfeld says.

"And she was so proud to be the girl having an affair with the President of the United States because that was IMPORTANT! She wouldn't always mention his name. She would sometimes say to me, 'You Know Who!'

"And of course I knew Who!

"She would say, 'I'm going to be with You Know Who again—he's so important, I can't mention his name.' Here she was in love with Jack and she knew I would do anything I could to help her see him. I don't think it was important to him. I don't think she was anything more than another girl to have an affair with. But to Marilyn, it was very important. She was going to bed with the President of the United States. She was awed by big names. She was awed by Joe DiMaggio at first, she was awed by Arthur Miller, she certainly was awed by the President of the United States—by You Know Who!"

That's how it stood that final week.

It was Thursday that she phoned Rosenfeld . . . this had a prior claim on all the plans she made on Friday. When she reached him, she ecstasized about returning the next week or so to New York.

"I want you to take me to Washington for the opening of *Mr. President*," she said. He declared that he would try. It was good business for a textile manufacturer to appear at such an event with Marilyn Monroe. Marilyn was, in her cunning little feminine mind, hoping to get together with the President again, and this time it was she who would pick out the "beard."

Besides, it was weeks away. It might conflict with resuming the picture—just as they'd clashed over it when she defied them and went to the birthday party. "I'm going, Henry, I'm going to Washington, and I want to go with you!"

Death stopped Marilyn from going. She probably wouldn't have enjoyed it—still, she might have! Jackie Kennedy was there in all her First Lady grandeur. The audience looked at her as much as it looked at the actors. The actors also looked at Jackie. They gave a bad performance. Irving Berlin considered the opening a bad one. President Kennedy missed the first act.

"He's probably got a date," one of the pack said.

"No, I think he and Bobby are watching the Sonny Liston-Floyd Patterson fight," another one thought.

The party at the British Embassy was glittery with celebrities, and nobody could have dimmed Jackie's brilliance but Marilyn, who had been dead since August 5. The Kennedys sat at sort of a ringside table, and the President danced and danced. When he danced with the girl with the snapping eyes, it was observed by one snoop that I know that he kissed her on the ear.

The strange death of Marilyn Monroe has become a chapter of American folklore more fascinating than Lizzie Borden, and if the paeans continue to gush from the typewriters of people who didn't know her, she will become the American Joan of Arc who was burned at the stake at Hollywood and Vine.

Her death was correctly explained, in my opinion, by the late Arthur Jacobs, who said, "I think she got drunk and forgot how many pills she had taken."

While it demolishes all the crackbrain theories of unrequited love and Communist murder plots, it corresponds with my conclusions. I interviewed several hundred people after her death in an investigation lasting several years. I determined at the time not to write a book about her because Robert Kennedy was still with us.

It's remarkable that Marilyn, a paradox in life, loved and worshiped by some who thought her one of the sweetest creatures on earth, considered by others a saleswoman of sex, should still arouse controversy as to whether she died accidentally or intentionally.

Going back to that last week. . . .

Marilyn hadn't had any spectacularly obvious sex life in months. In February, she'd visited ex-husband Joe DiMaggio, who was teaching batting to the New York Yankees in Fort Lauderdale. They seemed to have the penthouse suite at the Yankee Clipper Motel. He drove her to Miami and put her on a plane for Mexico. When he kissed her good-bye, they laughed off questions about reconciling.

"What do you like best in a man?" they asked her in a press conference in Mexico.

"Masculinity," she answered, wiggling in her tight-lime green jersey.

"What don't you like about a man?"

"Nothing I can think of."

Looking tired and red-eyed, Marilyn claimed that she was happy at the news that Arthur Miller had just married Austrian-born photographer Ingeborg Morath, whom he'd met while she was photographing Marilyn, Clark Gable, and the other stars in *The Misfits* in 1960.

"You're a three-time loser?"

"But I haven't given up!" And with that she went off to Cuernavaca and Taxco, looking for furniture for her home in Los Angeles with a Mexican motif. She was traveling with no men; only Pat Newcomb, her girl press agent.

Then came the picture, the President's birthday party, and the Hotel Carlyle afterward, and the quick trips on the Kennedy plane. . . .

Now it was Saturday, August 4. Without considering that conflicting and impossible schedule, she was still taking pills, though supposed to be fighting the habit. The world's most loved female could do as she wished. She had persuaded both her physician and her analyst to give her pills, evidently in such a manner that they were confused about whether the other was giving her pills. It was a small matter, anyway. The cuddliest of the sexpots could have cajoled almost any pharmacist's assistant to slip her some pills with just one little wiggle.

"I have to get some sleep," she was always gasping in that breathy way. A night's sleep, she thought, would cure everything.

"Why can't I sleep?" Sometimes she thought it was because of her nightmares. Horrendous dreams . . . of guilt. Frightening ghosts accusing her of the wrongs she'd done . . . Sleeping with married men . . . Promiscuous . . . Resentful of her mother for allowing her to be born an illegitimate . . . Mean . . . nasty . . . overambitious.

Hating her father . . . who would never admit his paternity . . . firing people who had helped her . . . suddenly dropping old friends through some whim. . . .

She remembered a friend showing her Goya's hobgoblins at the Metropolitan Museum of Art. "I understand Goya!" she exclaimed to her friend. "He understands me. I see ghosts and hobgoblins in my dreams every night." She shuddered.

She took some pills. . . . Sunday was going to be a busy day. . . . Tomorrow and tomorrow. . . . She had a bottle that held fifty. She would be seeing Sidney Skolsky tomorrow. She would be going to the beach. She had a lot of things to do. The thing to do was to get some sleep, and she'd have to get to bed early.

Peter Lawford and Patricia had a pleasant little house on the ocean in Santa Monica, where both the President and the Attorney General had visited them and where both had met Marilyn. Sometimes they said with a laugh that they were "bearding" for one or the other. The house is hidden from the Pacific Coast Highway and is hardly noticeable.

That Saturday afternoon, Peter realized that with his wife Pat visiting the Kennedys at Hyannis, Marilyn might have no companionship.

He phoned her. "This is Pee-tah," he said, giving it the English pronunciation. "Do you want to have dinner here?"

"I don't want to get in any all-night poker games," she said.

"You weren't even invited to play poker!" Peter retorted. "Do you want to come or not?"

"Let's make it early, I have a busy day tomorrow," Marilyn said.

"Seven o'clock," Peter Lawford said.

The remainder of that event was first described to me by Peter Lawford some months later as he sat in the house where it occurred. He repeated it to me several times later. It is one of the saddest stories in show business history.

"The *late* Marilyn Monroe" of course did not arrive at seven o'clock nor even at eight. At around eight, Peter Lawford phoned Marilyn's house.

She answered the phone in what he remembered as a weird, sleepy, fuzzy voice. His dinner guests, including George "Bullets" Durgom, the popular agent, were talking, and it wasn't easy to hear. But Peter recalled that he used the popular salutation of the day, "Charlie." Everybody was called "Charlie," regardless of sex.

"Hey, Charlie, what happened to you?" he asked Marilyn.

In words that were slurred, halting, and unclear, Marilyn said that she wasn't going to make it there for dinner. She was too tired. Pat Newcomb wasn't coming, either. They'd had a quarrel, and Pat had gone home. Peter Lawford decided from her uneven voice and enunciation that Marilyn was either drunk or half-asleep from sleeping pills. This was not an unusual condition for her at that time.

But what Marilyn next said gave him the scare of his life.

"Say good-bye to Pat, say good-bye to the President, and say good-bye to yourself, because you're a nice guy," Marilyn said.

She had said good-bye! This just wasn't an ordinary sleeping pill jag. Marilyn's voice faded away as though she'd dropped off asleep or let the phone fall from her hand.

"When somebody says good-bye, I figure that's terminal," Peter Lawford told me later.

Going into a mild panic, but concealing his concern from his guests, Lawford phoned his manager, Milt Ebbins. "I think I should go over there and see if she's all right," Lawford said.

With his client uppermost in his mind, Ebbins replied, "You can't go over there, Peter! You're the brother-in-law of the President of the United States. Your wife's away. Anyway, you're not the one to go. That's for her doctor or analyst! Let me get in touch with the doctors or her lawyer! They can help her!"

Marilyn had done this before in what seemed to be an attempt to get sympathy. She had been found naked on the floor at the Cal-Neva Lodge at Lake Tahoe with the phone off the hook.

"But she said good-bye to me. She may be dying," Lawford argued.

Beginning a phone search for the doctors and lawyers, Ebbins was frustrated by the clock. It was cocktail time and dinner time in Beverly Hills on Saturday night. Answering services answered.

It was probably a half hour before Ebbins located attorney Rudin at a cocktail party. Rudin began trying to locate Dr. Greenson. Rudin, who was stalling Marilyn on the new will, who was stalling her on making a new deal with Twentieth Century-Fox to resume the movie, because he wasn't sure she could do it, eventually got to Dr. Greenson, who said he believed that she was all right because he'd been with her before and she seemed OK.

"I still think I should go over there," Lawford said.

To satisfy Lawford, Rudin called Mrs. Eunice Murray, a psychiatric nurse living in Marilyn's house employed to look after her. She had a separate phone. Rudin said she found Marilyn to be OK. She told Rudin that Marilyn's record player was playing Sinatra songs, and that there was a light under the door. Rudin conveyed all this to Ebbins, who conveyed it to Peter Lawford.

"I want to hear it from Rudin himself," declared Lawford, still believing he should go there himself.

Another phone call, and another. Rudin personally told Lawford of Mrs. Murray's assurances that Marilyn was OK. At this point, Lawford decided not to press it further.

They didn't know at that time that Marilyn, a fanatic about

privacy, kept the door closed to keep Mrs. Murray out. The door being closed, the light being on, the records being played, really meant nothing.

Lawford blamed himself for not saving her after she was found dead at 3:30 A.M. lying nude and facedown on the bed with a phone in her hand. Attorney Rudin was among those who told him that it wouldn't have mattered much, for Marilyn was going to do it sooner or later anyway.

The significant thing to me was that Marilyn in her farewell message, as Peter remembered it, said:

"Say good-bye to Pat, say good-bye to the President. . . ."

Not to Bobby, not to the Attorney General, but "to the President."

Marilyn made many calls Friday and Saturday. She made one to Hollywood hairstylist Sidney Guilaroff Saturday night—considerably later, he believes, than her conversation with Lawford, which suggests she might have revived for a while and then taken more pills. "I am very depressed," she told him. That was the tenor of many of her calls. She seems also to have left a message for Ralph Roberts, her masseur, whom she often called when in the depths.

The rumor spreaders liked the gossip that Marilyn had been trying to reach Bobby Kennedy.

That was from those who believed that Bobby was her favorite Kennedy. If she was phoning any Kennedy, it was probably to get in touch with Jack, and if anybody knows that for a fact, it's probably Peter Lawford. And he isn't going to tell!

As for the wild rumors about murder plots. . . . If there had been any such thing, wouldn't the brothers Kennedy have had the FBI and the Secret Service crawling all over the premises for clues? That never happened.

The consensus is that Marilyn did not kill herself intentionally. Lee Strasberg told me that she had discussed it long before in the way that people do. "If she had done it deliberately, she would have done certain things," he said.

"Left a note?" I said.

"Not a general note," he said. "It would have been differently done. Because of something that she'd done before. . . ."

A mystery to the end.

Not entirely, however; because while she probably did not *plan* to kill herself, it's conceivable that once she felt herself slipping away, she fancied the idea as being a very romantic notion and surrendered herself to it as the goal she'd been drifting toward.

Otherwise, why would Marilyn have said farewell to Peter Lawford, Pat Lawford, and "the President"?

She knew she was going.

A bizarre but interesting piece of thinking came from Ralph Roberts, the masseur. "Marilyn could never have planned to kill herself," he said. "Because if she had, she'd have been in better physical condition for it!"

He meant that she'd have been beautified for the occasion with a new hairdo and certainly a manicure. Everybody shrank from mentioning that when she was found dead, beside the empty bottle that had contained fifty pills, she had shockingly unkempt fingernails. Ralph Roberts believed that if she had planned to die she would have done it more tastefully, grandly, and with a happy, flashy Marilyn Monroe flair.

President Kennedy had plans to be meeting Marilyn late that summer or in the fall in Palm Springs. She was dead. Not to have gone, however, would have tipped off one very interested party that he was to have met her there. He went.

How frequently they met, we'll never know. Peter Lawford could make a guess, but though he's no longer a part of the Kennedy group, he won't. Whether Marilyn was trying to reach the President on the phone that Saturday afternoon and evening, we'll never know from him, either.

The President was being very much a happy, devoted family man that Saturday and Sunday. He was at Hyannis Port with his children and with Jacqueline; she was leaving for Italy the next day for a much-headlined vacation on the yacht of the Fiat auto magnate Gianni Agnelli. The President had been described a short time before by the New York *Times* as being "in essentially good health despite a recurrent back ailment and tiny new lines around his eyes after sixteen months in the White House."

Marilyn's many phone calls that last Saturday included one to Hyannis Port.

At least it is the recollection of Peter Lawford that she intended to make one. When Joe DiMaggio took over Marilyn's body and the funeral arrangements, and barred all the Hollywood stars and celebrities from the services, he included the President's sister Patricia Lawford and her husband Peter Lawford in the non-invited.

"I was appalled that Pat Lawford would leave Hyannis Port to come to the funeral to learn without even asking 'May I?' that she'd been refused," Lawford said.

"I was so amazed," Lawford added, "because in one of Marilyn's calls to me Saturday, she asked for Pat's phone number in Hyannis Port."

What the two girls talked about, if they ever got together on the phone, would have been so confidential that we'll never know that from Pat. Marilyn's lawyer Milton Rudin protested so angrily to DiMaggio that he was admitted to the funeral after he'd said "You are keeping out her close friends."

"If it hadn't been for some of her close friends, she wouldn't be where she is," DiMaggio retorted.

Joe DiMaggio has grown in handsomeness and respectability in the years since Marilyn died. His face is always on TV and in the papers, in advertisements for a bank. Happening to meet him in La Scala restaurant in New York in May, 1973, I spoke to him about Marilyn for the first time since he once asked my wife and me to suggest how he could get her back shortly after their divorce. He was a sad, depressed hero in those days, willing to listen to advice from anybody.

This time I asked him if he knew of the new books about Marilyn. He did. "My sister sent me some clippings."

He was uncomfortable but courteous. "It's a sore subject with me and I have a lot of bad memories," he said. "I've always refrained from talking about it.

"But I don't think she took all those pills by intent. I don't believe it was suicide. Accidentally, yes."

I told him that Marilyn's executor, Aaron R. Frosch, had sent him a $5,000 check, as repayment on a loan, and that Frosch was mystified because DiMaggio had never cashed the check. Joe replied to me that he'd never seen such a check.

"No reason I wouldn't take it—I have as much right to it as some others," he said. The bitterness was still there.

But so was the love for Marilyn still there. I asked if he still sends the flowers three times a week to her burial place.

He nodded and answered in his firm and unemotional manner, "I pay the florist to send them. To never stop sending them."

I thought back to the day of the funeral when he was not in such good control and sobbed openly saying "I love you, I love you, I love you." He had kissed her before the coffin was closed and then murmured the words softly as he took a very long final look at the crypt where his ex-wife lay.

But now, 11 years later, Joe said a polite good night and walked around the corner and back to the Americana Hotel. He remains a bachelor without any obvious attachments or entanglements. The few girls he is seen with often seem to bear a resemblance to Marilyn. Today Marilyn would be nearing her 48th birthday . . . pressing toward half-a-hundred. She would have hated reaching that age. Because she would often shudder when somebody mentioned middle age. It was well that she died when she did. Today she might well be looking for movie roles for a character woman. She might be thinking of having a plastic surgeon remove the bags from under her eyes, which would be—horrible thought —like Helen of Troy getting a face-lift. God, or the fates, or whoever, was good in letting the Sex Symbol die when she was still young and lovely—and sexy.

President Kennedy's interest in Marilyn was strictly physical because they had little in common mentally. She wrote few letters because she had trouble with spelling. Once she called across a room, while writing a note, "How do you spell were?" This was the girl who was wooed and won by Pulitzer Prize Playwright Arthur Miller.

Still, she tried. Though some of the few letters she wrote were barely legible, she attempted to write poetry, and she undertook to paint. Once when she reversed the procedure and took my picture, she explained, "Joe bought me a Rolleiflex!" I never heard of her using the camera again.

Marilyn's achievements were largely in the field of the physical. Once at a night party at Toots Shor's restaurant, Marilyn, not wearing any pants that night, sat down on a chair and got splinters in her famous posterior. The splinters went through her thin dress. My wife took Marilyn to the powder room and extracted the splinters.

Robert Mitchum went with Marilyn by plane to a personal appearance in Seattle. The drum majorettes and the state police were out to greet her. Marilyn had to go to the ladies' room first. In the toilet, Marilyn discovered that the plumbing equipment of the toilet had been removed when the plane landed. "But when you got to go, you got to go." Marilyn went, forgetful of some state police waiting restlessly below the plane. Mitchum claimed that a couple of state policemen did not object in the least to Marilyn's thoughtlessness although it was quite disastrous to their uniforms.

She could be generous. "She bought some A.T. & T. stock for some friends of hers," Joe DiMaggio told me, "when she didn't have the money."

As one of the reporters who trusted her when she lived, I want to cite Marilyn for being as faithful to me on a news story.

It was the summer of 1960. She had arrived at Reno to film *The Misfits* with Clark Gable with a bottle of 500 pills. I visited her there and was amazed at the confusion and delay she'd already caused. She and Arthur Miller weren't speaking. Some months before, Miller, returning to their bungalow at the Beverly Hills Hotel to get his pipe, found her already in bed with Yves Montand. "Let's straighten it out and get the work done," Miller said grimly.

Marilyn was using the pills generously in Reno, had halted production while she went to a hospital, and had driven director John Huston to spending profitless nights at the Reno casinos.

But Huston got her out of the hospital and finished the picture. Back in Los Angeles, he told me, "I got her back to work by getting her off the pills. I got her to taper off on tranquilizers."

"Can I print that?" I asked Huston.

"Why not?" Huston said.

Here was a constructive story that might help other barbiturate users. But what were the details? Huston hadn't told me. I wrote it, but in reading my copy, I decided that in fairness to Marilyn, I should ask her consent to use it. It was a very personal thing, and her words would make it a better story.

I proceeded to outline my idea on the phone, when I returned to New York, to the late Arthur Jacobs, then her press agent.

Seldom had I been so pampered by publicists. He personally came to my office with two assistants to plead with me not to release the story.

"Marilyn wants to make a deal with you," Jacobs said. If I'd forget this story, she'd soon give me "a good story"—an exclusive.

It took only a little thinking to guess she was going to divorce Arthur Miller, and that would be my scoop—and a great one.

I agreed, but I was afraid. I was in New York, Marilyn was in

L.A. Louella Parsons, Hedda Hopper or Sheilah Graham might steal my story. I nursed it along, keeping in close touch with Marilyn through her publicists. Autumn came. The Nixon-Kennedy Presidential race was heating up. Glamor was missing from the front pages, which were filled with the campaign blasts.

Election week arrived. I was getting nervous about my story. What was keeping Marilyn from her announcement?

Came a late call. Marilyn's "good story" was about ready. In a day or two.

It would warrant headline display. I outlined the story to Paul Sann, the executive editor of the New York *Post*.

"I might have it for Tuesday," I said anxiously.

"Tuesday's no good," he said. "That's election day." He was thinking in terms of display and space.

"Yeah," I said. "Wednesday?"

"Wednesday's worse. The paper'll be filled with the election tables. Your story'll get lost on page ninety-six."

"Thursday then?"

"Thursday's not much better," he said. "Do you think you could possibly hold it till Friday?"

"Jesus Christ, Paul!" I screamed. "You're asking me to keep this story from those female vultures out there for three or four days! I'm not that good!"

"I'm just hoping you could hold it till a day when we can give it a ride," he said gently.

He was right—and I held on, but I'd never been so frustrated protecting a good story. The Wednesday and Thursday papers were choked with John F. Kennedy's defeat of Richard M. Nixon based partly on the close victory in Illinois which the Republicans later charged was stolen from them.

I was frothing for action about 1 A.M. Friday when I got the call from Marilyn keeping her word. I could release the story.

And there it was at the top of page 1 in the New York *Post* on Friday, November 11, 1960:

MONROE AND MILLER
SPLIT; DIVORCE NEAR   (Exclusive—By Earl Wilson)

The headline under that read:

GOP ASKS RECHECK
IN 11 CLOSE STATES.

There was a large front-page picture of Marilyn Monroe and Arthur Miller, arms around each other, Marilyn actually hugging the tall, professorial-looking playwright, taken back in happier days. It would be fair to assume that Marilyn Monroe never suspected that she would someday enjoy a dalliance with the man who occupied the rest of the front page that day, John F. Kennedy, soon to be the new President.

Exhibitionists "For Kicks"

I DON'T often have two in one day.

Not two like that anyway. Two interviews. Linda, of course, was the bigger celebrity. Linda Lovelace of *Deep Throat*, who had performed oral love feats that defied the laws of nature and anatomy, was in New York City promoting her book of confessions, *Inside Linda Lovelace*. Linda gave a press conference at the Gaslight Club where I overheard these comments:

"Linda's very hoarse."

"Yes, she sounds like she's got a frog in her throat."

"Not a frog . . . she's got a man in her throat!"

And the day I interviewed her I also discussed the same sexual exercises with a competing celebrity, Miss Marilyn Chambers, alias Miss Ivory Snow. That was Memorial Day week, 1973, which must have been the sexiest week in Fun City history.

Linda Lovelace, the face that sank a thousand ships, the girl who went down on history. What is Linda Lovelace really like? "I'll tell you what she's really like . . . she's a pig and a slob," a friend of mine told me, but inasmuch as my friend was also a pig and a slob at times, I didn't swallow his story.

It was sexy everywhere that week. The sex scandals erupted in Parliament. There'd been three murders in the sadomasochistic scene in Greenwich Village, according to *Oui* magazine, which specializes in that field. It also carried an article on "fuck music," make-out music, sheet music, saying Johnny Mathis had got more women pregnant than any man who ever lived. (With his sexy songs that got them in the mood for loving.) What else happened that week? Nothing much. Just Watergate.

One day it became my great good luck to be granted an interview with Marilyn Chambers, the Ivory Snow Girl who was one of the paradoxes of the Genitalia Generation. While her pretty picture, showing her as the mother of a small child, was being used by Ivory Soap in its advertising, Marilyn had another audience in the pornographic movie *Behind the Green Door*. I rushed off to see the film which was showing at the Orleans Theater on West Forty-seventh Street, where I'd previously seen the girl on *The Bicycle Built for Screw*.

Clearly, this was quite a girl I was going to see!

"She's insatiable!" I thought as I watched the movie, forgetting for the moment that this was a movie.

There was this lovely innocent-looking blond girl who is carried onto a bed naked and has her legs spread apart and her breasts kneaded and fondled by some women. Very soon thereafter she is having sex with four men. She is sucking a penis, she is stroking the penis of another man with her right hand, and another with her left, while a fourth man is licking her down below. There is no conversation, but there is some gurgling attesting to the authenticity of the oral sex.

The surroundings—in the movie—are those of a supposedly private sex club actually in existence in New York and other cities. Men and women in dinner jackets and evening gowns sit watching the sex athletics, wearing masks, and they get excited and start masturbating themselves or each other.

I felt as with the other pictures I'd seen that even the hottest of the sex grew monotonous.

In *Behind the Green Door*, there was, however, a break in the oral sex routine and the masturbation—when a large black man with an erection was brought in and, after oral foreplay, entered the heroine forcefully and copulated with her seemingly forever. The black man wore white drawers from which his penis emerged about a foot. His black face had been decorated with white markings rising from his eyebrows to his hair, suggesting Satan. He had been standing watching her as she had sex with the other four men, and now, like the champion, he took over, first with his mouth.

There was slow tomtom music that got faster. After he gave her cunnilingus, he kissed her lips, and then as he inserted his penis, she clung to him seeming to enjoy every stroke.

"Nothing phony about this, this has got to be real hard-core," I thought. After what seemed to be ten or fifteen minutes, she appeared to have a violent orgasm, and she was carried away limp and exhausted. The masked spectators were masturbating wildly.

The closing scenes showed semen dripping from the black man's penis into her lips as she strained to catch it on her tongue. This was repeated for emphasis, the droppings being pulled away, then brought closer, then being pulled away. The photography was surely imaginative!

"Explicit sex" is the term that Marilyn Chambers used to describe hard-core.

It was around midnight when I met Marilyn Chambers in her hotel suite (the St. Regis). While I have had varying reactions to actresses I've interviewed, I'd never quite had the shock I had now as I sat looking at this tall, sweet-faced blonde in her early twenties, remembering that an hour or so before I'd seen her on the screen having sex with three penises and a tongue at the same time.

With her were the famous Mitchell brothers, producers of more than 200 porno pictures; the wife of one of them, and Russell Fradkin, an advertising man representing the picture. Miss Chambers was sipping cognac, and there was a cognac bottle on the coffee table. It was strained and a bit embarrassing to try to interview a sex actress with an audience, and I was glad when Fradkin suggested they would go downstairs to the bar and leave us together. First, though, somebody asked if I'd seen the picture and followed through with "How did you like it?"

That was a difficult one for me to field.

"It didn't have much dialogue in it," I weakly answered. "But I didn't see it all." Having said that, I had to explain that I must have come in about the middle. They chose to leave for the bar at about this minute, which saved me further embarrassment.

They had just returned from the Cannes Film Festival where they'd been promoting their film, and there was an artistic film magazine, Zoom, on the coffee table.

There was shortly a call from another room, and before we really got started, the evening's heroine said, "Excuse me, it's my husband." I gathered that her husband, Doug Chapin, a San

Francisco mechanic "and a bagpiper," was either sleeping in the next room or calling from outside.

"*Behind the Green Door,*" Marilyn said, "is an old pornographic story that's been around for fifty years. It's been passed around on mimeographed sheets, and it's very well known, though nobody can quite be sure who wrote it. It's a sexual fantasy about a girl who's been abducted and taken into this private sex club. I used to work in New York and live here, and I know they have a lot of such clubs here.

"The story is that some men see this girl brought through the green door and they don't know what happened to her. . . .

"She's been abducted, and there's a woman who tells her that she's going to be used for sexual purposes, there's no way she can get out of it, and she might as well enjoy it. . . .

"And that's what you see in the film. There is no real reason for dialogue because all the talk is with the body, the eyes, and the emotions. Words would have blown it as far as I'm concerned. It was a challenge for me to act.

"Having actual sex on the screen is getting to be a very groovy thing," she said, leaning back on the couch while I sat listening to what was a sort of declaration of independence in this curious world. "Explicit sex is very honest," Marilyn continued.

"*Last Tango in Paris* is for the birds. I like the dialogue, but the sex is so unreal and phony and corny. It was also boring," she said.

Warming to her subject, she said, "Simulated sex is out. Sex has got to be explicit nowadays. It's got to be real and honest. It can't be faked; it can't be phonied up. It's got to be truthful. That's what the public wants now, explicit sex, and the producers and theaters are finding that out. We have another picture, *Resurrection of Eve*, which is explicit sex. Now it has a lot of dialogue and real great music."

"How explicit is it? How many guys do you have sex with at the same time in this one?"

"I don't know," she said with a laugh. "I haven't seen it lately."

Marilyn then sermonized about the value of the experience of having all that sex (in the film).

"Frankly, I had my doubts that I could do the picture to start with," she said. "Art and Jim Mitchell had no doubts, but I did. I was a little hesitant—because at first I didn't want to make it too dirty.

"But I think it helped make me a better person," she continued. "I'm more honest with myself about life. I don't feel hung up as much as I was before."

This was a defensive attitude that other sex actresses took, Linda Lovelace included. It is a part of the thinking of the Genitalia Generation which we would have denounced a decade ago but now take into serious consideration.

"I got rid of my hangups," Marilyn told me. This was simply saying that (before) she couldn't suck a penis in front of a camera, and now (after) she could.

"I think the people of the world are becoming more honest with themselves about sex," Marilyn continued. "I don't say, 'Flaunt it,' but I do intend to do a lot of serious talking and thinking about it."

I tried to find just how she felt she was a better person after having got over her guilt following these sex athletics.

"I just feel more honest with myself," she kept answering.

"And your husband?"

"He's become more confident of himself; he now likes to discuss it and to answer questions. In the beginning, of course, he wasn't anxious for me to have all that sex with different men, and he still has that attitude to an extent. That's great. I want to keep it that way. I don't want to lose him!"

It got to be comical trying to talk to Marilyn frankly about sex without talking dirty, as we used to call it. I was trying to be the polite little gentleman speaking in euphemisms. Frequently she stripped away the varnish and called a cock a cock.

Marilyn said she would have liked to meet Linda Lovelace and maybe discussed "trade secrets." They set up a "joint interview," as somebody facetiously called it, on the Long John Nebel (oh, oh!) radio program, but that wasn't carried forward because Linda's book promotion schedule was too complicated.

"There was a rumor that Linda Lovelace gets a shot of novocaine in the throat to enable her to take that penis so deeply in her mouth," I said.

Marilyn smiled. "But she said it's not true," I told Marilyn, who said, "Well, she surely would have to have some way to get some air down there to prevent her from choking on it."

"What Linda told me," I said, referring to my notebook, "is 'I have learned to control an involuntary muscle—the palate—so that I don't choke.' "

Marilyn thought over that reply. "Yeah, I don't think she took novocaine. I think she just practiced."

Visions of "Everybody out for fellatio practice" floated through my head.

"Well, how do you do it?" I asked.

"I do OK," she said.

"You surely do, but I meant, how do you swallow so much when you, uh . . ." I began to beat about the bush.

"You mean doing the blow job?" she said.

"Is that what you call it?"

"That's what it is, and that's what I call it."

"But how do you handle it?"

"Trade secrets." She laughed.

I wanted to avoid being clinical, but I told her that in her one memorable oral sex treatment followed by penetration by the black costar she seemed to be indulging with him for about forty minutes.

"Maybe it seemed like forty, but it was about fifteen," she said. "We shot it all at once."

"Now at the end there, after the orgasm, there are pictures of the sperm. . . ." I was trying now to be euphemistic again. I wanted to find how they shot the scene with the sperm dripping from the penis into her mouth.

"Oh," she said, without any nervousness, "you mean the 'come' shots. When the guy comes in my face."

"That's it," I said, relieved that she had supplied me the precise language. "How is it done?"

"Somebody jerks off in your face," she said.

"Who, your costar?"

"Oh, no, not just him. Different people."

"Different people?"

"Sure, one guy just can't keep doing it, of course."

"But," I said, still mystified, thinking maybe these shots had been patched together, "when these guys were dripping their sperm seemingly onto your face, you were there?"

"Very there!"

"Right there catching it?"

"Uh-huh."

"Did you mind?"

"No."

"What was your emotional reaction?"

"Well, in the picture, it's supposed to be humiliating when he keeps coming in my face, and it is humiliating in a way."

"But you did it?"

"All that jerking off and sucking and fucking and getting screwed and the guys coming in my face was just something I had to do in the picture," Marilyn said. "That's all it was, just a job of acting. You don't get hung up over it. If you do, you don't do a good job as an actress."

"How long have you been married?"

"Almost a year."

"And your husband doesn't mind what you did in the picture?"

"Oh, we had our ups and downs about it. Listen, I wouldn't do explicit sex if I didn't have him."

"I don't understand."

"He's my moral support. If I was on my own and screwing in pictures, I'd get discouraged and wouldn't want to come home. But when you're in love, you want to come home. During the film we learned an awful lot about each other, and we became better lovers. It helped our marriage incredibly," Marilyn said.

"He doesn't watch you shooting?"

"He says he just has no desire to watch me doing it. He saw a lot of the rushes, but he said, 'Why should I come to the set?' It takes a lot of guts for him to be my husband. I respect him for that."

Marilyn went back to the theme that has become familiar to me in talking to actors and actresses of all ranks about sex scenes. "It's like any part of acting. You're so involved in the acting part of it you can't get away from the fact you're supposed to be doing a scene for a picture. And like with any other acting job, you're tired and you want to get it over with and go home."

Linda Lovelace was already a household name when she gave a press reception, and a busy schedule limited me to remaining on the premises only a few minutes. Fortunately, the star of the occasion was on time. She had been delightfully prepublicized about her book in which she stated that her ambition was to be the best cocksucker around. This was openly published, of course, and distributed worldwide. A number of years ago when a famous woman used about the same words to the Kefauver Committee of the United States Senate, in explaining why she was financially supported by several mobsters, the committee sealed the minutes of the meeting and would never admit that she said such a horrible thing.

The Linda Lovelace buildup was quite candid, as it had to be with such a subject. *Playboy*, for example, had a photographic layout of her, not quite performing her specialty, but doing the next best thing—sucking her finger.

"Say 'Ah' " was the title. "It's just me acting naturally," she said, "doing things that haven't been done before. You're only here once, so enjoy life. I do what I do because it feels good."

"How do you do it?"

"I wouldn't want the whole world to know. I had to spend three or four weeks learning how to keep from gagging. After the first couple weeks' practice, I was still choking and turning purple. But now I can really get off that way. That's not the only way of course."

That's what she'd already said. When I went to her press conference, there was a tension in the place that I couldn't at first understand.

There were television cameramen and still photographers and reporters and columnists and press agents running around. One woman began yelling at a press agent who was trying to lead me to the star. Miss Lovelace finally swept in wearing that indescribably fuzzy hairdo which I didn't feel was quite right for her. Another reporter with a notebook was interviewing her while a press agent probably representing the book publisher came up and said, "You can have five minutes with her. You can't hog her, you know. There are others who want to talk to her, too."

"May I listen?" I said to the young man with the notebook, who courteously agreed.

It was then that I asked Linda the question about the novocaine that I referred to earlier. She replied that she'd learned to control an involuntary muscle.

"But the novocaine story?"

Linda laughed. "I never heard that before. Wouldn't that take the fun out of it?"

"Jesus, she wouldn't feel a thing. Who'd want to do that?" another reporter commented.

Linda went into an attack on the simulated sex films. "*Last Tango* is a ridiculous picture," she said. "I liked the dialogue, but the sex scenes are just plain silly. Even if the dialogue is good, who wants to ball with their pants over their head?"

That was a detail of the Brando film that I didn't remember. "The public wants to see real live sex on the screen and the old-line companies are going to have to merge with the X films," she said. "That's what it's coming to."

The tension, I discovered, was due to the fact that Al Goldstein of *Screw* magazine had come to the press reception. The book company publicist said he was not invited and they did not wish him there because he and Miss Lovelace were no longer friends. He had published a picture purporting to show Miss Lovelace indulging in her specialty with him.

There was such confusion at the press conference that it was decided to permit general questions . . . and there was Al Goldstein calling out: "Is it true you do it with dogs?"

(I had left before this interesting question was asked, but I was told that it actually happened.)

Miss Lovelace pretended not to hear the question. She privately declared that the whole thing was insulting and untrue, and he had a lot of nerve to get so personal. The rest of the questions were of general nature.

And the language was always guarded. The word "fellatio," for example, was almost never heard, and the expression "giving head" did not get employed either. The ladies and gentlemen of the media usually referred to "your special talent" or "your special technique."

"They called it anything but what it was," one of the press folk observed.

And Linda Lovelace in her shy way was just as cautious.

"I just have a special way of doing it," she said.

A specialist is what she is.

But let's have a look at the milestone movie that caused all the trouble. It made sex bigger than soundies.

Deep Throat, the controversial film about a girl whose clitoris is somewhere near her esophagus, which prevents her from having an orgasm unless she is trying to swallow a penis, was one of the most daring movies ever made. It was also one of the dirtiest, and in my opinion, had no redeeming social values whatever.

A friend of mine, Lou Perry, the first agent for Martin and Lewis a long time ago, was the nominal producer, and not proud of the fact. The first time I told him I'd like to see the picture, he discouraged me. Even though it was an enormous financial success, he didn't care to have his name linked with it.

Despite his warnings that I probably wouldn't like it, I decided that in view of the legal controversies that had arisen, I must go. I picked a night just before New Year's Eve, 1972, when the picture was being kicked around in a court fight.

Ironically, I had to ask Lou Perry to get me a seat. The news stories about one court closing the World Theater, on West Forty-ninth Street, where it was playing, and another court allowing it to reopen, had resulted in a long queue of young people waiting to see it.

"Sorry, there are no seats left," a young man at the door said when I arrived about two minutes before the scheduled showing.

"Oh, I didn't recognize you!" he apologized. "I'm holding a seat for you."

"Has it already started?" I asked.

"In about two minutes. They're running one of the short subjects first."

I'd heard about these short subjects. A sign was flashed on the screen that said: NO JERKING OFF IN THEATER. ORDER OF THE BOARD OF HEALTH.

There were stag scenes alleged to have been taken in 1919 involving much fellatio and cunnilingus and one pretty and naked girl trying to suck her own breasts.

I definitely heard a voice say, "Let's go home and do it," but whether that was from one of the cast or the audience or was part of the short subject, I'm unable to say.

Deep Throat then unrolled with proper tribute paid to Linda Lovelace, the girl whose clitoris is in her throat. As I sat in the dark theater watching all this begin, I had a feeling that there might be a raid. It was all very conspiratorial and naughty.

The "redeeming" part, I guess, was a fast quote from Freud, so fast that I couldn't get it all. And then there was a scene where a girl had her legs open and up in the air while a man was kissing her vagina and she was moving his head and lips about to give her more satisfaction.

The girl calls to Linda Lovelace, while she's getting cunnilingus from the man, "Give me one of my cigarettes, will you, hon?"

Then the same girl says to her lover down there, "Mind if I smoke while you're eating?"

"Not at all," he gurgles, and continues vigorously at his task.

Linda Lovelace is feeling bad about this because, as she confesses to her girlfriend, "I've never gotten off."

"Never?" . . . "Never. Do you think I'm not doing it right?" Her friend has some suggestions; Linda says, "OK, the way I feel, I'll try anything."

They proceed to what is apparently a brothel where a couple of "clients" come in and are given tickets numbers 11 and 12. Girls are spread-eagled all over the place with men manipulating them with their tongues and fingers. Into the room comes a homosexual type who is jealous of one of the other males and says, "What's a nice joint like you doing in a girl like this?"

Through all this sex orgy, Linda Lovelace is unhappy. She's unsatisfied. "How about seeing a doctor—a psychiatrist?"

The young psychiatrist, we soon figure out, is a sex maniac who doesn't even suspect what's coming. "Perhaps you had a traumatic experience that turned you off sex," he says.

"Oh, I'm not turned off to sex, I could spend the rest of my life getting laid," she says, "but I want to hear bombs going off and the ringing of bells. . . ."

"Well," says the doctor, "step into my office, I want to take a look at you." She takes her dress off, he takes her pants off, and he looks carefully into her vagina (he must be nearsighted, he gets so close) and says, "That's amazing!"

"If you tell me somebody left his watch in there . . ." she says, threateningly.

"You don't have one," he says.

Now he's got her worried. She looks into her vagina. "I don't have one? Are you sure?"

"I'm telling you, you don't have one. You don't have a clitoris. No wonder you hear no bells, you hear no bombs going off. . . ."

"When I get excited," she says, "I get excited here." She indicates her throat.

"Your throat? Well," says the doc, "open your mouth wide and say 'Ah.' "

"Ah," she says.

"Well," says the doctor again, like Columbus discovering America, "there is your problem. Your clitoris is in the top of your throat."

"Be careful," she warns him. "It's as if I said to you that your balls were in your ears."

Getting fiercely clinical, the doctor says, "Have you ever taken a penis all the way into the top of your throat?"

"No, I choke," she says.

"Try it, you might like it," the doctor says, and he sacrifices himself by lying down on the psychiatrist's couch with his clothes off, while she, with her clothes off, takes his penis in her deep throat. For the first time we see the depth of her talent as she fondles, strokes, kisses and seemingly almost swallows the doctor's most important instrument. They wallow in their lust for several minutes with Linda being the aggressor until finally the doctor starts hearing bells and hearing bombs go off. He's orgasmed and now so has Linda; she now hears the bells and sees the fireworks, all from that feeling in her throat.

"I am a fulfilled woman, I'm your slave," she says. "You've shown me the way, it's all I wanted, I need love."

The doctor has begun to fear that this might be too much woman for him. "You can come to work for me in my office," he says. "I'll make you a psychotherapist."

"I have no equipment," she says.

The doctor, looking over her figure and especially her throat, replies, "You have all the equipment you will ever need."

Linda is next seen in a white psychotherapist's outfit hustling around giving her deep throat treatment to assorted perverts. She also gives a lot of deep throat attention to the doctor, who is now a physical wreck, holding himself by the groin, finding it difficult to hobble around owing to her ministrations.

Next there's a fast love scene where a young fellow with effeminate mannerisms tells Linda he wants to marry her. She sighs that it's impossible.

"The man I marry has to have a nine-inch cock," she informs him.

"A nine-inch cock!" he exclaims. "I'm only four inches away from happiness."

He has a flash of a thought. Is it true that doctors can do things with plastic surgery and silicone? He phones a doctor who specializes in such changes. He states his problem. He has to have a nine-inch cock.

"Can you, Doctor?" he asks. *"You can!"*

He hangs up the phone and turns to his beloved cocksucker. "It's wonderful," he says. "We can get married. The doctor says he can cut my cock down to any size you want it." And then she has it in her mouth, and again there are the rockets, the bombs going off, and the bells ringing.

A happy ending.

But it was not a happy ending—yet—for the porno film industry. *Deep Throat* was the first salacious picture to be hit by the interpreters of the new Supreme Court obscenity rulings. The Hollywood filmmakers were in panic. Universal, making a picture titled *S-s-s-s*, decided to put a fig leaf on Adam's genitals on a replica of Michelangelo's "Adam and Eve." In the·Sistine Chapel at the Vatican, Adam's genitals had never been covered up in the original—but Michelangelo didn't have the Supreme Court looking over his work.

The Fun Lovers

🖎 A MINISTER'S daughter from the South who just loves her daddy and all he stands for was one of the chief copulators or fornicators in *It Happened in Hollywood*, a porno movie that "broke the Peter Meter" in *Screw* magazine and therefore surpassed *Deep Throat* in hard-core sexuality.

"What's a nice girl like you doing in a picture like this?" was a natural question to address to the tall, attractive, twenty-one-year-old dark-haired "Flo" from the Carolinas when we met for a drink and an interview in a Broadway restaurant.

"I needed the money . . . I was in debt . . . and I guess it was also an erotic impulse," she said, sipping some white wine.

"Flo" is not her real name, but in this film she's known as Flo Zeasily, and she's a member of a high-wire acrobatic team called "the Flying Fucks." She is naked and in body paint, bending over, when the male half of the act, with a huge dildo in front of him, flies off the high wire and drives the dildo into her anus causing her great joy.

But that is not her chief contribution to the picture. She rides a strange contraption called a Bicycle Built for Screw which has sexual devices to fill up nearly every opening in her while she's pedaling. Flo Zeasily feels a maternal pride in this Bicycle Built for Screw and walked down to the Orleans Theater, on West Forty-seventh Street, with me to take another fond look at it.

"He flies through the air and sticks it in her derriere" was one simple explanation of the performance by the Flying Fucks, but the Bicycle Built for Screw is more complex. First, there is a huge dildo on the handlebars that she is supposed to be mouthing as she bends forward and pedals, and as she bends forward, there's a false penis penetrating her from the rear. There are suction cups from the handlebars that hold onto her bosom and there are small penises that penetrate her ears. This is a one-woman orgy.

"I'd never posed nude, I'd never modeled, I'd never done any of this," Flo Zeasily assured me. "A guy I know who'd auditioned for one of their pictures and couldn't get the job because he couldn't get it up took me over to see the producers.

"When they asked me to ride the bicycle for the movie, I said, 'No way.' But it was good money, about two hundred and seventy dollars for the day, and suddenly I got one of those once-in-my-lifetime feelings. It was my thing to ride that bicycle that would blow my hometown out of its mind if it ever saw it. Fifty years from now I would look back on something crazy I did when I was young."

And so Flo Zeasily, after a trial ride on the sex machine, had to get a fitting—especially for the penis on the bicycle seat that was supposed to enter her anus. When she got naked and mounted the bicycle, with the false penis coming from behind, "I felt penetrated but not stimulated," she told me.

When she dismounted, there was applause from the crew and the cast, and she knew she had made good riding a fucking machine.

Flo Zeasily had to perform oral sex with another actor ("I had to ball the producer's son to get somewhere in sex films—that's the story line," she said). And in this performance she learned that the girls have an easy job compared to the men.

"I just didn't walk in coldly and perform sex with this fellow," she explained. "We were kidding around a whole day watching the others and we didn't get to our scene till about two A.M. It was funny—all day as we watched the others, this poor fellow was dying to get into it, and when we got around to our turn, he had had it. He couldn't get stimulated, and he wasn't stimulating me. Everybody was getting tired. There was another case of a guy who couldn't do it though the girl was on him for an hour and a half. He was lying on his back with his hand over his eyes, concentrating, and we were all cracking up.

"Finally he got hard, and she was kissing it and right away he was ready to climax; but the director said, 'No, no, not yet.' He said, 'Yes, yes,' and the director screamed, 'No, no, not yet!'

"The poor guy," she said, "almost blew his career."

The minister's daughter expressed sympathy for the unhappy stud. "I don't think it was lack of virility," she said. "A guy stands around stark naked, and then he's supposed to get it up for a girl he's just met. I don't know how a man can do it. A girl can fake it, and she can use lubricants; but a guy's got to perform, and everybody's watching, and it's enough to undermine his morale."

Actors find work hard to get, and these porno films help some of them make a living though they know they're dirty pictures.

"The directors always claim they're not dirty. Every director says, 'This is a work of art.' The same group of people keep getting parts, and it becomes like a family. I was called to do more, but I wasn't interested. I'd ridden my bicycle. I never went back. I never found the real name of the guy that I balled. His name in the picture was Putz Levine."

As we walked down Broadway toward the Orleans, Flo Zeasily, whom no passerby would ever have suspected of being a porno actress, asked me, "Did you ever get a little scared while you were having sex because there was somebody in the next room that might hear you or discover you? It makes it more dangerous and more fun. There's not a chance in a million that my daddy would ever find out about me because I was so changed by makeup. And my daddy's not the kind that knows about porno movies, let alone goes to see them. That and the chance that somebody else might recognize me made this exciting."

And so I was soon seated in a pornographic movie theater, the second I'd visited in my life.

Sitting there in the darkened house with about fifty others, I took notes. Then I wondered what to do with them.

If one's reporting on a pornographic movie, shouldn't one report the pornographic dialogue and the pornographic action? But wait, isn't this dirty, obscene, filthy? Or is it the language of the people of the 1970's and, therefore, literature? The speech of the hillbillies in *Tobacco Road* was considered filth when Erskine Caldwell wrote it in 1932, but today it's tame.

Felicity Split, the beautiful, sexually talented brunette heroine of the film, is ambitious: She wants to become a star in sex films. With this premise, the producers are able to claim that this picture is a spoof, a satire, on the film industry.

Felicity is preparing dinner for her lover, Elliott, in her apartment. She is a terrible cook; that is not her talent. "Are you hungry?" she asks him. . . . "Yes, for you." . . . "Not now, wait till after dinner."

As he is grimacing over each taste of food and jamming it into his pockets, Felicity confides she wants to be a sex film star. "But you'll be blowing every prick in town," he protests. . . . "But what's so bad about that?" She smiles.

As she pours him some wine, he grabs her, and she pours wine all over his suit, including his trousers, and when she tries to dry his pants by rubbing at the crotch, he says, "Don't stop!" Felicity says, "What do you want me to do, Elliott? Take it out?" Still at the dinner table, Felicity asks, "Shall I suck on it?" Then they're on the floor, and Felicity says, "Elliott, let's get on the couch . . . Elliott, let's sixty-nine . . . I want to eat you while you eat me. . . . Please, Elliott, fuck me in the ass."

In due time, Elliott concedes that Felicity might have a future in sex films. She's next seen stripping in a theatrical agent's office. He gets naked and auditions her, taking her on his desk, with many complimentary remarks about her talent for fellatio. Then he orders his secretary to strip and join in a threesome with everybody climaxing.

"This job is really nice, I think I'll like this work," Felicity says. She adds, "My pussy is so hot I could boil an egg in there."

And what looks like a boiled egg pops out of her vagina.

But Felicity has not yet made good. There's a troublemaker, producer Boris Ballzoff from Budapest. He's looking for a Delilah to play opposite Samson in a porno *Samson and Delilah*. He hasn't found any girls he likes. Young Putz Levine nominates Flo Zeasily with the Bicycle Built for Screw. Boris Ballzoff isn't impressed. "I saw that shit in Budapest before the war," he growls.

Felicity performs her specialty on Putz Levine's father's penis, and he requests an encore. "Is mine as good as the bicycle?" she asks. "Do I get the part?"

The story line got a little confusing to me here, but Felicity, as Delilah, arrives with a determination to use her talent at fellatio to learn Samson's secret of his strength. Samson has his detractors. "I think he eats Palestinian pussy," sneers one of his rivals. Delilah sweeps up and says, "The troops are horny as hell, Samson. They're out there balling my handmaidens." Samson has a majordomo, a little guy with a rabbi look, who warns Samson against letting Delilah work him over.

"Don't do it, boss, it's a trick," he says.

"Shut up, you runt fuck," snaps Samson, as Delilah puts her mouth where his strength is.

"Tell me your secret, Samson," she pleads, working away. "Stick your cock in my hot, wet, juicy cunt and in my tight asshole." It's time for comedy, and Delilah playfully hits him in the testicles with a hammer. "You're a tough nut to crack," she says. There's another one—a riddle: "What do you get when you cross a Frenchman and a Chinese?" . . . "A person that sucks your laundry." As for Delilah, she continues sucking away at Samson, and she saps his strength, and the walls come tumbling down around his head. That's the climax of the picture in more ways than one.

The scene shifts to the Fuck Film Festival.

Less important stars are getting their Oscars which are in the form of penises. One award goes to the performer who portrayed the asshole in *Bodily Function*.

But the most celebrated recipient is the ambitious little gal who told her boyfriend Elliott at dinner one night that she dreamed of stardom and thought she'd like the work besides.

"I'd like to take this opportunity," says Felicity Split in her acceptance speech, "to thank my lips, my tits, my tight ass, and my wet, hot pussy, without whom this award would not have been possible."

Felicity in real life was a surprise to me because she brought along her husband, a bright young photographer who had witnessed her making oral love to six men and not protested.

Felicity confessed to me without any blushing that she thought that all the penises she had to kiss and make love to were getting a bit much. "I kept thinking, 'Oh, not another one!' " she said.

The husband, to set me right on his acceptance of his young wife's performing fellatio on six men, explained, "My wife and I think that sex, love, and nudity are separate things. We are not possessive. When my wife wanted to do this, I thought it was best not to stop her. Besides, I didn't want to be possessive and felt that I wasn't. But when she started doing it to those other men, I found that I was possessive. It was an effort for me not to show it."

He discussed this as coolly as he might have talked about a

photograph he'd taken. He said they were both nudists and had gone to "swinging nudist camps," giving me the impression that mate swapping was not a shocking idea to them. They seemed to be happily married and spoke of a daughter. Felicity said she had insisted upon her husband going to the filming with her.

"I backed out at first," Felicity said. "They kept changing the script, making it wilder and more erotic."

Smiling, she added, "But the idea that I was to be the *star* of the picture—that's what they kept telling me: not just in it—but the *star!*" Clearly, she was flattered; she hadn't thought of herself as a startlingly pretty girl, and she was no actress. Yet she had a star's part, and even though she was principally copulating facially with men she'd never seen in a manner that many would consider degrading, she was the *star*—and she yielded.

"We made them change some things," she said. "They had a bunch of guys with still cameras shooting while we were filming the movie. I made them stop that."

Felicity told me she had no more desire to attempt other such roles. She claimed to be happy that the adventure was finished. Her husband said he had a contempt for one porno actor who works regularly in such pictures.

"He's such an egoist he says he can't do it unless he really turns the girl on," he said. "He came over to me and said, 'You don't mind if I turn your old lady on, do you? I have to do that to do my best work.' I guess he meant to get a good erection for her to play with. I said to him, 'I guess it's all right. She's here to do a job, and if that's her job, OK.'"

"Did you get turned on?" I asked Felicity.

"How can you get turned on," Felicity said, "when you got a camera on you, and all those guys watching you go down on an actor that's so conceited?"

Uncovering Burlesk

🖋 FOR three or four years, I'd known that the stripteasers in the surviving Broadway burlesque houses were taking it off all the way down to their pubic hair. But I'd never suspected that "burlesk," as it had come to be spelled, had produced an artiste like Monica Kennedy, the girl with the star-spangled vagina.

I researched modern stripteasing considerably before I got to Monica. The first time I heard that G-strings were no longer worn and that the strippers were revealing all that was once alleged to be woman's most precious treasure was in the late 1960's. I wasn't tempted to enter any of these houses that I walked past every day.

Then one day I was on the *Midday* TV show with my old stripteaser friend Ann Corio, star of the longtime hit *That Was Burlesque.*

"Come with me this afternoon," she said. "I'm going to the Broadway Burlesk at Forty-ninth and Broadway to scout for a tassel tosser for my own show." A tassel tosser is a talented girl who makes her bosom rotate clockwise on one side, counterclockwise on the other, and emphasizes this with tassels which snap, crackle, and pop and are therefore especially noticeable.

"It's really incredible what things they do now in burlesque," Ann Corio said. "You'll be amazed."

"It's like a meat market," said stripper-turned-author Georgia Sothern, who has also been on the TV show.

"What do they do that's so bad . . . masturbate?" I asked the two ladies of burlesque because I couldn't imagine what they'd been doing that hadn't been done.

I knew that some of the sleazy little taxi dance halls which nested in the same buildings as the burlesque theaters were guilty of strange conduct. I learned that some of the "taxi dance girls" were really men in women's clothes who made dates with some of the dance customers and later slugged and robbed them.

"It's worse than public masturbation," Ann Corio said. "There is a girl who uses a name I love, Penny Sillin . . .

"Well," continued Ann, laughing, "she put these little ping-pong balls down in her . . . and she fired them out at the guys sitting in front. . . ."

Ann conceded later that the ammunition that Penny Sillin fired at the men were actually pasties taken from her nipples which she inserted in her vagina. Then by very dexterous pelvic acrobatics, she "bumped" them out at the customers leaning their elbows on the edge of the stage.

First, though, Ann and I made a date to go scouting.

"See you in front of the theater and don't keep me waiting on

that corner with all those guys hanging around there!" Ann said.
Ann had been lamenting for several years that burlesque no
longer contains burlesque which is satire, lampoonery, ludicrous
parody, or grotesque mockery of a solemn subject. It is just raw
sex, and very raw, and the famous burlesque comedians who came
from those shows, and who satirized and parodized, are not even
remembered anymore. It is just girls doing their thing, and
showing it, and the old-time funnymen are not even copied or
imitated in today's shows. There aren't comedians on the bill
unless you count the girls who are showing off their frontal
nudity; some of them, poor creatures, do try ever so assiduously to
be funny, and at moments like these I had to agree that Women's
Lib had been right in protesting against women being just sex
objects.

I found Ann and her manager, Marty Kummer, sitting in an
upraised section of the "theater"—there was a stage and a
runway—in what would seem to be the royal box of the house.
They waved to me to join them. The house was quite dark; when I
settled down with them, I looked about and figured there would
be sixty men there. But sixty times the $5 admission price was not
bad, and if they could do that five times a day (they boast
"continuous" shows), they should turn a considerable profit.

Onstage, I noticed when I sat back to look at the "entertainment," was a revolting chunk of middle-aged woman who was
mostly exhibiting her anus.

She was trying to hang onto the conviction that she was still
"cute," and this was sad because she was rumpy, dumpy, and
lumpy, and in the manner that she bent forward, to show her
posterior to the men back of her, she was to me repulsive. That is
why I do not give her name. I imagine the lady needed the work.
She stripped off everything to her pubic hair and got a moderate
round of applause from the spectators who were perhaps more
interesting.

"Look, all the men are going to the john," Ann Corio remarked.
There was indeed a stream of them going to the room marked
MEN. There was one ancient fellow with a cane, one spastic, a
couple of graybeards who looked and leaned forward eagerly to
observe her tosses and twitches.

But now came the star—a much younger, more attractive girl,
Patti Wayne, who sang to us that she was "the Wall Street Playgirl
. . . Wall Street has been good to me, but I've been good to Wall

Street." Fondling her pelvic area, she said, "Boys, I carry my playpen with me!"

Ann Corio, who had been speaking to the manager, leaned over and said to me, "He says she's supposed to be bottomless but she said she won't be because we're in the audience. But in the end she will."

"They'd stone her if she didn't," Marty Kummer said.

She'd been wearing a lot, which she now started taking off. She had a large, well-formed, firm-looking bosom.

"Are those hers?" Ann asked the manager.

"No, but it's a good job," the manager said.

"She would be fully nude if I weren't here," Ann said. "I guess I should get up and apologize to all these old men."

Patti began rolling around on a circular couch which was covered with imitation fur, and soon she had on only a small triangular patch over her pelvis. It was held on by a thin string around her waist. She called out, "I still have goodies for you . . . come on, boys!"

Her predecessor had taken her G-string off, held it up rounded and lengthwise, and kissed it—in an unmistakable imitation of fellatio which the men immediately recognized and applauded. They had greatly appreciated her bending over with her anus to them so they could look up at it. The Wall Street Playgirl bounced around more on the couch, rolling off on the floor, simulating the act of love complete with the groans and howls and the climax.

Well toward the end, she took off the G-string and exposed her bush, to the applause of the viewers. She crawled around on the runway, face down, bottoms up, bottoms definitely up, going through the love movements of the centuries, using her bush for emphasis. I became interested at this point in the normal masculine reaction to a woman displaying her bush so publicly.

Sitting in the theater, I scrawled in my notebook this observation about femininity: "They show so blithely and quickly that which they used to withhold."

I referred naturally to the fact that one of today's strippers could expose her pubis in the middle of her act and without any enormous demonstrative buildup. It was getting so common now that one of these days the audiences would yawn and say, "Oh, that old thing again!"

Ann Corio was observant. When Patti Wayne began her half-man, half-woman sketch, which had been done in vaudeville and nightclubs for many years, Ann mentioned to me as Patti stretched out on the floor with a pasteboard figure of a man, "Did you notice his long tongue?"

God help me, I hadn't noticed.

Thinking it over, after we politely applauded, said thanks, and departed, I decided that the new features of "burlesk" were of course the exposed bush; the bottomless backside—that is to say the completely uncovered derriere—and certain "spread" postures used by the girls encouraging the men to look up into their private areas and salivate. It surely was a change from the burlesque that we'd heard about from fans of Abbott & Costello, Red Skelton, and Phil Silvers.

Just as I was about to conclude that there were no more significant changes than that (or those), I heard of a burlesque queen using the name Princess Sock-It-To-Me (an Indian maiden, no doubt). Enchanted by her name, I sought her out in a stroll around Broadway. I didn't find her, but I found my way into the Follies Burlesk at Broadway and Forty-sixth Street. The front was unimposing; a few small placards and signs, a narrow doorway, a stairway where one learned on the second landing that this was the entrance to the Pussycat Theater.

"The theater . . . where's the burlesque?" I asked a man at the Pussycat.

"One more flight," he said. I climbed onward, wondering whether there could be any activity in the midst of this comparative quiet. It was a Saturday afternoon on old Broadway, shouldn't there be girls, girls, girls? I climbed on.

"Yes?" a voice said. I had unintentionally walked past the box office. Keeping my head down, I extended a $10 bill to the man who'd stopped me.

"Aren't you Earl Wilson? Sure, go on in." He handed me the $10 back.

The show was on, and as I sat down in the back row of seats around the runway, I noticed a considerable difference from the Broadway Burlesk. There was an "orchestra"—a drummer and a chap playing away at a portable piano. A big sign over the runway: GIRL POWER! The audience included several young men, some with the long hair of the day. And when the first stripper, named Mona Lisa, came undulating out, singing a French tune, she soon addressed a well-dressed man of middle age who didn't seem today's burlesque type at all.

Maybe she knew him from a previous meeting. He sat as close as possible to the runway: the first row. Tall, black-haired, and statuesque, with a good figure, and still young, she picked him out and asked him, *"Parlez-vous français?"*

"Un peu," he said.

He did not pursue it with *"Voulez-vous coucher avec moi?"* nor did she. But Mona Lisa soon had everything off and strode about, her raven-haired black bush evoking a patter of applause when she exhibited it the first time. She held it high as she swung along the runway.

The announcer was speaking. "Once again it is star time—the Follies' Favorite—Randy Stevens!"

She was in black, even a black hat, a long black dress—looking what Ava Gardner might have looked like had she become a stripper. She wore a star hanging from her bodice, indicating, I guess, that she is a star. She was very soon bare-breasted and in a garter belt and long black stockings. She cupped her breasts, took off her G-string, with her bush standing out prominently between the garter belt and the stockings—no doubt her idea of super-high-power sex appeal. She ran her fingers down her pubic section, she sucked her finger, she fingered herself slightly, she kissed her breasts. Like the others, she performed the open-legged squat in front of the customers, getting as close to them as possible. The squatting, the bending over to expose the backside to the front row (in all its detail) are modern improvements of vaudeville.

It made the males want to reach and grope. Some did reach, but they didn't succeed in getting close enough to grope.

I was about to fold up my notebook and steal away when one of the producers said, "You must stay and see Karen Thomas, the last of the stars."

"The Georgia Peach," as they call her, was to prove the liveliest of all the sex queens, because she dared get close to the spectators, even getting off the runway and going almost onto one's lap, shaking her breasts over him and his face to the delight of the gentleman himself (who remained one) and to the envy of some of his neighbors.

Bare-breasted (and they were big breasts), Karen Thomas advanced to the edge of the runway wearing now merely a small patch and asked one man—the same chap who spoke French— "Hi, there, you want to play with me?"

"*Yes!*" he replied.

"I play grown-up games," she warned. That was all right with him. Now she was squatting open-legged a foot or two in front of him, her bush still covered by a patch, but the suggestion of it very strong because the patch was dark and thin. One looking from the back of the theater might indeed have thought she had uncovered herself.

"Hey, are you comfortable?" she asked, still in the open-legged squat, now moving even closer to him.

"Sure."

"I can make you even more comfortable." In the same open-legged squat she moved still closer.

"Can I get more comfortable too?" She teased him.

"Do you care if I get a *lot* more comfortable?" she continued. Now she began removing the small G-string and soon had completely exposed herself, not only to him but to the eyes in the heads of the crowd around him. "Can you see OK?" she asked.

"Wonderful!" he said.

While she was moving her exposed pubis toward him and the other men in the first row, she was fondling her breasts and squeezing them together. "I want to ask you one thing," she said. "Do you like milk?"

"Yes, yes!"

"In this kind of container?" She was almost kissing her own bosom.

"Yes, yes!"

It was then that she got off the runway and down onto his knees and shook her breasts in his face without, however, kissing him or "molesting" him as far as I could see. It was the first time that I had ever seen a stripteaser ever touch a customer. Her exposed pubis must have been around the gentleman's kneecap, but he kept in control.

"Maybe you'd prefer your milk in a bottle?" she whined.

"No, no!" he cried.

"Do you want any of the leftovers?"

"Yes, yes!" As he said this, a customer on the opposite side began summoning her. She said, "Oh, I'm coming, and I hope you'll be, too. But later." Now Miss Georgia Peach turned her breasts and exposed area to a long-haired young man who had been sitting next to the middle-ager who spoke a little French. I was surprised to find any really youthful spectators here, but there were at least half a dozen.

"Maybe you'd like some of my leftovers?" She wiggled and bumped.

"All right." He nodded. She was a young chick to these middle-agers, but probably an old woman to him.

"How about a cherry?" she asked him.

"OK."

She wasn't turning him on at all, and it was bothering her. "If I could find one," she said. "They're kind of hard to find."

"Yeah, I heard," he said.

"You wouldn't like to get real close to me?" She now was moving the tools of her trade closer and closer to him.

"OK." He shrugged again.

Now she bristled, for this was rejection in a place where they were all mad for her. It was the reverse of her usual adulation. She got out of her exposed open-legged squat, stood up to her full height, and strode across the stage. But as she went, she stopped to ask the young man, "How old are you?"

"How old do you think I am?" he asked.

"Twenty-five," she guessed.

"Twenty-one," he said.

"No wonder!" she said as if explaining her failure to herself. "You're not old enough to know anything yet."

She got back into the open-legged exposed-pubis squat and inched toward a man who had been calling for her. He was a lean fifty-year-old in a gray suit with glasses, a man I would take for a salesman or an accountant, a chap you might see almost anywhere, from behind the counter in a cigar store to a ticket window to a pew in your church. The Georgia Peach must have known him better than that.

"Oh, I know what *you* want!" she said, as though still angry at the twenty-one-year-old whom she hadn't moved. "You're in here every day!"

"Every *day!*" I thought. Those girls crawling on all fours at you with their everything showing—every *day!* The announcer was spieling his spiel. "Make it a weekly habit to visit the Follies Burlesk," he said. Weekly, maybe. But daily!

Walking along Broadway with me one night after her show, Miss Brandy Stevens from the Follies Burlesk was slim, attractive, and vivacious, and her conversation about her work—"shop talk"—was certainly different. There were male customers who came and stayed all day at some houses where she'd worked and yes, from the stage, she could see them masturbating. "I don't mind if they sit toward the back," she said. "I don't like them doing it down in the front row."

The trade name for the squat the girls do when they expose themselves is the beaver—and if they open wide, it's the split beaver. (This terminology is also used to categorize the porno-graphic movies, I learned.)

"I try to make a joke of it," Miss Stevens, who's from Hagerstown, Maryland, said. "I like the lights down to make it like a fantasy, and I work in a lot of fetishes that men are supposed to like. I tickle them with a feather, I hand them my shoe, I spank myself on my butt, I take my stockings off and tie them around my throat because some fellows like to be tied up and bound, I take my stockings and my panties in my mouth because some guys like panties and stockings. I try to keep it light and funny."

Brandy admitted, though, that much of her subtle spoofing of her art goes over the heads of the audience, and they are just waiting for her to do the beaver or the split beaver.

Some of the masturbators, she confessed, want to have their eyes fixed on her at the same time. "You're rolling around on the runway and this big eye is on you! It's bad, but you're getting paid, and if the place doesn't suffer. . . . One guy is everywhere I go. But he's harmless. He may follow you when you go out and say, 'Hi, want to have some lunch?' You say no, and that ends it. They're not too bright, some of them!"

After eight years of stripping, she had become philosophical. "When I started, the girls all wore net bras and G-strings, and the star did a flash at the end when she pulled down her G-string only for a second. But we had to keep up with the movies and other kinds of entertainment, and so you had to take more off to keep everybody interested. You have to compete. So everybody flashed. But now it's not simply a flash anymore. Halfway through the act you're down to your beaver and stay there. Now you have to do it, and it gets to be a farce. Nearly all the girls flash now. The only girl I know that doesn't flash is Tempest Storm. Look, you want approval, and exposing myself doesn't bother me, especially if I get a big hand!"

The less adventurous strippers look with disdain upon some of their wilder colleagues. There are girls who work with hot dogs and condiments, with champagne; they make noises with their vaginas. Miss Stevens knew of some of these specialties and was fascinated to hear of others. About the stripper with the hot dogs, she said, "That's nice of her. I wonder how much she spends a week for mustard and catsup."

"It's soft-core pornography, I guess," she said, trying to categorize her work. "Not hard-core, because there's no penetration. I tried some skin flicks but this is better. They got too demanding in the skin flicks, they wanted things with animals.

"I don't see the difference between wearing a G-string and not wearing a G-string. If they want to see it, they're going to see it and who cares? I try to keep it funny, and I'm not like anybody else, I'm just myself. I'm living with a guy, and I do what I want to."

These girls are practical, and they're almost unshockable. They do, however, shrink from using some of the language that might be lightly tossed off by women of a higher station of life. And they would generally consider themselves above the girls who pose for the open beaver or spread beaver pictures advertised in pornographic magazines. ("Spread Beaver magazines! Wild and wide-open poses by sexy girls. The world's finest open cunts. Only $7. Box . . . Minneapolis.")

While some of the burlesque strippers are doing just about what the girls in the photographs are doing, they consider that their "dancing" and their boudoir acrobatics make them some kind of actress. They are encouraged to believe this by a group of men called the Bird Watchers who are regular visitors.

"Most of the sex freaks are high-echelon businessmen," Brandy told me. "There's no doubt that some men get turned on watching other men masturbate.

"We have women coming in more than they used to, and some of them are lesbians. I've had some of them make me offers. And there are some younger men who are not much more than boys. They laugh; they're nervous. Maybe they never saw one before. At least they get to see one close up!"

Brandy was pretty sure that despite the open beaver or spread beaver proficiency that she displays, she would never be able to remove a $5 bill from a table with her sexual apparatus as was done forty or fifty years ago in Harlem at a place known to all the stay-ups of the time. It's referred to in the Billie Holiday film *Lady Sings the Blues* and was one of the contemporary art forms.

The first burlesque girl I ever interviewed while she was totally nude right down to her pubic hair which she had trimmed heart-shaped was Miss Monica Kennedy, from Boston. I had just witnessed her surprising strip act at the Broadway Burlesk where she kissed her own breasts and put a man's cigarette, and then a cigar, in her navel and made copulating movements with it. She also served about five bottles of champagne to the customers in glasses and paper cups, poured some of the champagne down her breasts and onto her pelvis, and let it run down her legs, after shouting out, "Bottoms up." I did not see her serve any of the champagne that had run down her own anatomy to the screaming males in the audience, but I understand she sometimes does this.

A high-spirited girl with a bottom that was bulgier than her bosom, she was obviously adored by the audience. When somebody yelled "Take it off!"—an unnecessary remark since she had already taken off everything—she pulled a few hairs out of her pubis and threw them at the audience.

At first she had worn a white cowgirl outfit with a sombrero and a couple of toy pistols. She had removed a belt that covered her femininity. The crowd of about 100 whooped when she began doing all the spread beaver specialties.

Now at past midnight she came into a hot stuffy little dressing room where I was waiting for her. She was wearing a transparent robe through which I could dimly see the blackness of her pubic area.

I believed that she would take off the robe and put on some pants or something. She took off the robe, but she didn't put on any pants or anything. She began rubbing a towel between her legs against her genitalia and continued this from time to time during the half hour I spent with her.

It would not be very flattering of me, I figured, if I turned my head away from her femininity and looked away from it. So in the interest of politeness, I looked at it. It had been meticulously barbered, heart-shaped at the top, like a valentine box.

"Congratulations on your hairdo," I said.

"You like it?" Miss Kennedy tossed her blond coiffure about proudly.

"No, not *that* hairdo. *That* one!" I pointed to the lower section. "Who does your hair?"

"*Me!* You like the way I do my pussy?" She kept toweling it. "I figured it would be original."

"I imagine it is," I said. "I have predicted that with pubic hair being shown so much, the day would come when women would have special hairdressers for their pubic areas."

Miss Kennedy looked down at hers with satisfaction. "But I'll still do my own." She was still standing and using the towel. "The way I figured this out, you want to say something risqué and also nice, like 'My heart dies for you,' so I dyed my hair and cut it out heart-shaped. I have also worn my pussy red, white, and blue. Patriotic!"

"For Fourth of July?" I asked.

"Any day you're supposed to be patriotic. I have had little red, white and blue wigs or wiglets I put over my real pussy hair. And I have little lights to light it up for the Fourth of July. That's really wild!"

I had brought with me a veteran Broadway publicist, Irving Zussman. He sat across the room from me as Miss Kennedy flaunted her most valuable possession. We exchanged glances. He had never witnessed an interview like this, nor had I ever conducted one so casual, yet so revealing.

"That thing you do with a man's glasses must not be very common," I said.

During her act she took a man's spectacles from him, and after rubbing them in her bare breasts and femininity, she seemingly inserted them in her anus. One could see the glasses protruding.

"I made it up myself," she announced. "I don't really put them up my butt. It's not really inside. It's in the muscle on top." She turned her rear end around and offered to show me with my own glasses. "I beat a case against me once on that point. I proved I didn't have the glasses up my ass but only inside on the muscle. It was in Schenectady."

"But the glasses did belong to some man at the ringside?"

"Oh, yes. He kissed them when I took them out and gave them back."

Miss Kennedy seemed happy recounting the times she'd tangled with the law. With one more pull of the towel between her legs against the heart-shaped pudenda, she said, "Another thing I got arrested for, I stood on my head and put a cigarette in my pussy and blew smoke rings. That was in Port Washington, Long

Island. They were very upset over that. I don't know why. The judge fined me five hundred dollars."

"I notice you also kiss your breasts," I said.

"Yes, I lick my nipples. In a circular motion. Some other girls can lick their tits but not circular like I do." She cupped one in each hand and began licking them clockwise while standing there bare all the way down. They were small and firm and obviously not silicone like most of the breasts in burlesque.

"Do you enjoy it?" I asked.

"Yes." She smiled, continuing to lick them. "It gets them hard. Look at that one!" The nipples were standing up.

"I was put off TV in Las Vegas for something I did," she said. "I put whipped cream on my tits, my navel, and my pussy. And I let a man eat the whipped cream. It's legal to eat it off of your tits but not off of your pussy. Well, I let him eat it off of my tits and my navel, and when he thought he was going to gobble it off me down here, I went *boom*, with a hell of a bump, and splattered whipped cream all over his face. They howled."

"Like Soupy Sales used to hit everybody with a pie in the face on his TV show," Irving Zussman spoke up.

"Yes, but I had my whipped cream on my tits and my pussy!" Miss Kennedy reminded us.

"Did you ever see girls who could pick up dollar bills with their things?" I asked. "They used to do it in Harlem."

"Oh, I can do that!" she assured me. "But my boss made me stop it."

"Why?"

"Too much heat. It's just muscle control. I squat down like this. . . ."

She started to show me, actually squatting down on the floor. "You learn how to squeeze with your pussy till you get hold of the bill." I believe she would have carried the demonstration through, but I wanted a little mystery left in femininity, after all, so I didn't encourage her to finish.

"I could even pick up a bottte with my pussy," she said.

"How big a bottle? Not a champagne bottle."

"No—like a chianti bottle . . . with the cork still in it."

"Doesn't it hurt?"

"No . . . well, a little at first. But," she added, "your pussy gets used to it."

My talks with Monica Kennedy were the most educational "dialogues" I've ever engaged in. If world governments could hold dialogues like these I've had with this stripper with the star-spangled pubic hair, they'd make progress. One midnight I climbed the stairs at the Broadway Burlesk, watched the last few minutes of Monica's show, and found her in what she called her "covered" mood. "I didn't know there was so much money workin' covered," she said.

Immediately alarmed, I inquired where and when she'd worked covered.

She held me off. "It's more intriggin'," she said. We were in her dressing room again, and she kept her robe on.

"That's what it is, the men find it's more intriggin'. Even though it chafes me between my legs when I wear a G-string, I can make more money bein' covered."

She had taken a couple of weeks from stripping and worked simply as a go-go dancer. "I made twelve hundred, thirteen hundred a week just in a little dump down by the meat market. Mostly in tips. I get ten dollar tips, thirty dollars, one guy give me fifty dollars just for dancing. Oh, I might give 'em a little flash, but I got it mostly covered."

"Where is this dump you worked in?"

"Don't print no names. It's in the market section where they bring in the meat. Downtown." It was getting warm in the dressing room, and Monica loosened her robe. "I don't want the other girls to find out about it."

"But you wouldn't want a career working covered?" I asked. She had me frightened.

"I might! There's going to be a slowdown eventually of this other stuff. They're showin' too much, the guys are going to want to see it covered." Monica repeated her favorite thought of the evening, "It's more intriggin'."

She was thinking of opening a small club on the East Side of the city, with only three or four girls, all covered. Huntington Hartford had told her he thought such places had a future. I mentioned to her that Hartford had a Midas touch in reverse. Just let him get behind an enterprise, and there was a good chance it would lose money. Monica reassured me that her angel would not be Hartford.

"You didn't wear your usual hairdo tonight," I said. I had

noticed that she wasn't wearing her heart-shaped pubic hair coiffure on stage. Or so it appeared to me.

"Oh, yes, I did!" She stripped off her robe and stood up for me to inspect it. "Oh, yes, it was different. The last time I guess I had the heart in red, and there were diamonds and stars around the edge of it."

"Ever had it photographed?" I asked.

"A snatch shot? No, I never took no snatch shots."

"Would you object to posing for one?"

"For a snatch shot? No, I wouldn't mind, as long as it was in good taste."

I thought that the star-spangled pussy should definitely be photographed and arranged to send a photographer at midnight to get the picture. I also wished to research one more point of her art—how did she learn to pick up coins, bottles, and other objects with her vagina?

"That's muscle control," Monica said. "Did you put down I had red, white, and blue hair for holidays?"

"Yes, I did, but what I want to know," I persisted, "is how you learned it. Who taught you?"

"Listen," she said, "did you notice, when I'm bending over, I'm making it talk?"

"No, I'm afraid I didn't. I wasn't that close."

"Well, I'm making it like snap." She held up her fingers and made a pincers movement with her thumb and forefinger. "I'm making it talk sweet things to you."

"I didn't get the message."

"These other guys did!" Monica laughed.

"But where did you learn it?"

"Some girls, it comes natural to them to make it snap. I can pick up a silver dollar, a dollar bill, even a pipe once. I told you I pick up a wine bottle, but it's got to have a cork in it. Or you would get suction. You might have to go to a doctor to break the suction if you don't have the cork in it when you pick it up."

But there was still more research to be done. "You told me you did your breast rotation different from other girls?"

"Well," she said, licking her breasts, "I take the bust up in my hand and instead of doing like this"—she was kissing the outer edge of the nipple—"I do the tip of the nipple just like a guy would do. It actually gets hard. Feel it!"

But I didn't, and I considered that noble of me.

"Look at this!" she commanded. And I did. The nipple stood up. "I'm very sensitive," she said. "And that's a good place to be sensitive."

"Most strippers tell me they never get sexually excited when they're performing," I said.

"Oh, are you kidding? That's a lie!" exclaimed Monica.

"You get a little worked up?"

"I'm oversensitive, but yeah, I get worked up. What turns me on is seeing a man, he's really interested, he shows his appreciation. That's what gets me excited."

Monica tossed back her long blond wig that fell down to her bare and well-rounded behind and announced with some pride, "Sure, I can pop twenty times to a guy once. I said to a doctor, 'I pop so quick, anything wrong with me, Doctor?' He says 'No, that's beautiful!' "

I considered my research—for that evening—finished, and arose to go. Monica, naked, with everything on display, gave me a kiss as I said good night.

The remaining undone chore was the picture taking. I arranged for an assistant, Tim Boxer, an orthodox Jewish young man, who never worked after sundown Fridays, to take the picture on a Thursday midnight which got into Friday morning. We met at the Broadway Burlesk at a little before midnight and watched Monica finishing her act. That night she was more than ever a nature girl romping around the stage barefooted, totally nude, with none of the usual hocus-pocus about being a stripper. She was just a naked girl up there with a pudenda that was spectacularly coiffured.

A young couple on the front row were getting sexually heated up as she poured champagne down her pubic hair, caught its drippings in a paper cup, and then drank them.

They were fondling each other and French-kissing. I'd never seen this in a strippery before.

When Monica was finishing her act with more than the usual use of her tongue, especially more licking her nipples, she ran off into her dressing room to get made up for the picture taking. Tim and I stood around in the now-empty theater waiting for her, and about twelve fifteen I got restless and announced we couldn't wait any longer.

One of the owners went to investigate.

"What happened," he said, "when she was dancin', her rhinestone fell off her box and she's got to put it back on."

"Her costume fell off," Tim said. "One rhinestone."

Still she kept us waiting. Now I went to investigate. She was standing facing a mirror, brushing . . . her pubic hair, of course.

"I just had to brush my hair and get my heart back on it," she said. She now came nakedly back into the theater and on the stage, while Tim Boxer focused his camera on her unique sex object. "What would you say in describing it?" I asked her.

"Just that I got a diamond-bordered heart-shaped pussy," Monica said. "I wore it like this five, six years. It's its regular color except that sometimes I dye it red, white, and blue to be patriotic. Sometimes I put little diamonds in it, little diamond chips. I have to be careful, though, I might lose them down there."

Without any prompting from me, Monica began doing bumps and grinds and stomach rolls, thrusting her pelvic area forward, the better for it to be photographed.

"How about would you like me to kneel?" she said. She opened up her vaginal area considerably, she did a spread, she cupped her breasts in her hands and licked them—she was not only cooperative, but imaginative.

Tim Boxer was practicing his photographic art very conscientiously.

"Hold 'em both up," he suggested, speaking of her breasts, of course.

She continued manipulating her tongue over them.

"Is that a wig you're wearing?" I asked.

"It's a wig, honey."

"What kind of wig?"

"Like a show girl wig."

Tim Boxer had now taken about thirty pictures and had, I felt, covered the subject. Walking up to Monica, who was still standing there naked, I thanked her for posing, and she thanked me back. She had no reticence whatever about discussing her unusual vaginal coiffure.

"How do you hold those rhinestones on it?" I asked.

Monica was eager to be helpful. "I hold them on it with surgical tape," she said, fingering the edges of her pubis to show me. "I cut the tape into small pieces and then make the rhinestones stick onto the edges of the hair. You see?"

I saw, very clearly.

"It looks easy, but it takes a lot of doin'," she said.

Once again she kissed me good night. Returning to my office at past 1 A.M., I thought to myself, "I'll bet Tim Boxer has found something that would make him work even on Jewish holidays!"

Sally Rand was looking forward to her seventieth birthday in 1974 and was going to continue dancing in and out from under those fans for years to come. But she had been to see burlesk shows and delivered a forthright opinion.

"When you stick a naked body out in those dreadful white lights, you destroy all the illusion," Sally said.

"But then this girl's entire pubic hair area is shown and it's not even well groomed . . . it's still parted from last night's orgy . . . well, that's hardly appetizing.

"And they all have fried-egg boobs and dirty toenails and bare feet. Who could be sexually titillated by anybody with dirty toenails?

"What else can they do besides showing their vaginas? One of them said to me, 'I bend over and have sparklers out of my ass.' And that's what she did. She twinkled her rectum."

I asked Sally now that she's near the end of her career to confess whether she was naked or not naked under those fans. She always left the illusion she was. She just smiled. "The Rand is quicker than the eye," she said.

"What about those gals who can pick up things with their vagina?" I asked.

"Snappers," Sally said. "Girls with snappers are very good in bed especially toward the end of the sex act. Acrobats are very good snappers because they have great muscle control, and since I'm an acrobat. . . ."

Sally gave the impression there was nothing they could do she couldn't do better.

It was on Broadway—in San Francisco—that the topless-bottomless battle, one of the most fascinating in the New Permissiveness, became not only furious, but also amusing. Carol Doda, the extraordinarily breasty blonde who pioneeered topless dancing away back in 1964, when bare nipples were pretty shocking, was shown on a large sign outside the Condor Club, and under the sketch were the words:

CAROL DODA
Every Body
Needs Milk

The connection between Carol Doda and milk was clear to everybody. This was an invitation to people to enter and behold Miss Doda's unbelievable bosom. When the city endeavored to end such advertising, the clubs asked, with pretended innocence, "Suppose a public-spirited nightclub owner puts up a sign like that because he just wants to help the milk industry . . . would that be a violation of the law?"

The city was using an ordinance which prohibited the "depicting of the human form or any portion thereof, partially clothed or unclothed. . . ."

While the ordinance makers undoubtedly intended to prohibit showing the bust, genitalia, etc., Superior Judge Ira A. Brown, Jr., declared: "it could include the face or the finger." Or the big toe, or the ear, or the elbow.

The clubs hooted at the clean-up campaign, claiming it was farcical. The police covering the uncovered Broadway area called themselves the booby patrol. The bottomless, topless girls went right on squirming and writhing in simulated sex acts as before.

The bottomless outburst in San Francisco brought forth some extremely candid news stories. The Department of Alcoholic Beverage Control of California announced it was going to enforce its rules and prosecute bars "where genitals and pubic hair are displayed."

"Bottomless" referred to pantslessness. There was no G-string, no patch, nothing. The girl was naked from the topmost hair of her head to the soles of her feet.

Newspaper readers may have been startled by this frank language. But the papers followed through by citing some of the rules which of course were public record.

With their liquor licenses at stake if they transgressed, the topless clubs were reminded that:

(1) No licensee shall permit any person to perform acts of or acts which simulate:

(a) Sexual intercourse, masturbation, sodomy, bestiality, oral copulation, flagellation or any sexual acts which are prohibited by law.

(b) The touching, caressing or fondling on the breasts, buttocks, anus or genitals.

(c) The displaying of the pubic hair, anus, vulva or genitals.

The bottomless brigade, the clubs, through their spokesman, Dave Rosenberg, an enterprising publicist, undertook to ridicule these rules, especially about "touching the breast, buttocks, anus or genitals."

"If you hear the national anthem, you put your hand over your breast, right?" he said. "When you salute the flag, you're touching your breast, right? These women are dancing. It's hard to control your emotions when you're dancing." In other words, they were artists, and if a totally nude dancer got emotional and touched her pubic hair and fondled her vulva, was that any different from touching your breast when you salute the flag? Well, why didn't they go arrest the fellows who were touching their breasts when they heard the national anthem? And if any female, even an old married woman, put her hand over her heart and touched her breast, wasn't she up to some sexual outrage of some kind? Shouldn't she be tossed into the paddy wagon?

The bottomless boys said they weren't simulating any copulation, masturbation, flagellation, sodomy, or bestiality, and they were already complying with that rule—but they'd be damned if they'd cover up the pubic hair by putting G-strings over them, by putting pants on the pantsless. It was their right, they maintained, to let the pubic go public.

For one thing, the bottomless battle was educational. The rules of the Department of Alcoholic Beverage Control forbade anybody to "permit any person . . . to touch, caress or fondle the breasts, buttocks, anus or genitals of *any other person*."

("My goodness, how long has this been going on?" one person asked in alarm. "Oh, a long time," he was told.)

One rule that was obviously quite old-fashioned prohibited display of the female breast "below the top of the areola." I have been writing about female breasts for many years but was driven to the dictionary to find that the areola is that ring of color around what is popularly (very popularly) known as the nipple.

The dirty-minded old Supreme Court took a lot of the friskiness out of Frisco by the end of 1973. The leering, laughing, bare-pubised and bare-bottomed beauties who had made Broadway, San Francisco, a land of promise for the sex-starved had been covered up, not by the White House, but by the Supreme Court. Believe it or not, the local judges had even ordered these poor creatures to cover up their areolae.

The Battle of Hookersville

✍ "THE Pussy Posse" was the name that some of New York's cops gave to themselves when they tried to run the whores out of Manhattan in 1972 and 1973. They chased the girls from Broadway for a while, and they moved over East; but later they returned when some of the cops in the Pussy Posse were transferred to fighting more serious crimes. There are still plenty of hookers in Hookersville. We don't like to face the bitter truth; but whores we will always have with us, and someday not far from Broadway there will be a legalized red-light district to serve the Johns of New York. The way things are going now, that New York City red-light district will not be limited to girls. There will be male whores for the homosexuals, and why not? There will be lesbians for the butch trade.

Just as Howard Samuels, the head of Off Track Betting, became "New York's No. 1 bookie," there will be some woman heading the red-light district who will have the quaint honor of being New York City's top madam.

Horrifying as this seems, it's likely to be part of the Genitalia Generation. There's too much of the latter for sale, and there are always buyers despite the paradox that there's so much of it that can be had for nothing.

When I first heard the expression "Pussy Posse" from a man who was head of it at the time, Sergeant John O'Neill, I was delighted with it linguistically and assumed that it was a New York term. But people more conversant with police told me that nearly every city has cops trying to hustle the hustlers out of town, and they all think of themselves as being in the Pussy Posse.

I was unable to share the expression with my readers since "pussy" is a word that's pretty hard to get away with in the newspapers. However, I could use "the prossy posse" or "prostie posse" and most people would understand.

Being on "pussy patrol" was certainly one of the most interesting, as well as undesirable, police assignments. And I went out on patrol with the Pussy Posse a few times, watching the Battle of Hookersville first hand.

The streetwalkers just around midtown Manhattan numbered 100 to 200 and were the cheapest, dirtiest, lewdest, crudest tarts imaginable. It made me sad to think that some of these creatures had been driven to this by existing social and economic conditions that made it almost impossible for young girls to live decently on their salaries. By the time she paid her taxes and rent many a respectable girl saw the wisdom of "doing a little part-time hookering." They might become "models" or call girls and deteriorate, when older, into streetwalkers.

Directing them in the battle with the Pussy Posse, of course, were their pimps, nearly all young blacks, wearing floppy wide-brimmed hats, sharp clothes and jewelry and driving expensive cars which the police called pimpmobiles.

"Hooker Hill," or "Hookerama," the battlefield, was New York City's Casbah. It lay on dark, ugly Eighth Avenue. It had been an eyesore street of pawnbrokers, cheap bars which advertised topless go-go dancers, gypsy fortune-tellers, and movies whose marquees proclaimed "all-male casts." The hooker section stretched from the West Forty-second Street area that the late editor Abel Green of *Variety* named Slime Square northward to about Fifty-second Street. That, in the old, old days, had been the westernmost end of Swing Street.

I lived just a few blocks north of Hooker Hill and walked through the outer edge of it for several years when going to my office without observing any shocking transformation.

Then people began asking me in astonishment, "Have you tried to walk down Eighth Avenue lately?"

A woman remarked, "I'm afraid to go down that street anymore."

At first had come the streetwalkers, and then "the pussy parlor" had emerged.

The GI's, "the servicemen," the foreign seamen, had found plenty of prostitutes on Eighth Avenue in the late '60s. The girls enticed them into mean-looking little hotels. But around 1970 we began hearing of the body-rub dives, the massage parlors, the pussy palaces.

The massage parlors were not new in Europe, but they were

fairly new in New York City. A dozen years ago, in Rome, Americans marveled at ads in Italian papers, luring men to get massages from beautiful and shapely masseuses. These ads often described the assets of the masseuses: They were beautiful, blond or brunette, and had sensational measurements. These assets were expected to make the massage more enjoyable.

"How do they get away with printing ads like that?" Americans would wonder.

In the beginning in New York, the sex entrepreneurs were rather timid. They hawked nude models for photographers. And for those who didn't have a camera, they offered something called "psychedelic body painting" or finger painting. Then along came *Screw* magazine and all its imitators, and they were out in the open with their full menu.

The June 28, 1971, issue of *Screw* which had the headline GERMAINE GREER ON MASTURBATION, had an ad for the Scandia Studio, 31 West Forty-sixth Street, a little east of Hooker Hill. THE CLIMAX AT SCANDIA, it read at the top. A picture of a large bare-breasted blonde with her pubic hair showing topped the ad, and in the middle of the ad was a picture of a naked girl seeming to be masturbating.

"You Fancy It—We've Got It," Scandia told the world.

"Sensuous and very experienced masseuses. . . . A unique type of massage geared to turn you on and totally satisfy you. . . . Have your own harem with 2, 3 or more girls. . . . Group sessions. . . . Nudist colony weekends. . . . You owe it to yourself because you've never had it so good. . . . So just come in and indulge yourself."

Club 252, at 252 West Forty-sixth Street, off Eighth Avenue, and exactly in the nub of Hooker Hill, was just having its grand opening, according to its ad. "Erotic, stimulating rubdowns our specialty," it said. "Our girls will make you feel like a new man. . . . The most liberal model show in town. . . . Plus live continuous sex shows. . . . New sensual waterbed massage."

The Ram Studios, 694 Third Avenue, showing a nude girl in a spread shot, her legs wide open exhibiting her pubic hair, announced it had "14 voluptuous, erotic damsels awaiting your brush or camera. Don't phone—Just Come!"

So that's what New York had come to! Whorehouses disguised as massage parlors, advertising their whores as masseuses!

Screw magazine took much of the glamor out of the massage

parlors with its candid reviews of their activities. Prices ranged from $15 to $20, plus a $3 to $5 membership fee, entitling a customer to a half-hour private session with "the model" for the photography or the body painting. (Everybody was supposed to be a painter or a photographer.) A generous tip was required if the customer expected the model to be especially nice to him.

Screw's reviewer said that Club 252's rooms "are bare and have only a curtain over the door." . . . Deep Purple: "Each room has a door and a bed but the top of each compartment is open." . . . "Studio Erotica is small and cramped; its rooms have minimal privacy with a curtain across the door" . . . and Stallion Studios, 714 Lexington Avenue at Fifty-seventh Street, "is the only studio with male models catering to the gay trade. It has half a dozen private rooms, each with a bed, and carpeted."

Only The Casbah was complimented, for its molded plastic that gave it a cavelike environment. "The girls are also attractive. Massage only," it added, and since this was the only "model studio" where the reviewer added "Massage only," the impression was obtained that the others offered more than mere massages.

During my walks to work on Eighth Avenue, I saw two of these massage parlors spring up, one on the corner of West Fifty-fifth and one between Fifty-fourth and Fifty-fifth. They were both secretive-looking, with windows generally boarded up and girls and men coming furtively in and out. When the door was opened narrowly once when I was passing, I saw two girls sitting, fully clothed, on a couch as in a waiting room. For a time the other massage parlor displayed sex books in its window, and I saw a girl clerk seeming to be selling pornographic books and sex devices.

While the readers of *Screw* and its contemporaries knew about the inner workings and behind-the-curtain goings-on in the massage parlors, the general public didn't. The Broadway theater owners, producers, and press agents and the Times Square restaurateurs must have suspected. They were certain, anyway, that there were more prostitutes around the theatrical area than they could remember.

And they began screaming their protests to Mayor John V. Lindsay and the police.

Just by soliciting, and lingering and loitering in doorways and whispering, "Want to have a party, honey?" they were contaminating the theater. These cheap whores in their miniskirts and their slacks, with their seductive glances and "How about havin' a good time?," were keeping decent people from going to see the Broadway shows. Such was the charge against them by the producers who were suffering hard times.

They were talking about the streetwalkers rather than the "models" and "masseuses" in the massage parlors. The latter were now an additional problem. And to make it more difficult, some reformer would go on TV and declare that the problem would never be solved until prostitution was legalized.

"And where would we have the New York red-light district?" somebody would ask.

"Why not keep it right where it is now—on Eighth Avenue?" some wit would retort.

The Broadway Association, after many overtures to Mayor Lindsay, decided to get tough with His Honor. They warned him that unless he properly policed Times Square and cleaned out the vice, they would install their own private police to mop up the area, and tell the world that he (then the would-be President of the United States) had failed at his job.

The Mayor promised, the producers raised a fund for better lighting of some dark areas . . . and thus the stage was set for the Pussy Posse to expel *les girls,* or at least to begin the battle.

The great brains of the world have wrestled with the problem of prostitution and concluded that it will always be with us because men want sex and will buy it, and women can supply them with sex and will sell it.

"The way to get rid of prostitution is to get rid of the pimps," a police matron told me. "When one pimp is driven out, about eight girls go with him."

General headquarters for the Battle of Hooker Hill was the Seventeenth Precinct Station in a dreary-looking old building on West Fifty-fourth Street between Eighth and Ninth avenues. I went over there one afternoon to see the then Deputy Inspector Charles F. Peterson, the youngest deputy inspector in the city, only forty-one, and the possessor of three college degrees. Tall, red-haired, and good-looking, he had a law degree and particularly hated the procurers.

"There's a West Fiftieth Street bar that's the pimp headquarters of the Western world," he told me. "I'll close it if it takes five years.

"Every time I try, I get five assistant DA's after me claiming I'm violating their civil rights and that I'm harassing them. I'm harassing them, all right, in the name of the law!"

It was from him that I learned first of the Pussy Posse, although he never used that term. He boasted to me that he had a sergeant and eight patrolmen trying to chase away about 200 "hard-core" prostitutes, including perhaps 100 in the massage parlors.

"They're running this town down, and I've got to clean it up," he said. "You don't see so many of the pimps' pimpmobiles around now, do you?"

He smiled an Irish smile over his triumph. "I put their cars in the pound in Queens in the rain and snow until they can prove their ownership, which usually they can't.

"The pimpmobiles are like their status symbol; it's their ad to the girls that they're prosperous and successful, and that if the girl gets arrested, they can take care of her."

But let's look at the way prostitution works in New York City. A streetwalker accosts a man on Eighth Avenue or any number of streets and solicits him. After discussing the price, she takes him to a cheap nearby hotel unless he has a room in a good hotel, they have sex, and he pays her. That's the old way. The massage parlors introduced the body-rub idea where the man pretends for several minutes at least that he's there primarily to get a massage. Of course the masseuse is naked, and naturally he gets that way very quickly. He is there to get massaged, isn't he?

Reporter Larry Kleinman did a fascinating series of stories on the massage parlors for the New York *Post* and undoubtedly spurred on the police drive. He had first promised his wife and his city editor that he was going to avoid having sex with any of the masseuses. He was going to pose as a would-be customer and then decide at the last moment, after he'd obtained all the information he could, not to go through with it.

He got around to asking most of the girls, "Do you fuck?"

About half of them said they would if the price was right.

They also offered to perform fellatio, again for the right price. Very few refused to give a "hand job"—to masturbate him.

A girl reporter, Lindsay Van Gelder, went on a tour of the massage parlors pretending she wanted to get a job as a masseuse and found that it was all more revolting than she'd anticipated.

She told the bosses, who were usually young swinging types, that she was married to a writer currently working on a sex novel that should make a lot of money but that now they were broke.

"My husband doesn't know I'm here, but I think he'll let me take the job once I get it . . . on one condition.

"I don't want to fuck anybody," she said.

(To her surprise, they didn't throw her out.)

"I know my old man wouldn't like that. But any other kind of sex would probably be all right with him because we really need the bread."

One of the bosses, named Dick, nodded and, having looked her over (with her clothes on) says she's to consider herself hired (she hasn't definitely decided yet whether she wants the job)—but that there are certain rules.

"The customer must take off his clothes completely, socks and all, before I begin to undress.

"I am never, ever, to suggest anything beyond a massage. Let the customer suggest sex."

These are for the place's legal protection in case of an arrest. The club promises to pay her legal fees in case of an arrest.

Dick was cautious in talking about the sex stuff following the massage. He said the tips "would amount to a lot."

"Most of the men who come here are married, they have kids, they're not bums," he said. "The important thing is to be nice. No matter how you feel, you've got to act like you've been waiting to see him all day."

Then Lindsay Van Gelder said, "with enormous politeness, Dick asks me to strip.

" 'It's a routine procedure, we just have to see what the customers will see.'

"I panic and say I'll strip tomorrow after I get my husband's permission.' Dick shrugs. 'Nobody's forcing you,' he says.

"The next day I phone and say my 'husband' said no. We wish each other good luck."

She found from the masseuses, though, that Dick hadn't told her the entire truth about the massages. One girl is a chubby redhead wearing a granny dress and a shawl and she says the customers include a lot of "creepy creeps" and "whip-me types" and that she had one strange session "with a guy, all he wanted to do was look up my rear end."

She got a $50 tip from a man who wanted her to tell him dirty jokes while he masturbated.

"After about fifteen minutes I ran out of jokes, so I kept saying,

'Fuck, suck, fuck, suck, fuck, suck.' That was fine. He really dug it. I didn't even have to touch him to make him come." She giggled relating the experience.

There was a hip-looking brunette named Margo who boasted that she was the new girlfriend of a man who in recent months had become the darling of the celebrity lecture circuit. He got $800 to lecture for an hour, and that impressed Margo.

Until recently she hadn't revealed to him what she did for a living.

"Finally I just came out and told him, 'I'm a prostitute,' she said.

"You know what, he wasn't even that surprised. He didn't mind, either. He said, 'Margo, the idea of you fucking all those guys all day long and then coming home to me really turns me on.' "

There was a black masseuse listening to this rendition, and she said, "I wish I could find a guy like that."

The girls discussed other massage parlors and claimed that some of the "very fancy" East Side places catering to doctors, lawyers, and even psychiatrists were colorful because "they're the sickest." One of those parlors was closed by police not because of the sex activities but because one of the supposed nineteen-year-old girls turned out to be fifteen with a fake ID card.

The girls discussed their astrological signs and their male ideals.

"Do any real cute-looking men ever come in here?" Lindsay asked.

"If they're cute," the redhead said, "you know what?"

"What?"

"They don't have to pay for it."

In trying to maintain that they were respectable, the massage parlors claimed they would give massages to women clients or "members." They even advertised they offered "co-ed facilities." This got to be funny when Lindsay Van Gelder went to some of them and said she wanted a massage. They hadn't expected any woman to believe those claims, evidently.

"When I bound up the stairs at 219 East Forty-sixth Street, the man at the desk gives me what can only be described as a bewildered sneer. Am I a lesbian? A lady cop? Or just plain stupid?"

Nevertheless, probably figuring she's a policewoman, they went ahead with the pretense. Miss Van Gelder wrote that they gave her a masseuse, a tall, slim black woman who was very bored with her and couldn't wait to get her out of the place.

"When I get on the massage table, she seems to be waiting for me to make some unspeakable offer. I do—I ask her if she'd mind massaging my left ankle, which was broken in a car accident and has been giving me trouble lately. This turns out to be a horrible mistake. Ankles are clearly not her specialty.

"The second my massage is over, Yolanda (the masseuse) gathers up all my clothes and tells me not to forget any of my belongings. 'I'd like to finish my coffee,' I say, but Yolanda stands there fidgeting and tapping her foot. Feeling I've just been crowned Leper for a Day, I finally take the hint."

At the Magic Carpet they hadn't had a co-ed customer before, and the manager felt like a pioneer. "There is a lot of fussing and consulting while he finds me a place to undress (the men change in an open locker room) and a closet long enough to hold my maxi-dress. Then he elaborately clears the sauna for my private use.

"I'm such a novelty as a customer that three Atlanta business-men loudly offer fifty dollars just to let them peek at me in the sauna. It's more weird than flattering."

The masseuse here is a college dropout who'd majored in psychology and later become a Wall Street secretary. When Miss Van Gelder informed her that she just wanted a massage, and would that be OK, she said she didn't mind but that some of the girls got uptight at such requests.

"But I'm not a complete money grubber," she says.

Her conclusion from visits to several places with "co-ed facilities" was that it was possible to get a simple backrub, but that a girl didn't get any of that Queen of the Nile treatment that the men get.

The language used by the girls with the men consists usually of a few expressions: "blow job," "hand job" and "fuck." One masseuse told Larry Kleinman, "Most of our customers are fifty-year-old men whose wives have never even heard of a blow job. We perform a real service."

"I had a cop once," one of the masseuses was quoted, "and I knew he was a cop because he didn't want to take his pants off, but he finally did. Then he told me he was a cop and he was going to bust me. I said, 'You going to get up in court and tell everybody how you took your pants off?' He smiles and says that in court he's going to say he kept them on. 'OK,' I told him, 'I've been sitting here studying your genitals, and when I get into court, I'm going to describe them, the color of your hair, birthmarks, everything.' He decided not to bust me."

The question "Will you fuck?" got varying answers, but a typical reply was, "Sure, but I have to charge you forty dollars for it. All we get are our tips. But I'm worth it, I assure you."

There were occasions when a masseuse didn't want to comply sexually because she was having her period, and one girl said she'd ordinarily be happy to give him a blow job, "but this cold has me coughing too much to be very good at it today." She was sucking a cough drop. "How about me masturbating you?"

While the New York *Post* was running this series about the couple of dozen places, the police were raiding some of them, and it was found that a special deluxe massage might consist of an orgy on a water bed with two girls for ninety minutes, costing $200.

But the girls could be bargained with. One detective got the price for the two girls down to $140.

The detective offered to pay cash, but the manager preferred to be paid with an American Express credit card.

"They don't like to do business with cash," the detective said. "They're afraid if there's an arrest, the cash will be confiscated."

One raid on a "key club" was right across from my own apartment building. It could be accurately described as posh. In fact, I had attended the opening, a rather elaborate cocktail party, when we were all led to believe it was simply a sauna place for the tired businessmen. My wife went to the opening with me, and I remember us saying, "Isn't this nice?" Some of the waitresses and attendants reminded us of hostesses in other famous men's clubs.

Police said that while they were lounging in water seats beside an indoor pool, two of the masseuses wandered up and, in the soft glow of the psychedelic lights, offered their sexual services for prices ranging from $10 to $20. The police arrested fifteen women—and closed the place. But it reopened—the charges were dismissed.

I wished to ask a very simple question. I therefore dropped into the ancient, dusty, depressing West Fifty-fourth Street police station, where some of our Very Best People have been jailed and handcuffed. It was total confusion. Phones were jangling, one heard sirens and alarms, and at the desk a man in handcuffs was having his pockets searched by a cop who'd already taken from him a small whiskey bottle which now was on the desk. The man was bitterly protesting this search and seizure. I found a uniformed sergeant momentarily unharassed and asked him my question. He turned and echoed it to the room.

"Who has the Posse tonight?" he asked.

It was a Friday in June, 1973, and I wished to be up to date.

"Sergeant O'Neill . . . he's been transferred . . . Sergeant McNally, he works days. . . . Sergeant Eugene Rooney . . . he's in charge, but he's off till Monday night. . . ."

O'Neill, McNally, Rooney—do you have to be Irish, are the sons of Erin better at those things? Such a thought had I when the sergeant suggested I should talk to Sergeant Gilmartin of the Eighth Avenue Task Force.

"I do not have the Posse," he succinctly asserted.

"Well, then, can you tell me who does?"

"I would say nobody on the weekend."

"Not on the weekend! I would have thought you would have needed the Pussy Posse mostly on weekends."

Quickly explaining that he had nothing to do with the Pussy Posse and was simply trying to help me, he said, "Well, the prostitute activity is heavier during the week. The city tends to empty out on the weekend."

"But what about the convention delegates?"

"They come in Sunday night or Monday."

"And the tourists?"

"Small. Don't you know, it's a lot of your New York businessmen, yes, your New York businessmen, that are away over the weekend . . . and they're the ones who patronize the prostitutes!"

So it was probably people I knew or types I knew that were keeping prostitution flourishing in New York. And the hookers were loyal to the theme of Melina Mercouri's movie, "Never on Weekends."

While I was waiting, however, I saw half a dozen afternoon hustlers being loaded into a police van to be taken to downtown court. While some are young and some are beautiful, I have often been impressed by the fact that some of those picked up seem to be grandmotherly and spectacled and totally undesirable. One of these hags now resisted being assisted—that is, being shoved—into the police van.

"I'll have you know I was once married to an FBI man!" she said.

"Who was it? J. Edgar Hoover?" one of the cops asked.

One development of the Genitalia Generation not only in New York but around the country has been doorway copulation led by the ladies who then slug, beat up, rob, and occasionally even kill the male customer, especially if he's got a poke—that is, some money.

It starts with a man being enticed into a doorway by a prostitute who kisses him in the dark, fondles him, and opens his trousers.

"How about a blow job, honey?" She promises she can supply him this while he's still standing in the doorway. If it's late and he's a little drunk, she works better, but if it's 10 or 11 P.M. only, and the customer is fairly alert, she may have the need of help from a couple of co-working hustlers who stroll by. They pounce in while she's got his penis in her mouth and go through his pockets taking everything.

He's hardly in a mood to resist; for one reason his pants are probably down around his ankles. If he starts to scream for police, he finds out these girls carry knives or scissors in their purses. Three girls were actually observed giving this treatment to a male customer very near the Hilton Hotel in New York recently. One girl became angry at a friend of mine who was watching the whole operation and said, "Get movin'!"

"I like to watch," he said. "I'm a voyeur."

"Get movin' or you may get your balls handed to you," the girl warned him. They had the man with his back to the wall, and he seemed to be perfectly happy while one sucked him and two others robbed him.

As for the professionals, who have given a lighthearted air to what we once considered pretty serious stuff. . . .

They purge themselves by talking freely about their sex-for-pay to almost anybody who asks. That justifies it, in their eyes.

Before the Genitalia Generation, the girls didn't talk honestly, or at all, but now they all seem to want to outdo Xaviera Hollander's screwing confessions. "It's an easy life and I like fucking, I love fucking, and I love guys to eat my pussy, and I love to eat cocks, big cocks," says a typical nonpublicized hooker. "They say we do it for the money, and we do; but even if we didn't get paid, I would eat cocks because I love to eat cocks and I love to have somebody eat my pussy."

This is a young one no more than twenty-two, and though she has her own little brothel on the East Side in the Fifties, you are afraid she is not going to last very long in life, because she is vulnerable.

"I get mighty fuckin' scared when I don't get any customers for a few hours," she says, mentioning that she's got a goodly rent, an expensive dog, a huge phone bill, and frequent visits to the beauty parlor. She's made an application for an expensive gymnasium and health club where Jacqueline Onassis is a member.

"Wouldn't that be a laugh? Jackie and me! She should look as good as me!"

This young one confesses that she's got a business manager— not a pimp, she keeps saying, more a businessman type of lover—who really loves her and can suck her all night, but he also manages to bring her some clients.

"He goes around town, and he gets guys to talkin' about fuckin' and suckin', and he gets them excited, and he says, 'Have I got a broad for you!' He says, 'Wait a minute, I hope I didn't lose the number.' Then when he gets the guy ready to jerk off, he gives them my number, and I know from the phone call that he set it up.

"Sometimes he sets it up so he's watchin' when I'm givin' the guy a fuck.

"He's very commercial. He wouldn't let me fuck or suck nobody just for love. I got to get paid. He may set me up to five or six tricks a night or even more, but that's about all I can handle because I give 'em a good time and work them over till they get a damn good orgasm. I may not come, but I make damn sure they come so they will want to come back.

"It doesn't matter to me whether I come. If I can suck their cocks and make them come, I feel very relieved. And there are very few cocks," she adds, "that I haven't been able to make come!"

The prostitutes in the Genitalia Generation start in their teens because they've learned from reading and from talk shows that they're worn out by the time they're twenty-five and that the well-paying customers like young stuff, by which they mean the teeners.

"You know I've heard guys call a girl an old bag that wasn't more than twenty-three. I guess screwin' a half a dozen guys a day gives you wrinkles and lines so you have to get it when you're young. But Jesus, you can make fifty, sixty thousand a year, and that ain't bad if the income tax guys let you alone. And all those cocks besides. Slurp, slurp!"

She adds, "As you can see, I love my work."

Strong-muscled young male hookers working as masseurs in massage parlors for homosexuals are part of the sex of the seventies.

I found they were easy to talk to because they are anxious to expose their guilt and air it in conversation.

At first, I thought they were mostly very young blacks, and while there are some such in the field, those I encountered were white men from out of town, some close to middle-aged and quite surprising in appearance. If one had told me he was a minister, I could have believed him because that was the attitude of so many.

They were primarily masseurs, and they were probably very good at giving massages. Yet, just like the masseuses working in the hookerish massage parlors, who ever judged one by her massages?

"I'm a hustler," one of these male hookers said. "I've been at it since I was seventeen when I came here to try to be an actor. I couldn't get work as an actor, and I was too lazy to be a waiter, and I found out I could get a nice living buggering some of these older guys. I learned all the moaning and panting and trying to make it look like I'm having a ball.

"The trouble is, life as a hustler is too good. I eat too good, and I drink too good, and I put on weight. I can't hustle much longer; they want younger meat. I'm lucky I lasted this long. What'll I do? Well, you know what some of them do? Kill themselves."

Coke

✍ "I HAD an orgy with eight chicks—just me and eight chicks and my coke," a Broadway choreographer recently bragged to a friend of mine. "Yep, eight chicks, balling them all at the same time, and my thing stayed up. Coke, man, never lets you down."

The popularity of "coke," or cocaine in show business, is due in part to the belief that it's a powerful aphrodisiac, that it helps a man sustain an erection. My friend who received this information is a sex addict but a dedicated nonuser of drugs and wasn't moved to try it although he was enormously impressed.

"Eight chicks?" he said. "Wow! I've balled three chicks at once, but eight sounds greedy and an awful waste. How'd you collect eight at one time?"

"Dancers I know, including some students," he confessed. "My dong never failed me. You said you've had three at once. When I've only got three, I'm like tapering off."

Cocaine is so loosely sniffed or snorted in the music section of show business that it's become known as "Brill Building Aspirin," the Brill Building being a onetime famous locale for the music business. Coke gives off no smell, as burning marijuana does. And it becomes so chic—phony chic in my opinion—that it's almost a status symbol to snort.

The disgusting society types who are using cocaine to multiply their arrogance and contempt for those below them are enough, however, to give cocaine a bad name. If they don't, the kickback and payola guys in the record business will, and in a couple or five years it won't be so fashionable. But surely there'll be a big surge of popularity for coke for a while because of the sex angle.

"It gives me stamina to satisfy all the celebrity fuckers and the groupies still hanging around." One of the rock stars grinned recently as he fondled the gold coke spoon such as he and his fellow users wear around their necks.

"But the ladies ball better, too; in fact, I think it makes them wilder than it does us studs," he said. "You give 'em coke, and they won't crawl off of you the whole gahdamn night. And they want to do them multiples. The three-four-five girl-guy scene. I'm not knockin' it!"

Again it's the sex lure that makes it fashionable. And one reason is that the gentlemen have found varying ways to use it. There's a school of cokeheads who put cocaine on the head of the penis claiming that it deadens the feeling, prolongs the copulation, and delays the ejaculation.

"I also persuade the chick that it has an interesting taste, and she should lick it off of my cock," declared one of these pioneers.

Oscar Wilde, Sir Arthur Conan Doyle, and Sigmund Freud of

course used "High C," as it's been called, and perhaps were forerunners of the sophisticates of today who think it's smart to be stoned on the little white powder.

As far back as September 21, 1972, I wrote in my column, "A Government source says cocaine's the new 'in' drug of the wealthy movie stars, authors, tycoons—and pimps."

Pimps! How chic can you get? The showoffy procurers with their big hats and pimpmobiles had to try to emulate the VIP's. A Broadway writer and publicist, Marc Olden, discovered many pimps using cocaine and sharing it with their whores. He reported it in his paperback book *Cocaine*. Marc Olden, a black, has proved more convincingly than anybody that cocaine is just as unchic as horse manure but that the chic people don't know it because they're either stupid or blind.

Have you ever wondered why certain famous people are so superior and so arrogant?

So have I, and wondered why they were humble and almost human last night and arrogant tonight. Well, no names, now—but could they be cokeheads?

A celebrated European female who'd been eased into a drugatorium for treatment after an extended cocaine binge gave me the clue to these suspicions when she said that cocaine "gives you a total delusion of grandeur about yourself. You feel you can get away with anything."

Bizarre clothes, bad manners, impudence, canes, walking sticks: attention-calling devices bespeaking phony grandeur.

They get to consider it a part of their power, and power is all. There's got to be power when you consider that you've got a taste that may stand you $500 a day.

During the investigation of the record business payola and its link to cocaine and other drugs, one of the moguls of the record world was swinging around his opulent offices stoned on cocaine most of the time.

"Sure, he's a big user," one of his acquaintances said, "but then you know with him, it's either lightin' up or snortin' the whole day. But I'll say this. He did make the whole office quit smoking grass at work. It got too heavy in there.

"So they went to cocaine, them that could afford it, like him.

"But damned few of them can afford it. They smoke grass on the outside, I guess."

He was rich, he was "entitled," but he was nervous because his own link to some of the business' questionable practices was known. And his whole empire might crash down on his head. For that reason he was worried—and he was getting stoned constantly.

It helped him feel arrogant and grand and above those other people beneath him. He felt like a prince or a king; that's what coke did for him.

The fashionable cokeheads swear that they've never met anybody from organized crime but it could well be that they're getting their High C from those ruffians. And the ruffians can play ruff. Anybody using drugs risks running up against the hoods behind drugs.

There's a story told, as fact, that a recording artist of great reputation wished to break his record contract. Two "visitors" to the record firm held him by the feet and dangled him head down from the fourteenth-floor window until he became satisfied with the contract he had.

The tie-up between cocaine, payola, and organized crime was money. The music business was no longer limited to the Brill Building, to 1650 Broadway, to Jack Dempsey's restaurant, and the late Turf restaurant, where the pluggers and certain composers always went to have lunch. The music business was no longer limited even to New York. It was very big in Nashville and Memphis and of course Los Angeles—and London, where British rock groups were busted on drug charges.

Nor was it limited to guys who wore suits.

Some of them wore jeans and beards and long hair and beads and hung out in strange places in Greenwich Village and were usually with their "lady," to whom they were not married but who went along willingly with their "life-style."

I would bump into them in a couple of hangouts mostly noted for always having beautiful girls around. They were not big names—except in the music business.

But they had become suddenly wealthy and "gotten into coke." It took a lot of money to "get into coke."

A steady user could get into $500 a day. The guy just getting some together to show his chick the joys of cocaine for a night would go for $200 or $300. There was a tendency when guys were showing off to their chicks to be wasteful and to rub some coke over their testicles as well as their penis. They were not in agreement as to the most often expressed conviction that it desensitized the organs. But they agreed that it produced "one hell of a come."

They had offbeat tastes in music when they were relaxing. They were titillated by what they called "rock and rouge."

That was the name given to the music of men usually dressed as women who did not consider themselves transvestites. They weren't quite sure what they were except they wore makeup, hence "rock and rouge."

In the back rooms or the dressing rooms of some of these places, coke would be passed around or even be made available on a table in the center of activity. But the chic practice especially in the upper financial reaches of the record business was to hand out a blow of cocaine using a crisp $100 bill as a snifter.

The bill was rolled up so as to be thinner than a pencil, the white powder inside, the bill used as sort of a funnel. The bill was twisted and tightened so the coke would not fall out and was handed briskly by the giver to the receiver. This was considered the height not only of luxury but of friendship.

Lavish parties became part of the music business—they were always "honoring" somebody—and at one of these gatherings they were bold enough to have some $100 snifters passed around at the dais.

The lesser people in music—the record promoters—passed this custom along to their contacts, the few disc jockeys and station people whom they could buy off. They would secretly hand out a snifter in a bill, but sometimes the traffic would not stand for a $100 bill, and they would use a $50 instead.

That was usually appreciated, too.

I heard the term "drug culture" a thousand times. The "drug culture" of the music business, "the drug therapy" of the record world. . . . Drugs were talked about even more than songs, and the drug they talked about was not horse, or heroin, as much as coke.

The "narcs," the narcotics officers, say that drug users are faddists and that coke happened to be their choice in the early 1970's because "shit" (marijuana) and acid (LSD) had had their course.

I succeeded in getting one cokehead to talk about it one night at a crazy party on Central Park West where the air was full of pot.

"I use it because it's not messy," he said. "You'd never get me on horse, never, never. And I've graduated from shit, which I'll always think of as shit because they love to keep using that name for it. Coke is nice and clean, and no needles, and no problems afterward."

"But you get dependent on it psychologically and physiologically, they tell me," I said.

"Yeah, who tells you? The narcotic agents? Some of them use coke."

"Can you prove it?"

"I don't have to prove it!" He suddenly got that feeling of arrogance and superiority that the cokeheads find familiar.

The "glamor" of coke is artificial and is part of the fad. The amphetamines and the hallucinogens were passé. Some admirers of the movie *Easy Rider* had remembered the happy cocaine smiles on the faces of some actors. The rock musicians started finding out about coke.

Along with references to coke in certain lyrics of rock songs came the fad of wearing "coke spoons"—personalized, of course. A cokehead wore the tiny spoon on a bracelet or around the neck, and simply dipped the spoon into it when offered a "blow" and lifted it chicly to the nostril as with snuff in the old days in Dixie.

The magazine *Rolling Stone* reported that coke "became the high of the Stars." The fans of the stars followed suit, but they, for the most part, couldn't afford it. The luxury folks in so-called society could.

It was an unreal world where these jaded people in search of new titillations found Madison Avenue jeweler Arthur King offering them filigreed coke spoons selling for from $200 to $400. Reporter Jan Hodenfeld of the New York *Post* found a "head shop," whose owner insisting on anonymity sold solid gold cocaine-carrying vials for $500; a 14-karat pail and shovel, very tiny, to be worn as a pendant; the pail for stashing the powder; and the shovel for shoveling it. He had small folding spoons that wouldn't be noticeable to nonusers, for $70; a curved straw for snorting which was part of a bracelet for $275.

For the completely satiated cokehead, he had a miniature gold penis, the testicles used as a place for storing the stuff ("the stash"), and the penis shaft as the grip.

A diamond-studded inhaler was a steal at $1,000 at another shop. The president of a large "respectable" corporation had one.

You could also get a whole Cocaine Kit for $250 (in gold); it consisted of spoon, straw, decanter, and a razor for chopping up the stuff.

For a laugh, one dealer invented a Snuff-Sniffer of pyrex, looking like a tuning fork, with a tiny scoop at one end leading up to two barrels, snorting through both nostrils simultaneously. It prevented the powder from getting caught in the hairs of the nose—"always a bloody nuisance." This idiotic little thing was just a joke, really, since it cost only about $5 and offered a pyrex straw as a snifter unlike the gold spoon that was more popular with the substantial trade. If the inventor of the Snuff-Sniffer could turn these out in gold, he might get $500 and make the gadget respectable.

Movie star Robert Mitchum, the first hippie, the original Apostle of Pot, told me during one of his four-letter word interviews at the Sherry-Netherland that he was worried about the spread of the use of cocaine. Because it wasn't controlled. Marijuana, he seemed to think, was controlled.

Once Mitchum told me that drug dealers in Africa offered marijuana of different types for various uses. One type for musicians, one for athletes, one for sex maniacs.

"Do they have one for acting?" I asked him.

"Don't advertise that!" he commanded, with a smile.

But for the cocaine dealers, he had enormous contempt.

"They had the whole drug picture pretty well sorted out, now comes cocaine," he said. "There was one dealer who came up with a supposedly highly refined cocaine. They analyzed it. Nothing! Nothing but strychnine, talcum powder, milk sugar, dirt, and one one-hundredth cocaine. Oh, well, the guy made a couple hundred dollars, bought some guns, and held up a bank."

Mitchum linked cocaine to crime just that casually.

"These cats come up to you with a hell of a lot of cool," he said. "One comes up to me and says, 'Look, man,' and he flashes a rock on me. He says, 'Look at that rock! I snorted a whole rock.'"

Cocaine comes in powder form and in hard form, like small pebbles; the latter are called rocks. This man was offering cocaine in pebble form and was boasting that he had blown one pebble up his nostril.

"What do I do about it?" said Mitchum. "I run like a thief."

The high-salaried musicmakers, the satiated socialites, and the low-down cocaine pushers had a relationship with another class of people: the artists themselves.

Very few of the major artists ever got busted for it. You knew about them. They were the tops.

Along came the movie *Superfly,* with the male protagonist Ron O'Neal helping glamorize cocaine for the lines of black young people who stood in line outside theaters on Saturday night waiting to get in. It was a hard look at drug peddlers in Harlem, at corrupt cops and at Fat Freddie, a street man, a dealer who wanted to make a killing without getting killed and get out of the dirty business. It had some naked black gals, too, and it was a good picture. And while it was anticocaine, of course, it could have excited some weak-willed young black people into using coke for stimulation, because *Superfly* was supergroovey and superhip.

Soul musician Miles Davis was one who got busted about this time. He had the respect of the music world for his talent, his trumpet and creativity. The police got to him twice in '72 and '73, charging once that they found a gun in a West Side apartment building which he owned, also "three small tinfoil envelopes containing cocaine"—"three blows," as they say on the street.

Davis was charged only with possession of a weapon. Pleading guilty to that, he was fined $1,000. Nothing more was said about the three tinfoils of cocaine.

I had mingled with the likes of Jim Morrison, Janis Joplin, and Jimi Hendrix at parties where the acrid smell of pot was overpowering. Then I had helped write their obits when they were very young. Jim Morrison, the young "king of orgasmic rock," I remembered from the time he lowered his trousers and masturbated onstage during a concert in Miami. Janis Joplin was author of the admonition "Stay stoned and stay sexy." Doing her forty-five-minute performance of rock songs, she said, was like having a hundred orgasms. This was largely, as she called it, "fuck music" in the half second of history that spawned a "drug society."

Unquestionably these superstars had two talents: making music for the world and making trouble for themselves.

But now they were ashes, with nobody grieving for them, and Janis Joplin's image was being chopped down by published tales of her lesbian love.

And now we had the stars of the Genitalia Generation. Jim Morrison playing with himself was a little ahead of his time in the Genitalia Age. The rock stars John Lennon and his wife, Yoko Ono, evidently believed in genitals.

Their nude picture of themselves on the cover of their album *The Virgins* was considered unspeakably daring at the time. How innocent we were!

In the summer of '73, *Women's Wear Daily* kidded Mick Jagger and his wife, Bianca ("Emperor and Empress of Decadence"), and mentioned that their favorite pastimes included "snorting."

Well, in contemporary language, "snorting" has only one meaning.

Sexy Mick of the Rolling Stones was the pet of the set. This rebellious young man who had charisma before the word became a cliché had been in trouble in England over four "pep pills." His worshipers thought the charge was ridiculous. He proved he had bought the pills legally. Now he was around New York, Ireland, France, the Caribbean, where he had homes, reveling in being a millionaire. Sexy Bianca, his Nicaraguan queen, evidently loved him devotedly. They often dressed unisex fashion.

They were the suddenly rich in the one corner of the big-money music world that everybody wanted to edge into, and their fame was such that they could do just about as they wished.

The sad, dirty, messy, scummy world of drugs that killed off Jim Morrison, Jimi Hendrix, and Janis Joplin was the sub-sub-sub-basement of life.

The recording company biggies who played around with the $100-bill snifters never suspected the number of killings in the world of cocaine by the people bringing them their "blows."

The killings were usually in slum sections of Harlem and Spanish Harlem where they stashed, processed, and cut the cocaine.

They were miserable human beings, often using the drugs themselves, willing to kill a competitor or intruder, now that there was no death penalty, no electric chair anymore.

"You get caught, man, well, maybe you can serve a little time and get out a lot smarter and with a lot better connections. Maybe you can even make yourself a deal with the Man and become a stoolie."

For half a century at least, top law enforcers have privately admitted that some of their greatest successes were often due to their stool pigeons.

These informants, though mostly human debris that hung around cheap bars gathering scraps of information which they turned over to their bosses, sometimes developed into rich men . . . rich on the money the government paid them for turning in their friends.

Once found out, they were of course ticketed for death, destined to be gunned down or stabbed to death or set on fire by their former associates.

And that accounts for a paradox that seemed incredible. In Harlem, some ex-narcotics dealers, who were actually well off on the money paid them for being informers, were in danger of their lives, likely to be shot by those they'd turned in. So the government supplied them with bodyguards to protect them from the coke merchants and peddlers.

If these recording company aces knew of this slimy background, would they have continued to seek paradise through the little white powder? Probably, because of the vigor and arrogance and sex power that it supposedly brings.

Of course it wasn't always so low-down. One Harlem stoolie actually was rich enough to have his own jet. He had turned in some big ones, some giants.

And there were college dudes selling cocaine right on the campus in one university in New York.

"One blow, away you go!" That was an effective selling speech.

Two black roommates had been hustling it right out of their room, as Marc Olden reports in his book. They got an anonymous phone call to desist. They ignored it, but it made them nervous and worried. They had one more deal that would be good for $10,000, man. A guy they'd sold some coke to was bringing them up a big-money friend.

Their guy brought the big-money friend to their room early one night. They were little more than amateurs and weren't anticipating trouble. They were both shot four times and killed. The anonymous phone call had been from a big-time, serious type of coke dealer who didn't want any amateur competition. Let this be a lesson to the rest of you college bums. . . .

As for the guy who'd brought the potential customer to the college roommates, he was paid off in heroin, which was his problem.

The music chaps around Broadway and Fiftieth Street probably never looked into cocaine half as seriously as I have, and I've never snorted once and don't plan to.

They mostly just smile slyly. They don't admit anything, but their smile indicates agreement.

I asked federal narcotics men to classify cocaine for me.

Was it as bad as some authorities said?

"Heroin is number one," they told me. "It's the greatest threat to society; it's addictive and deteriorative.

"Cocaine generally follows as number two, but though it's not considered addictive, its physical damage is more serious than heroin. It destroys tissues. It does cell damage. It does brain damage. People do develop a dependence on it. The inside of the nose begins to decay. Large doses produce anxiety, fear, and hallucinations. . . ."

"And the sexual stimulation?"

"The users think so, but as everybody knows, there's a lot of that in the mind. . . .

"Anyway, cocaine comes from the cocoa bush in South America and comes up here in girdles, brassieres, pubic hair, soles of shoes, false bottoms of trunks, in little girls' toys their mothers are using as instruments of smuggling, in bandages, in stuffing that's supposed to make women look pregnant.

"The Incas used to chew cocoa leaves. The warriors thought that besides giving them sex drive, it gave them great vigor for fighting. They thought it was a sacred plant."

It's getting sort of sacred in the music world, too.

And why? Because the record business is the richest part of show business—more than a billion-dollar industry—having surpassed films. And the record business thrives and survives on the simplest thing: "Air play."

The disc jockeys spin the records, and air play sells records. Billions of dollars' worth.

And if cocaine is the way to the record spinners, why not use it as a sales tool?

There are many disc jockeys who are untouchable. But there is a slice of this influential area that is approachable, via coke. You'll be hearing more and more of the grim details as one investigation after another hits the front pages.

Brothel in the Desert

STRICTLY for purposes of research, I visited a legal house of prostitution in Nevada and met a shapely little blonde named Lana who instantly adored me. We became lifelong friends in about five minutes.

I'd been gradually convincing myself over several months that I must investigate, personally, the whorehouses in the only state in the Union where they're not illegal. On a midnight in the summer of 1973, I happened to mention this itch for research to a cabdriver named Charlie as we were riding along the Las Vegas Strip.

"You'd like to go out to Sally's?" said Charlie.

"Sally's? Is that the madam's name? Where is it?" I became instantly attentive.

"Fifty, sixty miles," he answered. "Pretty long trip."

"But why would anybody go that far to get—?" I didn't finish the sentence. Las Vegas was popularly regarded as having literally hundreds of prostitutes available on busy weekends. It was an established fact that you could pick up one in bars in even the most respectable hotels. Somebody had said that taking a girl to Las Vegas was like carrying coals to Newcastle. Why, then, would any man want to ride so far to visit a brothel?

"Some guys just get their rocks off that way," Charlie said. "Some of them never been to a whorehouse. Four, five of them get to drinkin' and go out and have a party."

Charlie'd been on a couple of trips there—he thought it was to Sally's. "I picked up a girl at the airport. She was going back there to work after her vacation. I'd say she was about twenty-two, and I guess she was all right; if she didn't have that job, she'd be behind the counter in a five-and-dime."

"Was she sensational-looking?"

"Nope."

"But I still don't understand the lure that gets men to go so far to get what they can get in their hotel room!"

Charlie shrugged. "Some guys are nuts," he said. Charlie figured it would cost me about $50 taxi fare if I went at a slow time—say 2:30 A.M. My passion for research was now so overwhelming that I couldn't be stopped.

Still, there were moments when we started the trip, out past Nellis, Nevada, turning left on Highway 93, up north toward Lincoln County, when I said, "What am I doing here?" We were in deepest darkness and in true desert with no towns in sight. I fell asleep, woke up, and went back to sleep as Charlie piloted us through the night.

"What's it going to be like?" I asked.

"Like a ranch house," Charlie said. "There's a bar and then the girls got their rooms."

"Is there any show, anything like that?"

"The show is the girls," Charlie thought.

It must have been near 4 A.M. when two buildings sprang at us out of the darkness. Around the roof of each was a string of red lights. Everywhere else around was pitch-dark and quiet.

Parking the taxi, Charlie then led me into the brothel through an entrance that read BAR. Another said GIRLS. Charlie said we were now in Lincoln County, where prostitution isn't forbidden, having come from Clark County, where it is. I drew a long breath as we stepped inside, then suddenly realized I was within the law. Sheri, an attractive brunette behind the bar, smiled at us, served us drinks, and never said she was the proprietress. I thought she was just a barmaid.

Now all full of excitement over my research project, I stepped into the next room, which was like a living room, and about as sinful.

I wish I could compare it to the bordellos of Paris and Rome and London. It was more like Akron. Eight girls in slacks and dresses sat with men visitors in an atmosphere reminiscent of a high school or fraternity parents' day. Two attractive blondes sat on a couch with a man. The blondes moved over to make room for me on the couch.

Lana, the smaller, bouncier blonde, on my left, seemed a likely research project. We told each other our names, me giving my right one.

"I'm here to do a story, a chapter for a book," I said.

"Maybe I can help you!" she said. I hastily added I wasn't there for sex. "I'm just getting material," I explained.

"You won't get anything else here—this is a very clean place," she said. "They inspect us every week, and we wash everybody's peter very carefully before and after. . . ."

"But if I'm just here for research, I guess I can avoid that," I said.

"I just hope I can convince Sheri you're just here for research," Lana said, a bit doubtfully. I asked Lana and her friend if they'd have a drink. They declined. I tried to make small talk. But as it was four in the morning, Lana understandably wanted to get to the main point of the evening: business.

"Which of us girls do you want?" she asked me with a broad smile.

"You!" I said. Her hand reached out for mine.

"But it's just to talk, not to have sex," I said.

"All right. But you have to pay me for my time," Lana said.

"I understand that." And she popped up from the couch and led me to a bedroom in the back. It was just a bedroom as far as I could see—no mirrored ceilings, no dirty movies, no pictures of her as a child. She dropped onto the bed, and so did I (I've mentioned that I was sleepy), and we began talking. She was from California, was working here strictly for the money, had never been away from this area, and had no desire to see the rest of the world. I became her career planner and suggested that "in your line of work," she might be able to work anywhere and everywhere in the world—Paris, Rome, London. I sketched out the glories of those great cities as they might open up to a whore who made good use of her leisure when she wasn't, so to speak, working.

"I don't have any ambition." She yawned. "I hate to bring it up," she suddenly said. "But I have to ask you for something."

"What?"

"Some money."

"Of course!" We had become such conversationalists that the commercial aspects of our meeting escaped me. "How much, do you think?"

"A hundred?"

"Just to talk!" I said. "How about fifty?"

"All right," Lana said. "It's deductible, you know."

I told her I didn't think so. She said she'd read in a paper that an Internal Revenue Service agent had decided that when sex was prescribed by a doctor for medical treatment, it could be listed as a medical expense.

"I shall definitely consider this as good for my health," I told Lana. "No, wait! This is strictly for research. It is a research expenditure, a business deduction, like buying stationery, type-writer ribbons, and carbon."

"Whatever you say." Lana smiled. I handed her a $100 bill.

"You don't want to go for the hundred?" she said. "You can have a very nice party."

"Strictly for research, remember?" I watched her hustle out with the $100 bill and was surprised, somehow, when she returned with two $20's and a $10. Having heard all my life how prostitutes never gave you change, I suspected she would take off across the mountains on a horse and that I would never hear from her again.

But there she was: I had my $50, she had given the madam her $50, and we had time on our hands. What do we do now? Lana was more disturbed about that than I was. I could always talk. But Lana as the girl doing the "entertaining" wasn't properly briefed for such a change in program.

"I guess there's no point in me taking my clothes off . . ." she said. "Unless you want me to. You're entitled to that."

"Don't bother," I said. "No point in me taking mine off either." I shrugged. "Although I think I will remove my jacket." I hung it on the back of a chair.

"Usually at this time I would wash the man's peter in a washbasin and make sure his peter's sanitary," Lana explained.

"But we're skipping that," I said, hastily. "What would happen after that?"

"Not so fast!" Lana pretended to give me a little slap. "I would take your peter in my hand and move it back and forth and squeeze the top of it. . . ."

"*Ouch!*" I said. "I'm terribly sensitive."

"Then," continued Lana, "I would dry off your peter with my towel and lead you over to the bed, and we'd get between the sheets and . . . how do you like it? Straight, French, half-and-half, sixty-nine?"

"Just browsing," I reminded her. "Research!"

We must have lay there talking for twenty minutes, and it reminded me of a Harry Hershfield story about a man from Jersey City who'd met a sexy lady in Paris. She asked to buy him a drink, and he thought, "Well, this isn't like Jersey City." She asked to show him her lush apartment, and he thought, "Well, Jersey City surely isn't like this." She got undressed and into an expensive perfumed negligee and began stroking him. "Well," he thought again, "Jersey City isn't like this!" Then she became bold enough to ask him for some money, and he gave her some. "And from then on," he said, "it was just like Jersey City."

I didn't learn much new about the business except that the girls usually buy their jobs and get 60 percent to the proprietor's 40 percent. I saw no black girls or black customers. When I finished my research, Lana said I'd better go because I'd already taken up $50 worth of time.

This was a little bit of a blow to my ego, as I thought I had been pretty entertaining. "If you want to go for another $50 . . ." Lana said.

I took my leave of Lana, who, I noticed, was already bouncing about the living room, sizing up other prospective customers. I met Charlie, the driver, at the bar. Sheri, the proprietress, offered me a free drink and said business was good. She said the prices there are reasonable, starting, she said, at $10 for something quite ordinary. I am sure she said $10, although when I repeated this to specialists in this area, they were sure I was mistaken.

"It's not really in the high rent district," I had to concede because it was truly 60 miles from no place. Now as I left with Charlie I saw that it was between 5 and 6 A.M. and daylight. The morning was coming over the beautiful snow-topped Nevada mountains, and the lonely setting looked more stark than I had imagined it in the darkness before.

Farther along the highway was another brothel called Betty's.

It looked much the same except there was a letter out of the GIRLS sign. It read GI LS. We looked in briefly. Charlie was going to be late getting back with his taxi. Alongside was an airstrip. A few customers fly up with their private planes. Business is not primarily at night. They get some "traffic" at 9 A.M. Some fifty or sixty girls are employed in the two houses, and they are quietly operated without any hell raising. The community would close them down otherwise. They survive by the grace of their neighbors, and they keep that in mind.

I slept beside Charlie riding back to Las Vegas and felt strange coming in from a brothel around 9 A.M. and going to my room at the Riviera.

Assistant District Attorney Chuck Thompson, an accommodating young man, told me that the idea of legal brothels has been studied in Clark County (Las Vegas) owing to the fact that fifteen of the seventeen counties already have county option. The district attorney, Roy Woofter, was experimenting with a new enforcement plan: jail sentences for every second offender.

"They don't want even one hour in jail," Thompson said. "This is scaring some of them out of Vegas already."

There's a *Bordello Guide* published for those who like to shop around. There's always been prostitution in Vegas. It's said that a couple of locally famous women started that way and became popular matrons and housewives. Stories are told of prostitutes' bodies being found in the desert when they left one pimp for another. The authorities generally are "pragmatic" and know that girls do loiter about bars and pick up men. "You can tell them," Chuck Thompson said. "If a girl sits alone in a bar looking around and smiling, trying to catch your eye, what do you think?"

"Of course we do get some schoolteachers, secretaries, and salesgirls who come down here and hustle for a weekend. And housewives, too.

"What we want to do is to eliminate the extortion and burglary that go with prostitution," Thompson said. "We want to get away from these girls rolling a customer and from girls getting a bunch of room keys together and cleaning a place out. How about when some customer here from Nebraska gets rolled and gets his brains punched in?

"Listen," he said, "we know that if a gambler here is a twenty-five-thousand-dollar customer and wants a broad, the house is going to make it possible for him to get one, don't we? And it probably won't cost him anything, either. . . ."

"And is it the cocktail waitresses, the show girls?"

"Don't you know the facts of life yet, Mr. Wilson?" spoke up a friend listening in. "Cocktail waitresses and show girls go for bartenders and musicians!"

One terrible afterthought, following my visit to the brothel in the sands: I forgot to ask Lana for something. A receipt.

What's Bigger Than Sex?

✍ I WAS walking through one of the Las Vegas casinos with a man friend who was heading for his room. As we parted, he was approached by a strikingly beautiful brunette who looked no more than 22. I heard her say to him, "Where are you going?"

"To my room," he said.

"Can I go with you?" she asked.

"No," he answered brusquely.

"I'll show you a very good time," she said.

"Get away from me!" he snapped.

And he went on his way to his room—to dig into his bag upstairs for a checkbook to get some more money for the crap tables. It is a fact that a true gambler would rather gamble than copulate.

The urge to gamble is more popular today in America even than the urge for sex.

At first this may seem a ridiculous statement. But consider the millions who are betting on horse races, baseball, football, basketball, and hockey, or playing the numbers, or buying lottery tickets, or indulging in church bingo games, or taking up the new backgammon fad, plus the millions who rush off to the nearest gambling casinos, and you will agree that there are more people doing that for a longer time more concentratedly than there are people in bed having sex.

Yes, and sex is over in a few minutes, while the delicious pain, or whatever it is, of gambling can continue for hours. There are millions of people too old for effective sex who are still able to throw the dice or toss a chip on a roulette number.

Gambling and gamblers may eventually rule the country. Today the appetite for gambling exercises an incredible amount of control over one of the country's largest, most exciting industries —show business.

In a Canadian city on an afternoon in December, 1972, a whiskery middle-aged man, who looked a little seedy as well as needy, picked up a phone and reached the local branch office of a top Las Vegas hotel noted for catering to high rollers.

The manager of the branch office in the Canadian city was anxiously alert and respectful when he heard who was calling.

"I got the urge to play a little baccarat," said the whiskery man, a big lumberman we'll call Mr. L. "I feel lucky today. How soon can we get goin'?"

"I'll get tickets and call you back in two minutes," the manager said. "I'll go along to see you get well taken care of."

"I don't need no baby-sitter, I'm a big boy," Mr. L laughed.

"I may want to play a little myself," the manager answered.

Four hours later they got off their luxury flight at McCarran Airport, Las Vegas, and the man who looked seedy and needy was limousined to the hotel and shown to the Presidential suite. Within ten minutes, he was at the baccarat tables, where the dealers are in black tie and dinner jacket even in the daytime. Mr. L was welcomed with smiles and bows despite his unpretentious look, for he was a well-known high shooter who at times could become what they call "a gambling degenerate." He had $50,000 credit.

That same afternoon a New Yorker named Mr. Z, well known in the garment industry on Seventh Avenue, felt bored and weary about business conditions and desired excitement. He was not a "dame guy," or a boozer, or a narcotic experimenter. He was middle-aged, respectable and respected, flashily dressed but not excessively so, and he felt a sudden inclination to "get away," to gamble, to shoot craps. He phoned the New York branch office of the same Las Vegas hotel, which lately had got "very hot."

"You want to go out a few days, Mr. Z?" the local manager said. "Our pleasure! You're our guest all the way. Mrs. Z going, too? Good! Let me get you the plane tickets. . . ."

Mr. Z had the confirming word almost immediately. "We're sending a car to pick you up at two to leave Kennedy at three thirty," the manager told him. "You're on TWA first-class 747. There'll be a limousine at the airport to take you to the hotel. Good luck at the crap table."

The local manager had been in touch with the manager's office in Las Vegas about Mr. Z's arrival. "Is the Presidential suite available? He wants to stay till Sunday."

"The Presidential suite's gone, but we'll put him in the Alexander the Great suite," Las Vegas said.

"Shit!" New York said. "You guys should have five or six Presidential suites. Mr. Z might go for two, three hundred, you know."

"Hell, there's nothing cheap about the Alexander the Great suite! It's got a bar bigger than the 21 bar."

"OK," New York said. "But let yourself go on the flowers for Mrs. Z. Not that Mr. Z will ever see them."

It was dusk and dinnertime when the visitor from the garment district and his wife rode to their hotel, but the lights and the neons lit up the sky over the Strip proclaiming the existence of the Sands, the Dunes, the Riviera, the Hilton, the Landmark, the Stardust, the Desert Inn, the Frontier, the Tropicana, the Aladdin, the Flamingo, the Thunderbird, Caesars Palace, Circus, the Silver Slipper, the Westward Ho Motel, the El Morocco Motel, the Fashion Center, and a couple of wedding chapels that gave twenty-four-hour service.

"This goddamn town has two new hotels every time I come out here," the New Yorker said to his wife. "Now they got that new MGM hotel and the Marc Antony. It's gettin' like Miami Beach used to be."

"Yes, sir," offered the chatty chauffeur, "they've got seven thousand new rooms under construction."

As Mr. and Mrs. Z walked into the lobby of the hotel, they were met by a surge of people. It was wall-to-wall bodies. They were accustomed to expect a lull in the month of December, but this place was jammed, and there was a line of people waiting to check in. Red, the bell captain, had already seen Mr. and Mrs. Z and took them quickly to a special penthouse elevator.

"What the hell's goin' on?" Mr. Z asked in astonishment. "What're they all doing here?"

"They're here to catch Mary," spoke up his wife, who read the columns carefully and was speaking of "the hottest new act in show business."

"I can't wait not to see her," her husband said. "I'm here to shoot craps!" Once inside the Alexander the Great suite, which, he observed, was big enough to play basketball in, he unpacked his bag, got out a shaving kit, doused his face with shaving lotion, and paused to comment about the three-foot-high floral arrangement. "Must be Arbor Day," he said.

"It's beautiful, isn't it?" his wife said.

"You gonna be all right?" he asked her.

"Do be careful, honey," she said.

"Don't tell me what to do!" he flared up, and then was instantly sorry. "Here." He counted out five $100 bills. "Keep playing number six for me."

"What about dinner?" she wondered.

"Didn't you eat enough on the plane? I did. I'll page you in a couple of hours." And he shot out the door en route to the elevator and the crap tables.

The queue of people waiting to get into the show room to hear the new hot comedienne Mary, celebrated for her risqué material, stretched past the crap tables and back to the blackjack games. While waiting to see her, there was one well-tanned, fifty-five-year-old, sideburned gentleman in a dark-gray suit who was not wasting his time. He was shooting craps after leaving a woman friend to hold his place in the line. She spoke to a member of her party about him.

"He's such a nice man," she said. "He's crazy about big shooters. He keeps saying that's all he wants, to go where the big shooters are."

"What does he do?"

"He's in oil."

"Petroleum?"

"Olive oil, dummy!"

"Mafia?"

"You said that! I didn't."

"He must have pretty good credit around here."

"A hundred thousand."

All these people were eager to play. There were two others, however, who were not. One was a famous TV comedian, a skinny, nervous little man, who was now sitting in the coffee shop just off the casino with another man who was using a table telephone.

People seeing the famous TV comedian at this hotel wondered about his presence here because it was a well-advertised fact that he was supposed to be starring at a competing hotel.

"He walked out on them," one of the casino security men who'd dropped in for coffee, said.

"What happened?" a waitress asked.

"He blew forty thousand dollars and they wouldn't give him any more credit."

"They shouldn't! How can he ever pay that back?"

"He could work it off. He probably gets about that a week. But he ain't about to. Instead, he walked, and they had to replace him, and he got drunk and came over here and started throwing markers around till they cut off his credit here. A guy can ruin himself in one or two days like that. He can ruin himself for life. Know what else happened the same time? His wife sent him a divorce summons."

The skinny TV comedian was biting his nails. "Waitress," he called out, "a double scotch."

"That's not going to help you any!" said the man with him, who was his manager. "I gave specific orders to the casino manager over there not to give you more than a hundred dollars' credit a day."

The TV comedian laughed bitterly. "But I outsmarted you. I countermanded your instructions. I told him it was my money, and I could do with it what I wanted to."

"But how could you lose forty thousand dollars!"

"It's not so hard. You just buy five hundred dollars' worth of chips and. . . ."

"Yeah, and pretty soon you lose everything you got in the world. Well," declared the manager, "you've blown this town, the best spot in the country! What do you plan to do now?"

"Anyway, this'll take care of my divorce settlement." The comedian shrugged. "I can't divide with her. There's nothing to divide."

"What I got to do," the manager said, getting busy at the phone again, "is get them to take you back in over there."

"And work it off? And work for nothing? Oh, no, no indeed!"

"Listen, you idiot, that's the way it's got to be! I only hope they'll take you back. You weren't doing so well over there, I guess you know."

"That's it!" snapped the comedian. "Give me confidence."

In one of the lesser suites upstairs, a woman from Kansas City was entertaining a friend who had been her high school classmate long ago. This suite cost about $150, according to the little slip they got when they checked in. "What would you like to drink, Janet?" the woman from Kansas City asked her old classmate.

"Vodka and tonic, I guess. You got any tonic?"

"Sure. Jack takes vodka and tonic, too. Jack is betting so heavy now it worries me," she said.

They could hear him shouting into the telephone in the next room. "Not only does he shoot craps here, but he bets football," the wife said. "Five thousand on one game!"

"Five thousand! I never knew they bet that kind of money."

"And everybody on the junket plane was gambling even before the plane got here. You see, there were over a hundred of us on the plane, everybody getting free transportation and free rooms. They got two, three junkets a month. Only thing is that my husband or whoever the gambler is has got to buy a thousand dollars' worth of chips, and he's supposed to play them at this hotel. But that's a small amount because the crap games are unbelievable."

"Do you play?"

"Never," the wife said. "Jack won't let me near the table when he's shooting craps so I hang around the quarter machines or play a little roulette. Jack says I'm bad luck to him, and I can't stand to watch anyway. It makes me nervous. It doesn't seem right to me. People throwing that kind of money around. Then Jack gets to drinking the free drinks the cocktail waitresses bring him, and he gets nasty and impossible when I try to get him to quit."

"I know a way you could cure him, I'll bet," the other woman said.

"Tell me quick!"

"Well, they've got some lovely shops down on the first floor."

"Of course, I've been through them, looking. . . ."

"Well, go down there and buy yourself four or five of those dresses at five hundred dollars or one thousand dollars apiece. That'll shake him up. If he doesn't like it, just tell him it was your turn."

The woman from Kansas City shook her head no. "I could never do that."

"Why not?"

"Because," she answered, "then we'd be more in debt than we are now."

The new MGM Grand Hotel has six penthouse suites whose announced rental is $800 a day each. They are probably seldom rented, yet always occupied. They are "complimentary" to the high shooters. The high-rolling visitors have 5,000 square feet to

Queens of the bellydance, bellyrinas Little Egypt and Nai Bonet. Photo/ *Tim Boxer.*

Photo/ *Earl Wilson.*

The first topless secretary—Xav era Hollander. When she was stil a happy hooker, she visited Ear Wilson's office in this non-attire Photo/ *Tim Boxer.*

EVERYBODY NEEDS MILK
EVEN CAROL DODA'S

Carol Doda, who started the topless rage in San Francisco, was certainly a giant in the Silicone Set. Her topless club, the Condor, used postcard advertising—not French postcards—American postcards.

Lisa Loughlin started in show business as a Jackie Gleason Glee Girl and later made headlines in a divorce case.

Marilyn in the famous skirt-blowing scene in *Seven Year Itch*. Joe DiMaggio, after watching Marilyn shoot dozens of retakes, all night long, with a score of photographers enjoying their work, left in a huff and later separated from her.

Gina Lollobrigida and Marilyn Monroe get introduced to each other at Trans-Lux Theater in New York in 1954 by Earl Wilson.

Marilyn, with a red rose in her cleavage, in El Morocco's Champagne Room in their happier days in 1954.

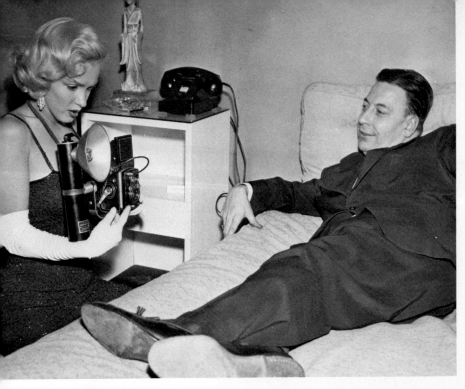

Marilyn shooting Earl Wilson with camera Joe DiMaggio gave her.

And pretending to enjoy one of his books, Beverly Hills Hotel, 1953.

Marilyn trying out one of her lines on Wilson at a cocktail party. Notice: no exposed cleavage.

Earl helps a model keep time to the music at a showing of "knee watches" for hot pants. Photo/*Tim Boxer*.

Sexy actress Edy Williams, estranged wife of producer of sex films Russ Meyer, in Gallagher's restaurant's deepfreeze. Photo/*Tim Boxer*.

Shirley Bassey always is SRO at the Waldorf and almost always undresses her back like this.

Ursula Andress in the *Dr. No* swim outfit that first attracted attention to her in 1962.

Sexy Sylva Koscina as she appears in *Three Bites of an Apple*.

Ann-Margret—sensational sex siren and terrific actress.

Sarah Miles getting over her tears after thanking Earl Wilson for saying something nice about Burt Reynolds. Photo/*Tim Boxer*.

Maureen Stapleton and her favorite playwright, Tennessee Williams. Photo/*Tim Boxer*.

Above left: Marlon Brando with Elizabeth Taylor in one of his not-so-good pictures, *Reflections in a Golden Eye*. Above right: Burt Reynolds is interviewed by Earl at the New York apartment where *Shamus* was filmed. Below: Ingrid Bergman tells all to Earl in Rome.

Michael Caine and the pregnant fiancée, Shakira Baksh, a former Miss Guyana whom he married shortly after this picture was made. Photo/*Tim Boxer*.

Donna Jordan and Jane Forth, underground superstars from Andy Warhol's movies. Photo/*Tim Boxer*.

Gay activists dancing together at the Rainbow Grill (the manager wasn't happy about it). Photo/*Tim Boxer*.

David Frost and Diahann Carroll in 1971 when everybody—including they—thought they might get married. Photo/*Tim Boxer*.

play around in—that's as much as in an ordinary home. There are two of everything, including bathrooms, bedrooms, and TV sets.

The MGM Grand, bankrolled by the movie company of the same name, also provided its big shooters with a little privacy—an exclusive penthouse casino where they didn't have to be bumped into and shouldered by women slot-machine addicts carrying their quarters in their Dixie cups.

One trouble with a big shooter from a hotel's standpoint is that he is slippery and may get off the hook. High rollers can't be controlled. They have been known to arrive in Las Vegas and take over a complimentary suite and begin playing, then decide to try the gambling at a rival hotel, which, to keep them on the premises, gives them another complimentary suite.

"I know one of these dudes who had two such complimentary suites on the Strip," said Jack Binion, one of the operators of the Horseshoe in downtown Las Vegas, "and came down here and stayed with us because he liked our poker games better'n what they got."

Although it looks to be a rather simple thing for these hotels to funnel all those $100 bills from the visitors' pockets into their own boxes, it isn't. The gigantic Caesars Palace handles about $24,000,000 of food and beverage business a year, $10,000,000 room business, and $150,000,000 a year in gambling. The successful gambling business is supposed to win 19 to 20 percent of its handle which means it should win $30,000,000 a year.

You can begin to see why Dean Martin was able to get $3,500,000 for his 10 points' holding in the Riviera Hotel when he left there. Ten points—he had 10 percent of the joint!

"What's the biggest loss you ever had, if that isn't too embarrassing a question?" I asked Billy Weinberg, a "country boy" from Cleveland who was in charge of those departments at Caesars Palace.

"Half a million on dice," he answered, and didn't even look sad. "That wasn't just in one day," he said. "That was over five days."

"What could you do about it?"

"Nothing. Just hope that he comes back."

"Did he?"

"We're still waiting."

"How many have a hundred thousand dollars' credit?"

"Not too many. Twenty-five or thirty. That's Caesars," he said. "We don't know about other places."

Of course they do have information about what's going on at other hotels, and any bad news about a high roller's getting drunk and disorderly and becoming pugnacious spreads around pretty fast.

A gambler doesn't establish credit just by walking over to the cage and saying he'd like to have some credit. It's done in the big leagues through banks and correspondent banks since sometimes these gamblers are from distant cities and often from another country.

While I was talking to Billy Weinberg, he took a call from somebody who wanted to cash a check for $500. To my surprise he approved it with a call to the cashier.

"Somebody you know?" I asked, because this end of the conversation indicated that it was somebody he didn't know.

"No, but from somebody that knows somebody I know," he said. As if to warn me, he added, "We never discuss a man's credit."

"Nick the Greek" is long gone, and most of the other characters have grown old. But now and then you hear of one who's a Hindu and of an eccentric from Montreal called Murphy.

"Murphy used to carry around a satchel. People thought he had money in it. He had peanut butter sandwiches."

He interrupted himself to ask me, "You don't want to go to Honolulu, do you?"

There was a trip returning to Hawaii, and they had some space. "They're leaving at five o'clock." The easy traveling, the $100 bills, and the enormous amount of building still impress me about Las Vegas. And of course the heat—115 often in the daytime—the pretty cocktail waitresses, and the noise at the crap tables at four, five or six in the morning.

One night—it was really Monday morning—I sat in on a $45,000 "hold 'em" poker game at the Horseshoe downtown. In Glitter Gulch the lights never dim and the doors never close. Unfortunately, most tourists stay on the Strip without visiting downtown where the poor people gamble. There are no floor shows at the Horseshoe. They come to gamble.

The players in this poker game were shirt-sleeved and rather country-looking except for one they called Laughing Alan. He wore a neat checked jacket, a tie, and a beard and sat there unsmiling and grave.

"He's the only player not from Texas," Jack Binion, the son of the founder, said. He sat next to me with a neat pile of $100 bills in a rubber band beside him and a stack of $100 chips in front of him.

"Laughing Alan just played for four days and four nights," spoke up Doyle Brunson, a plump chap from Houston with a nice smile. "When was the last time you were broke, Alan?"

"Yesterday," replied Laughing Alan, allowing himself to smile.

"Two hours ago," Laughing Alan corrected himself.

As about $15,000 exchanged hands, Jack Binion said to me, "This isn't really any big game."

"Isn't it?" Laughing Alan said. "When you think I had only thirty dollars when I started." He thumbed his own stack of hundreds. "I borrowed two hundred fifty dollars. I got a partner. Who raised it, you, Buck?"

"Do you have any Nick the Greeks around here anymore?" I was foolish enough to ask.

"Nick! They come in here in droves better'n him," Doyle Brunson said.

They meant nothing disparaging about Nick the Greek, who was of another age. Arizona Slim is one of the characters now. Big Jack Strauss, who sat on the other side of me, was now in his forties. He studied education in college. He made the mistake of losing $7,000 betting on a football game.

"I didn't feel I wanted to work a year teaching making up that seven thousand dollars, so I began to play poker," he said. They were family men, husband types. Jack Strauss took his wife and two children hunting in Mozambique, Africa, last year. They talked little and concentrated quietly on the cards. In fact, their conversation was conducted solely in politeness to me.

"Too bad you didn't get to meet my dad," Jack Binion said. "He's at the ranch.

"He went to jail for income tax evasion and we lost the joint. He did three years and somethin'. Hell, he paid five hundred thirteen thousand dollars' back taxes. He thought he wasn't goin' to jail and he had one hundred thousand dollars in his pockets. He thought he had a fix. Well, then we got the joint back, and I got to playin' a lot of poker. I got to thinkin' I was a good poker player."

"You're fair," Laughing Alan said, glaring at Jack's hundreds.

"I just play for fun," Jack said.

"Sure," Laughing Alan said.

"We got the highest limit anywhere," Jack said. "We're a

gamblers' gambling joint. Real gamblers come here. Bookmakers, guys that want to get a decision. You can get ten thousand dollars on a throw of the dice here if you're a good customer.

"We had one customer here, on one roll of the dice, he won ninety-eight thousand dollars. Did he quit? No. In fact, we ended up beatin' him for a lot of money.

"This guy was fabulous," Jack Binion said. "He comes to town with a million dollars in a satchel. He comes from a very rich family. He goes to Caesars and he says, 'I want to gamble high.' He lost a lot, and he goes to the Sands and loses there. He's got suites both places, and he ended up stayin' here because he liked it. He took the bed out, put a mattress on the floor, and slept on that with a beaver sheet he brought with him. In sixty or ninety days he loses over three million dollars. He had an excess of money. He had a crap system that he wanted to try out. He tried it out. It wasn't a very good system, really.

"Another guy a few years ago"—he gave his name—"was the head of a distillery. He loses around three million.

"He couldn't make the payments he was supposed to make, and he went back to sellin' whiskey for the company he used to run. Well, he's still sellin' whiskey—and he's still shootin' craps.

"But we been beat plenty—for two hundred forty thousand dollars in one night.

"One night we beat a guy for one hundred ninety-eight thousand dollars. My brother takes him out to his car to get the money. He had it in his car. He was going to console him and say anything you can say.

"The guy pays my brother, and then he says, 'Wait a minute, I'm goin' back in with you.' He comes back in and wins three hundred sixty-six thousand dollars. Besides gettin' the one hundred ninety-eight thousand dollars back.

"Does it bother me? No, because I know you're not gonna shoot us out of our bankroll if you keep coming back.

"Like Dad says, used to be, if a guy had one hundred thousand dollars, he could be a substantial partner. Now he can't get one percent for that.

"We got a guy—I'll introduce you to him—he's a greeter now. Bob Carnahan.

"He played craps. Well, around 1946, when the Golden Nugget opens, he wins forty thousand dollars. They didn't have that much money in the cage. They want to give him five percent of the joint.

He wanted his money. He had connections in Wichita, where there was gamblin' then, and he goes out and gets more money and then he keeps playin' till he ends up losing two million dollars. Yeah, he lost it, and he's here working for us."

Jack Binion took me back among the slot machines and beckoned to a neatly dressed, scholarly-looking, soft-spoken gentleman in his seventies. This was the man who turned down 5 percent of the Golden Nugget, which proved to be one.

"What I can't understand," I said, "is how you get two million to lose."

He nodded his comprehension of my lack of comprehension.

"When you have so much money, you forget how much it is you're losing," he said.

And that's the secret of Las Vegas. "You forget how much you're losing." Then you get into a panic to get it back, and you lose some more. And the panic increases, and the losses increase, and. . . .

That's how Las Vegas is able to pay those enormous salaries. Robert Goulet can sing for twenty weeks at the Howard Hughes hotels for at least $50,000 a week, making him much more than $1,000,000 for a year. The Barbra Streisands, the Elvis Presleys, get around $150,000 a week. They're the bait that gets the suckers on the hook. The hotels hire the biggest stars to lure in the customers, but the real gamblers don't really care about the stars. They go to see the shows only as a relaxation from their serious business of gambling. Altogether it is an unbelievable world that was started by Bugsy Siegel and a few slot machines a little over a quarter of a century ago.

Sarah Miles Weeps for Burt Reynolds

ROUGH, tough, sexy man-eater Sarah Miles suddenly began crying softly while we were having a quiet lunch. We were talking about Burt Reynolds and David Whiting's famous suicide of a few weeks before.

It was Friday, May 25, 1973, at the Sea Fare of the Aegean restaurant on West Fifty-sixth Street, New York. Looking back on it now, I'm convinced that she wept because I'd said something nice to her.

"Somebody should write something nice about Burt Reynolds!" she'd been saying.

"I'll do it," I said. "I know Burt. I believe what you say about him."

"Do you?" That's about when she began sobbing. And she laughed about it as the tears dried. "I don't often cry," she said. "I can be as tough as anybody, and when people are nasty, I just laugh. But when anybody's nice, I cry and collapse. I'm not a toughie at all." And she looked up at me through the glistening tears, and I collapsed.

The Whiting death from an overdose of drugs, the coroner's jury's investigation, the suggestion that Whiting—he was her business manager—might have been murdered were all behind Sarah the day we met. I did not plan to question her about it all over again. However, nobody had warned me that she didn't want to discuss it. We sat down and each had a glass of dry white wine and began talking.

"One of the times I remember seeing you," I said, "was in England at a deserted airfield when you were filming *Those Magnificent Men in Their Flying Machines.* You had a small car and a big dog."

"Yes, that was Addo, my Pyrennean mountain dog who died last year," she said sadly. "After he got old, I said I wouldn't make a picture while he still was alive because he pined for me, and I'd never work out of England till he passed away. I also had a minicar then. I have now gone up to a Volkswagen."

I told her that ironically I knew much about her from an article that David Whiting had written about her before he presumably killed himself for love of her. It referred to her as "The *Maiden* Man-Eater," the subheadline saying that she "uses words that would make a construction-worker blush, but from her they sound refined."

"It was a brilliant job, very colorful and entertaining and true," Sarah Miles said.

"Do you remember the opening anecdote?" I asked.

SARAH: Yes, it was actually what happened. This was at a

dinner party, and this gentleman before dinner knew that I was very keen on breeding horses. He told me he had bought this stallion for an enormous amount of money, and he simply couldn't get it to ejaculate. And I felt terribly sorry for this gentleman. So after the meal I stood up and raised my glass and said, 'I do hope your stallion ejaculates tomorrow.' But unfortunately I'd got the wrong gentleman, and the woman who was with the gentleman I'd made the mistake to gave me a look I'll never forget as long as I live.

E. W.: I was impressed with the title he gave to the article, "The *Maiden* Man-Eater." You weren't a maiden certainly?

SARAH: No, I was Mrs. Robert Bolt and had been for a long time.

In a sweepingly general way, Sarah confirmed some of the other stories about herself. She was once seeing a blue movie which had nothing much to it except a man with a gargantuan penis. A man sitting next to her grew upset at the instrument's hugeness and finally turned to Sarah and asked her, "Is that an average-sized cock?" Accepting her role as an expert on such matters, she replied, "About average. Maybe a little smaller."

Once a girlfriend of Sarah's couldn't stop her hiccups. Remembering the belief that hiccups can be stopped by fright or shock, Sarah reached up under the girl's dress and pulled down her pants. She stopped the hiccups. Sarah says words like "cunt" with ease and "wee-wee" more easily. Whiting told how she always said, "I must have a wee-wee. There's nothing to be embarrassed about. It makes a pleasant sound—tinkle, tinkle—and it does relieve one so."

E. W.: How many pictures have you made?

SARAH: I don't know. I don't keep count of anything in life. I just take it one day at a time.

E. W.: What was the first one?

SARAH: *Term of Trial* with Sir Laurence Olivier.

E. W.: At what point did you make *Blow-Up*?

SARAH: I don't know except that was the time that I retired for three years.

E. W.: Why did you retire for three years?

SARAH: *Blow-Up.*

E. W.: I thought it was a very interesting picture.

SARAH: I didn't hit it off with Antonioni very well.

E. W.: I remember standing up in the audience after it was over and asking people what it was all about and they didn't know either.

SARAH: That was precisely my point. You make a film like that and the intellectuals and pseudointellectuals will read into it what they wish to read into it at the moment.

E. W.: What did you think of it?

SARAH: To me it's just a pile of rubbish.

Sarah was suddenly laughing. "What are you laughing about?"

SARAH: A friend and I tried to watch it on TV last night and neither of us could follow it. And we both said, "What the hell is this movie about?"

E. W.: I feel better now because that's what I thought the first time I saw it, and then I saw these ecstatic reviews, and I thought I must be very stupid.

SARAH: People get influenced by other people's opinions, but they shouldn't. One should see a film and criticize it oneself and not listen to what is fashionable at the moment.

Inasmuch as Sarah took her clothes off quite a lot in her first films and got the reputation of being a sex kitten, I felt it only fair to ask her what she thought about the trend to total frontal nudity.

"Sex has nothing to do with flesh," Sarah answered. "Sex is in the mind," she endeavored to explain. "Show a pair of naked breasts, and they're either good breasts or bad breasts; but they've got nothing to do with sex. It depends on the circumstances. Not on the actual body itself."

E. W.: Then anybody with a pair of bad breasts can have as good a sex life as somebody with a pair of good breasts?

SARAH: I think that's precisely true. Otherwise, nine-tenths of the ladies wouldn't get laid at all. It's one's attitude. Not what one physically looks like.

E. W.: Now Carroll Baker used to take the attitude that the actress had to have an affair with her leading man to make it realistic on the screen.

SARAH: Oh, really?

E. W.: Do you have any feeling about that?

SARAH: I feel it's a lot of nonsense. It's like saying you have to get drunk to play a drunk scene. Nonsense! You'd play it much better if you were sober. I would.

"I remember Carroll Baker's husband at the time [Jack Garfein] telling me that Carroll thought she should have an affair with

Robert Mitchum. She said it would be good for a picture she was doing in Africa with Mitchum."

"I was going to do that picture!" Sarah laughed. "Yes," she continued, "it goes back to my dog Addo. I was offered to do that movie and I accepted it only if I could smuggle Addo to Africa with me. I got a gentleman who said he would do it. It was for a phenomenal amount of money, but I didn't mind that if I could have Addo out there. It was all arranged, but about a week before I was to set sail with my smuggler, he ran off, he did a double on me, so I had to cancel the movie. The other reason I wanted to do that film was that it involved an elephant. My one mission in life is to own an elephant."

"Own it!" I asked. "Why do you want to own it?"

"Love it!" she said.

"Anyway, Mitchum said he wasn't interested . . . maybe that was just good acting . . . you know Mitchum pretty well. . . ."

"Yes, I know Mitchum pretty well . . ."

"Well, what do you think? Do you have to go to bed with your leading man off-screen in order to go to bed with him on-screen?"

Sarah gave me a flash of an understanding smile. "I don't think so, but we're getting into a lot of sexual areas, aren't we? Aren't there some other areas we can progress to? Are you enjoying your salad? You haven't touched it yet!"

"Should it have been handled differently?" I asked. I referred to the fact that David Whiting, who'd been hopelessly in love with her, according to most accounts, as well as an employee she and her husband couldn't get rid of, had died under such circumstances that she and Burt Reynolds didn't seem to want to discuss it.

"Mr. Whiting had a death wish!" she said.

"I've heard that he was so close to you that you sometimes have a feeling he is still alive and that you were heard to say just a couple of days ago, 'David will take care of the tickets.' "

Sarah shook her head. She didn't remember saying that or feeling that.

"David"—she called him both his first name and "Mr. Whiting"—"wasn't in love with me. He was in love with F. Scott Fitzgerald," she said. "He always carried a copy of *The Great Gatsby*. He was always very flirtatious with death. Of course he never told me he was married. He was in love with extremes.

When he left our home in the country and went to live with us in Chelsea, he took an enormous amount of pills."

"I've heard that you've caused three suicides," I said.

"I have been *associated* with three suicides," she corrected me. "Not that three people died for love of me. One woman and one homosexual and then David. The woman was a school friend who brought her little boy and came to live with me and wouldn't leave. My husband finally said, 'This is ridiculous, she has to go.' I said, 'Robert, I can't tell her.' He finally told her it was no longer possible to support her. She left, and the next day she jumped off a building.

"Was she in love with you? Was it a sex thing?" I asked.

"Oh, no, she had many boyfriends. She had been in a mental home."

Sarah waved that away as just another person's life she'd become hopelessly involved in.

"The man, the landscape gardener, was living on my property. He hadn't paid me rent in two years. If he was in love with me, he didn't tell me. One day the police said, 'Did you know Johnny put his head in your oven?' "

The light manner of speaking probably didn't indicate her real feelings but undoubtedly was more a mask for them, I decided later. For the moment, I said, "But David Whiting. . . ."

"David was a man of so many words. Of course he was unbalanced, which we didn't know at first. He never had a home. He had made a muddle of his life. He had a wife, which he didn't tell me about. She was a stewardess. He told us his father was a director of Pan Am. . . ."

"But the mystery?" I said.

"Where's the mystery?" Sarah demanded. "There's no mystery. Poor Burt. He's as innocent as a babe! All he did was help a damosel in distress.

"Listen, I was there the whole time in his room. It was his birthday, and poor bugger was getting a massage and getting dressed. There had been the trouble with David, and the producer wouldn't let me go back to my room. Look, this was a motel. You couldn't go someplace else. There was no other place to go.

"I finally said, 'I'm going to get out of here and find my son and nanny.' I went into the room, and there was David dead. I was the first one to see him. . . ."

I truly had no great wish to grill Sarah Miles about David

Whiting's curious death. She had suffered enough. The authorities at Gila Bend, Arizona, had evidently decided there were no more questions to be asked. Why should I be making up some? I asked her instead, "What do you want to do next?"

"Not a question of what I want to do. I'm booked up till I'm a hundred," she said. "I want to work. I hate being off. I hate the sun. I bought a house in Malibu. I swim about two miles a day, not up and down a pool with people sitting on the edge drinking champagne. But in the ocean. It comes right up to my veranda. It was some lady's home, and I got it very cheap. I take occupancy in a month; then I let it while I go to Argentina to do *The Plumed Serpent*. Then I come back to it in December, when I do *St. Joan* on the stage."

"Is that the *St. Joan* of Shaw's?"

"Yes. So many people have had a go at it. I did it at seventeen. My father, who's my strictest critic, said it's the best thing I ever did. He's near eighty. I want to make him proud of me once more. His name's John Miles, and he's a consulting engineer. My mother'll come over, too, and they'll all stay at Malibu."

"Has the tragedy had an effect on your career?"

"Yes." Her answer was sharp. "It has had an effect on me. The thing that I deplore is that it has made me a hot property. It shows how sick the world is. That a private tragedy—and it was private—was turned into a fiasco is proof to me of the sad collapse of the world we live in today."

I was surprised that she placed such significance on the curiosity that the press had displayed. It seemed just about normal to me.

She closed the subject on that, like a woman snapping closed the pages of a book, but she could reopen it.

"There have been things suggested about Burt Reynolds and me. I didn't even know Burt Reynolds. I don't even know Burt Reynolds now!"

I gave her a look indicating, I hoped, my lack of comprehension of that remark. By normal standards, she certainly did know Burt Reynolds. She was speaking on another plane. It reminded me, if I may digress, of a talk I had long ago with the popular author of his day Jim Tully, who had a brother who was a groom and lived in a completely different world. Jim Tully said to me, about his brother, "There are rooms in my soul he has never entered." I thought that was pretty high-flown and literary at the time. Now this once-upon-a-time sex kitten was saying she didn't know Burt Reynolds, and I hoped I was getting her meaning.

"He is in love with Dinah Shore," she said clearly and with seeming conviction. "Somebody should say Burt Reynolds is innocent. All he did was protect a lady who had been given a pretty bad battering. I still don't know Burt Reynolds. Except that he's a much better actor than he's given credit for!"

"I agree," I said. "Two, three years ago, before the *Cosmo* centerfold, he was more respected as an actor than he is now. He wasn't as well known, but those who did know him knew he was a good actor with a flair for comedy. And very good on the talk shows."

"Yes, yes," Sarah nodded. "And because all this thing has been foisted on him, his talent is forgotten. Christ almighty," she exclaimed, "you've got another Clark Gable on your hands!"

After a second, Sarah added, "He's a kind and lovely gentleman, and he loves Dinah Shore."

"But Dinah's a lot older than Burt," I pointed out.

"I told you that there's no such thing as age or years," she said. "Age should be abolished."

"But it hasn't been."

Sarah smiled. "It's what you are inside. Gladys Cooper was a friend of mine. I knew her very well. She was the sexiest thing on two legs. She swam the Thames. . . ."

She said that she, Sarah, has two birth certificates, to confuse how old she is. "On one my mother says I'm thirty-one, but my mother says I'm twenty-nine. Age is irrelevant, except that my mother says she's going potty because of the two ages. My father's near eighty, and my mother's fifty-two or fifty-three. They're all so vague about age in my family. My father's an engineering consultant, but he won't retire. He says working keeps him young."

It was at about this point that I looked down and saw Sarah Miles crying. The storm had come up during our discussion of Burt Reynolds when I had agreed that he was a good actor and had said I would write something good about him. This was a little too much for a girl who had been talking with people who were attacking both of them.

"People think I'm a toughie," she said now. "I give the impression that I'm hard, but as soon as they're nice, I let go.

"You see," she said, "when anybody's nice, I burst into tears. I don't often cry. I can be as tough as anybody. It's been a devilish day. I finally had to say to one woman, 'Get out of my life.' " And, she added, "The talk about the tragedy again. In Cannes nobody mentioned it. I had felt fine. And then this incident with this woman.

"She flattered me," Sarah Miles said, "and because I'm a cunt, I believed her."

Though Sarah is famous for her plain speaking, it was about the only nonladylike term I'd heard from her.

"I'm a failure," she said, looking tearful again. "I shouldn't be acting. I should be breeding the best horses. That's what I love to do. But I'm a failure at that, too, because they're too beautiful to sell and I can't let them go. I could be a very rich Sarah Miles if I would just breed horses, but I am making myself a very poor Sarah Miles.

"I'm very insecure," she said.

("They mostly are," I thought.)

What I Said to the Naked Lady or It's My Broadway

✍ I HAVE an office on what's alleged to be the most colorful street in the world, and one of the visitors to it has been a famous girl in the nude. I don't usually have naked girls running into my office. She, indeed, has been the only nude I've viewed (in my office).

My office in one of the Broadway theaters in what was formerly the heart of the hooker district is a disgrace aesthetically. It's mostly notebooks that should have been thrown out, and glamor girl photographs, and dirty windows.

The late Mike Todd, when he was poor and had not yet married Elizabeth Taylor, once occupied the office that is now mine. When he was rich, he had offices on Park Avenue. When he was broke again, he would move back to Broadway. As he was often broke, he often had the office that I now use.

Police have moved the hookers out of my block, but one night when hookering was at its height there, I counted seventeen girls in that single block. A ham-and-eggery across the street was once so popular with the girls that the cops named it "the Hookerama." It is now, as they say, "under new management" and closes at 8 P.M. to avoid the hooker trade.

Strange people and some good people hang out in my neighborhood. One of the good types is saloonkeeper Sam Leibowitz, who has a Zsa Zsa Gabor accent. He runs the Cordial, on Broadway next door to the Ed Sullivan Theater, at Fifty-third Street, and has the most popular toilet on the street, as he will be glad to tell you, with plenty of Hungarian indignation thrown into his speech.

"Razzberry Joe," the angry little man who sits on a wastebasket on a curb giving the Bronx cheer to passersby, operates somewhere near the Jack Dempsey restaurant. He is supposed to be mad at the world because he was a trumpet player and lost his lip. It is very distressing to be walking along the street and suddenly have a bearded little stranger start making rude noises at you.

We don't see Billy the Kid anymore. He was a tall Southern boy who sold some heroin that turned out to be aspirin. His customers shot him to death.

The police didn't seem to care much who did it. "Saved us the job," one of them said.

We don't see Isadore Glass either. He dealt in foreign cars and often carried as much as $25,000 in his pockets as he went upstairs to his office there in the CBS Building which houses the Ed Sullivan Theater. Somebody must have known about that big roll that he carried. He and his black wife were strangled in their apartment, and police have never arrested anybody in the couple of years since.

But about that naked lady.

It was the summer of 1970. A fat lad named Hal Stone often came into my office boasting that he had nude girls and topless go-go dancers doing a good business in his nude model agency.

"Exclusively nudes," he said. "You need any nude girls for anything? I'm loaded with 'em."

"Thanks, anyway." Hal was so pleased with himself in his role as flesh peddler of nakeds that he was hard to resist.

One afternoon, I didn't resist. "Do you happen to have any topless secretaries?" I asked him.

I only said this to arouse my own secretary Julie Allen who had a low regard for Hal Stone's enterprise. When she looked up with a glare, I was content.

"Topless secretaries?" Hal Stone said. He confessed he hadn't any.

One day later my assistant Tim Boxer came in grinning guiltily.

"Wait'll you see," he said.

A beautiful blond Scandinavian from the Hal Stone agency had come up the stairs, stepped into a back room, and shed her light raincoat, under which she was wearing nothing.

Now here she was, naked, even barefoot, with everything hanging out and down and showing, topless and also bottomless. And she strutted immodestly across my office to my secretary's typewriter, plopped her bare bottom down on my secretary's chair, and began typing furiously.

My own secretary was shocked but no more than I was. Out in the great outdoors, nudity was OK, but in the great indoors of an office, it wasn't.

Suppose somebody came in? It would be hard to explain this bare-behinded, bare-fronted typist.

"I think you'd better leave," I managed to say. I probably wasn't very polite about it. Hal Stone had delivered a topless secretary, sure enough! When she had wiggled out, put on her raincoat and departed, and my secretary and I had sort of settled down, I went to the typewriter to see whether the topless, bottomless typist could really type.

She definitely could.

She had written "fuck" about ten times.

A year or more passed, and one night I got a call from a young Scandinavian madam who'd just been arrested as purveyor of girls to the rich, influential, and celebrated. She wished to supply me with some colorful details of her career. It was a big news story, and she had figured that I would be writing about it.

I was a little scornful. Why was she calling me personally?

"You *know* me!" she howled. "You saw me bare-assed. I was your topless secretary. I wrote 'fuck' all over your typewriter!"

"Oh, yes," I said. I took some notes about her brothel and then I asked her, "What do you say your name is?"

"Xaviera Hollander," she said, spelling it carefully. Thus was I introduced to the Happy Hooker.

In fact, Xaviera told me in that conversation that a friend of mine, Robin Moore, was writing a book with her about her career and that they planned to call it *The Happy Hooker*. I told her it was a funny title, but of course nobody would print it. "We think we might get someone to publish it," she said. Everybody now knows how she went on to fame, fortune, and deportation.

"But what were you doing in my office that day?" I asked her.

"That was just a gag, I was doing a favor for Hal Stone," she said. "You chickened out, or we might have had some fun."

The next time I saw her was at a party, and she blew in my ear, a trick that those ladies have, and hinted that if I visited her place of business, which she was then still operating, I might get certain press privileges.

George Jessel's speech of farewell to Xaviera after she'd become a celebrity was a dear thing. He was off to Israel, and he hated to say good-bye.

"Now, Xaviera, you be true to me," he said.

Personally, I never encouraged Xaviera, and I fear I must confess that I did not help her along her way. However, I did see her potential long before most people.

A hooker was also the heroine of one of the most popular things I ever did in journalism—getting mugged on Broadway.

It was a blizzardy night in February, 1969. At 1:40 A.M., I felt an extraordinary compulsion to eat an egg sandwich.

It was now Monday morning, and because of the blizzard, nearly everything around the neighborhood was closed, including the little hot doggery downstairs and Sam's Cordial restaurant. But the ham-and-eggery we called the Hookerama was open. I would mush over there for one egg fried hard, toast, and coffee.

I left my second-floor office, walked downstairs to the front door of the theater, unlocked it, stepped out onto Broadway, and turned to lock the door of the theater behind me. I turned back to the very lonely street—and was confronted by two white youths. One of them thrust a very hard object in my stomach.

I couldn't really see the object that he stuck in my stomach, but I thought it was an automatic. I meant it felt the way I was sure an automatic would feel.

"Give us your wallet," one of the boys commanded.

"OK," I said, and quickly brought it out of my pocket. The automatic was going deeper in my stomach (if it was an automatic).

"Here it is, but let me keep the cards," I said. I was too

frightened to think of anything else, and I knew that I was at a disadvantage with these two boys, who seemed to be in their twenties. The boy who didn't have the hard object in my stomach took the money and gave me back the wallet.

Their business with me finished, they took the $75 or thereabouts that I'd had in my wallet and ran north on Broadway.

I ran south on Broadway—toward the Hookerama. But when I looked back, I saw them joined by a third man who must have been their lookout. "What a waste of manpower," I thought. "They didn't need three men to rob me. One would have been more than enough."

My final look at them was as they ran up the street and turned eastward about Fifty-fourth Street looking back to see whether I was doing anything about pursuing them or calling police. I wasn't. I was still going to have that egg sandwich.

Snow was falling as I crunched into the Hookerama. I was shaken but still hungry. I sat at a counter. Several girls sat at tables over their coffee and cigarettes. They were black hookers.

One of them, who was ambitious, left her table, and slid down beside me at the counter. Nobody tried to deter her.

"How about a party, honey?" she said in her lowest, sultriest voice.

I was waiting for the egg sandwich. I had to laugh despite my still nervous condition. Mugging or not, business went on as usual at Ye Olde Hookerama.

"Just my luck," I said. "I meet a gorgeous creature like you and I'm broke. I've just been mugged."

"Where? Where? When?" She was excited and angered by these malefactors although she was one herself.

My egg sandwich that had cost me so much—$75 for a sandwich!—tasted delicious. I put some strawberry jam on the toast. Meticulously, I described the mugging to the hooker and how I had bravely handled the situation by running the opposite way they ran. My hooker friend was seething with indignation. She was now on the side of the law.

"They were amateurs!" she snorted, fiercely.

"Amateurs! How do you know they were amateurs?"

"Anybody can see that, honey." She looked down at my hands. "You got your ring, you got your wristwatch. Did they take all your money?"

"No, they didn't get into this pocket," I said. "I got a few bucks."

"I tell you, amateurs," the hooker nodded. "But that's what's happening all over. Amateurs are ruining my business, too."

The Shack-Up Society

⚑ ONE problem that I as a glamor reporter have now that the world has—if you'll forgive me—"gone pubic" is trying to keep straight who's coupling with who.

People used to say they read Walter Winchell to see "who's sleepin' with who." That's too mild now. Nevertheless, a directory would be helpful. Not merely a Social Register, but a fat red volume that would politely tell Who's Screwin' Who in America.

This would be a very practical book for hostesses, social secretaries, public speakers, merchants, and fan clubs. It might clear up some of the confusion about couplings that's resulted from the blithe attitude about matrimony taken by the refreshingly frank but sadly amoral young people of show business.

They don't get married; they don't get engaged; they don't live together very long. They nevertheless have children, and then as one rather callously said, "We don't know what to do about the little bastards."

Rod McKuen told me in an interview, "It used to bother me when I found out that I'd been born out of wedlock. Then I realized some people spend their entire lives becoming bastards and I'd had a head start."

To prove he considered it no disgrace, he fathered an illegitimate child himself and spoke openly about it.

"Shack-Up Society" of today doesn't give a damn about such niceties as marriage. Thirty or forty years ago, before Levi's, before the Pill, before vibrators, before group sex, there was a horsey crowd they called the Mink and Manure Set, and they gossiped about one member who had always been thought to be illegitimate. Then his legitimacy was established, and one of his true friends—and there were true friends in those days—said, "He may not be a bastard, but he's still a son of a bitch."

The Shack-Up trend probably got its start about the time that Ingrid Bergman gave up Dr. Peter Lindstrom and went off to Stromboli with Roberto Rossellini in 1949. There was a Hollywood joke that expressed the then shocking attitude:

Hollywood Dialogue: "Blondie Bigbosom just announced her engagement to Tommy Tighttrousers." . . . "No kidding! I didn't even know she was pregnant."

Today it goes this way: A happy daughter rushes to tell her mother joyous news. Her boyfriend has just whispered the three magic words, "Let's shack up."

Not "Let's get married," as in her mother's day. Some shocked parents criticized me for printing that story. But every teen-ager knows the trend. Warren Beatty and Julie Christie enjoyed a long relationship without getting married. Elliott Gould and Jennifer Bogart had a baby and parted when she was pregnant with her second, without benefit of a minister. Vanessa Redgrave and Franco Nero rather improved upon the shacking-up system. They were in love, but they had a baby without actually living together for any long period, seeming to consider the shacking up unnecessary.

Weddings and engagements they report in the papers, but shackings-up, not yet. Couldn't it be done in excellent taste under "Liaisons"? What's a liaison? "An illicit sexual relationship between a man and a woman." And what is illicit? "Not permitted, or authorized; unlicensed, unlawful." It being "unlawful," it could not be lawfully recorded, and therefore the shackers-up, the pillars of Shack-Up Society, will never be completely recognized.

What a pity, what a cheating of their devoted fans who only learn of these liaisons in carefully worded "blind items" or in the more energetic and less cautious fan magazines! To think that there are repetitions of the Katharine Hepburn-Spencer Tracy relationship going on today among stars who are almost equal in fame and box-office appeal and that they can't be tattled to the world.

And I swear to you that they do exist and I am going to be most cautious in giving the details, because of taste, good manners, a sort of ethics, and because of the laws of libel and slander. The latter are misty and vague, and I don't wish to go hunting for lawsuits. I would prefer to keep the public in ignorance of some liaisons I have just learned about, and avoid being sued.

Yet the show business connection made it glamorous and exciting . . . supposedly. I give credit to men who are great operators, as we once called them, with the girls. Once I was interviewing one of the most beautiful girls in the world in her suite at the Hotel Plaza. While she was busily denying to me that there was anything serious in her relationship with Warren Beatty, who should be barging into the next room of the suite with a lot of clothes being removed from another suite, but Warren Beatty?

It was an awkward, embarrassing moment.

"Oh, hello, Earl," he said in some surprise, "what are you doing here?" He was holding a couple of suits on hangers.

"I was about to ask you the same thing," I said.

("But I see I don't need to," I thought of adding but for once held my tongue.)

The young lady was right, I have decided since, in maintaining that there was nothing serious going on with Warren Beatty. Nothing as serious as marriage, anyway. I have been most respectful of Warren Beatty's tightrope walking on the matrimonial high wires since and believe I would almost unqualifiedly list him as the champion nonmarrying eligible bachelor. Warren is such a slick operator that he always leaves them happy that they've had an opportunity to revel in his charm. There's nothing like a satisfied customer, and his are always not only satisfied, but almost ecstatic.

I had a completely different experience with a famous black actor whose privacy I am going to respect although there is really no reason that I should. Handsome, prestigious, talented, he became the lover of a beautiful white actress who got pregnant. The black press reported the situation with the names spelled out. My policy has been to publish these stories only if the participating parties wish to acknowledge them.

Reaching him by phone at his office, I said, "I have heard about the baby that was born to you and——. Do you wish to say anything about it?"

"You mean, for publication?" he said.

"Certainly—for publication!" I said.

"You know I don't want to talk about it," he said.

"Well," I said, "you never know. Sometimes there are fathers who *do* want to talk about it and are proud to do so."

I thought that might shake him up, but it didn't get through to his chivalry, his gallantry, his pride of fatherhood. And so the story has been printed so far only in the black press. Thinking back over his case, I must give credit to Sammy Davis who, when he fell in love with the blond Scandinavian beauty Mai Britt, came right out and said so and married her. Sammy declared he didn't care what color their babies might be—"I wouldn't care if they were polka dot," he said. Maybe Sammy was less discreet than the man who wouldn't speak out at all, but his courage put the other to shame.

Leaving Shack-Up Society for the moment, let's look at show business' contributions to Orgy Society. The most famous case in thirty years, involving a big male star who was caught bare-bottomed at a New York party, is said to have been hushed by a studio with a $50,000 payoff here and there. I heard about its horrible details when I began writing a column in the 1940's. The male star is still with us, his career unblemished, for the story never got the headlines it deserved.

A pretty young actress and model (of that period) was the heroine of a sensational tale involving a playboy millionaire. He got her pregnant but didn't want to marry her, because he suspected he might have had accomplices on the job. He was on a plane flying to Florida which got in very rough weather, and all passengers feared for their lives. He prayed to God for his life to be saved and promised that if he survived, he would marry the girl. He lived, he married her, and eventually, he gave her millions.

He himself became an orgiast. He had a weird fondness for little girls. He invited big girls but gave them little girl dresses which they were supposed to wear, with the crotch cut out. He gave them lollipops which they were supposed to suck. He would say, "You've been a bad girl," pull them on his knee, yank down their panties, and spank them.

The girls were from Show Business and could well use the $500 fee he almost always paid. A man of varied tastes, he also engaged lesbians, whom he liked to watch making love to each other, and homosexuals, who would also perform for him. And he liked to be whipped. A girl going to call on him by appointment had better be sure to take a suitcase full of whips. He had a Chinese doorman who greeted guests nude, but for some reason, the host himself was usually dressed—at least, he wore shorts. It was a big loss to show business when he died recently, and around the theatrical restaurants, more than one girl said, "I wonder if he took his whips with him."

Syndicated Hollywood columnist Sidney Skolsky and I occasionally fill each other in on Who's Shackin' with Who. Skolsky mentioned that George C. Scott, after three marriages and divorces, shacked with Tricia Vandevere and then got happily married. "They previewed it," Skolsky said.

"You know about Tony Perkins and Berry Berenson becoming parents and going off to Europe to tell her relatives?" I said. "And the time that Juliet Prowse talked casually on TV about how she and her boyfriend were on the way to get married and she got stricken with labor pains?"

We were having coffee at a back table in Schwab's drugstore in Hollywood. "Twiggy and Justin Villeneuve share London's most fabulous flat where she has sculpture and fur-lined furniture," Skolsky said.

Michael Sarazen and Jackie Bissett had been together about three years. . . . "They were afraid marriage would spoil their romance." . . . Patti Duke and Desi Arnaz, Jr. . . . everybody'd known about that. . . . beautiful Brenda Vaccaro and Michael Douglas, Kirk's son. . . . Carrie Snodgrass and Neil Young . . . Stella Stevens and Skip Ward. . . . And then there was the interesting story of Liv Ullman, the greatest Swede since Ingrid Bergman. Miss Ullman divorced Dr. Hans Jacob Stang in 1960, and the famous Swedish director Ingmar Bergman divorced his fourth wife. Miss Ullman now has a five-year-old daughter named Linn by Ingmar Bergman. It was a scandal when Ingrid Bergman did it with Roberto Rossellini, in 1949. When Ingmar Bergman did it in 1973, it was a popular contribution to culture.

Sometimes the Sex Wave got almost overpowering here at home and I wanted to get away from it. One pleasant Sunday forenoon in London, I left the Savoy Hotel for a stroll along the Strand.

I was thinking nice clean Sabbath thoughts when suddenly near the Charing Cross station, I saw a newsstand with an array of sex magazines such as I hadn't yet seen in the United States.

I bought one of each from the newsdealer who must have thought I was a sex-starved Yankee. He managed to find a huge chunk of wrapping paper for me to carry away my burden.

It appeared that the English had outdone the Americans in covering this subject. One magazine called *"X" Films* featured an interview with Sue Hattsson, who said she was depressed by her movie roles—"pretending to be raped, seduced or gang-banged by half the studs in the film world."

At fifteen, while she was still a virgin, she met a photographer who got her into these pictures, and now everywhere she went men were saying "how they fancy your tits and asking whether you go the whole way on the set. Men think I will screw with anyone who possesses a penis.

"Since most of the ones I have met have that piece of equipment, it would keep me pretty busy.

"I know the limitations of my ability.

"My boy friend's agent told me that I needed an image which would enable directors and casting agents to immediately identify me.

"If you go to a few directors you'll find that they sample the wares before the screen tests even begin. The director screws himself into a state of exhaustion trying to find the perfect starlet for his movie. Then he hasn't the energy to put up any resistance when the producer suggests it should be some no-talent girl whose mouth needs to be sealed."

Miss Hattsson said she decided to try to get identity, so she began going to clubs featuring sex shows and pretending that she had become so excited that she had to take off her clothes and perhaps masturbate onstage. "Sometimes I walked around in the nude and let the men feel my fanny. What does it matter? It's only flesh and bone!

"Most of the clubs didn't like me getting in the act so I had to offer a little more than usual. I started the whole thing of lifting pennies off the table with my you-know-what. Naturally I often got arrested but all I ever received as punishment was a fine, a smile from the judge and plenty of great publicity.

"Once I had my boy friend in the audience and we climbed on stage and pretended to make love. I say pretended but actually it had gone far beyond."

She had made three blue movies when she needed the money, and she said "It wasn't as bad as it sounds. I had to meet boys and girls, then we would undress and all make love. You only need a couple of scenes with them actually penetrating you.

"Most of the rest is simulated. Sometimes you fellate a guy. You don't even have to take it in your mouth. The punters like to see the stuff spurting over your face. The ones I disliked were when I had to do it with women.

"Most of them were lesbians and they would really go to town on you. Well, one thing would lead to another and you found yourself really digging the chick between your legs, and I'm no lesbian. Every day after that type of scene I had to get dead drunk and lay as many men as I could."

To her, life was full and good, and she had no complaints.

"The life I lead would probably drive most women mad with envy. I use my body and ability to the utmost and earn money from allowing men to look at my nakedness.

"It fills me with delight that I can think of myself beautiful enough that men actually pay for the privilege of seeing me. These women's liberation people are always saying what a disgrace I am to their sex. What they never realize is that I am the exploiter. It is men who get worked up looking at my picture, not the other way around."

But enough of Miss Hattsson. The film reviews in *"X" Films* come from a new school of film critics. Their style is blunt. *Last Ride to L.A.*, a Nestegg Production starring Jenny Makeman, William Custer, and Paul Turler, concerns seventeen-year-old Lucy, whose parents want her to visit a dying aunt. "Sexually mature" Lucy gets so angry she goes to her room, flops on the bed, "lifts her bottom from the bed and runs both hands across her flat stomach.

"She is a wonderful sight as she slides her fingers through the abundant pubic hair which nestles thick and black between her legs. She spreads her legs wide, giving us a view of her most intimate parts, a superior shot I have never seen in any of the hundreds of films I have had to review.

"She parts the lips of her vagina and the camera dives into the open cavity revealed there, her fingers find the wet entrance and slip up into it. This scene, I am sure, is far from being faked—the expressions on her face are those of sexual excitement and when her final release comes, it is not with the usual 'cinematic orgasm' which throws its subject wildly around but with a heave of the hips, a final thrust of the fingers and then a sigh of peace which one can almost see float over her body."

Lucy reluctantly decides to take the train to L.A. and meets Phil and Bob, whom she copulates orally as the train rolls across the country. She goes to live with them in their pad "in a rather tatty area of the city."

"The next problem they have to face is that of sex—obviously they both fancy having Lucy around. Lucy herself solves this problem when one night she leaves the bed they have made for her in the living room and waking Bob up, she takes his hand and leads him to Phil's bed, the two of them then climb in beside Phil and the problem is solved."

The critic declares that "the three of them begin to reach an understanding of one another which is rare in the field of human relationships. This comes across superbly in the film, and the sense of honesty which comes from their union is enough to give the most dedicated pessimist a little hope for humanity.

"The sex in this film is not there for sensational effect and it is definitely not a skin flick, it is a well made, intelligent film which has a point to make and makes it in the clearest way possible."

To this critic, the picture "may well be a landmark in erotic cinema, since it is the first which has done anything to justify sexuality as a communal way of life and succeed. These three people are typical of the generation which for the past few years has been trying to create a way of life centered around freedom of sexual expression—in James Whitman the generation may well have found the mouth piece it needed," he concludes.

"Group love" is freely dealt with in British publications of this type; in fact there's a book, *Group Sex*, which has an introduction by Dr. Robert Chartham.

"The chief feature of group sex is that all activity must be in public . . . though the party may be so large that two or more rooms may have to be used, no couple may occupy a room alone," Dr. Chartham says.

Make Way for Mechanical Orgies is another title that caught my attention: about wife-swapping groups making use of vibrators together. They called it "gimmick night," and the equipment included several vibrators and dildos, men applying the vibrators to women and vice versa.

The groupies and supergroupies that follow the rock musicians and singers around and try to go to bed with them have imitators in Britain—"the supersirens of the buses."

In Liverpool, young girls waylaid bus drivers. Enthralled by the muscular looks of some of the young drivers, these girls would board a bus and ride to the end of the line, when the driver often had a half hour rest period. The driver would turn off the lights in the bus and proceed to make love to the groupie, who was not in a group but all alone waiting for him.

These girls were called the Goosers, and they were addicted only to bus drivers. They were not prostitutes; they were young girls who had not been fulfilled sexually and wanted to be. One was called "the Northerly Nymph." She had been riding the bus drivers and fornicating with them since she was a much younger girl. "I only go with the drivers I like," she said. "I decided life was for living and I was going to get my share of it." One of the bus drivers confessed that he wasn't sure why he and his fellow drivers attracted these girls sexually. "I guess it's my uniform they're interested in," he said.

Once there was a word that was used in all discussions of this kind. It was "morality."

The word's no longer fashionable. I believe it's used principally in sermons.

Playbill, the program magazine for theatergoers, published an article, "Sex and the Actor," by Stuart Little and Arthur Cantor, in December, 1972, which said:

". . . there seems to be a definite theater sub-culture whose distinguishing character is laissez-faire morality. . . .

"Openness about sexual promiscuity, ease and frequency of sexual encounters, preoccupation with sexual perversion and toleration of homosexuality" were part of it.

"A Manhattan psychiatrist with a group therapy practice that includes many theater people says, 'Actors are more aware of their feelings than other people. They cater to those feelings and therefore are less strict with themselves in their behavior.'

"To young people first entering the profession, the abundance of sexual opportunity is sometimes bewildering," Stuart Little and Arthur Cantor continued.

"One actor said, 'I'm thrown into situations you don't usually face in a normal job. When you meet a girl offstage, you know nothing about her, but she knows who you are and everything about you. If you want to, you can go to bed with her that night.'"

(This was not Earl Wilson, the gossip columnist and scandal-monger, saying these alarming things. This was from producer-publicist Arthur Cantor and a longtime observer of the theater, Stuart Little).

"The actor is most susceptible to these casual encounters at the very time they're most likely to occur—right after a performance," they continued.

("Not during?" I wondered. That's what I'd heard.)

"An unmarried actress describes the heightened state of sexual awareness she experiences when she's acting, and acting well. 'I have what I think is a normal interest in sex,' she says, 'but when I'm acting, I want to be wild. And the better I'm acting, the more intense the feeling becomes.' "

Older actors admitted their phenagling and tried to justify it. "A love affair within the cast is like a convenience when you're on tour," one man said. "I need female companionship. When I'm in a strange town and it gets to be 11 o'clock, I don't want to go back to my hotel room alone. Not a season goes by that actors don't meet in a stage love affair, fall in love, divorce their respective spouses and marry each other."

While the older actors hunted excuses for their conduct, the younger performers didn't think there was anything that needed to be justified. They had seen and experienced so much sexual freedom that it was all normal to them. They didn't know about morals or morality.

"Morality?" It was just as Carol Lynley had said to me subsequently, it was a word that nobody ever used any more.

Brando, Front and Backside

🖋 WHEN Wally Cox's wife, Pat, found him dead in their Bel Air, California, home at about 7:30 A.M. on Thursday, February 15, 1973, she immediately went into a state of shock. But she remained sufficiently in control of herself to say that one person who should be notified at once was Marlon Brando. Wally and Marlon had been friends since they were seven, both living in Illinois. That had been more than forty years before. But they had discussed death, funerals, and cremation, and Marlon Brando would know exactly what Wally would have wanted done. And he would have the strength and the authority to get it done.

"But I couldn't get through to him in Tahiti," Mrs. Cox has said since, "and I wasn't of much use trying to find him. I kept saying that Wally was only in a coma, while the firemen who had come to try to resuscitate him kept saying he was gone.

"Marlon, it turned out, was on his way to Honolulu," Mrs. Cox said. A plane flying low over his island of Tetiaroa had dropped a message to him. He immediately began the trip back to Los Angeles. Arriving the next morning, Brando did more than take charge. He used his talent for gentleness to make it possible for Patricia Cox to live in the house where Wally had died.

"I couldn't stand to go into the room where I had found him," she remembers.

"Marlon not only stayed in the house while I went to the home of a friend, but he made it beautiful for me to go back into the room. He kept telling me Wally would have been upset if I thought it was repulsive to see him dead. This was when I was still trying to think he was only in a coma. Marlon slept there, and his sister, Jocelyn, stayed there, and also his stepmother. They stayed there on and off for three weeks. He made me able to come back to my own home."

I dwell at length on this because it's the side of the sexy, swingin' Marlon Brando that few people know. He was also the dominant figure at a wake at the Cox home the following Monday which columnist Army Archerd reported in the Hollywood *Daily Variety*. It lasted most of the night, and it was attended by about 200 friends, some from the *Hollywood Squares* TV show. It was also attended by Wally's dogs, cats, and pet goat.

Brando, who would be forty-nine in a couple of months, was about eight months older than his small, spectacled, far-from-robust friend. He was already figured to be a runaway for the Oscar for *The Godfather* and his picture had been on *Time*'s cover three weeks before: "Sex and Death in Paris . . . MARLON BRANDO in 'Last Tango.' " He was undoubtedly the biggest personality, male or female, in the entertainment world at that moment. But he hated caste, and he was helping pour the cheap wine or the beer that Ursula Andress and Mrs. Kirk Douglas had set out for the mourners.

"The cheap wine and beer was a good idea because nobody got drunk and riotous," Mrs. Cox said.

Rattling around in his wheelchair, Cliff Arquette may have attracted more attention than Brando, but Marlon had no competition from anybody else—except possibly the goat. To Brando was subsequently assigned the scattering of Wally's ashes after the cremation.

This required delicacy. A law had to be broken. Wally did not want his ashes scattered at sea. He wanted them strewn somewhere else. I'm not permitted to say where. But it was someplace nearer home. And it would be slightly illegal if done that way, because ashes were supposed to be scattered at sea and not upon the good clean earth.

The last part of the wake was the handing out of stones which Wally and Pat had themselves polished by hand and with the help of a machine. Some of the stones had been polished when they lived in Long Island several years before. They had meant much to Wally, and he would have wanted his friends to have shared them. So thought Pat and Marlon.

And following that, it was made known—not exactly announced but "leaked," "bruited about"—that Marlon Brando had taken Wally's ashes onto a boat belonging to another friend, Bob Schiffer, and scattered them at sea. This wasn't quite the truth, but it got in the papers that way, and no harm was done to anybody. I repeat, I don't know quite where the ashes went, but greater love hath no man than he who doesn't scatter a friend's ashes at sea but says he does.

"What were your impressions of Brando the first time you interviewed him?" a reader asked me.

Always he's been pictured as a rebel, and always Marlon Brando has been a rebel, although today's rebels probably don't consider him sufficiently rebellious to be called one. It seems incredible even to me that I have known him for close to twenty-five years and that he has been of rebellious temperament every one of those years.

He had brought along a sack of cherries that day in 1950 when I first met him. He was barely twenty-six and already celebrated for wearing T-shirts and blue jeans—and for starring in *A Streetcar Named Desire* with Jessica Tandy.

He was dressed up for our interview. He wore a rumpled jacket, a two-day beard, and his hair had been combed . . . some time.

He was thin-faced then, with a lot of hair, and a youthful chin and a narrow neck unlike the neck of a bull that he has today. He had come to my apartment at Fifty-fourth Street and Seventh Avenue to meet me—he was accessible to the press then—and we had proceeded to a nearby Child's restaurant. From time to time he dug some cherries out of the sack.

I mentioned his T-shirt. In a nice way, he put me in my place.

"I don't care much about perpetuating this blabber about my clothes," he said. "It's just convenient to dress like this.

"Oh, I have a suit," he added contemptuously. "You see millions of people walking around like me." He simply dressed like a common laborer. He got more publicity for his manner of dressing than Orson Welles got for his beard (which was unusual at the time) and Errol Flynn (and Van Johnson) got for wearing red socks.

"I've been on the unemployment line, and this way of dressing is very appropriate there, too," he said.

His first movie, *The Men*, was behind him. "What do the people who invite you to Hollywood parties think about you dressing like this?"

"They don't invite me . . . that's the laugh," he said. He didn't care anyway. He had wanted to meet Charlie Chaplin at a Norman Mailer party. "But so many people were sitting at his feet drooling and adoring him with open mouths that I couldn't get to him."

Alan Ladd was a big celebrity. "I don't want to be an Alan Ladd and have that bobby-sox crowd around me. I'd rather shoot myself," he said.

He'd been on the stage in one of the worst shows I ever saw on Broadway, *The Eagle Has Two Heads*, with Tallulah Bankhead.

"I got bounced from her show." He laughed. "The play was no good." (It wasn't; it was horrible. But it had a long monologue for Tallulah which made it seem good for her, and to her.) "Every day they had the janitor in to help rewrite the script.

"Tallulah didn't like me much. She thought I was a weirdo. She always wanted to go out and order champagne. Then she'd say, 'Oh, do let's paint the walls with fish.' I just about left my mind."

Four years later, I was lying on the grass out at Twentieth Century-Fox one day in July, and Marlon was stretched out beside me, bare-chested, getting the sun, wearing the trousers he used playing Napoleon in *Desiree*. His face had begun to fill out now, and his head seemed larger. After all, he was in his thirties now.

"Why are you always having trouble with the press?" I asked. (It is one of every columnist's weaknesses to consider himself important, powerful, and indispensable.)

"My troubles really began when I was in *Streetcar* in New York," he recalled. "There was a woman columnist from Hollywood who thinks she looks young. I'd never met her. She came into Jessica Tandy's dressing room, and I walked in. I don't see well, and I didn't have on my glasses. I looked at the woman and I said to Jessica, 'Don't tell me! It's your mother!'

"It was Sheilah Graham.

"Well, you know, she's never liked me since."

Sheilah was then one of the most important Hollywood columnists. In those days, Louella Parsons, the Queen of gossip, allowed the stars to come to her big home, where she would interview them amid luxury. They were summoned to her residence as though to a royal court.

When Marlon was summoned, he wouldn't go.

"I didn't see why I should go to see her. I didn't see why she shouldn't come and see me," he said. "It wasn't long before she began writing things about 'that naughty boy Marlon Brando.'"

The subject of his relationship with the press seemed uppermost in his mind—and that was two decades ago.

He was one of the first to be contemptuous of the fan magazines. He felt himself mentally above their standards, and he was right, for the standards of some of them were the lowest possible.

"I have the satisfaction that what they get they have to snoop for," he said. "There is an unfortunate ritual here that you're supposed to divulge every part of your personal life. Anyplace else this would be considered outrageous. They write about you as though they were sleeping in the next room . . . with only a thin wall between. They're so pious. But I don't blame the writers. It's the people who read it. I go out of my way not to help those who excoriate people they don't even know for the sake of making a slimy dime."

You can see he'd thought it over most carefully and was in a mood to make almost a crusade of it. I tried to argue with him, because I felt some of his accusations were too sweeping. He was contending also that we were writing about foibles and secret characteristics, when we should be writing about acting.

"But there are some of us," I said, "who are not assigned to write just about acting. We write about personalities."

He had been moving around on the grass, trying to stay in the sun, to stay out of the shade. He leaned up on an elbow and said, "That's just it. If they wrote about me as Napoleon, all right. But about me as Marlon Brando is what they write, and I feel that nobody gives a damn about Marlon Brando."

"But they do," I said. "And the reason they do give a damn is that today in motion pictures, you have more of an audience than Napoleon ever had."

Brando sat up sharply, and his eyes swept the scene.

"I've got no answer for that," he admitted. I wondered if I might have given him a hint for the first time that he was interesting copy. If I did, I made no lasting impression, because he continued for another two decades to blast away at those who wanted to write about him and not Napoleon.

But though he's slugged away at us for our alleged lack of responsibility, Brando has often been most unreliable as a source of news about himself. Back about 1963, he told me he was on the point of retiring, which would have made him a senior citizen at around forty. When I next asked him about it in 1964, he was putting it off until 1968.

This was a dark period for Brando. The 1950's had been his. But this was a decade later. His brutal Stanley Kowalski in *Streetcar Named Desire* was a T-shirt prototype who would influence James Dean, Paul Newman, and other young actors coming along. He started out the 1950's with that, playing opposite the flighty, fluttery Vivien Leigh who won an Oscar. Three years later his Terry Malloy character in *On the Waterfront* won him an Oscar. But now in his restless way he was hunting and groping for roles and settings that would enable him to escape the "rebel" pigeonhole that everybody wanted to stuff him into.

He was moody and brooding one day in '63 when he invited me to lunch at his hotel (for the purpose of publicizing *The Ugly American*) and talked for two and a half hours—much of the time about me.

But I suspected at the time that he was employing that stratagem to keep from revealing things about himself.

Yes, he told me, roaming about the room while room service brought in the lunch, he was going to "get out of this dodge," this movie-actor racket.

"Whether I'll become a director, or whether I'll change my profession and alter my interests is a question of time and not fact," he said.

"And get out of the picture business entirely?"

"I think it's conceivable." He nodded. "The fact is, I will quit acting. I don't know when.

"And now," he added, after blasting *Time* magazine for printing tales about his private life, "I'll interview you." He seemed to be genuinely interested in how I wrote my column, which, to me, seemed to be a very dull subject.

I didn't get him onto the subject of *Time*'s reporting on his love life. He brought it up. "I'm inviting disaster by doing this," he admitted.

"But I have children to bring up and their mothers to protect from scandal and embarrassment, and I'm going to do that to the best of my hopeless ability."

There was the suggestion that he might well be ruined by *Time* for these words. That was a little amusing more than ten years later, when *Time* gave him a cover story on *Last Tango in Paris*. Evidently it forgot, even if he didn't. He also battled with the late *Saturday Evening Post*, which portrayed him as a megalomaniac superstar totally lacking in professionalism. He was pictured by various publications as a real-life mutineer in *Mutiny on the Bounty*. He played Mr. Christian as an effeminate eccentric with a comic accent. Brando had evidently chosen to think of himself as a comic, if not a comedian. However, the critics didn't think he was funny, and he was on the decline.

Still trying to get out of the mold, he searched for more unexpected roles. In '64, I witnessed him in a painful scene on the set of *Morituri* at Twentieth Century-Fox in Hollywood. He was playing a German officer with a German accent, and one scene was so long, so difficult, and so unsuccessfully done that afternoon that I would have understood if he had said, "To hell with him—I ain't seeing anybody for a week!"

I stood in the sun watching Brando trying the scene over and over and over—there was a long speech; too long, I felt. I was sorry for a millionaire actor. When he was dismissed for the afternoon, we went indoors and sat stiffly on a couch where he thoughtfully inquired if I would like to have some coffee.

When I said I would, he looked around for somebody to get it for me, but found nobody, and he got up and went off to get it himself. He brought back the coffee, though not having any for himself, and I drank it feeling quite self-conscious and also impressed by his hospitality and courtesy.

Having waited to see him hoping I'd get copy, I couldn't merely sympathize with his having a bad afternoon, and thus asked him about Anna Kashfi and the glamorous Tarita. Those questions were unproductive of news, and I reminded him of the prophecy the year before that he was retiring.

"I still want to," he said. "I sold my company last year. I had contracts for seven pictures to fulfill"—*seven!*—"one of which I've done this year, two of which, hopefully, I will do next year, leaving four more. . . . After that, I've thought of writing . . . and directing.

"Do you know," he suddenly asked, with his trick of turning a question on an interviewer, "what you'll be doing four years from now?" Four years from then, 1968, was the new target date for his retirement that never happened.

One picture that didn't help Brando when he was on the toboggan going down in the sixties was *Reflections in a Golden Eye* which he did with Elizabeth Taylor. The filmmakers, producer Ray Stark and director John Huston, thought the Brando-Taylor "chemistry" would revive Brando's box-office appeal, but the fizz turned into a fizzle.

Brando was, nevertheless, trying.

I remember how he fumed when I asked him how he felt playing a latent homosexual Army major with an inordinate fondness for a young stableboy Army private played by Robert Forster.

That was rather daring for a he-man of Brando's reputation in the year 1966.

I rode out to Mitchell Field, Long Island, to watch him in one scene, at around midnight. There was a special tenseness around the quiet set. Brando was in his trailer. People were talking in low voices. It was all in deference to Brando, who, at that time, didn't really rate all that respect because he wasn't getting offers of the best scripts.

The picture, based on a classic story by Carson McCullers, had a scene in which Brando as Major Weldon Penderton picked up a candy bar wrapper just dropped by the stableboy private and kept it as a souvenir because he had a fixation for the private.

During a break in the shooting, I talked to Brando. We were standing under the trees in the glare of the camera light. Brando was in his major's uniform, looking very military—but he became more militant than military when I asked him about the homosexual angle.

"So that's how they're selling the picture!" he snapped. "Sure, that'll get 'em at the box office. It's got the smell of money in it. It vulgarizes everything that Carson McCullers wrote!"

He was in a quiet, restrained rage at the film company trying to sell the picture by playing up the idea of him portraying an officer in love with a private. He twisted his neck around in his collar. He jammed his fists deeper into his pockets. As always, he spoke his mind.

"It's not dirt! It's about a very human problem," he said.

"Did you have any fears about it when you decided to do it?" I asked him.

"No, I didn't," he said.

John Huston said, however, that Brando had been hesitant "but his conscience as an artist overcame that reticence." Ray Stark told me that Richard Burton and Lee Marvin had both been interested in the role and they had no qualms about playing a latent homosexual. Although Brando was furious at them for using the homosexual angle in selling the film, they evidently didn't use it enough because the picture didn't do well artistically or financially.

Elizabeth Taylor was box-office tops then. The picture, though laid in an American Army camp in the south, was mostly shot in Italy—because Liz lived there and it was convenient for her.

It seemed to me that Brando was always trying to appear hard and brusque, and accidentally revealing that he really wasn't.

That night a woman from *Life* magazine stepped up to him to say good night. She departed, and when she was ten feet distant, he tipped his major's cap.

"Little late," he said to me, "with tipping my cap."

Charlie Chaplin's *A Countess from Hong Kong* didn't help restore Brando's prestige either. Besides, he had some problems with Sophia Loren. Brando was sick for a time. He confided to a friend, who confided it to the world, "If I die, Sophia will show up at my funeral and get into all the photographs."

Chaplin, making a comeback at the age of seventy-eight, had cast Brando as the son of a rich oilman, just appointed ambassador to Saudi Arabia, who discovers Sophia, a Hong Kong dance hall girl, as a stowaway in his cabin with nothing to wear but an extremely low-cut evening gown. Brando lends her some pajamas —and then tries to rip them off her. It was old-time Chaplin comedy, and there was such great hope for it that the wealthy Jules Steins of New York and Beverly Hills gave a plush party attended by the leaders of London society, including Princess Alexandra, the Duke of Marlborough, and the Douglas Fairbanks. Of course I flew over for it.

Before the party, I asked Chaplin about the Brando-Sophia difficulties. Sophia didn't attend the party. Chaplin said, "It's all over now, but sometimes I had to remind them that this was supposed to be a love story."

There were reports that Sophia didn't go because she didn't care to run into Brando again. Brando did some good acting at the party at the Hotel Savoy, pretending he was happy, when he must not have been, because Brando fans said he gave one of the dullest performances of his career in that film. He didn't seem to have any interest in it, so these Brando enthusiasts maintained.

But he was affable with all of us at the party, becoming a social lion, devoting himself to Princess Alexandra, who sat next to him at supper and then slid into his arms during the dancing.

The photographers rushed to photograph him dancing with the princess.

He held up his hand like a traffic cop signaling stop.

"Not while we're dancing," he told them. "Give us a break, will you?"

They didn't, of course.

It was the only time that I can remember seeing him in a dinner jacket, and he was handsome and shaved, not sloblike as he was in so many films. He seemed to find it hard to smile and was scowling even when he was dancing. He was on his good behavior to the point that he seemed to realize he was the evening's main attraction and he had better dance with everybody important or there would be criticism. He would dance, and perspire, and return to his table, and mop his brow with a napkin, and look around to see who he'd missed. Maybe he could have been more discreet and sat down at the table to mop his face with the napkin; instead, he did the mopping while he was standing and looking around.

"Oona, it's your turn," he said to Oona O'Neill Chaplin, Charlie's wife and the mother of eight, and that seemed to be just the right thing to do because he'd not asked her up to then and people were beginning to notice it.

Poor Marlon! But when he asked Oona to dance, somebody noticed that he'd been dancing with Princess Alexandra and had left her on the floor alone, not having remembered that he should escort her back to their table.

But by then it was getting to be almost 2 A.M., and nobody was remembering the niceties anyway.

"What did you think of your performance?" I asked Brando that night.

"I stank," he said. "I never did know why he wanted me in this picture to start with. But it was Charlie Chaplin whom I'd always worshiped, and I was too flattered to refuse."

It was unfortunate for Brando that the English critics had never been kind to their fellow Englishman Chaplin and flogged him and his picture cruelly. They said with great contempt that it was old-fashioned. Chaplin replied that they were "baby brains" and "bloody idiots." He said, "It's about a multimillionaire who gives up his lovely wife to marry a whore. What's so old-fashioned about that? It's rather current."

Brando went down with the picture, farther down than he'd been.

Liza Minnelli, who was twenty-one then, and just beginning to star in the supper clubs—this was in 1967—attended that big London party and said to me with a slight gasp, "I'd just like to look at the celebrities." It's probably safe to say that she never suspected that in the year 1973 she would win an Oscar for *Cabaret* just when Marlon Brando was refusing one for *The Godfather*. Much happened to both of them in the next six years.

(Later the reason why Sophia developed a coolness for Brando came out. At the beginning of a love scene, the devil in him took charge of his sense of humor, and he couldn't resist saying to the glamor girl, "Do you know you have black hairs up your nostrils?")

Marlon's defiance of convention and his wild sense of humor

were constantly against him—or for him, according to how you looked at it. When he was still comparatively unknown, he hung around with the Irving Hoffman-Eddie Jaffe-Joe Russell set in an apartment on West Forty-eighth Street in New York, where impossible events became possible. These imaginative, fun-loving friends of Brando's had numerous enthusiasms. One of them was a spiritualist who held séances where the table moved as you sat holding onto it in the dark.

At one séance, pennies seemed to spray the room and the participants. Even the spiritualist was baffled by this. He knew he wasn't doing it. He suddenly turned on the light during the penny shower.

"There," one of the participants reported to me, "sat Marlon Brando with a mouthful of pennies."

There's a familiar anecdote illustrating his sense of humor. Arriving in Hollywood for his first picture, very much spoiled by the flattering words of some of the New York drama critics, he was asked by those who welcomed him just what they could do to make him happy. He was just an average-looking citizen—except that he was traveling with a pet monkey. "Is there anything at all we can do for you?" they asked him.

They may have expected him to ask for a girl or two. Instead, he said, "Yes, get my monkey fucked. He's been trying to make love to me."

He'd begun to get a reputation as a stud in New York long before he went to Hollywood. Years after their boyhood together in Illinois, Marlon met Wally Cox in New York. "Hello, Marlon," said Wally. "Hello, Wally," said Marlon. They soon had an apartment together, where Brando began making himself known for being a surly, unappreciative, and ungrateful kind of lover that masochistic girls could weep over. A couple of rather famous older actresses batted their eyelashes at him, but he scratched his behind, belched rudely, and walked away from them.

In those days, Maureen Stapleton's apartment was a gathering place of the young actors of the Stella Adler and Elia Kazan persuasion. One night Marlon's roommate, Wally Cox, still a silversmith, did a routine, his impression of an Army sergeant.

"You've got to do something with that!" Maureen said. He was auditioned by Barney Josephson, then operating the Café Society Downtown in Sheridan Square.

"He went in one night, and next morning he was a star," says Tony Randall, who was among those present.

With his bragging that he'd never finished his high school "education," because he'd been expelled for dumping a slop jar's contents onto a teacher, Brando was looked upon, in the beginning, as a kook.

I saw Brando make his Broadway debut in *I Remember Mama*, starring Mady Christians and Oscar Homolka, on October 19, 1944. It was John van Druten's adaptation of Kathryn Forbes' book *Mama's Bank Account*. I was more impressed with the audience than the play itself—especially with the lovely glamor girl of the period, Maria Montez, who was wrapped up in ermine.

While I didn't write about Marlon Brando, playing Nels, the son, critic Robert Garland did in the New York *Journal-American*. He wrote: "The Nels of Marlon Brando is, if he doesn't mind me saying so, charming."

His name was also mentioned, along with Frances Heflin and Carolyn Hummel, in *PM* by Louis Kronenberger, who said they "are all good as the children of the family." In a small part, Brando had come off well, and he treasured those clippings, and justifiably.

Two years later, in Maxwell Anderson's *Truckline Cafe*, he did even better. Critic Robert Garland of the *Journal-American* had undoubtedly become a fan, for he wrote, "After playing Frankie to Ann Shepherd's Johnnie, Marlon Brando has himself a high old actorial time before giving himself up to Robert Simon pretending to be a California cop. A graduate of the role of Nels in 'I Remember Mama,' young Mr. Brando distinguishes himself in this, his second professional part."

"There is an effective performance from Marlon Brando as the young wife-murderer" said Ward Morehouse in the *Sun*. And Vernon Rice in the New York *Post* said, "But long after they and the play are forgotten we shall remember . . . the poignant playing of Ann Shepherd and Marlon Brando as the ill-fated husband and wife."

There was little wonder that young Mr. Brando was beginning to show his egocentricity.

"Marlon was the first one of us that got a job," Maureen Stapleton says. "He was our 'celebrity' because he was working! My apartment was on West Fifty-second Street over Leon &

Eddie's. Marlon's was downstairs. My place was convenient. Nobody ever went home. Marlon was something to see in those days. The other boys got his rejects."

Although it's been said that Brando learned his mumbling, grunting, and scratching from the famous Actors Studio, Brando has remarked, possibly in jest, "Bullshit, I taught the Actors Studio how to mumble, grunt, belch, and scratch your ass."

He was already working effectively under Elia Kazan's direction in *A Streetcar Named Desire* in 1947 when Kazan, Cheryl Crawford and Robert Lewis launched the Actors Studio. Nobody can say he came up through the ranks of the Method studio because he was already established before it was.

Marlon concocted a new supply of eccentricities for himself to go along with his outrageous success in *Streetcar*. His first fan, Robert Garland of the *Journal-American*, said he was "our theater's most memorable young actor at his most memorable." The New York *Post*'s Richard Watts, Jr., said, "I have hitherto not shared the enthusiasm of most reviewers for Marlon Brando but his portrayal of the heroine's sullen, violent nemesis is an excellent piece of work."

Brando was roaring around town on his motorcycle, getting barred from restaurants because he wasn't better dressed, and scribbling messages when he gave autographs which were merely scribblings. He thought it was a joke on the autograph fans to leave them scribblings to try to decipher, when that's all they were: scribblings. (The artist William Steinberg does this too.)

He and Wally Cox shared a pet raccoon. Brando also engaged in some boxing for amusement—and suffered a smash on the nose that broke it.

"He was so good-looking I thought he might be ruined," Maureen Stapleton remembers.

The reset nose wasn't as pretty as the original. There was a lot of worry about the effect on his career. But eventually the experts on such matters decided that the new nose was an improvement. It wasn't as beautiful, but it gave him increased sexuality. It gave him a hardness and brutality that he hadn't had before.

"I should have had somebody break it before," he has said.

He was suddenly making more than $500 a week and getting invited to restaurants like 21 up Fifty-second Street from his strange apartment. The 21 Club set would mostly have thought of him as an undesirable neighbor because the visitors that he entertained were often nothing more than oddities. Marlon remained hospitable to them, though, even though he didn't always know just who they were.

"Marlon's a prince—there's nobody like him when you're in trouble," Maureen Stapleton says. "He shows up when you need him. As long as you're OK and don't need him, you may not hear from him. But when you do. . . ."

From *Streetcar* on, Brando probably never had any real financial worries such as other actors had. That is, he could always live well, because the publicity and the excellent reviews had made him a marketable product. They wanted him for this or that show—the motorcycle, the grunting and scratching, the sex appeal were all worth money. When he began going to Hollywood, he frankly said that it was just because he was so weak in conscience that he didn't have the honesty to say no to that money they offered him.

Brando the Lover has been a man of mystery, rejecting stylish, sophisticated ladies known for their intellect or talent for young women who seemingly appealed largely to his libido. With a few exceptions, he has not been interested in great beauties, having said, as other men have, that they are mostly too shallow and interested in themselves. (They wouldn't give him a chance to talk about him!)

I used to see him with Joan Collins whom I considered one of the great beauties of modern times. When they went out in public together, the photographers never knew which one would steal the picture. Both would be trying . . . and Brando was better at mugging than Joan—he was older and more experienced. Marlon never got interested in "a typical American girl" and surely never in a girl next door.

When Shelley Winters was considered a sexpot, she was one of his dates, and they had laughs. But his taste ran to France Nuyen, Pier Angeli, and Rita Moreno, in various stages of seriousness on the part of the young women. Then there was Katy Jurado, Francesca Scaffa, Susan Cabot, nearly all of whom had been properly warned not to take him seriously.

These exotic types seemed to be part of a pattern he had of educating himself. He was going to learn some French from France Nuyen, some Italian from Pier Angeli, and some Spanish from Rita Moreno—and some passion and some femininity from each.

"I'm not tying myself down," he warned them.

Like most men who brag they'll never be tied down, Brando was in danger of having it happen to him. Anna Kashfi hadn't surfaced yet.

First, he discovered himself engaged to Josanne Mariana Berenger, a French actress and model under twenty whom he'd met in New York at a party. Although the engagement announcement by the girl's parents shocked Marlon's friends who hadn't considered their dating a serious romance, Marlon confirmed their plans and declared, in the winter of 1954, that they would be married very soon.

They weren't.

They never were.

Marlon blabbered a couple of times about wanting to have a home and children. But those who knew of the ease with which he made conquests didn't believe him. Ostensibly he was still engaged to Josanne Berenger in the fall of 1957 when he suddenly and with little warning married Anna Kashfi, who he said was an Indian actress. Anna said the same.

Marlon was being exotic again, but apparently he wasn't as exotic as he thought, because from Wales came a disillusioning statement by a factory worker, Pat O'Callaghan, saying that Anna had lied when she listed her parents as being Devi Kashfi and Selma Ghose of India.

"She's *my* daughter," declared Pat O'Callaghan testily. "Her name's Joan, and she was born in India when I was supervisor on the Indian State Railway, and she has no Indian blood."

Anna, he said, had passed herself off as Indian to get a break in Hollywood and had evidently used the same ruse to capture Brando, who had been so taken in that he'd been going around in Indian garments. Anna was already expecting a baby when they got married. The dispatches from Wales and the goddamned inquisitive reporters got the marriage off to a rocky start, which got rockier and rockier as the years went on.

Considering his great movie image as a tamer of women, Marlon was a horrible disappointment to those who knew the truth. Anna confessed that she hadn't loved him; but she'd been pregnant, and marriage had seemed the proper course. She contended that he had no loyalty to her and that he copulated with another girl in their own bed—and that she caught them. Her favorite term of endearment for him at one phase of their honeymoon period was "you son of a bitch."

Their son, Christian Devi, just a few months old, became the prize in a legal tug-of-war that continued for more than fifteen years. Suing him for divorce, Anna got half a million and custody of the son. Almost every year since, Marlon has been charging she's an incompetent mother and she has been charging that he's an irresponsible father. It was all stirred up again after Marlon's picture *Last Tango in Paris*, when Anna declared through her attorneys that some of those sexual acts including sodomy and other love manifestations were unacceptable in today's world and that Marlon therefore should surrender custody to her.

Anyway, Marlon found out one day that he was married to Movita, an electrifying Mexican actress, and that he had a son, Miko.

Marlon had romanced Movita while making *Viva Zapata* in 1952, and eight years later they legalized it. Anna Kashfi didn't learn about it until Marlon thought to tell her the next year, and then she wanted to kill him.

"Marlon just thought he was being gallant by telling her about his second marriage," a friend explained. "What burned hell out of Anna was Marlon's suggestion that his two boys get acquainted and play together."

Somewhere in this busy schedule of working and loving, Brando found time for the beautiful Puerto Rican Rita Moreno, who would eventually get recognition for *West Side Story*. She was as beautiful in her way as Joan Collins was in hers, and it was not surprising when she got an Academy Award as Best Supporting Actress. Nor was it surprising, I suppose, that she took an overdose of sleeping pills while she was in love with Brando and that the press assumed it to be an effort to commit suicide. Brando tried to console and comfort; his conduct was correct.

"He still likes Rita," a friend of both remarked to me recently.

It was now getting so that you couldn't tell the wives and girlfriends without a score card. While he was making *Mutiny on the Bounty*, he began an affair with a Tahitian waitress, Tarita Teriipaia, who was to become known to the world simply as Tarita. He gave her the role of his leading woman, Maimita, after he'd auditioned many native girls for the part. That may have been one of the reasons for Marlon's love for Tahiti. Marlon took it upon himself eventually to let it be known that he and Tarita had a son, Tehotu, by this time two years old.

Anna Kashfi didn't like it when that became public.

Nor did his Mexican wife, Movita, who was in his home in Beverly Hills, not divorced from him.

It seemed that in Tahiti, the arrangement that Marlon had with Tarita didn't require marriage; therefore, Marlon wasn't in any rush to separate legally from Movita, although eventually that was done, with Movita growing extremely upset when the lawmen came to oust her from her home, even her very bedroom, where she was defying them.

Brando's private life today is more messed up than it has ever been. Besides his three sons, one by Tarita, he has a daughter by Tarita, also named Tarita. The Tahitians give him all the privacy he demands and protect him from intruders. The Anna Kashfi problem is never going to be settled as long as they are both living, but Brando has generally protected the son Christian from the public spotlight.

While Brando and Tarita apparently have never married, the liaison seems to work better than many marriages. Brando flies back to Tahiti after sporadic visits to Hollywood and is never seen out cheating with any of the many women who would still find him exciting.

He has lost some of his looks.

At least Maria Schneider, his partner in *Last Tango*, thought so. Exploding the idea that they had indulged in hard-core sex in the film, she said he was a bit paunchy and too old for her, besides.

When I interviewed her, she kept sneering at me, "I didn't come here to talk about Marlon Brando." She wanted to talk about her! That couldn't be love.

"He's almost fifty years old!" she exclaimed. "He was very fatherly to me."

In the first filming of the sodomy scene, Marlon had removed his trousers. Subsequently he performed with his pants on. He felt it looked more respectable that way—if that could be respectable —and also sexier, which will always be a question in the minds of some experts.

A surprising revelation was that there was considerable film showing Brando frontally nude which was never used and was presumably saved for the hungry Hollywood archives.

The anus has evidently always appealed to Brando. In his youth around Fifty-second Street, he got into something that he considered funny: baring one's behind to shock people. He may have picked this up from his realization that dropping one's pants was considered very funny in burlesque. The Brando disciples picked up his "mooning" game which was simply showing one's bare derriere to people at unexpected moments. To flash it, for example, from the window of a passing automobile, while going past a crowd. Brando got some of the cast of *Godfather* participating in the game. They were capable followers, they learned well and rapidly, but they said that Brando was the champion at showing his bare ass.

Mumblin' Marlon's tour de force in public relations was not in his dispatching of an Indian maiden to reject an Oscar for *The Godfather*, but his prodigious fist swinging at the mouth of free-lance photograper Ron Galella, breaking the top of his jawbone. This provided some of the best, if cruelest, laughs of the summer of 1973. Because one day later, Marlon was discovered in a New York hospital with an infected right hand, suffered when the hand came into contact with the photographer's mouth.

"Serves Brando right!" a few thousand people said.

Being human, they laughed at his getting paid back.

Some of my contemporaries, even among the press, thought Brando was justified, though most thought he had suffered temporary dementia. Galella, the undiscourageable pursuer of celebrities, had so enraged Jacqueline Onassis that she got a court order keeping him fifty yards distant.

"Galella should get an injunction making Brando stay fifty yards from him," commented one Broadway fellow, noting that Galella had been staggered by the wallop, gone to surgery for two hours, and been sewn up with nine stitches.

"Brando should either be arrested," thought another, "or be given another Oscar."

The great punching occurred in Chinatown, and photographers were warned to beware of Brando, because in Chinatown, an hour after you've slugged one photographer, you want to slug another one.

One-punch Brando's very sad night was brought on by himself. He had indicated that he would like to go on Dick Cavett's ABC talk show, possibly to talk about his refusing the Oscar and to speak his piece about inhumanity to the Indians. He was *not* badgered or cajoled into it by publicists; in fact, the publicists had been woefully unable to communicate with him. Even when he arrived at the ABC Theater on West Fifty-eighth Street in New York, having been helicoptered from La Guardia after flying from Los Angeles, he was playing it coy. He would see no reporters; he would pose for no pictures. The press would have to keep its distance.

Tall, forty-two-year-old, freewheeling, and frequently pestiferous Ron Galella greeted Brando—already running late—at the heliport. He took a few shots. Brando was trying to get into his limousine. He was wearing dark glasses. The glasses annoyed Galella. They spoiled his pictures. He asked Brando if he would take off his glasses. Brando didn't say, "Go to hell," or anything. He didn't answer.

Brando's limousine shot off to the theater. One can imagine Brando hoping he had seen the last of that photographer. Little did he know. . . .

Sitting in the theater watching the program (after Brando had been rushed in by a flying wedge of pages), I was struck by Brando's increasing baldness—and his very soft voice. He was in good humor and able to laugh and appear human.

Cavett asked him if he had it to do over, would he reject the Oscar in the same way?

"Well—uh—I don't think so," he answered. Unaccustomed as he was to public speaking on talk shows, he wasn't a very good guest. He took too long to answer, and his voice at times was monotonous. Nevertheless, this *was* Brando, and even when dull, he was a spectacle to be observed carefully. Because you probably would never see him on TV again.

Cavett had several biographies of Brando in front of him.

"Have you cracked these? How do they get away with it?" Cavett asked.

"People sell items," Brando said, with his usual disdain for journalism. "There are items worth one hundred dollars, items worth one hundred thousand dollars, and there are items worth two dollars. I find that people don't believe all the nonsense they read."

But Brando said he knew the need of a TV interviewer to be sparkling. He mentioned that "I threw manure out of a window" and "They want to see me describe how I threw the manure," and "If you don't ask me whether I threw the horse manure, a lot of guys in shirt sleeves drinking beer are going to turn you off."

Having shown he knew this, Brando proceeded to perform as though he didn't know it. He wanted to talk only about the Indians.

With all the television audience waiting to hear him defend *Last Tango in Paris* for its sexuality, Brando said, "I haven't seen the movie, and I don't know what I could say about it."

That firm statement cut off what could have been a brilliant half hour and left Cavett struggling. Cavett tried cleverly to trap Brando into doing a commercial.

They were complimenting each other (Brando obviously with great sincerity). Brando said he admired Cavett's ability to handle commercials. "I don't think I could play the role you play now," Brando said.

"Let's see if you can do it," said Cavett, holding up a product and a speech for Brando to read. "As they say in commercialdom, 'Have fun with it.' "

"No, I won't do it!" Brando snapped firmly, sitting up straight.

Cavett, who'd probably never expected him to do it, exclaimed to the audience, "The man's incorruptible," and said to Brando, "I'm glad you didn't."

Cavett made one more but futile effort to get Brando back to show business.

"Did you like the way *The Godfather* came out?" he asked him.

"I don't want to talk about movies," Brando answered. "We have so little time to talk about the Indians and so much to say. But then I'm your guest, and I don't want to horn into your program. . . ."

But hadn't acting been good to him?

"It's been a good living," Brando admitted. "But if you were in the lumber business, and you went on the Dick Cavett show, and somebody said, 'How do you like the lumber business?' " The sentence dragged off. Cavett gave up and brought on the Indians who had been waiting to tell their story.

There followed one of the most boring chunks of television I've seen, with one of the Indians absolutely incomprehensible to me—for several minutes at a stretch.

Just as a viewer, I felt cheated by Brando for not saying fascinating things that he could have. Irritated by the Indian talks which seemed confusing, with the Indians unable to agree with Brando on who their friends are, I wrote longhand in my notebook: "One of the dullest 1½ hours on TV. Dick Cavett found what reporters have always known. Brando is a dull, stubborn fellow not half as interesting as the press has shown him to be."

Columnist Rex Reed said the next day, "The most infuriating, embarrassing and utterly worthless 90 minutes I have ever seen."

Cavett and Brando lingered around onstage and then went to Cavett's dressing room after the program. They'd now become close pals, evidently. Remembering Brando wouldn't see any reporters, I skipped away to another appointment.

Deciding about an hour later that I had erred journalistically in neglecting to ascertain Mr. Brando's plans for the evening, I casually phoned Dick Cavett's apartment to seek information from Dick.

A voice full of exasperation answered. It belonged to Mrs. Cavett, the actress known professionally as Carrie Nye.

"I don't know where Dick is," she confessed wearily. "I've had about thirty calls. His supper's waiting for him. I suppose he's gone somewhere with Brando." She said all this in a manner that I considered quite restrained for a wife who'd not even had a call from her mate a couple of hours after his colossal interview.

Anxious to locate Brando by now, I phoned and visited some restaurants without getting a clue, then again phoned the Cavett apartment.

"We don't know where he is," a man said. "His supper's still waiting for him."

I began to envisage an iceberg developing in the Cavett ménage. The taped Cavett program was to go on the air at eleven thirty. Surely Cavett would be home with his wife to watch the program. At eleven twenty-five, I phoned once more, confident that Cavett would be sitting there in his slippers ready to watch himself. Mrs. Cavett answered.

"Dick's still not home and hasn't called." Her voice tapped its foot. Her manner was getting crisper than a Krispie. She had no clues to where Dick and the Tahitian tangoer might have tangoed.

"They're probably out for a quiet beer," she said. "I've got more serious things to think about than where Dick Cavett and Marlon Brando are." (She had an early rehearsal next day.) "I'm going to bed.

"And turning the phone off!" she added.

Apologizing to the patient and harassed lady for bothering her, I hung up and resumed my telephonic *cherchez Marlon.* A couple of hours later, around 1:30 A.M., came a call from a friend—and this was just a rumor—that Robert Mitchum had slugged Ron Galella.

I began trying to find Galella and discovered him at Huntington Hartford's *Show* magazine club on East Fifty-second Street. Yes, he had been punched.

"Not Mitchum! *Brando!*" And he poured out the story, after explaining that the novocaine in his mouth was beginning to wear off and he was suffering.

"After the program," Galella said, "Brando and Cavett got in a car and went to Chinatown. I followed them with another fellow, an amateur photographer.

"They got out of their car and walked a couple of blocks asking people the way to a certain Chinese restaurant. Brando already had dark glasses on, and Cavett put dark glasses on.

"At first Brando was nice and friendly. I walked ahead of them taking their pictures. I took about six shots as they walked toward me.

"Finally Brando said to me, 'Why are you continuing to take the same picture?'

"I said, 'Editors like a little variety. For variety, I'd like both of you to take your glasses off.' "

Brando, whose lack of interest in what editors want is notorious, seemingly was more than irked by this request.

"*No, I won't!*" Brando said, according to Galella.

"It was dark, and I couldn't see very well, but he whipped his right arm at me and hit me square in the center of the mouth. He was coming at me, and he said, 'You want more? You want more?' I was gushing blood, and I didn't look back.

"I rushed to Bellevue Hospital, and I was in surgery for two hours. He broke the top part of my jawbone. They gave me six stitches inside and three outside—nine stitches—and a brace in my mouth to hold my jawbone together. And novocaine."

"Before he hit you," I asked Galella, "wasn't there any further discussion, any argument, any quarreling?"

"That was the unfair part of it—there was nothing, not another word spoken," Galella insisted. "I started taking pictures, and he didn't object. Sinatra'll say, 'No pictures,' or, 'Get lost.' This guy said nothing. That was the bad thing—lack of communication."

Galella, who's six one, about a head taller than Brando, said, "It's like you're talking to a guy and all of a sudden you get bashed in the face. *Boom*—I'm staggering in the street. Had he not had his glasses on, I could have seen an indication of anger and that he was pissed off and wanted me to get lost. He did it impulsively. He probably thought I had enough pictures."

Actually, he didn't have so many—he took thirteen with his motor-driven Nikon at the heliport and half a dozen with flash in Chinatown on Bayard Street.

Curiously, Galella picked up a witness to the punching by helping out a Brando fan. When the program was finished and Galella was determining to follow Brando, he ran to his car, hoping to pursue the limousine carrying Brando and Cavett.

"A lot of fans got on my car and in it. I let one of them stay . . . an amateur photographer. Well, he was with me and saw it all happen. He can swear that there was absolutely no hostility shown by words or gestures."

After Galella had been sewn up at the hospital—two teeth had been driven through his lower lip—he decided he wanted to have a photographic record of the damage that had been done to him. He proceeded to the Hartford *Show* club where a girl took pictures of his broken jawbone and the brace in his mouth and the swollen nose.

It was there that Galella delivered the classic line "I can't understand Brando. He talks about how people mistreat the Indians. Look how he mistreats the photographers!"

The Brando-Galella collision might never have become public property but for the erroneous tip to me about Galella having been slugged by Bob Mitchum.

"I didn't want any publicity on it, and I wasn't going to report it," Galella explained. "Things get twisted and I get the blame. Then *you* found out about it. . . ."

Galella then said a touching thing that sort of explained his tenacity which Brando found too much to take. I asked Galella, whom I'd seen at every news event but never with a girl, whether he was married.

"No, I'm a bachelor," he said. "I'm married to my career. What a career, huh?"

The flash that Brando was in the Hospital for Special Surgery with an acute infection of the right hand, coming the next night, evoked laughter in about the same way that we laugh at the man who slips on a banana peel. I never heard one person say "Poor Marlon." I believe everybody laughed a little at the idea of the Mighty Mumbler having been brought down.

Brando's stay in the hospital confirmed that he had belted Galella smartly. He was getting antiobiotics intravenously, his temperature was normal, and he wasn't seeing anybody or talking to anybody, so the hospital said. He was, however, seeing Dick Cavett, who wasn't talking despite his great reputation as a talker.

"I was there," Cavett said on one of the succeeding shows. "Brando was on one side of me, Galella was on the other side of me—and I saw nothing."

He was right, of course. Anything he'd have said would have been wrong. Brando was his new pal. He couldn't go against him. Galella would raise the issue of a free press. Dick Cavett was a pal of the free press, too. He couldn't go against the free press. If he did, the editorialists would blast him. He had better keep his mouth shut, which was a hard thing to do, not only for Cavett, but for any TV talker.

And while Brando languished in bed in the hospital, who do you think was watching and waiting for him to try to leave?

Not Ron Galella and his motor-driven Nikon. No, he wasn't able. But a photographer friend of Galella was lurking near.

"Want to get a picture of him with his hand bandaged," Galella explained. He didn't, though. This time Brando got away. A lawsuit, for the broken jaw, was awaiting the great friend of the Indians and would be another chapter in the Brando story.

The Incredible Gabors

🖋 ONCE, in a pique at Zsa Zsa Gabor, I referred to her as "the unbelievable Zsa Zsa," and explained, "She's unbelievable—you can't believe a damn thing she says."

As the years went on, I concluded that although she has playfully told certain untruths, they were usually fascinating fibs and may have made life more interesting. Anyway, she seems to have been on a truth kick lately. Successful in business, still keeping her beauty and on her good behavior generally, she is one of the ornaments of our nutty world. I've also decided that Zsa Zsa doesn't always know what she's saying.

In Paris at a small gathering once, she excitedly told her listeners, "Dollings, So-and-So is the only man I vill ever love, but he is qveer for little boys." We didn't believe she meant it and thought she was probably having a little quarrel with him at the moment.

When Zsa Zsa was having a wild, mad, front-page romance with the late Porfirio Rubirosa, I took my wife and son to visit Rubi at his home in Paris one Sunday noon at his invitation. He was playing polo that afternoon. His houseguest Zsa Zsa was accompanying him. We must come along. But first he opened a bottle of champagne. We had time for one glass. He showed me his exercise room. Then we were off to the polo. I took some pictures of him receiving a cup as a trophy. That was the extent of our visit with Rubi and Zsa Zsa.

A few weeks later, a friend told me, "Zsa Zsa is saying the most horrible things about you. She says you and your wife and son were stranded in Paris, and she and Rubirosa had to put you up at his house."

"Oh, she couldn't have said such a thing," I said. "Somebody must have misunderstood her due to her Hungarian accent."

Nevertheless, the story kept coming back to me. I still didn't believe she'd said it. I didn't see her until the night of July 4, 1958, when the late Prince Mike Romanoff gave himself a Hollywood party at his own restaurant celebrating his becoming a citizen.

The guests were heavily imbibing, moving around the restaurant, mingling. Along came Zsa Zsa, arm in arm with the prominent Hollywood publicist Warren Cowan, a longtime friend of mine.

Warren gave me a handshake and said to Zsa Zsa, "You know Earl Wilson, don't you?"

"Of course, dolling!" she bubbled. "He and his vife and little boy stay vith Rubi and me at Rubi's house in Paris."

"What was that?" I said. "I've been hearing that you've been spreading that story and didn't believe it. Now I've heard you say it with my own ears. Why did you tell a lie like that?"

Zsa Zsa shrugged.

Warren also shrugged, as though it was a mystery that one should not try to solve on such a festive night as this.

"It's a terrible lie for you to tell!" I repeated to Zsa Zsa.

"Vell, anyvay, dolling," she said, "I rather do for a living vot I do than vot you do."

She had topped me, and that's when I said she was unbelievable.

Zsa Zsa has her own peculiar social standards. For a while she was having a romance with a Las Vegas headwaiter, a sexy fellow who'd been intimate with several Hollywood beauties. He wanted to escort her around town. She was horror-struck. "I don't mind sleeping vith him, dolling, but he vants to be *seen* vith me! Imagine, a headvaiter!" Zsa Zsa said.

Hank Greenspun, the Las Vegas publisher, happened to see her having breakfast, or late supper, and his paper subsequently printed that she and Joey Adams were "dunking doughnuts at 3 A.M." Zsa Zsa was indignant and declared she would sue Greenspun for $1,000,000. Joey couldn't understand her anger. What was wrong with the item? "You're always talking about your sex life in the papers!" Joey said.

"Dolling," she said, "that is romantic. This dunking is vulgar, a lady vouldn't do that!"

One of her own stories is that she saw George Sanders on the screen and determined at that moment she was going to divorce Conrad Hilton and marry Sanders. They had a wild and tempestuous marriage. Then Porfirio Rubirosa came into her life. It's a part of the show business mythology that once when she and Rubirosa were making love, Sanders walked into the room without announcing himself. It was Christmas, and he thought it was open house.

"Oh, pardon me!" said Sanders, with a cough.

Unperturbed, Zsa Zsa exclaimed, "Dolling, I'm so glad to see you. I have a present for you. Look under the tree."

The question of the ages of the Gabors fascinates people, and yet it's usually Zsa Zsa's age that is discussed most, with much less interest in the oldest, Magda, and the youngest, Eva. Once when I asked Zsa Zsa, "Which of you Gabors is the oldest?" Zsa Zsa answered, "She would never admit it, but it's Mama." At the Adolph Zukor hundredth birthday dinner at the Beverly Hilton Hotel on January 7, 1973, I asked the VIP's if they wanted to live to be a hundred. Zsa Zsa said, "If I vas a hundred, I would only admit to ninety."

Mama, surely close to eighty, is the director, the boss, the driving force of the family. She gives remarkable parties in her New York apartment, which is notable for a chandelier in the kitchen and for Mama's youthful-looking husband, Edmund De Szighithy, pronounced Ziggety as in Hot Ziggety.

In her own mind, Mama is just as glamorous as her daughters, whom she regards as the beauties of the world. At one party, Mama took me aside and said, "You could ron my picture vunce in a vile, too." And she presented me with an 8 x 10 glossy print such as the young models send me.

Ladies who are inclined to aggressiveness in pushing themselves and their families say that Jolie is the champion in that field and maintain that she's "cute" about it. They don't criticize her for giving parties where she promotes the sale of her costume jewelry or endeavors to get more patients for her favorite face-lifter.

"We forgive Jolie for everything," they say.

Upon arriving at a Gabor party, you immediately become conscious of a definite old-world flavor. Mama and her husband greet you warmly in Hungarian accents. "I vant you to meet the gooverdnor of Tschicago," Mama says taking you by the sleeve. It may turn out to be the lieutenant governor of Connecticut, but you may be halted to get kissed by the singer Hildegarde. Mama calls her—and nearly every other woman—"the fourth Gabor sister," and they are all flattered, and Mama knows they are flattered.

Mama has been trying to make this particular party the occasion for introducing daughter Eva's new boyfriend, the millionaire Californian she's going to marry. But something has gone wrong with Eva's plans; she has not come in from California with her intended. That does not reduce the gaiety of the group. Three strolling musicians are playing and singing "You're looking swell, baby." Wealthy Mrs. Laura Johnson of Park Avenue, a Rumanian, is phoning El Morocco about a table reservation in accents not much different from the Gabors'. Jolie swings and swirls around the party, leaning over her guests, getting them drinks, urging them to eat.

"I am szure your Beautiful Vife won't eat nuzzing, I am szure of it," Jolie says. My Beautifil Vife is also "the fourth Gabor sister" and is on a diet.

In the kitchen under the chandelier a woman is preparing food while watching a program on a portable TV set.

"I hear Eva's vadding is off," somebody says to Mama.

"Oh, no, eez ze great lovv of Eva's life!" cries Jolie. (It always is.) "You have food, no? Ze line is over zere!" She steers you to the buffet table. "Have wanna zeese meatballs, dolling?"

"Are they Italian . . . Chinese?"

"No, dolling. 'Awngarian!"

By now the strolling musicians are singing "You're looking swell, JOLIE!" and Jolie is confessing to me that this party, planned to announce Eva's engagement, is also a party without any of her daughters being present. She is the Queen Gabor, and the daughters aren't particularly missed.

Zsa Zsa is in California getting rich, and Eva is in California with her rich beau. Zsa Zsa tells Jolie, says Jolie, "Please get me a husband, I don't like to be alone." Having given up, or been given up by, the movies several years ago, Zsa Zsa has done enormously well in commercial fields and has kept her love life a secret. Jolie, to keep the party swinging, is now singing "Never on Sunday," which she almost always sings at her parties, and is encouraging others to sing, but she is doing all this between urging them to have some of the spaghetti and 'Awngarian meatballs. People are still arriving. "Cahm een, dear," she says, pulling them forward, "bot vy you so late? Cahm, I vant you to meet the gouverndor of Tschicago!"

Music is in the air, and the Brazilian singer Rosina Pagan, formerly of Broadway and Hollywood, now the wife of a rich Canadian, Bert Nesbitt, begins belting out some favorite songs which are saluted with "Olé!" One song, aimed at the white-haired gentlemen present, contains the lyric "When there's snow on the roof, there's fire in the chimney."

Six nights before this party, Mama has tipped me off to the prospective marriage of daughter Eva to a very rich man and has not discouraged me from printing it, which I take to mean that she's happy to have it bruited about. I'm not suggesting that Mama was planting ideas in the gentleman's head; I'm just saying she didn't protest when it came out in print.

It is Larry Doyle, "a big shott on Vall Street and a sveet man," who makes the announcement. "All stand up, please, and raise your glasses. I would like to make a little announcement. . . ." He says Eva is engaged to Frank Jamieson, vice-president of North American Rockwell. The musicians strike up "Here Comes the Bride," somewhat prematurely, inasmuch as the engagement never did get announced. "None of the three daughters are here tonight, we're doing all this for Mama," says Larry Doyle. Mama finally says as she sinks down in a chair, "I need a little rast." She has gotten another daughter married off—well, engaged off, anyway—and if it didn't take, it's hardly her fault. Eva is a comparative virgin, having been married only twice. "How often has Zsa Zsa been married?" Jolie replies almost apologetically, "Only five times."

It's hard to believe now that for the first half dozen years that she was in America, Zsa Zsa was known as "Georgia Gabor" and "Sari Gabor." When I first met her in the 1940's, she was "Sari," she was the wife of Conrad Hilton, she was a bit chubby, she was not as ambitious for a show business career as Eva was, and she had red hair and wore red dresses. She had been Miss Hungary of 1936, and though she'd been known over there as Georgia, the name Sari Gabor was beginning to sink in here.

Not that there was so much news to be written about her; in fact, her first splurge into print after her marriage to Hilton concerned a book she was writing, *Every Man for Herself.* Zsa Zsa has been writing books about that idea ever since.

Sari flitted around frequently to El Morocco, where eventually she got into a fight with the late proprietor John Perona. Subsequently she went into the West Hill Sanatorium, where she received thirty-three treatments. It was messy but in a clean, legal way, as Dr. Manfred Sakel, a psychiatrist, sued Hilton for $5,150 in fees for treating her. Hilton, no longer married to her—he was twenty-five years older than the bouncy Hungarian—replied through attorneys that she was getting enough alimony to pay for her psychiatric treatments herself. Sari shuddered and acted out recollections of terror and fear when I saw her around 21, El Borracho, and other places and she discussed these treatments. "Connie had me drugged for six months vile I suffered hallucinations and nightmares," Sari Gabor told me.

This was part of her divorce battle with Hilton; she herself admitted that she'd had a nervous breakdown—from worrying, she said, about her parents who had been in Budapest while the Nazis invaded Germany.

Sari was a pretty picture when she described her alleged "imprisonment" for the psychiatric care. Remember that now she was in her thirties, there was a little more bounce to a few more ounces, and she was seemingly from a world of make-believe anyway. Sari was always smoking cigarettes; she had diamond bracelets on her wrists and diamond rings on her fingers. She wore sequins frequently, and they played a musical accompaniment to her excited chatter.

"I vas very seldom avake for six months," she said. "They put an injection in me vith a needle and gave me eighteen sleeping pills a day. There vas such a noise outside my room in the morning vith other patients, I guess, I thought somebody in my family vas being murdered. I felt like I vas in a concentration camp right in the heart of Hollywood. Ven they let me vake up, and I vas conscious, I vas in a room alone, vith a sveater, a skirt, and a hat, and I only veighed eighty pounds."

Sari was still battling her way up through the gossip columns and the front pages to be Zsa Zsa, but she hadn't made it yet. Sari was as careless with accusations as Zsa Zsa got to be, and she has great talent for embroidering an incident to glamorize herself. She showed up with a patch on her nose in 1945 and told me and other reporters that she'd been hit with a poker by a "jealous vife" in "Vashington" and that her nose had been broken.

Then, she said, she went to El Morocco "vith my broken nose," showed a clipping about the "jealous vife," and got into an argument, bringing about her ouster from the club—forever.

El Morocco said the "broken nose" had nothing to do with it. She'd got into an argument there with proprietor John Perona and had thrown champagne into the face of a woman who sided with him. And it was true: She was henceforth not welcome.

But "the broken nose" caused by "a jealous vife vith a poker" . . . vell. . . .

A plastic surgeon, Dr. I. Daniel Shorell, emerged to say that he'd put the patch there after performing a ninety-minute operation that straightened a bump on her nose. The "jealous vife" and the "poker" had been Sari's way of fictionalizing her own life, making it more interesting by rewriting it. Sari has done this throughout her life in the United States. Perhaps she should have been a novelist instead of a glamor girl.

(When Sari got to be Zsa Zsa, the new circle of women she met always wondered whether she'd had her nose fixed. It has taken an old researcher and rememberer like me to tell them with certainty that Dr. Shorell said she did.)

"Sari Gabor Hilton" was mastering the uses of publicity as few women ever have. When she was a middle-aged lady, in 1970, known as Zsa Zsa Gabor and starring on Broadway in *Forty Carats*, she had a front-page jewel robbery. Dropping in on her backstage at the Morosco Theater on West Forty-fifth Street and hearing her jokes about the robbery, I had a strange feeling of *déjà vu*, I've been here and seen this before. I checked back through the mists of memory. Her 1970 robbery at the Waldorf Towers was a very nice robbery as jewel robberies go, but back in 1947, she'd had one with bigger headlines when she was still Sari.

The newspapers made much of it when she was Sari.

RAFFLES WAS JITTERY
IN HOLDUP, SAYS SARI—New York *Daily News*

BANDIT GETS $600,000 GEMS
IN RAID ON PENTHOUSE HOME
MRS. SARI HILTON, HOTEL CHAIN OWNER'S WIFE,
REVEALS HIDING PLACE OF JEWEL BOX AFTER
INTRUDER THREATENS TO SHOOT BABY—Page 1, New York
Times

It had all the dramatics, even in the *Times*. Mrs. Sari Gabor Hilton "surrendered at pistol point yesterday morning a king's ransom in jewels to a lone bandit who forced his way into her nine-room penthouse at 8 East 83d St."

"It's the biggest jewelry robbery by one man I ever heard of," a high police official said of the Hilton theft, the *Times* continued.

Sari, then in her late twenties or early thirties if it's true that she was "Miss Hungary of 1936," word-painted for the police and the press an intriguing recollection of the bandit. Trust her to be thinking about his sex appeal and other masculine charms. He was well dressed, he was nervous, he trembled and shook and gasped from excitement, but he was also very brutal. However, he didn't try to rape her; he was there on business. (She wondered a little about his not trying to attack her.)

"Mrs. Hilton" was in bed at about 10:30 A.M. when the buzzer sounded. Her six-month-old daughter, Constance Francesca Hilton, was in a crib in the nursery. A maid, Lulu Barth, opened the door to discover a pimply-faced fellow twenty-five to thirty forcing his way claiming he had come to repair the wiring. He didn't take off his snapped-brim brown fedora hat or his dark glasses; but he whipped out a pistol, and when Mrs. Barth let out a shriek, he sent a crashing blow to her jaw and knocked her to the floor.

"I vas terrified ven he come and pulled me from my bed," Sari recounted. (You will note that "I vas terrified" is one of her expressions.) "Ven he dragged me past the nursery, I could see Connie's crib, and it vas empty. I vas afraid he had done something vith my baby. Then I could see the baby on the bed across the room. Mrs. Barth had put her there to change her before the man got there."

Sari endeavored to talk him out of the heist.

As she related it to the smiling police, Sari said to him, standing there in her negligee which he had permitted her to put on, "You are a nice young man. You can make an honest living. Vy are you doing this?"

He cut her off with "Where's the rest of the jewelry?"—having already scooped up from a night table a pear-shaped diamond and a platinum necklace with a 20-karat stone, a diamond and platinum engagement ring set with a 20-karat emerald-cut stone, and a platinum and diamond wedding ring. Sari pleaded with him to allow her to keep the wedding ring, but he brushed her off. "Where's the rest of the stuff?" he demanded.

Then, she said, he dragged her around the floor and threatened to shoot the baby.

Sari hesitated, noticed how he trembled and shook, then she saw him moving the gun as though aiming it at the baby, and she told him, "Move the chair. You vill see a box under it. Under the chair—under the chair!" she repeated in panic.

The bandit found everything in an ordinary tin box which was open and he took everything in it except a religious medal which he may have declined because he was religious—or because it wasn't valuable.

He tied up Sari and Mrs. Barth with some brown twine he'd brought along, then tied them again to a wrought-iron love seat. He happened to notice in tying them up that Sari wore a diamond ring that had escaped his attention, and he took that. He paused to look at a closet of fur coats belonging to Sari but evidently felt that would be too big a burden to carry and left them all.

There was one touch to this robbery that was seemingly original. The bandit had brought a pair of tan pigskin gloves—it was in October—evidently to cover up fingerprints. He dropped one of them on the floor, and Mrs. Barth kicked it under some other furniture. It was about the only clue.

Sari got loose by biting away the twine bonds with her teeth; then she freed Mrs. Barth, and they called police. It was such a big robbery that at least twenty-five detectives were working on the case—which amounted to a detective for each piece of jewelry. One interesting thing about the robbery aside from the crime was brought out: She and Conrad Hilton had entered a divorce in California in 1946. This was not to be final for a year. Within that period, she went back to live with Hilton, and also during this time, daughter Constance (for Connie) Francesca was born. Hilton had a permanent suite at the Hotel Plaza in New York, and during the time when the front pages carried stories about "Sari Gabor Hilton" which referred to "the Hilton penthouse," he was not there. It is relevant that come January, 1970, Zsa Zsa starred in an act at the Las Vegas Flamingo and Conrad Hilton was there sitting with their daughter, then called Francesca, and said by Zsa Zsa to be nineteen years old, although other statisticians figured that if she'd been born in March, 1947, she'd be close to twenty-three.

"Don't be mad vith me," Zsa Zsa said to him across the heads and the tables at the Flamingo opening. "Connie," she said, for she always called him that, "vas so busy building an empire I only saw him ven he was opening a hotel. For a divorce settlement, I got one million two hundred thousand Gideon Bibles."

"And never opened one of them," Hilton retorted good-naturedly.

Barron Hilton, by this time the head of the Hilton empire, laughed, too. After all, he was Zsa Zsa's stepson; she was his stepmother. "I came here to see Mother work," he said. "I'd never seen Mother work before."

Sari shrewdly got rid of the Sari name and acquired the Zsa Zsa label some time during the George Sanders period in the early 1950's. It was an almost unique name for a unique woman. Sanders knew her as Sari in the beginning of their romance. But by that time the press was acknowledging the Zsa Zsa by printing it "Sari (Zsa Zsa) Gabor Hilton." She was being compared to great beauties Lupe Velez, Hedy Lamarr, and Gene Tierney. It was reported that she was born in either 1920 or 1921, or 1922 or 1923, so she was about thirty when the Great Brawl with Sanders began. (Columnist Sidney Skolsky said she was born on February 6, 1923.)

The first explosion came during a Tallulah Bankhead show on radio from Radio City with big-name guests. Zsa Zsa's reputation for loquacity was sufficiently established that Goodman Ace and other writers of the program knew of the value of a skit which called upon George Sanders to say, "We've been married a couple of years and I haven't spoken a word to Zsa Zsa since she said, 'Yes.' "

It was a better line than they knew, for Zsa Zsa walked off the show. Sanders tried to explain that it was all a joke. Her sense of humor went blank. She demanded that he walk off the show with her. He refused. Somebody else read Zsa Zsa's lines.

"When I got home," Sanders said, "Zsa Zsa asked me to pack and move out. I did. I moved into an apartment. I can't do anything with her."

"I'm his vife," Zsa Zsa blazed. "I von't have him talk to me even on the radio like he talks with other vimmin." Of course they got together again—90 or 100 times.

I was on the inside of the flashiest, most glittery chapter of Zsa Zsa's career as a glamor creature and love object. That was when Porfirio Rubirosa, the love machine, was marrying skinny Barbara Hutton, not curvy, well-developed Zsa Zsa, in 1953.

"I tal you Rubi vill come back to me!" Zsa Zsa predicted. "I vill give their marriage not even a year."

Zsa Zsa was right. Rubi and Babs, the Woolworth dime-store heiress, broke up after ten weeks, and Rubi went back to Zsa Zsa. She never married Rubi, and I believe it was because she wasn't sure he had money. She also knew that he could no more be faithful to a mate than Xaviera Hollander. Zsa Zsa and Rubi were both of the belief that you might as well marry somebody rich as somebody poor. Zsa Zsa succeeded in earning money of her own, of course, and George Sanders once told her, "I might remarry you. I find your money a great aphrodisiac."

The suave, pencil-waisted, soft-spoken, dark-complexioned Rubi was the sex catch of the forties and fifties. Girls melted in his arms when he danced body to body with them in El Morocco. His prowess as a lover was well advertised. He was thirty-nine and Doris Duke was thirty-four when they were married in Paris in 1947. He attracted the attention of the world by smoking a cigarette during the ceremony. Doris was heiress to a $30,000,000 fortune from her father's interest in the American Tobacco Company, but to smoke a cigarette while saying one's marriage vows—after all!

Doris and the dashing Latin lived together twenty-three days. When he was next heard of, wooing Barbara Hutton, the rumor spread that he had said he was going to marry America's three richest women one by one.

It was New Year's week, 1953, and all a lot of froth and fun. As Rubirosa confirmed to me that he and Barbara would be getting married at the Hotel Pierre, Zsa Zsa declared in Las Vegas that he had blackened her eye with his fist when she refused to marry him and then said, in spite, that he was going to marry Barbara.

Quite willingly, Zsa Zsa posed holding an ice bag over her shiner. "It vas the first time I vas ever hit by a man," she said, "and it vill be the last. He kept asking me to marry him, and I tried to slam the door on him. He lost his temper and hit me vith his fist. He vent back to New York, and he called me five times asking me could I reconsider and marry him."

I found Rubirosa was staying at the Midston House on East Thirty-eighth Street, phoned him, and we made a date to meet at the bar at midnight.

As I look back now, it's marvelous what a charmer he was. His words of love for "wonderful Barbara, who has brought something new and different into my life," sounded logical and believable, and I'm afraid he made me think he was sincere.

Drinking scotch and munching popcorn at the bar—"my bachelor dinner," he sighed—Rubi said, "I will not be like her other husbands. I will make her happy—at last.

"And as for what Zsa Zsa is foolishly saying about me wanting to marry her. . . .

"Barbara is such an intelligent girl"—she had then been married four times—"she understands human nature so well, she'll know it's all ridiculous. She's one of the most intelligent women anybody ever met. Zsa Zsa," he added, a little sternly, a little impatiently, "is just trying to get publicity out of Barbara and me. I don't think it's very ladylike."

"How does it feel to be able to marry the two richest women?" I asked.

"I don't need anybody's money, I have money of my own," he answered. (One of his envious admirers among the studs said "That's true—Doris Duke gave him a million.")

Zsa Zsa kept giving out statements about Rubi's love for her, and this stirred up the flames among Barbara's friends, relatives, and financial advisers, who tried to talk her out of it. "Barbara's going to fool around and give money a bad name," one of them said. One skeptic said, "Zsa Zsa isn't marrying Rubi because she can't afford him." He had been the Dominican Republic's minister plenipotentiary to Paris (appointed by his former father-in-law Rafael Trujillo), but that title had been taken from him as a slap on the wrist when he was named corespondent in a divorce action brought by golfer Robert Sweeney against the former Joanne Connelly. Now after he married Barbara, he was going to get the title back, and Barbara was going to become a citizen of the little Caribbean republic.

And so it happened. Barbara became Mrs. Rubirosa the day before New Year's Eve. There was a very private wedding reception (only about twenty-five people), and I was the only reporter present. "Mrs. Rubirosa" got to talking to my wife about babies and gushed out a confession: "Oh, I would like to have another baby . . . a child for my wonderful husband . . . it would be such a great thrill . . . but I am probably too old . . . I'm forty-one."

And meanwhile back in Las Vegas:

"Vot the hal, he called me just an hour ago," Zsa Zsa said. "He sends me flowers every hour on the hour. He is mad for me and vill be back ven this is over. He vas bagging me and bagging me to marry him. Somebody says I can't afford him. Maybe he can't afford *me!*"

Zsa Zsa, with her press bulletins, was almost as prominent in the wedding reports as the nervous bride, who kept saying at the reception that she felt as if she'd been hit over the head. She had been in Doctors Hospital for a run-down condition and appeared unsteady on her feet. At the remarkable reception, the guests stood around with drinks in hand, quietly making jokes about Zsa Zsa. Nobody made any about Barbara. The jokes were not any great tribute to Zsa Zsa, but then "vot the hal?" as Zsa Zsa so often says.

The remarkable thing about the reception—to me—was that I was there by invitation—not by crashing.

While I was interviewing Rubi the night before, he said, "You must come up after the wedding and have a drink with us."

He scribbled my phone number on the back of an envelope.

"That's the last I'll ever hear of that," I thought.

But the next day came a call from his aide inviting my wife and me to the reception. Arriving at the hotel, I was met by some security people trying to steer people away by telling them the reception was off. I got on the house phone, and Rubi's aide sang out, "Come right up, we're waiting for you!"

Rushing around the suite was the late James Woolworth Donahue, Barbara's favorite cousin, who grabbed my overcoat and dumped it onto a bed in one of the bedrooms, then rushed to the door. "It's Ma!" he shrieked . . . the celebrated wealthy Mrs. Jesse Woolworth Donahue, whose arrival sort of gave a seal of approval to Rubi. He gave her one of the hand-kissingest hand kissings you ever saw.

As everybody wolfed the canapés and tossed down the champagne, the cheerful bridegroom, Rubi, talked freely about the furor with Zsa Zsa. I'm not sure that this would be approved by modern etiquette specialists, but when Barbara was in another room changing her jewels, Rubi said to me, "Zsa Zsa says I hit her and she got a black eye.

"If I ever hit her, her head would come off," he said, smiling charmingly, but demonstrating with tightly twisted hands just how he would like to do it.

Despite all this brave talk, Rubi would be having his own neck twisted, figuratively, by Zsa Zsa within three months. Sad-eyed Barbara, who had complained that she had grown ugly and hated to look in the mirror, had fallen out of the competition for Rubi even though she was his wife. She bought him a private plane, a converted B-25 bomber, as a wedding present, and he did an ungentlemanly thing. He took off in it. The marriage was over, and he returned to Zsa Zsa.

When I visited Rubi and Zsa Zsa in his beautiful 150-year-old home in Paris in July, 1955, which was eighteen months after his marriage to Barbara, Zsa Zsa said in the same juicy Hungarian accent, "Vot else can I do? Rubi vants to marry me. Vot about my career? I give up four thousand dollars a veek Hollyvood money just to come see him."

Zsa Zsa suddenly remembered she wanted to chastise me about something. She rebuked me sharply for implying that she had an accent.

"Vy the hal you do that?" she demanded.

The great romance of Zsa Zsa and Rubi continued into

1956—its third year—when Rubi, at forty-seven, tumbled for a very busty French teen-age actress, Odile Rodin. She had no fortune, no great name, and his admirers were mystified.

Had the excesses of sex cut him down in his best years? Why was he no longer a playboy scandalizing the world of the rich? Were there too many rings on the trunk of the old tree? The gossips who had so widely advertised Rubi's virility when he was young now declared that he had lost his sexual prowess. This was worse, much worse, than a great baseball pitcher losing his curve. On July 5, 1965, his powerful Ferrari sports car, which he was driving at over 100 miles an hour at 8 A.M., leaped a curb and smashed into a tree in the Bois de Boulogne. The wooden steering wheel on his car crushed his chest, and he died in an ambulance. His wife was alone, wondering what had happened to him, when she got the tragic news. He had spent the night out, as was his custom, and was alone in the car when it sideswiped a parked car on the Avenue de la Reine-Marguerite. It seemed a peculiar accident for one who'd been a skillful race driver.

When Rubi died, black columnist Langston Hughes said in the New York *Post*, "In his youth, Rubirosa was a handsome colored boy," but that "mulatto Latins, in their own Caribbean or South American lands, are not classified as Negro in the U.S.A. sense of the term. . . . Had he been an American citizen by birth, the headlines probably would have read NEGRO PLAYBOY DIES."

Zsa Zsa had him as her lover when he was in his prime and for much longer than Doris Duke and Barbara Hutton. He once said that he regarded that day lost when he did not make love.

Soon after Rubi's onetime father-in-law Generalissimo Rafael Trujillo was assassinated in May, 1961, Rubirosa came to New York. I received a call between 2 and 3 A.M. from a night owl friend that a man resembling Rubirosa was on Broadway near my office (in the Broadway Theater at Fifty-third Street), seemingly waiting for somebody.

I hurried downstairs to the street. And Rubirosa was indeed there standing under the marquee of the theater.

"Whatever are you doing here at this hour, Rubi?" I asked him. The neighborhood was dark and lonely at that hour.

"I'm just waiting for my car," he said nervously. That was surely not an honest answer. I asked him a few questions about his ex-father-in-law's assassination and then, having no excuse to prolong the conversation, turned and returned to my office.

The informant who had phoned me about his being there was watching, however. He reported that a few minutes after I left, Rubirosa strolled away with a streetwalker. Presumably he hadn't made love yet that day.

The Gabors are just incredible ladies. Consider that Zsa Zsa married George Sanders, who later married her sister Magda, and that he parted from Magda and appeared to be about to remarry Zsa Zsa when he died. "Vy George never married Eva?" Jolie said once.

Eva became a TV star in *Green Acres* and had a brief thing with Frank Sinatra after breaking up with her husband Dick Brown. From time to time, the sisters feuded and didn't speak to each other, but Mama got them back. They all found out how to make money, Mama included, because Jolie has homes in Palm Springs, New York, and Connecticut, and Zsa Zsa recently took over Howard Hughes' home in Bel Air, California, next to a house she already owned there. The comedians had Zsa Zsa in mind when they told a joke about an actress being a good housekeeper. "She always keeps the house."

They have lent some laughter, as well as beauty, to our scene. I don't think they've wrecked any homes. Eva sounds just like Zsa Zsa, and they all sound like Jolie. Eva played summer stock in *Applause!* in 1973. After saying, "Hello, sweetheart," to me, she said, "Jolie vill come to see me, Zsa Zsa vill come, but not togadder, darling. Dey're staggering.

"Dey de dancers, dolling, pick you up and sving you through the air right and laft vile you kick your legs . . . dey could drop you!"

She did suffer a spill and had to perform in a cast which probably helped the box-office owing to the publicity, but as far as I could learn, it was legitimate and not a stunt.

It was only a few months after Jolie had endeavored to announce Eva's engagement to Frank Jamieson at the party which Eva and Mr. Jamieson failed to attend. I asked Eva about that enagagement.

"Vot the hal," she said. "People don't get engaged anymore, sweetheart. People don't get married anymore."

"You're right, vot the hal," I had to admit because as I wrote this piece, Magda was splitting from her latest husband Tibor

Heltway, both Zsa Zsa and Eva were single again, and the only Gabor who was married was Mama.

But hold the presses! On Friday, September 21, 1973, about ten months after the announcement party, Eva Gabor and Frank Jameson did get married, in a chapel on the grounds of the Webb School of California. Mama Jolie flew from New York to Beverly Hills for the reception, a resplendent event attended by sisters Zsa Zsa and Magda. Jolie's husband—only her second, mind you!—and I worked out a little score card on the Gabor marriages. Two of Zsa Zsa's husbands, Herbert Hunter and Josh Cosden, were a little vague in our memory. Nevertheless, the three sisters had racked up fifteen marriages, and were running neck and neck, five each, and Mama's two brought the family total to seventeen marriages. If there is any family that can do better, stand up and let me count your husbands!

Woody Allen, Sex Maniac

THERE have been several Allens who became well known in and around show business. Fred Allen's worshipers considered him the greatest humorist in the world in the 1930's, 1940's, and 1950's. Comedian Steve Allen was the first of the TV talkers. Then there have been wild-haired Marty Allen and Nazi-impersonator Bernie Allen. My secretary Julie Allen made her contributions. Once when I boasted of attending Heidelberg, she inquired, "The college or the brewery?" She has also asserted: "Anybody who says life is just a bowl of cherries is bananas."

And bananas bring us to inconspicuous, unshaven, dirty-sneakered, lean, little Woody Allen who had a picture called simply that (*Bananas*) in 1971. There are many devotees who now acclaim Woody Allen as being today's Charlie Chaplin and others who believe he is the first important comic actor and filmmaker to kid sex, as he surely did in *Everything You Always Wanted to Know About Sex (But Were Afraid to Ask)*.

It's only when all his works are pieced together that it's seen that little Woody's discovered to be the sex maniac among the filmmakers, but a latent case.

Bananas was more memorable for the fact that while making it in Puerto Rico, Woody came out strongly against bathing and taking showers. Reveling in getting to be known as No. 1 on the Worst Dressed List, Woody wouldn't get dressed up to do a TV show, and they were happy to get him out of the studio.

"Bathing is snobism," Woody said to me one afternoon when we were sitting around in the Hotel Sheraton in San Juan. It was raining, and Woody couldn't film. "Bathing isn't good for you. It washes off the natural juices that keep you young. Sitting there naked in a bathtub, immersed in water—it makes me nervous. I don't want to be caught nude."

Woody denied that he smelled. "I douse myself with talcum and liberal helpings of spices," he said. "I break down and have a shower about every third day, but I hate it."

You always have a feeling when talking to Woody Allen that he is kidding you and probably also himself, and yet there is a gravity in his delivery that is puzzling. That he is a phenomenon was clear to me during 1972 when Groucho Marx gave a one-man show at Carnegie Hall. Woody Allen, sitting on the aisle, was allowed no peace by the hundreds of autograph hunters and fans. Woody Allen also speaks sagely at times. I discovered in going over some notes that when I talked to Woody in San Juan in June, 1970, I asked him, as part of the nonsensical conversation we'd been having, whether he had any message for me to take back to President Nixon.

"Yes," he said, from under a decrepit hat, "tell him he's in the wrong business!"

Watergate was three years away.

The headpiece he had on and kept on almost matched his dirty sneakers for style. "I bought it in San Francisco two years ago," he said. "I was looking for a hat to be worn by a man in a chain gang—the most brutal hat I could find. This is it."

"What kind of hat do you call it?"

"Ugly hat," he said.

One of the curious parts of the saga of the new Charlie Chaplin is that I helped start him on his way when Woody was fifteen or sixteen. I didn't "discover" him. In fact, when he became known as a nightclub star, at first I didn't remember having helped him.

It was he who brought it up. He was kind enough to say, "You know, you helped me get started by printing my jokes."

Years went by, he grew famous enough to be *Time* magazine's cover boy on July 3, 1972, and I checked it with him again. Had he forgotten my help by now? He hadn't.

It was a most unusual cover for *Time*. There was a strangely eerie owlish picture of Woody, hair frazzled, brow creased, lips turned downward, sitting, his knees up and arms around them, patches on his blue denim seat, his sneakers not overly clean, but OK by today's standards, and his eyes staring straight at you through his horn rims. Inside, under "Show Business & TV," we read: "Woody Allen: Rabbit Running."

And then one of Woody's lines: "I don't believe in an afterlife although I am bringing a change of underwear."

Newsweek was supposed to have had a cover story on Woody the same week but went with Senator George McGovern instead. I remember thinking, "Time will tell which magazine was the more journalistically astute."

On a very hot noontime the following week, I was looking around in Sardi's restaurant, when Jimmy, the maître d', said, "Woody Allen's over there."

"Where?"

"Under the hat."

"He's wearing a hat?" I said.

"Can't you see it? You ought to be able to," Jimmy said.

I couldn't for I'd just come from the glary sunlight. What the hell was Woody Allen wearing a hat for, inside, on a summer day?

I walked toward his table, but he seemed to be lunching with a girl, and I didn't want to interfere. Comedian Jackie Mason was at a nearby table discussing a movie he'd made, *The Stoolie*. He asked me to sit at his table, and Mason proceeded to discuss Woody, and in a prejudiced way, because they were after all in the same business.

"That hat," Jackie Mason said, "keeps Woody from being recognized. He definitely is not interested in attracting attention. So you look at this guy sitting indoors wearing a hat, and right away you notice that he's the guy that doesn't want to attract attention."

"That hat" was a crushed tan felt hat that I thought of as being a safari hat, which was amusing in a way, because Woody was not on any safari—he was on Forty-fourth Street, New York City.

To Jackie Mason it was an attention-grabbing thing, but with Woody I think it was more his zany approach to life. I think Woody already had all the recognition his ego needed. (I must add, that's my opinion only.)

Finishing his lunch, Woody started out with the girl, still wearing his hat. I spoke to him near the door. "May I speak to you a second?" I said. "Certainly," he said cordially.

"First, what kind of hat is that?"

"This hat?" His tone contained the comment that this was quite normal. "Why, it's an Abercrombie & Fitch hat. That's all. Keeps me from being recognized."

Then I asked if he could refresh my memory about me printing some jokes he'd written when he was a boy.

"Sure," he said. "I told *Time* magazine about it for the cover story. I was about sixteen and was going to Midwood High School in Brooklyn. I can't tell you too lucidly, but you did publish me in a fairly consistent manner."

"And you got a job as a gag writer out of it?"

"That's right. I had to write fifty jokes a day."

"Do you remember how much you made?"

"Yeah! Twenty-five dollars a week. You got me all the good jobs!"

Woody and the girl left on that note, and I returned to my office and began going through the files. It had been almost twenty years before that his name and jokes began appearing in my column. I had a fictitious show girl character named Taffy Tuttle who was supposed to make stupid remarks. Various gag writers would submit Taffy Tuttle jokes in which their names or the names of publicity clients would appear. It was not uncommon for young hopefuls to submit contributions to the columnists. Leonard Lyons had sent material to Mark Hellinger and become a columnist himself.

My file yielded up some of the early Woodyisms.

"Taffy Tuttle told Woody Allen she heard of a man who was a six-footer and said, 'Gee, it must take him a long time to put his shoes on.' "

"It's the fallen women who are usually picked up," says Woody Allen.

"Woody Allen boasts that he just made a fortune downtown— he auctioned off his parking space."

Not sensational, but not bad for a sixteen-year-old. I decided I should try to do an interview with Woody about those days when he was starting as a joke writer. I phoned one of Woody's publicists, Richard O'Brien, who was nice, but not sure he could set a time because Woody was very, very, very, *very* busy just now. This attitude irked me considerably, but I reined myself in.

"I'll only need half an hour," I said. "He must eat somewhere. I could do it over lunch."

"He's very, very busy," O'Brien said.

"Listen," I said, and now my feelings were really beginning to get hurt, "he's not all that busy. He was at P. J. Clarke's last night!"

"Let me see what I can do, but I'm going on vacation."

I went off to Puerto Rico to be one of the judges of the Miss Universe contest. When I returned, I asked again about the Woody Allen interview. O'Brien's secretary hadn't been able to set up a time yet. Then O'Brien returned. He wasn't able to nail it down.

I was just about to seethe.

Woody Allen wasn't able to find time to see the great Wilson who had printed his first gags!

"That's the way life works," I said. "You discover them"—by now I had discovered him—"twenty years ago I was too busy to see him, I just printed his jokes . . . now he's too busy to see me. I'm just supposed to go on printing his jokes."

That was a test of my sense of humor, I suppose. Trying to prove that I had some left, I wrote a column saying that I had made this bum a big man and now he wouldn't deign to see me.

But before it got in the paper, O'Brien phoned. The picture editing, the ads were all under control. Woody now had time for the interview.

"At Mike Hutner's office at United Artists, 727 Seventh Avenue, Friday at three o'clock," O'Brien said. "You said only a half hour, right? Because he's got something else he's got to do at three thirty."

I got it—a little nudge that I wasn't to take up too much of the movie mogul's time. I was beginning to develop an acute dislike for Woody Allen, the man whom, I had about decided by now, I had practically put in business, whose success I was undoubtedly responsible for. "That's gratitude for you," I was thinking.

But before Friday, there was another call.

"Could you make it four instead of three? And it's still a half hour? Right?"

I broke an appointment I had at four to make it. This had now become such an enormous enterprise that I walked into Mike Hutner's three minutes ahead of time. Waiting there for me was Richard O'Brien.

"We have an appointment here with Woody Allen," O'Brien said to Mike Hutner.

"Woody Allen!" exclaimed Hutner. "He just left here not three minutes ago!"

"He left? But our appointment was here."

"He didn't mention it," Hutner said.

"Oh, for God's sake," I said. My feelings got hurt all over again. Obviously the dirty-sneakered little creep with the nutty hat had forgotten the important appointment he had with the man who made him what he is today.

"He couldn't have forgotten it," O'Brien said. "We just mentioned it to him an hour ago."

"Oh, the hell with it," I said. "It was a lousy idea to start with."

O'Brien got on the phone calling Woody's manager's office. No, they didn't know where Woody was going. O'Brien groaned, and I groaned. O'Brien suggested that I return to my office, which was just a few blocks away, and that he would find Woody and deliver him to me. I was so disgusted when we got into the elevator that I didn't even want to mention Woody Allen's name again.

"You didn't see Woody Allen, did you?" O'Brien said to the elevator operator.

"He's down in the lobby," the operator said. "He's waiting for somebody."

And as we stepped from the car, there he was with his manager Jack Rollins, waiting for me, for he'd been under the impression we were to meet in the lobby. I'd begun to think of him as tall, fierce, and bullying, a nasty monster, in the weeks I'd been trying to make this appointment. Now, looking at him, I saw a docile, owly-eyed little boy with a strange hat, sneakers, and a soft, gentle voice and manner.

"I was afraid we'd missed each other," he said, putting out his hand. "How are you?"

I proposed that we go to a bar and sit down. Nearby was the Brass Rail, which was far from posh.

"Will they let me in like this?" Woody's concern over his clothes seemed little-boyish and genuine.

"I'll just have a club soda," he said to the attractive waitress, who didn't recognize him. He explained that he hadn't been able to see me earlier because the picture (*Everything You Always Wanted to Know About Sex*) had been edited right up to the opening day and that they'd used "practically a wet print.

"There was the advertising to work on, to make sure the ads were right. It kept me busy. But the picture is breaking records, and there is a big demand for it everywhere."

"Do you think that's due to you or to sex?" I asked him.

He took the question as a serious one. "Most people want to see a real sex comedy," he said, answering it straight.

"I don't think there has been a sex comedy before. One that is really sexual like this one. I guess there is a lot more sex today, and in this picture, there's sex for everybody. There's perversion for the whole family."

"Do you know all about sex?"

"I'm still learning about it."

"Where did you learn what you know?"

"I managed to pick up things about it on the street, and now I've put it on the screen. I know enough to get through the evening."

"What kind of girls do you prefer?"

"Uh . . . yeah . . . well." He seemed to be half-smiling for the first time. "Practically all kinds."

"I heard of a fellow," I said, "who said, 'All kinds, as long as they're breathing.' "

"No, that isn't even necessary in my case. I've had some that didn't breathe, and it didn't bother me."

Sitting there under the hat, which he said was a rain hat—it was a hot day with no hint of rain—he reminded me of the vulnerable little bloke Chaplin used to play, the underdog the cops were always chasing.

"Do you feel you're Chaplinesque?"

"Some people have said that, and I see what they mean. I don't aspire to it. It's not the kind of thing you aspire to. You just do what you do and hope some people will like it. There's more of a Chaplin quality than there is of a Jonathan Winters."

"What would you say is your favorite Woody Allen line?"

"I have no favorite lines. I hate them four minutes—no, three minutes—after I write them. I never like to reread my stuff, and I don't like to see my movies over and over. When you see them again, you want to improve them."

"Was your early gag-writing technique 'switching' jokes as *Time* magazine said?" I asked. *Time* took one of his divorce jokes and attempted to show it was updated Oscar Wilde.

"That was another of *Time*'s conclusions that had no basis in reality," Woody said. "Comedy was always something that interested me. I was always a big fan of comedy. I was the neighborhood wise guy who yelled things out to the movie screen, and I still do, at other people's movies."

"When you became a gag writer working for a press agent, putting your jokes in the mouths of Arthur Murray and Guy Lombardo, did you resent them using your material?"

"No. It was a big kick. I had a whole slew of funny fellows I wrote for. I wrote thousands of jokes and didn't save one."

"Why is it you're such an easy guy to get along with but such a hard guy to be married to?"

Woody looked painfully surprised at that question.

"I think I'm an easy fellow to get along with as a husband. Sure, the first time I was married, it lasted five years, which by today's standards is a long time. I was only nineteen at the time. Yes, my first wife sued me over some references I made to her in my act. Believe it or not, we are still friendly, and if I'd run into her now, we'd be friendly."

"You plan to stay single?"

He nodded. "I'm strictly a bachelor."

"Now back to your hat. What is the story of the hat?"

"It's just a hat that I can pull down over my eyes and I don't get recognized." He seemed to speak with sincerity.

"But why do you keep it on in a restaurant at lunch?"

"If I take it off, my hair gets mussed and looks silly. The fact is, it's my disguise hat."

"Do you wear it to bed?"

"I don't mind being recognized in bed," he said.

Woody's leap from a picture like his *What's New Pussycat?* to *Everything You Always Wanted to Know About Sex* is the story of the Sex Rebellion. The latter, in tune with today's thinking about sex, had a scene involving sodomy with a sheep.

When I ran into him in Paris in October, 1964, when he was

appearing in *Pussycat* after having written it for producer Charles Feldman, Woody was primarily concerned with the revisions. It was his first movie. He claimed that he was sneakily rewriting it so that he could steal the picture from Peter O'Toole and Peter Sellers.

"Who's going to get the girl?" he said to me at a cocktail party. "Woody Allen!"

Feldman was trying to funny it up and kept asking for more rewrites. As each new page of script came smoking from Woody's typewriter, Feldman found hilarious new lines for Woody Allen.

"You've fattened up your own part," Feldman howled.

He wanted to be a sex symbol even though he looked like a guy who went to Paris to buy dirty postcards. He cast himself in the picture as a towel boy at the Crazy Horse Saloon, the famous stripteasery. He helped put the towels on—and take them off—the luscious beauties. The movie story was wild in other ways. Peter O'Toole was the sex-crazed feature editor of a Paris fashion magazine. He fell in love and wanted to marry. He went to a headshrinker, Peter Sellers, who was more of a stud than he was. There was a lot of bedroom farce with the flavor of the Marx Brothers who were Woody Allen heroes. The picture eventually made money and launched Woody on a movie career although Bosley Crowther in the New York *Times* said, "Nobody in his right mind could have written this excuse for a script."

Skip along eight years now, and it's sodomy time with the sheep.

An Armenian shepherd has fallen in love with one of his own sheep named Daisy. Actor Gene Wilder plays a Jackson Heights doctor who, upon being consulted, decides this isn't a case for a GP but a veterinarian. However, the doctor, upon meeting the sheep, finds himself also smitten by the beautiful Daisy.

Unable to control his libido, he arranges a rendezvous in a hotel and softens Daisy up for the sodomy by serving her white wine, caviar, and some tasty fresh grass.

"What Is Sodomy?" was the title of that sketch, which brings up the horrifying thought that Woody Allen beat Bertolucci and Marlon Brando to buggering. Woody's contention in serious moments was that he was endeavoring to ridicule the American book-buying public's hunger for sexy subjects.

"Are Transvestites Homosexuals?" was another one. This is of course a grave subject in Transvestia, but Woody kicked it around by having Lou Jacobi play a middle-aged Jewish fellow who likes to cavort in women's undies and falsies and gets caught and found out, most embarrassingly, during dinner with some future in-laws. Woody displeased both homosexuals and transvestites with that just as he probably outraged all sheeplovers, shepherds, and shepherdesses with the sodomy treatment.

Lynn Redgrave wore a chastity belt in another, and Woody tried to undo it and her. As Woody was trying to unlock the thing, he said in a line that might have come from Groucho, Robert Benchley, or S. J. Perelman, "I must think of something quickly because before you know it, the Renaissance will be here and we'll all be painting."

"What's My Perversion?" and "What Happens During Ejaculation?" got the same spoofing. Woody wrote, directed, and starred in the film and made money with it.

A lot of people didn't like it. Archer Winsten of the New York *Post* and Kathleen Carroll of the New York *Daily News*, both Woody Allen boosters, said they were disappointed. The Woody Allen cultists adored it and proclaimed that Woody Allen was superior to Chaplin, W. C. Fields, Laurel and Hardy, the Marx Brothers—all of them combined.

Woody's professional life has been a battle to make people think he's funny, to agree with him that he has a great sense of humor and isn't just spewing a lot of nonsense.

When he was twenty-five, in 1961, his managers, Jack Rollins and Charlie Joffe, decided he should be speaking his own lines instead of writing them for others and booked him into a Greenwich Village club, the Duplex, where he was so scared that he got a vomiting attack and quit (every night). He was to go on and on to the Bitter End, the Blue Angel, and Basin Street East and later to the Royal Box at the Americana. It took him a couple of years to get going.

"He's proving he's the funniest monologist in town," Martin Burden wrote about him in the New York *Post* when he was at the Blue Angel in June, 1963.

He was presenting himself as a fumbling little Milquetoastish guy who was so anxious to be liked that he tipped process servers. He maintained that he'd been robbed so often in his one-room apartment, "subdivided by the landlord into living quarters," that he hung a sign on his door, "We Gave."

"I was mugged," he said, "and when the police came along to arrest the mugger, they didn't. They took his side."

He was beginning then to tell jokes about his first wife Harlene. "We didn't get along," Woody said. "When I was taking a bath, she'd walk right in—and sink all my boats. When I brought her home, my parents liked her, but my dog died. She had a change-of-sex operation six times. They couldn't come up with anything she liked."

Woody said, "I made a settlement with her and she got everything. In the event I remarry and have children, she gets them."

He has always presented himself as a fumbler, a kind of Walter Mitty at times, frustrated and unable to cope with life, and often just about to cry.

"I can't pass a shoeshine boy on the street without getting a shine," he has said. "And I always wear suede shoes. I went to a school for emotionally disturbed teachers. I varied between below average and way below average. I failed to make the chess team because of my height. I went with a girl who had a child by a future marriage."

Woody has always been punching out those one-liners, and some of them are pretty wild. He contended once, "The meek shall inherit the earth—right in the mouth." He spoke of going to a damaged animal pet shop that sold "bent cats, white-on-white zebras, and a dog that stutters. It says B-b-bow-ww-ww-wwwwowww!" He's afraid to fly, he says, because on his first flight to Europe, they showed a movie, *The Life of Amelia Earhart*.

At times he gets graphic. In his *Don't Drink the Water*, about an American family in Europe, Estelle Parsons, playing a mother in the film version, says to her daughter, "Your father will get something out of Greece."

"Yeah," says Jackie Gleason, the father, "four more days of diarrhea."

That had been his first play for the Broadway stage with Lou Jacobi and Kay Medford in the leading roles, and it wasn't a spectacular success for the young playwright who was just thirty. The critics thought he had some very funny material but that the one-liners came at you as on a conveyor belt and were too mechanical.

He was always struggling to be different and to win acceptance for his zanyish look at life. The same week his first stage show was opening, his first movie, *What's Up, Tiger Lily?* was premiering. This was as wild as, or wilder than, others of Woody's enterprises. He had taken a beautifully photographed Japanese spy film, which was also a terrible movie, and supplied it with crazy English dialogue which was funny to Woody Allen disciples. In one scene, two men are watching an exotic dancer getting very erotic.

"Isn't she fantastic?" asks one man.

"She was even better in *The Sound of Music*," says the other.

Well, critic Judith Crist found it "a very funny, refreshingly original movie."

Besides doing plays, movies, and nightclub acts and writing humor articles, Woody demonstrated his originality on TV. In one TV special, he interviewed the Reverend Billy Graham respectfully, tastefully, warmly, and amusingly.

WOODY: Can I ask you what your favorite commandment is?

GRAHAM: Well, right now, with a lot of teen-agers, it's to honor your father and mother.

WOODY: That's my least favorite commandment. . . . I'm saving up my money, as I get a little successful in show business, and when I get a little older, I'm going to put my parents in a home.

Woody then said: "Mr. Graham, I read that you don't believe in premarital sex relations. Is this true?"

GRAHAM: It's not a matter of what I believe, it's what the Bible teaches. The Bible teaches that premarital sex relations are wrong.

WOODY: To me that would be like driving a car—you know, like getting a driver's license without a learner's permit first.

The evangelist replied that most psychologists and psychiatrists would agree that there were serious problems involved and that God did not forbid immorality just to keep people from having a good time or having fun.

"Yes, He did," argued Woody, still trying to keep it amusing.

"Mr. Allen," inquired the pastor, "what is the worst sin you ever committed?"

"I had impure thoughts about Art Linkletter," Woody replied.

The result of the interview—with Woody asking Billy Graham whether he could get a white robe and wings if he got converted—was that most people felt Woody had been amusing and that Billy Graham had been a very decent guy to go along.

On February 2, 1966, Woody married actress Louise Lasser and didn't let that prevent him from doing his scheduled act at the Americana Royal Box. It included the jokes about his ex-wife. One of Woody's proud possessions was a billiard table that left little space for anything else in the small room. Although Woody professes to be lonely and antisocial, he and Louise Lasser gave a New Year's Eve party in the first year of their marriage that was memorable.

With the show *Don't Drink the Water* doing well, he invited the cast and 200 friends. The idea was to turn the house into a discothèque and have topless waitresses. Mrs. Allen vetoed the idea of the topless waitresses. It was a strange party. Salvador Dali couldn't come but sent several proxies. Security guards stopped ninety-three would-be gate crashers by actual count. Miniskirts were in fashion. Tom Poston wore minipants. One woman came in pajamas, which was fortunate because she got sick from overimbibing and went to bed in the pajamas. Woody stepped in to break up a slapping involving a woman who lost her husband.

The party went on and on. Woody and his wife were seen sneaking out.

They couldn't take their own party. But unlike most hosts, they had the guts to leave.

I heard rumors about Woody and Louise and went backstage at Woody's show, *Play It Again, Sam,* on the night of June 5, 1969. Yes, Woody said, they had separated. How long were they married?

Grimly and unsmiling, Woody said, "Four years come Groundhog Day."

But they have remained friends, and Louise appears in most of his pictures. They often lunch together, Woody wearing his hat.

To watch Woody Allen now in a stage show or nightclub in Las Vegas—the only place that can afford him—is educational. He uses his body just as commercially as Elvis Presley, Tom Jones, or Engelbert Humperdinck. Or as Jayne Mansfield and Mae West have done. But Woody does it in reverse. He doesn't play his body up; he plays it down.

Hands jammed deep into his pockets, he shrinks into his shoulders and walks out to face the killers. With twitches and lip biting and by squeezing his shoulders together across his thin chest, he conveys that he's nervous, embarrassed, scared, terrified.

He pushes his hair down into his eyes; he keeps lifting his foot like a horse tied to a hitching post; he wriggles and squirms and massages the inside of his left leg with the knee of his right leg. He makes that audience believe he's a nervous worried little shlump. But like any comedian who has learned to move an audience, Woody Allen is enjoying the hell out of it.

He's putting us on.

A Free Soul Named Elliott Gould

I LIVE in a world of weirdies. One afternoon in May, 1964, I visited the new penthouse of Barbra Streisand, who was then twenty-two. It was commodious. It had four terraces, six chandeliers, and a big EXIT sign that lit up. Despite this seeming affluence, Barbra had thumbed a ride that day on a truck.

"I don't have a chauffeured limousine or anything," Barbra explained. "Last week I couldn't get a cab, so I asked a truck to take me. And I took a truck today."

Barbra giggled telling it and mentioned that being the star of the stage show *Funny Girl* subjected her to many pressures and consequent stomachaches. She hadn't had to worry about money since she started bringing out albums at eighteen.

"You have to start thinking about the show at five o'clock. You can't eat too much. It stops your life!"

"What about your husband?" I asked, referring to Elliott Gould, who had just finished a film, *Confessions,* in Jamaica.

"He's going to be a movie star, a big movie star," she predicted, as she was showing me around the patent leather bathroom. The large mirror had the words I LOVE YOU printed—in bath soap, by Elliott Gould. "He's the American Jean-Paul Belmondo!"

"Another Humphrey Bogart?" I said. "In France, I've heard them call Belmondo the French Bogart."

"He'd love you to say that, and it's true. That's just what he can be. Remember I told you!" Barbra leveled a finger at me as she led me into the paisley kitchen, the next stop on my tour of her castle on Central Park West.

I remembered her words seven years later when I went snooping for Elliott Gould, by this time divorced from Barbra, and found him living with Jennifer Bogart, nineteen, the daughter of Hollywood director Paul Bogart, at 58 Morton Street in Greenwich Village. Jennifer was awaiting his baby. She was to have two by him without marriage. Then they would part, in one of Hollywood's more bizarre examples of the New Morality.

Barbra's prophecy had been accurate. Elliott Gould had become the hottest movie male in the country.

The Night They Raided Minsky's was his first, then he went on to *Bob & Carol & Ted & Alice, M.A.S.H., Getting Straight, Move, I Love My Wife,* and *Little Murders*. Then Swedish director Ingmar Bergman, impressed by the fact that there were Elliott Gould movies competing with each other on Main Street, U.S.A. as well as Broadway, signed him for his first English-language picture, *The Touch*.

But in 1971 something happened to Elliott Gould.

Suddenly he walked off a movie he was making in New York, *Glimpse of a Tiger*, and his producers, Ray Stark and Jack Brodsky, couldn't, or wouldn't, explain his departure. But some horrendous rumors got around—he'd freaked out or had a nervous breakdown or become a religious nut. He was reported to have a wild pad in the Village where God knows what went on.

I found some of this to be untrue once I got the address and phone number and arranged an appointment. A free soul, though, he certainly is . . . really a part of swinging show business.

I saw him three times and believe I have drawn a fair picture of him through his own words. His apartment I did not find to be "wild," although I'm sure that he must have been responsible for the EXIT sign in Barbra's penthouse, since his own living room was commanded by a shoeshine chair. He was pouring either lemonade or punch and said to me as we climbed the stairs and confronted the shoeshine chair, "Would you prefer punch, lemonade, or a shoeshine?"

Little Jennifer Bogart wore Levi's, a sweat shirt with "Puerto Rico" across the front, and an Afro hairdo. She was worshipfully quiet as he talked. He was barefoot the first time we met, not uncommon in the Village. He wore a heavy black beard. He didn't look freaked out or like a religious nut, but his hair was long—medium long.

"There are a lot of stories about what happened to you," I said (swilling the punch like mad).

"Nothing's wrong with me!" He hoisted his bare feet onto his desk. He was very pleasant.

"You're out of things."

"I'm not a social guy. I just stay quiet. I don't have to explain myself to anybody. People say, 'Oh, look at him!' But they smell me, and they can't smell anything. I bathe every day, and I'm sanitary. I'm fine. The stories they spread about me were creations of a lot of cowardly, scared people." He added, "Corrupt people."

Jennifer, obviously pregnant, was playing with a neighbor's little girl. She served us another drink.

"Did you two get married?" I asked.

"Did we get married?" He repeated my question. "To us, we did. We looked in each other's eyes."

"What'll you name it?"

"Either Molly or Max. There'll be nothing legal or religious. I don't want legal things."

"Was the divorce from Barbra difficult?"

"It wasn't difficult except for all the legal bullshit." He grimaced, saying this. And he spoke warmly of his son by Barbra, Jason, four, who was then in California with his mother. "That's my son's room down there when he's here," he said. "We're going to have him with me on the beach later in California."

He had an athlete's build and spoke like a baseball pitcher as he talked of his acting career. He was a stickball guy and still loved to chew bubble gum. He sometimes went out into the Village streets and played ball with the kids. He mentioned that he'd done pretty well before this thing happened—he'd made four pictures in one year. He couldn't have sounded more confident.

"I had a lot of raw stuff I wanted to get down," he said, moving from the desk and to a couch, pulling Jennifer down beside him. "I'm like a pitcher. I'm just working with a curve and my fast ball. Wait'll I open up. I haven't shown fifteen percent of my stuff."

"Will you be making another picture soon?"

He waved that aside with a dark glower.

"Those stories about me are the fantasies of a bunch of businessmen trying to protect themselves. They say I'm a loner. I've always been alone. But anybody can look me in the eye and see I'm OK."

He'd been "frozen out," he said, and it had been costly. But he said, with his bare feet up on the coffee table, that he'd be OK. Eventually he wanted to direct.

As I thought it over, maybe his apartment was "eccentric"—if not wild. On the wall were some posters with room for one's own home graffiti.

One poster bore longhand scrawlings, several inches high, saying "fuck you," and "hey, wanna suck?"

Thirteen months later I returned to Morton Street. Elliott, opening the door for me, was clean-shaven now and much better-looking than with the beard. His face was long, and his heavy eyebrows were dark. His shirt was open to the middle of his chest, which was hairy. As we passed the room which I remembered was the one used by his son Jason, when he was visiting in New York, I remarked that I was soon going to be seeing Barbra Streisand in Africa where I would be covering the shooting of her picture, *Up the Sandbox*.

"Oh, say hello to her for me," he said.

When I laughed, he said, "No, I mean it."

By now Jennifer Bogart had given him a daughter and was pregnant again. He held her in the curve of his arm and said, "She won't marry me. She's too smart."

"Too smart?" I said.

"She says it's more romantic this way."

Elliott was on the way back. He had even shortened his hair. He was no longer being "frozen out" of pictures. He had the role of a private detective in a Raymond Chandler story, *The Long Goodbye*.

"Want to see a current picture of Jason?" He whipped one out. "Isn't he great? Here's one of Jenny and Molly. She looks a lot like her mommy."

Speaking gravely and without any humor, Elliott said that he had suffered severely in trying to buck the big business jungle of show business. He had lost heavily when he pulled out of *A Glimpse of a Tiger*

With his hands jammed into his pockets, he said, "I discovered the business world is a rough place. You can't go in there. You'll get burned to death.

"A lot of people's bodies could be in there. It cost me a lot. My accountant figured out I'll have to make four movies to get even."

"But you're recovering?"

"I have had to broaden my perspectives . . . to accept a lot of things that aren't the way I thought they were. I'm a very serious person, and I have learned from experience."

Jenny was there throughout, quiet and mousy, strikingly unlike the very vocal Barbra Streisand—in fact, such an opposite that I wondered about the popular belief that men constantly choose women like their first wives.

"Jenny was pregnant the other time you saw her, and now she's pregnant," Gould said. "She's due at the end of the year."

"Have you changed your image?"

"Because I shaved the beard and cut my hair? That's the way they want me for this picture. Now I look like the client that my agents want to represent." He ran his hand through his hair. "I still don't comb it. I'm just one of those people that don't have to comb their hair."

Jennifer, whose own Afro was long and flaring, spoke up in his defense. "It's hard to comb his kind of hair," she said.

"Is this a comeback?" I inquired.

"It is to me not a comeback. I don't know anybody like me. I feel I'm one of the best. . . . Pardon my humility."

"What will you do next?"

"Candidly, I'm looking for a job. Nobody's paying my rent. I'll take them one by one."

He took Jennifer by the hand and led me down the stairs to the front door. "What I'm trying to do is reestablish myself. I'd like to direct some children's classics. I have three or four—and, listen, I know how to make film."

I said I hoped to see them again—after the next baby was born. I left them on the sidewalk, seemingly a very happy unmarried couple with a growing family. . . .

Once more I returned to Morton Street and Elliott Gould. It was just over three months later, September, 1972.

Jenny wasn't there. Jenny didn't live there anymore.

Elliott wasn't depressed now. He was happy with the picture. He said it in the language of the business office: "I think it'll make a lot of noise."

"I hear you and Jennifer have broken up," I said. "I wonder if you might be sort of a spokesman for this new generation of people who think it's all right to have children without marriage and then move on."

"I speak for myself. Nobody else."

"But you are broken up?"

"The whole idea of breaking up is, well . . . yeah—no—we're friends and we're not living together anymore. Would you call that breaking up?"

"Where is she?"

"She's living with her folks in California, which is the best place for carrying a baby. It's better than belaboring things when we can't live together. I speak to her, and I'm looking after her."

"You are having another baby?"

"You know," Elliott said, "children must not complicate things, no matter how painful it might be."

I confessed never having heard this view so forthrightly expressed and mentioned that it might be considered a very selfish attitude.

"It's the best for all concerned," he said. "She has one child and one which hasn't been born yet. It's the most honest thing to do. I've never been able to pretend anything I don't feel. It's difficult for many people to accept, but for me it's the right thing."

"What is your reasoning?"

"That we're not living together anymore! That's where it's at. I've always stood up for my responsibilities. We're no longer living together, but our children are and will be taken care of in happy surroundings rather than in an atmosphere of parental hostility."

Elliott gave a long, deep sigh. "It ain't easy," he said. "I'm sort of living in solitary here now."

"I wonder if you'll get much approval for your position," I said.

"You can't think of approval. You can only hope for understanding. Everything is understanding and trust, you have to have those for life to go on. The only important thing is life. Stravinsky said that which we love we do harm to a little.

"Well, Jenny and I learned from each other. We have understanding and trust. She and me ain't makin' no more kids. But there ain't nothin' wrong with what we did. What we did was OK. 'There are no accidents on a place called earth.' "

I was impressed with this "lesson in morality" and philosophy from a movie star and repeated that some people would violently disagree and have some bad names for him.

"Those I care for and trust will support my position. I know I'm not bad. I know I'm good!" He laughed at his conceit. "Nobody wants to hurt anybody down deep where we live.

"Even with killers, it's not personal. They might have to kill, but they don't want to."

"Does Jenny feel the same as you do?" I asked.

"I hope so," Elliott said. "She's twenty. She understands it. It *is* delicate," he conceded.

"What about your in-laws?"

"They're looking after her, and she's living with them. Do they approve of it? What choice do they have? That guy Paul Bogart—I respect him. He's doing the best he can, and I'm doing the best I can. Anyway, it's between Jenny and me. I'll take care of her. If somebody doesn't approve of it, that's their tough luck because we're livin' it!"

"Is it that you don't believe in marriage?" I asked him.

"I got married one time—and I do believe in marriage," he fired back. "I'm a more serious character than I like to admit. Oh, I do believe in marriage, I do, I do. I have a very strong definite code. I'm for law and order. The fact that we weren't legally married doesn't change the fact that I *considered* myself married."

"What do you call a woman you lived with but didn't marry?"

"A past mate of mine, a young woman of mine, or a girl of mine."

"Won't people think of that as being caddish?"

"Yeah, I'm a walking contradiction, I know."

"Yet you married Barbra."

He nodded. "Yes. You ain't jokin'."

"So?"

"But I'm pretty much together now. It ain't bad what I've done as people might say. It might not be ideal, but I challenge people who will judge me, the people holding onto their past lives and pretensions for fear of exposure and embarrassment, to match their lives with mine."

"Will you be there when the second baby is born?"

"If it'll be any comfort to Jenny, I will."

"What did you name your daughter, inasmuch as you didn't get married?"

"It's Molly Gould on the birth certificate."

"Have you discussed Jenny with Barbra?"

"No. Though I believe she knows Jennifer and likes her. I am Barbra's friend, but she can't be my friend. She doesn't understand me. I have been her friend even before I saw her." After a pause, he said, "She's got her own problems."

"What are your plans?"

"Just to make the most out of my life. It's a lonely place for an honest man who tells the truth. People don't want to hear the truth.

"And so," he said, "a new beginning is on its way."

"Do you think you'll have a relationship with somebody else?"

"I hope so—you kidding? I'm living in solitary now but I don't want to forever. . . ."

A teen-age kid from the neighborhood who had been waiting to play catch with Elliott had sat through this entire discussion, hardly listening. I thought to myself, if he had listened, he would have heard the New Permissiveness carefully outlined by one of its principal practitioners. But then the kid probably knew it all, anyway, and wouldn't have been a bit astonished.

I wanted to complete the odyssey of Elliott Gould. About seven months later, on Tuesday, April 10, 1973, while at the Beverly Hills Hotel in Beverly Hills, I found his phone number and called him at the Windsor Apartments at Seventh and Catalina. I asked if we could get together. "I have to look at some film," he said, "but I could be there about one thirty."

When he strode up the walk at the hotel, I was waiting for him. He always seemed unexpectedly tall and rangy like a basketball player which he had obviously wanted to be, and his very dark mustache was longer than I remembered it from our last interview.

"Do you want to go to the pool or to the Polo Lounge?" I asked. He wasn't wearing a tie, but in Beverly Hills it doesn't matter especially in the movie colony.

"The Polo Lounge," he said. As we walked through the lobby, he whisked out a color photograph. "I brought you a picture," he said. It was a scene from his latest movie, *Busting*, in which he played a vice cop. The photograph showed him emptying his revolver at some lawbreaker. His mouth was wide open in a yell of triumph.

"I shoot about three people," he said, seeming to relish the idea. "It's a very entertaining picture and is gonna sell a lot of popcorn."

I burst out laughing. He had generally been extremely serious, and I couldn't remember him making a deliberately funny remark.

He was getting commercial and materialistic as he grew older. He and Robert Blake had been the lowliest police in this movie.

"They make us work in men's rooms, looking for fags and hookers," he said. "In my next picture for UA, I'm going to Paris and work my way up from the toilets. I play a spy. Any basketball players coming through, have them look me up."

He ordered a Bloody Bull which is a bullshot with tomato juice as well as bouillon. As it was arriving, he said that financially, he was straightening himself out.

"In four or five years," he said, "I'm free."

"You're a slave meanwhile?"

"I ain't no slave." He smiled.

Cautiously, I asked about Jennifer.

"Everything is going good," he said. "We got Sam." Sam was their son born on January 7, 1973, at 5:15 A.M. in the kitchen on the kitchen table while *On the Town* was on TV. "We got movies on TV all night in L.A.," he said. I asked why the baby was born on the kitchen table. "The doctor said it'd be easier to clean up things later in the kitchen."

"You were there?" I asked him.

"I held her hand, and I had my face down in her belly."

"What is Sam's middle name?"

"Bazooka, like the gun. I hope when he plays basketball, he shoots like a bazooka."

"What is Molly's middle name?"

"Sapphire. Molly Sapphire. I hear my boy Jason talking about his brother and sister. I never had a brother and sister." He said this with a tone of regret and loss, and I felt that it meant that in his mind he had missed much.

"Jason's got a terrific brain," Elliott continued. "He said to me, 'I say what I mean and mean what I say.' That's my six-year-old."

"Is Jennifer living with her parents? Are you living with her?" I asked, for this to me was the most interesting part of this relationship.

"Am I back with her?" He often repeated questions I asked him as though thinking how he should answer. "Sometimes I stay with her. We see one another. We understand each other better than we did before. But I'm not back living with her.

"I'm a very formal dude," he said.

"Do her parents think you should get married?"

"I'm sure they think we should get married but I don't know

how anybody should *feel* we should get married," he answered. A nice distinction, I thought.

"Do you still feel the same about children not being allowed to interfere with one's life?"

"That I remain free of any problems? Yes," he said, ordering another Bloody Bull. "I want my children and my children's children to know me. I just can't pretend all the time; I can't pretend to stick around. And that has nothing to do with loving. That doesn't mean I don't love them.

"My ambition," he said, "is to settle down. Some time! When I settle down it has to be on my terms—at the expense of a lot of social conformities. And I believe I'm winning. You must be true to yourself, and that's what I'm trying to do—to be true to myself."

Jennifer, he said, was living with her children, separate from her parents and separate from him. "How old is she?" I asked.

"She'll be twenty-one later this month. She has nothing to worry about. I got her her own home."

"How about Barbra Streisand? The last time we talked, you said you weren't friends. At least that she couldn't be your friend."

"We're friends. She admits she doesn't understand me very good. And that's very possible!"

"What of your own future?"

"I have utter confidence I'll be able to do what I want to in my time. I would like to have a good relationship with the world. I trust myself. I'm still not being asked to act with girls. That's just around the corner. I'm doing action and adventure pictures. I can't work in the cities where I want to work. . . ." This was a return, I felt, to his fear that he was being frozen out by mysterious forces working against him, going back to his contention that they were getting even with him for leaving *A Glimpse of Tiger*.

"They can't hold me down," he said. "I'm so thick they can't hurt me."

Since the entire Hollywood community was talking about Marlon Brando's refusal of the Academy Award for himself, I asked Elliott what he thought of Brando's influence.

"I think Earl the Pearl Monroe, the basketball player, is a better actor," he said. "Marlon Brando is my favorite actor. But I believe Charles Laughton was the daddy of Marlon Brando. He was the first Method actor. Laughton directed *Night of the Hunter*. There's an anecdote I like about Laughton. He was on his deathbed in a coma. He woke up and said, 'I don't think this director knows what he's doing.' "

It was a good closing note. We got up and said "So long" till next time. As he walked away from me, I hoped that he knew what he was doing. Surely, he was as free a soul as I would ever meet in show business.

The Happy Edith Piaf

◢ A GREAT movie could be produced, but probably never will be, about Edith Piaf's having been one of the happiest girls in the world in her tempestuous forty-seven years. The idea that she was a child of tragedy who lost her great lover, Marcel Cerdan, when he was flying to her, has been drilled into us so persistently that we forget that she had other loves later, tremendous professional triumphs, and comparative wealth for one who had scrounged for food as a child. The overpowering climax of her remarkable career which she as a tragedienne would have enjoyed was her astonishing funeral which was attended by 15,000 other confused people and me one hot October Monday in 1963 after 40,000 of us had visited her Paris home, or tried to, the day before. I scrambled and stumbled among the gravestones at Père Lachaise Cemetery after the services, bumping and pushing my way among the other mourners, reached a phone, and cabled back a story to New York: PIAF SRO AT THE CEMETERY.

The newspapers, reporting Piaf's tragic final curtain, wrung the last teardrop out of the occasion, which actually was a big mob scene, a little bit circusy, but a true tribute to the girl from the streets from the people still in the streets.

The Parisians—the Poor People of Paris, *Les Pauvres Gens de Paris*—idolized her and saved their francs to buy tickets to hear her sing her sad songs. They and their worship were part of her happiness that she blended with her tragedy. With her lovers, her drinking, and her drugs, "The Sparrow" was a suitable name for Piaf because she was often in the clouds, flying.

Only a stubborn, professional skeptic like me would try to tear away some of this glamorously romantic picture of a soul always in torture.

She lived two lives, and in one she had ecstasy.

It is necessary to be truthful. She could have ecstasy because she had made so much of so little. She was not a great singer. "She is consistently off key," wrote Brooks Atkinson, then the critic of the New York *Times*, after her first New York appearance.

Yet she soon became the "must see" singer at the great Versailles nightclub a few seasons later. She was the darling of a lot of dressed-up Americans who didn't know enough French to know what the hell she was singing about. They were snobs of a sort. Piaf raked in the money and got more lugubrious and more French. If they wanted sadness, she could give them buckets of sadness.

Sexually, she had an insatiable appetite, and here was another reason for her to have ecsatsy.

This poor little creature was down to about 80 pounds a year or two before her death, and when she was 115, she was fat. She was flat-chested, she had no curves, she never wore false bosoms, she looked as though she had just uncombed her hair, she avoided makeup, and she could hardly have been called beautiful.

Yet she got more sexual athletes into bed with her than the big-breasted sexpots, and afterward she bought them gold lighters, and ties, and suits of clothes. She was the happiest invalid in the world.

Piaf did in fact laugh at the way the chic people took her up although she shocked them by wearing beltless, waistless, unpressed black velvet gowns with sleeves rolled up like those of a dishwasher. She also laughed at the hairdresser snobs who ruled the lives of other people but not Piaf's. Some singers of that day, and this, couldn't make an appearance without spending half a day with the coiffeur. But Piaf gave the impression that she'd taken a swipe at her hair with a comb and missed. The hairdressers were privately annoyed but publicly exclamatory about the little bird who was so careless about her greatest glory.

Jean Cocteau said her hands "were like lizards darting over ruins."

Such high-flown appraisals of her talent also amused Piaf, who was a pragmatist about singing and mannerisms. She became the master of the sock-it-to-me repeated word or phrase style years before the rock stars did it. When she sank into the melancholia on the stage and cried, *"Mon amour, mon amour, mon amour,"* or a word such as "Milord" over and over and over, her intensity of emotion multiplied with the repetition.

"Piaf had found out that her talent was not to make people laugh, but to make them feel or cry," Eddie Elkort says. "She chose her material with that as the measuring stick. If a song didn't move the audience emotionally, the hell with it—out it went." (Elkort was her American representative.)

In real life, it was the other way around. Piaf clung to the things that made her happy and threw out the things that didn't. She liked to drink. Brought up, as everybody knows by now, in a cheap bordello with a bar in it, she had been drunk at age three or earlier. Once her mother, who habitually abandoned her, didn't have any food or milk for her, but left her with a cheap bottle of red wine for nourishment.

Drinking made her happy, and she refused to throw it out of her life. A couple of years before she died, she was in the American Hospital in Paris for cirrhosis of the liver. She was of course forbidden to drink. She had the nurses under control, however, and the story is told that one night she persuaded the nurses to take her to a nearby bistro for "just one beer." After all, the nurses would be with her to watch over her. It got to be more than one beer, and Piaf sneaked away from the nurses for a while. When they recaptured her and returned her to the hospital, she was in a coma for four days.

When Piaf thought of her money problems at all, she would shrug off the present. "There will be money coming in from other engagements. . . ."

Edith sold her life story to Warner Brothers for a movie for $50,000, and a script was written about a year before her death.

To me, the funeral should be the great scene in the real Piaf movie, and of course that could not have been written yet in the first Warner's story.

It's doubtful that there was anybody with a more confused and disputed life story. Simone Berteaut, who says she is a half sister, contributed to the confusion with a book called *Piaf* in 1969. The book said among other things that the half sister knew Edith's lover Marcel Cerdan and was intimate with the famous fighter before Piaf was.

"I never heard Edith speak of a half sister," Eddie Elkort said.

Nevertheless, another woman, claiming to be a certified half sister, Denise Gassion, appeared in court in Paris to challenge the authenticity of Simone Berteaut's claims to being a half sister. The book pictured Piaf as a nymphomaniac, alcoholic, and drug addict. It became such a best seller that bookstores kept stacks of it close to the cash register. The certified half sister and a brother, Herbert Gassion, declared the book should be banned because it was false and slanderous. They claimed the so-called half sister had no blood ties with Edith Piaf.

Simone Berteaut scoffed at all their accusations and said she had really played down many of the Piaf characteristics and adventures in high living.

"They know I didn't tell everything out of friendship for them and out of love for my sister," she said.

That itself would have been funny to Piaf: all these supposed "close" relatives now worried about her reputation. Her answer would have been the modern equivalent of "*Now* they tell me! Why didn't they tell me then?"

I have access to the Piaf life story that she herself approved— and it makes no attempt to cover up or gloss over the distasteful events of her childhood.

Nor of many other events that she might have preferred to forget.

The Sparrow was written for Warner Brothers by J. P. Miller in 1962, and its contents were known not only to Piaf but to her longtime manager, Louis Barrier, of Paris, and her husband at the time, Theo Sarapo.

Prepare yourself for some melodrama.

It is a day in Normandy, France, in 1922, four years after the close of World War I, half a century ago.

A shiny old automobile chugs through the French countryside proceeding up a hill into the cobbled streets of the town of Bernay.

A goateed middle-aged gentleman steers the car to an ugly house. He is carrying a black leather bag. Hesitating as though in doubt that this is the correct address, he finally enters a parlor with a small bar at one side.

At the bar, a painted lady and a man with whiskers are laughing at a joke.

Still in doubt, the goateed gentleman sets down his satchel and walks to the bar. The bartender taps a bell.

The painted lady turns, smiles at the goateed visitor, greets him—and simultaneously several other girls appear, including one who is Chinese. They flirt with the gentleman and try to look their prettiest and sexiest.

It is immediately apparent that he is in a house of prostitution and that the girls think he is a customer.

"I—uh—good afternoon," he says. He is confused. "I was looking for Mme. Gassion."

A large middle-aged woman comes in shimmering with beads, lace, and chiffon.

The prostitutes cluster around her. The large lady states that she is Mme. Gassion and what is the gentleman's pleasure? (Does he have something unusual in mind?)

"I am Dr. Descombes, the eye specialist, from Rouen," he says, whereupon Mme. Gassion becomes greatly flustered, turns on the girls, and snaps at them, "You idiots, get out!"

Apologetically, Mme. Gassion explains that she has called him to look at her tiny granddaughter, Edith Gassion, later to be Edith Piaf.

Carrying a lamp, she leads the doctor upstairs while he is clearly disapproving of the setup here. Mme. Gassion says her son is a big circus star. He wanted to take the little daughter with him, but traveling is not good for a little girl who is blind.

They enter a dark room.

With the help of the lamp, they see a tiny child sitting on the floor holding a doll. She has been unable to see for three years. As the grandmother brings the lamp close, the little girl turns her head away and tells her grandmother to tell the man to go away. The doctor coaxes her, and finally the little girl relaxes and allows the doctor to look at her eyes.

By now there is tension all over the bordello. The girls know who the doctor is and that he is conducting an examination of little Edith, their favorite child, who cannot see. They are huddling together at the bar downstairs awaiting his decision.

Slowly, the doctor descends the stairs. Mme. Gassion hands him his fee, which she has counted out from an old safe.

"I am very sorry, madame," he says, gravely.

Some of the prostitutes are crying as he leaves.

He has said as the other specialists have said that there is no hope for Edith's sight.

Mme. Gassion turns to the mournful group. "I say there is hope. We shall go to the biggest specialist of all—God."

She tells the bartender the girls will not be working tomorrow.

The next morning, dressed in their best, with little Edith wearing a bandage over one eye, the girls and Mme. Gassion travel in a noisy day coach to the Shrine of Ste. Thérèse at Lisieux. They get many disapproving glances on the way because their profession is obvious. Edith is led into the cathedral by "Aunt Marie," who is Mme. Gassion's daughter.

"Tell me how it looks," Edith says.

"Tall and beautiful with a big round dome," Marie says.

"Ohh, we're inside, I can feel it," Edith says.

At the tomb of Ste. Thérèse, the little collection of prostitutes are hushed, but their lips are moving.

Mme. Gassion's prayer is heard:

"If you will only consider her worthiness and her past suffering without complaint, dear Ste. Thérèse: born on the sidewalk in a snowstorm, abandoned by her mother at two months, treated like an animal by her maternal grandmother, locked in a room at the age of three for days at a time with nothing but a nursing bottle full of red wine for company—drunk at the age of three!"

Mme. Gassion prays for an hour, Edith on her knees beside her with Aunt Marie on the other side.

Mme. Gassion continues to pray: "And you will forgive me if I ask one thing for myself. You see, my name is Louise, and the twenty-fifth day of August is the day of St. Louis, my name day, and if you could see fit to have this miracle happen—to give this child the gift of sight again—on my name day, I'd know then that it was because of my prayers. Edith could run and play and see her father."

"My papa can do flips and walk on his hands," Edith interjects into the prayer.

Mme. Gassion says, "I, Louise Gassion, will give ten thousand francs to your shrine in your memory, for your sacred works. Amen."

The prostitutes return to their brothel not without hearing scornful remarks about themselves from passengers on the train. A few days pass. Marie enters Edith's upstairs room to tell her she's made a beautiful fondue because it's Grandmother's birthday.

Suddenly Edith seems to be choking; then she screams.

"I can see! . . . I can see you, Auntie! I see your eyes, your face! I see you! I see you!"

Mme. Gassion hurries in. "Grandma!" Edith shouts. Mme. Gassion opens the curtains, Edith runs around the room, touching things, looking at her own hands, looking at the girls, who cross themselves and fall to their knees. Edith stares at the girls wondering about them, and they feel embarrassed.

"My miracle . . . my miracle," says the dazed Mme. Gassion, who has now had a sudden thought of fear.

Her son from the circus will want to take Edith away with him now that she can see. Edith won't be able to stay in the house in Bernay any longer.

There are none alive today to attest to the authenticity of the religious miracle that gave Edith back her sight. It was of course a period of bliss and rejoicing for all. For a while, Edith was the happiest of youngsters. But then her father did reclaim her from the brothel. Louis Gassion was an itinerant acrobat whose stage was frequently a street corner in Paris. As Edith grew into her teens, he used her in his act. He proclaimed to the street audiences that in addition to seeing him do his incredible backbend, they would see his daughter do a triple flip.

Edith was toughened by the street crowds. Once when Edith missed a cue, her father told them that Edith couldn't do the triple flip that day because she was sick.

"*Fraud!*" cried out a heckler. "I saw them pull the same swindle a month ago!"

Her father slapped her around. She probably was sick, from hunger, from living on wine and cheese, which was about all that her father and his mistress of the moment could afford. Edith would nevertheless bring his act to a rousing climax by singing "La Marseillaise." And the audience would contribute a few coins depending on its degree of friendliness and appreciation.

This was the beginning of Edith's singing career, and she dramatized her rendition of the anthem with overdone gestures while her father was doing his "incredible backbend."

Edith began to see raw sex as practiced by her father and his mistresses, and sometimes it was pretty tawdry with Edith being in the same cheap room.

Once, according to the stories collected about Edith, she was doing her street act with her father when a well-to-do woman approached them. The well-dressed woman was especially interested in the little girl and kissed her. Edith grasped the drama of the moment.

The woman was her mother. She was with her new husband.

The woman attempted to persuade Edith's father to take the act to America. Edith's father quarreled with the woman and insulted her husband. They left, Edith's eyes following them. But there was no further conversation and Edith did not kiss the woman who had kissed her. That was the first and last time that Edith was to see her mother after her mother had left her when she was a baby.

Edith at fifteen was beginning to enjoy one of her great happinesses, sex. Her father loudly protested that a street boy, Louis, was following her around, interfering with her work and his act. Reduced to sleeping wherever her father and his mistress could find a room, Edith sometimes spent the night in a hallway or under a bridge.

Asking her father for money for food, she was told to eat some of the cheese.

"I'm tired of cheese," she complained.

"Then you're not hungry!"

Louis, the street boy, got a job as a messenger. He also found them a room. He was probably her first lover.

By sixteen or seventeen Edith was pregnant, apparently by a bricklayer.

Now the tragedy resumed. Edith gave birth to a daughter, Marcelle. The bricklayer-father was unhappy with Edith's singing in the streets—she was singing at the Place de la Tertre (a favorite spot of visiting American tourists) in Montmartre. He took the baby from her. Edith continued singing. The baby suffered meningitis, and her condition grew worse.

The baby died. Edith was nineteen. She did not have money to bury the baby.

The next part of the drama is in dispute. Edith's own story as sold to Warner's glosses over other versions.

Edith and a girlfriend supposedly got drunk on Pernod after the baby died. They still needed ten francs to bury Marcelle, even after their friends around the cafés had contributed to a fund.

"I'll make it myself," Edith announced. Her intention was clear.

She had been around whores all her life. Now she would turn into one.

Edith picked up a passerby and prepared to go to bed with him. Crying, she explained to him, in the room, why she was doing it. He gave her the money and left. She had the money for the baby's burial and had not committed the ultimate dishonor.

Sad as it all was, Edith's real singing career commenced with the baby's death and the departure of its father. Edith's friends relate that Edith was singing in the rain in Place Pigalle one night when a gendarme reminded her that street singing was against the law.

However, the kind gendarme asked her to sing "Valentine," good and loud, while he went around the corner so he wouldn't see her violate the law. He gave her a coin.

As she was singing her heart out, along came Louis Leplee, a middle-aged bon vivant who managed Gerny's cabaret.

Even in the rain, he was struck by her voice.

Interrupting her song, he called out to her: "You must be a little crazy. You'll ruin your voice!"

"I'm going to ruin my stomach, too, if I don't eat," Edith said.

Leplee asked her to audition for him. Edith didn't believe him. She had been getting money from a pimp named Albert. She refused to be his prostitute but helped him steal by visiting dance halls, finding women with money or jewelry, and directing Albert to them. He would dance with them, try to escort them home, and then slug them and grab their jewelry and money and run—and meet Edith.

"That I was going to audition for anybody sounded crazy," Edith said. Leplee foresaw a future for her, changed her name to Piaf (meaning Sparrow)—and that made her cry.

"I want to keep my own name, Gassion," she pouted. Leplee, a man of power in the café world in Paris, "introduced" her with an opening far beyond what she was entitled to at this point. Chevalier, Fernandel, and Mistinguett were cheering. Edith had knitted herself a sweater but had finished only one sleeve. In the middle of her performance a white scarf she wore over the sweater fell to the floor, and she stood there in a sweater with only one sleeve. That was something the celebrities could understand. They felt pity and admiration, too.

Chevalier stood up leading the ovation. "She's got plenty of guts, that kid!"

That was it: guts. After such a happy and unbelievable debut, Piaf was on top of the world—but then Leplee was murdered. Edith was one of those questioned but was released. Without Leplee's help, Edith was reduced to job hunting again. Raymond Asso, a composer who had been attracted by her at Leplee's club, found her. He taught her some song techniques, became her lover, and helped her start all over.

Through him, she became the pet of Paris—and the sweetheart of one after another, Yves Montand among them—and then Cerdan.

The torrid romance that Edith had with Marcel Cerdan, which is the centerpiece of all the tragic stories about her, lasted for less than a couple of years, from 1947 to 1949, unless you count Piaf's attempts to reach him by séances after his death. However, two years was quite a long time for Piaf to be in love with anybody and be true to him.

She was thirty when they met in a Paris club and was already a big name. He was a big name, too, in his world. But it wasn't love at first sight. Piaf had been collecting and discarding lovers since she was fifteen. She must have had hundreds of affairs by that time, not surprising when you remember that her early childhood was spent in a brothel and that her companions when she started singing in the streets were prostitutes and procurers. When she began singing in the cheaper clubs, the whores were always there. Piaf's love affairs were often quickies, one-night stands. But at times she would tumble madly for somebody and suffer desperately until he returned her love. And when he did—it followed a pattern—she would cheat on him with somebody new.

Marcel Cerdan didn't set off any sparks when they met in Paris about 1946.

Then Piaf's career led her to America. And right here, on my Broadway beat, is where the romance blossomed. I reported it, and so did Walter Winchell, Ed Sullivan, Leonard Lyons, and Louis Sobol, in our Broadway columns, although of course we didn't recognize its importance, its depth, or the impact it was to have.

We all loved the Versailles nightclub on East Fiftieth Street where Piaf was to have her greatest American success. It was lush and plush and expensive. It was operated by "Nick and Arnold," two affable gentlemen of Italian extraction whose boss was said to be another affable gentleman whom we saw from time to time, named Johnny Bogiano. It was the smart kind of supper club which no longer exists in New York. Dwight Fiske might appear there singing his songs with the risqué lyrics. When Elsa Maxwell, the tireless hostess, decided to make a supper club appearance, she chose the Versailles. The cuisine and the wines were distinguished, and so were the entertainers. There was no better place to work in America.

The Piaf-Cerdan romance centered there in that club that was later to be known as the Round Table, a rendezvous of bellydancers and later of male entertainers, and also as the site of Jackie Kannon's Rat Fink Room.

But that was much in the future. Piaf's first performances in America hadn't overwhelmed the public, and Cerdan was just getting known. Piaf's half sister asserts that she herself had had Cerdan as a lover on the beach at Casablanca long before Piaf had him. Cerdan, the Casablanca Bomber, married and a father, was looking for adventure one night and was strolling the beach. He found adventure all right . . . in Piaf's half sister.

The half sister reported that they got to know each other almost as well as any couple could. Piaf and the half sister parted because Piaf's last previous lover had objected to having her around. After her fling with Cerdan, the half sister returned, considerably later, to Paris, and rejoined Piaf, who was breathless with ecstasy over her newest lover.

To the half sister's astonishment, Piaf introduced her new love, Marcel Cerdan.

Both kept discreetly silent.

It was in 1947 while Edith Piaf was starring at the Playhouse in New York with Les Compagnons de la Chanson that they found each other, the two strangers to New York. Although it had been pointed out that Edith sang off-key practically all the time, New York *Post* critic Richard Watts, Jr., liked her. His reviews have always been fair and honest, and I have valued them highly. He wrote:

"Mlle. Piaf is a small, intense, sad-eyed young woman with a forlorn air of wistful valor about her, who sings songs, chiefly of a gallantly melancholy nature, with mocking dramatic power, a suggestion of great inner fire, and a hint of unquenchable tragedy of heart. In one way the lady's admirers have been deceiving me. . . . She had overwhelmed them despite notable defects in her vocal and visual qualities. . . . I don't know what they were talking about. The more academic music critics might find flaws in her voice and I certainly wouldn't hail her as one of the great beauties, but her strikingly effective singing, even technically, is far beyond the merely adequate, and her looks seemed to me extremely satisfactory."

A remarkable review considering that he added: "Edith Piaf is clearly one of the distinguished performers of the postwar era."

But Edith was dissatisfied working with the Compagnons, thinking they could do better without her and that they did not help her. Deciding she had to work alone, she made a deal to go into the Versailles for considerably under $5,000 a week. That was pretty good money. She had determined to learn English and swore that she would stay in her dressing room between shows studying English rather than to go table-hopping.

There are the usual contradictory stories of how Cerdan and Piaf got together in New York. One is that Edith learned of his presence at a cocktail party and went to greet him. Another is that Cerdan, in New York for a championship fight with Tony Zale, phoned her, asked if she remembered him and their meeting in Paris, and took her out. Regardless of the beginning, it was the beginning of Piaf's *La Vie en Rose*.

I have always followed one rule in column writing: never to write anything that would tip off a husband or wife that a spouse was romancing somebody else. If the spouse knew about it, then it was OK to mention it, but I must never be an informant, a marriage wrecker. Walter Winchell had established that rule in our strange profession long before I entered it.

Cerdan's romance with Piaf fell within the prohibited area for a time because he was a married man whose wife didn't know about Piaf. In rereading my columns, I find that I carried this to extremes. I mentioned Cerdan going to the Versailles without mentioning that Piaf was singing there. It is as though I were trying to cover up for him.

Marlene Dietrich and Maurice Chevalier, a couple of romantics, were in New York and around the Versailles at the time, cheering on *La Vie en Rose*. Edith was in ecstasy. It was claimed that Piaf was singing her songs to Cerdan, who was in the audience many a night. It was claimed that she wrote some of the words to "La Vie en Rose" with Cerdan in her heart and mind at the time.

Especially the lyric *"Quand il me prend dans ses bras . . . Il me parle tout bas . . . Je vois la vie en rose. . . ."*

These, anyway, were very, very happy days for Edith in her real life, although she was the usual tragic figure at night singing of her broken heart at the Versailles. This is what I mean when I refer to the happy Piaf. Brought up as she had been, Piaf was contemptuous of all rules and regulations, and it didn't occur to her that she should observe an old rule in the sports world that fighters should not be going to bed with their girlfriends or any other girls while training for an important fight. To Piaf, it was simply that she had an enormous sex drive, and she wanted to have her lover make love to her, and why in hell shouldn't she and Cerdan sneak off somewhere and get in bed together? And to hell with the rules and with Cerdan's opponent, Tony Zale.

There are New York sportswriters around today who will tell you that Piaf succeeded in sleeping with Cerdan at his training camp in the Catskills, that she was smuggled in and spent many nights with him, that it was done so secretly and cleverly that his closest associates didn't know it.

And there are other sportswriters, considerably advanced in years now, who will tell you: "Listen, I was around that training camp a lot! If there'd been any whispers about Piaf being up there on the sneak, I'd have known about it."

It was a hazardous undertaking, especially dangerous to Edith because she was sure to be blamed in case he should fail, and it would have been a national tragedy in France. Marcel's managers knew of Edith's tenacity and warned her but she would not be deterred from having her normal round of lovemaking with her man.

La Vie en Rose. . . .

Thank God he won. He was the new world's middleweight champion. The year was 1948.

Surrounded by French friends, the shy, modest Cerdan went to the Versailles and relaxed, drinking champagne and eating a big supper, while his proud mistress sang to him and told the audience, "Tonight I am very happy."

That perhaps started the stories that Cerdan had become a playboy and was training on champagne. And the word spread that Piaf was responsible for his being in bad condition later when he lost the title to Jake La Motta. Cerdan read stories about it in the papers and told Piaf not to feel guilty. It was his own fault. He knew the rules about training. He should have kept away from her. But how could he?

"You will win it back, *chéri*," Piaf promised him. "I will not let you near me."

Again Piaf was to open at the Versailles in the fall of the year, 1949. She was the darling of the sophisticates now, and her salary had gone up a couple of thousand dollars a week. The papers exclaimed about her return to America alone—without Cerdan. But it was known and explained that he would follow very soon to prepare for his attempt to regain the title. All was peaceful in the Cerdan-Piaf paradise, the world was assured.

But Piaf grew restive being alone in New York. (It was dangerous for her to be alone anyplace, but especially in New York.)

She pressed Cerdan not to come to New York by ship as he had planned but to come by plane, because she couldn't wait to see him and make love to him again.

He took a plane with the result that we all know now.

On Tuesday, October 25, 1949, my column said "Marcel Cerdan arrives Friday to train for the La Motta fight in December."

Friday was to have been the day of their reunion. She would be singing at the Versailles that night and they would be together afterward.

Nineteen forty-nine is a long time ago. One of the suddenly famous movie stars of the day was Paul Douglas. Gene Autry and Roy Rogers were getting rich from their Westerns. Humphrey Bogart was having panda trouble at El Morocco. Tyrone Power and Linda Christian had arrived from Europe after getting married in Rome and remaining there for seventeen months. A reporter told them, "While you were away, Al Jolson made two comebacks."

The news that Cerdan's plane had crashed in the Azores on Friday was flashed to the world by radio. Piaf was asleep in her apartment. A couple of women friends at the apartment, horrified by the news, tried to keep it from Edith until it was confirmed that everybody aboard had been killed.

"My God, it's impossible, I can't believe it," she sobbed when they told her about 2 P.M.

Running wildly around the apartment, weeping, listening to the radio, waving everybody away, she said she would be unable to sing that night.

"It would be an insult to the French people," she said, "if I sang tonight. My God, how can you take a father away from his three children?"

A spokesman told one newspaper that Cerdan and Miss Piaf "were just good friends" and that there was no truth to a report they'd gone into the trucking business in North Africa.

As evening came on, she strengthened and went to the Versailles, held up by two women friends who were afraid that she might collapse. The word spread that she was trying to summon the spirit to go on. Walter Winchell and I were in the crowd outside her dressing room on the second-floor mezzanine while she was inside crying and deciding.

"She's going to sing . . . no, she can't make it!" Bulletins like that came from inside the dressing room. Photographers and other reporters were waiting.

The door opened. There was Piaf, her face dark and pinched, her eyes blood-colored. She knew Winchell and me, but she didn't acknowledge us, she didn't acknowledge anybody, as she propelled her thin tiny body to the stairs and moved like a robot down to the main floor toward the empty stage waiting for her.

As she stood in the spotlight in her usual gown of plain, unrelieved black velvet and faced us dry-eyed, we rose in a standing ovation, causing her to call out, "I do not want any applause tonight. Tonight I am singing for Marcel Cerdan alone."

But love and life ripple on! On September 3, 1950, about eleven months after the end of the idyll with Cerdan, I broke the story that Edith Piaf, back at the Versailles supper club to open a new season, had become engaged to American-born crooner Eddie Constantine.

Big, rugged, and rangy, thirty-four years old, he had been getting nowhere in Paris until he met Piaf who commandeered his life. He made such progress as her new man that he was referred to as "Addie Cawnstantine, the Sinatra of the Seine." He sang in French, wore foulard scarves which she bought him, and helped her with her English.

He wrote her a song, "Hymn to Love," for her opening at the Versailles.

Eddie Constantine had the usual problem of Piaf's guys—he was married.

"But it's all working out," he told me. "Helene and I"—that was his wife, a ballet dancer from Chicago—"have discussed divorce."

Eddie discussed it all so freely with me because I'd known him when he was just another chorus voice, singing at Radio City Music Hall with the group or with Ben Yost's Vikings at the old Latin Quarter. They were eight muscular fellows belting out songs nobody got excited about; I always felt they were a stage wait until somebody important like Milton Berle or Sophie Tucker swept on and took over the evening.

"I'd never been able to sing a note on my own until I met Piaf," Eddie'd told me.

Eddie and Edith could compare hardships and heartbreaks although Eddie's couldn't match hers. He'd been able to study opera in Vienna at sixteen and had a strong voice. Back in America before he knew Piaf, he had been fired from the Music Hall when he and Helene Mussell went on a sudden honeymoon without giving notice that he'd be away. Helene eventually got a dancing job in Paris, and they floundered around there for a while, with Helene the moneymaker and Eddie trying to find something. They had children, and the times were rough. Eddie was frequently alone. He began going to music hangouts and met Piaf, who was ready to fall in love again. He was soon installed as the master of her ménage, and she was buying him lighters and suits.

Their plans were as rosy as hers with Cerdan had been when I talked to them after she brought him to America. They would open a club in Paris to be called the Club Piaf, and they planned to do a musical show on the radio. Edith had been looking at wedding rings, and the only obstacle remaining was Eddie's wife, who, Eddie said, was being quite reasonable about the whole thing.

"The persistent rumors that Eddie Constantine and I are inseparable are absolutely true," Edith said. Edith liked that line, which Eddie had taught her and kept repeating it when somebody asked.

Eddie was going to Chicago next day to see Helene and discuss the divorce. . . .

About five years went by, and I was in the Hotel Berkeley in

Paris one night when I heard people buzzing about somebody named "Addie Cawnstantine" being there with a girl.

"The big movie star, the French love him because he's American and he slaps women around," a friend explained to me. "Addie Cawnstantine is the biggest thing in France."

While I was wondering how I could reintroduce myself to him and see if he'd remember the old days with Piaf, he came to my table and shot out his hand.

"It's been five fantastic years," he said. "I've made eight French movies, and there seems to be no stop to it. My salary's bigger than anybody's except Fernandel's, and now I finally record my own songs."

In a remarkable series of confessions that appeared under Edith's signature, she said that six months after Cerdan's death, she became a drug addict. Not because of her grief, but because of the pain she suffered after an auto accident in France. "They pulled me out of a heap of scrap iron, with cuts and bruises, a fractured arm, and cracked ribs." They gave her morphine. After she was taken off morphine, she persuaded a female friend to bring it to her hidden in a purse.

"I got down on all fours to find the syringe that I hid by turns in my bed, in the wastepaper basket, behind the bathtub, so that my friends couldn't find it."

Mysterious dope pushers smuggled drugs to her and she paid them outrageous sums. "I was so frantic that I no longer took the trouble to boil the needle and the syringe to sterilize them."

She put herself in the clinic, she thought she was improved and was allowed to go home, but she wasn't cured, and one day she decided to kill herself. Just as she had the poison and the glass ready, some merry-making partners arrived to say hello. Their accidental visit prevented her suicide.

While she was fighting the drug, she was also singing on tour in France, and the same woman was smuggling morphine to her. For four years this went on, and three times she went into a clinic. Four attendants held her down on the bed when she tried to leap out the window because they wouldn't give her an injection. Edith claimed that by gradual withdrawal she conquered the habit and that for eight months afterward, she stayed alone in her apartment, afraid to go out and face the world again.

Characteristically, Edith was having a love affair—with a married man, a bicycle rider. He moved his belongings to her place, and his wife had the police raid Edith's apartment and charge her with receiving stolen goods. Just as this romance collapsed, she met Jacques Pils. His pianist, an unknown Frenchman named Gilbert Becaud, brought Pils to her with a song Pils said he had found for her—"I've Got You Under My Skin."

During two weeks of rehearsing the song, Edith discovered she was in love again—and, miracle of miracles, he was single.

Pils was not a come-on strong guy. He was reticent, and when he finally said, "I love you," Edith replied, "You must prove your love, Jacques! If I ask you to marry me, will you do it?" He embraced her, and she made plans for the wedding . . . and then Pils had to make a confession.

"My God, he's married!" she figured. No! He had lied to her about his age. He had said he was 39 but he was really 46.

They were married in New York City in October, 1953, with Marlene Dietrich as her bridesmaid, Edith wearing white.

Jacques helped her—in fact, forced her—to continue the fight against drugs. Piaf told him about all her weaknesses, especially about her inclination to cheat on every man, to be unfaithful. He had promised never to take off his wedding ring. One night she visited him at a concert and the wardrobe mistress came into the wings and said, "Don't forget to take off your wedding ring, Mr. Pils."

Enraged, Edith felt another romance blowing up, but this was more: this was a marriage. Edith was singing at the Versailles, Jacques was singing at a club called La Vie En Rose. They were also apart on tours. Edith succumbed to the sweet words of another man, liked it, and admitted it to Pils, who said, "Before the catastrophe, let's separate."

It had lasted a couple of years, and now it was over in a couple of months. There was no bitterness, and Edith said, years later, that she would have remarried him if he had asked. Edith, however, was on the search again for a new lover—and found one—"a real louse," she said, who smashed her in the face while she was singing at the Waldorf-Astoria, and sent her to a hospital.

Edith was not only faithless, she could torture a lover. Although she helped develop Yves Montand by using him in her show and getting him to change his style from cowboy songs to love songs, she also made him jealous by pretending to hide letters from other men. At the same time, however, she might have two other affairs going with two other men.

Yet when she was introducing him in his own show at the Theater de l'Etoile, she personally phoned 400 people to say "I am presenting a new performer; come and you will see." An hour before he went on, she took him to church to pray. He was such a smashing success that Piaf had trouble getting the audience's attention when she followed him.

She was broke because she squandered enormous sums on men—and herself. The designers were waiting for her; she bought costly gowns and never wore them. She set up a specially decorated design for her suite in a Paris hotel, at a tremendous cost, and then couldn't sleep there. It was too rich; the blue satin bedroom was too beautiful and grand.

Edith bought some dazzling jewelry to bemuse one new lover. He jilted her. Edith fixed him. She took the necklace, the earrings, bracelet and pin and flushed them down the toilet. It should be added that Edith was drinking at the time, because she was an alcoholic, too. At least she so confessed, and said she was also capable of ingratitude. Once a man who had befriended her came to her for a loan. He had lent her money; now he was asking a loan from her.

She had bought herself some gold ingots that she hid during the day and looked at in fascination at night—signs of temporary wealth. She would have to sell them.

"No, I'm sorry, I cannot." She hung up.

And lived to regret it because the time came when she was broke.

A lover who was faithless to her not only left her but took the gold ingots with him.

Piaf could change lovers like dresses. In June, 1962, she was in mourning for Doug Davis, an American artist, who was killed in an Air France jet crash at Orly Field. He was going back to America to help arrange an American concert tour. By October, she was over that mourning and getting married to a former barber, half her age, Theodore Lamboukas, twenty-nine, also known as Theo Sarapo. He had become her singing protégé (just as had so many others).

By now Edith seemed to be over her alcohol period. Friends had sent her to take the cure and she was as tortured as she had been when she was a drug addict. She kept seeing little men—dwarves.

Her wedding with Sarapo, who somebody called "the Greek barber boy," was a public riot, with photographers battling the gendarmes when the couple went to the mayor's office in the fashionable Sixteenth Arrondissement for a civil ceremony and then to a religious ceremony in a nearby Greek Orthodox Church.

Cameramen were manhandled by the police; doors in the mayor's office were barred; the crush was so great that the bridegroom almost had to carry the bride (in black velvet) into the mayor's office. Later the mayor was worried over the validity of the marriage because it was behind closed doors.

"Piaf, Piaf!" cried the crowd as six cops formed a ring around her, trying to get her to the church. Five vans of police had been called; the crowd had reached thousands. Piaf, despite the scene of rioting, loved it. It added something to her marriage—which had already caused much speculation.

"Let them talk!" was Piaf's attitude. It was her business whom and how she married. She was always talking and thinking of death, now, and she wanted to have fun. Theo tried to find some for her. When her secretary, Claude Figus, another would-be singer, brought Theo around, Edith found him boring. But he kept coming back, bringing her gifts, and finally he offered to do her hair.

"You're a barber?" she laughed. That was one thing Edith hated—having her hair done. Furthermore, she was getting bald, and she didn't think she could be becoming to a man—a bald lady. It both amused and touched her—and he did her hair.

Later, as the romance between Edith and Theo headed toward marriage, the secretary, Figus, mysteriously killed himself.

Tragedy again—but Edith surmounted it and was riding high, going to restaurants with Theo, even going to beaches, and planning Theo's singing appearance at the Olympia Theater.

"He's using her to help his career," they said.

"It's true," he said. "It's true that if I didn't know her, I wouldn't be on stage with her at the Olympia. But I have my own talent and I will prove it."

"Don't you feel like a gigolo?"

"Not at all. I merely prefer being with Edith to being with someone my own age whom I do not love and who does not love me."

"Does your wife give you spending money?"

"Why should she? I'm making good money now as a singer, and, even before, my family was well off in the hairdressing business. My material life hasn't changed one way or the other."

This was a happy time—emotionally—for Edith, even though she was still suffering from her repertory of illnesses that was as big as her repertory of songs. Name an illness, a habit, and she had it, or had had it. She was fighting her illnesses, and she was fighting the cynical public which at first didn't know how to take young Theo as her husband.

But Paris loved Piaf and when she was introducing him as part of her act at the Olympia, the crowd broke into roars of applause for both of them.

Locked in each other's arms, they sang together, and the crowd yelled and stamped and applauded; Theo was victorious. That is to say, Edith was victorious. She had put him over.

They were outwardly a happy couple racing around Paris in a white Mercedes. The French press was generally friendly now and Piaf thought her health was improving. Her assorted pains, her arthritis, her scarecrow thinness did not bother her as much as they had, or maybe she was overlooking them as she tried to convince herself that she'd finally found the love that had eluded her through her own fooling around with it over the years.

Her friends contributed to her contentment by keeping out of sight a piece written by an American journalist, Joseph Barry. He reported that there was a sad story about Edith Piaf whom he called an "aging femme fatale." Her voice was gone. He put it less harshly. It was "failing."

Life was rosy, she was so-o 'appee with Theo—that was what she kept repeating—but while she may have been complimented to have Theo so attentive, she was getting to be very sick. She'd been disfigured by pain in a clinic in Besançon, France, and now in April, 1963, she was back in a Paris hospital, and Louis Barrier canceled her bookings. She got a blood tranfusion to start.

"I am sorry, but Edith is very tired," Barrier wrote to Elkort, her American representative.

She claimed in the hospital: "Each pain gives you some happiness inside. The more pain you have, the more joy. I have had great joy in my life because I have had so much pain. You have to have one to have the other." It was something that Edith had reasoned out for herself.

She fought off the pain in the hospital and took injections to help. She wanted to go back to America, to present Theo at the Versailles and at the Mark Hellinger Theater, where she'd been booked. She didn't know that she'd sung publicly the last time on her tour of France just before she went into the hospital.

"They'll adore you in America!" she assured Theo. He was six feet seven to her four feet ten. He became almost her nurse. As her pain increased, she was given more pain-killing drugs, and she was at times in a dream world. Theo, on his own, decided to take her to the Riviera for the summer; but in the villa they took she did not respond well to the sea, and so Theo took her off to the mountains. But she became unconscious there several times, and Theo moved her again to a little hideaway near Grasse, not far from Cannes.

"We'll be celebrating our first anniversary!" Edith told Theo from the bed which she hardly left now. Yes, it had been a year since the riotous scene in Paris, and for Edith it had been mostly pain, cirrhosis of the liver, and ulcers. She was down to 65 pounds, but the spirit was there. She exclaimed to Theo how well they would be received in America, in New York, Washington (where she wanted to have him sing for President Kennedy), and of course Hollywood, where they would want to put Theo in the movies, because he was so tall, so handsome, and such a good singer. Edith was in a happy delirium much of these nights and days in the month of early October, 1963.

They were together on their wedding anniversary, October 9, 1963. Edith was getting more injections, and there could not be much of a celebration; but Theo was there holding her hand and lifting her about. Finally it was clear that she had only hours to live. An ambulance was called, and Edith went home to Paris, the city that loved her, and that she loved in return. It is not clear precisely what hour or minute she died, but it was said officially that her death took place in her home in Paris, although one of the myths is that she died there on the Riviera and that she was dead when they placed her in the ambulance.

She is listed in the records as having died of an internal hemorrhage on October 11, 1963.

October was not a good month for "The Sparrow." It was in October, 1949, that Marcel Cerdan was killed. Curiously, Edith's *La Vie en Rose* with him had ended fourteen years before, and she had since had two husbands and many, many sweethearts, as well as rich professional triumphs that brought her happiness envied by the greatest stars. Yet in almost every obituary we read that Piaf lived a life of tragedy made tragic by the death of Cerdan.

Actually, Edith Piaf, in her tragic life, had a lot of fun.

I came into Paris that day from Copenhagen where I'd been attending a highly festive fiftieth birthday party for travel writer Temple Fielding. It was the Friday on which both Edith Piaf and Jean Cocteau died. Paris was stunned when it heard at breakfast that its beloved little bird had passed away. That's all that was talked about at the restaurants on the Champs-Élysées—and then about seven hours later it learned that its famous intellectual Jean Cocteau had also died. By coincidence, Cocteau, who had once written a one-act play for Piaf (about a woman hopelessly in love with an arrogant lover), had just eulogized Piaf for the press a few hours before he died.

As I went about the city that Friday and Saturday, I could feel Paris' grief building up. In the lobby of the George V, at Fouquet's, where I sat outside having a drink, the melancholy mood of the city got hold of me. Of course, I knew that Paris loved Piaf, but my own view of her had always been that of a detached American watching her from the ringside at the Versailles in New York or the Mocambo in Hollywood.

I went to the kiosk at Fouquet's for a paper. Paris *Soir* headlined: PIAF TRIBUTE STAGGERS PARIS.

Amazingly, even in death, she was having trouble, she had not found complete peace. She was denied a church funeral because of her divorce from Jacques Pils and subsequent marriage to Theo. It was an "irregular situation," according to the church.

The crowds trying to get a look at Piaf in an open coffin in her home were enormous, the papers reported. I recoil from funerals and wakes, and I did not intend to go.

But on Sunday afternoon I decided that as a newspaperman it was my duty to brave the crowd. It was a sad, emotional, quietly mumbling crowd that I got into on the Boulevard Lannes, it must have numbered thousands, and it had been moving by endlessly for hours before I got there. It reminded me of the thousands who filled the streets of Washington for the funeral procession of President Franklin D. Roosevelt in 1945. There were traffic jams, typical Parisian auto accidents, drunks, girls suspected of being prostitutes, many, many, gendarmes, and now and then a touch of humor.

I had anticipated difficulty getting in.

But there was none. The gendarmes knew they had a respectful crowd, and they had the line of six people moving slowly up the street to the home. They were in berets and sweaters and light suits—it was a sunny autumn afternoon—and they were mostly the common people.

Perhaps that's why it was easy to get in. The great people of Paris had already paid their respects at a private viewing. When it came my turn, we filed into a small room. There was the casket with the tiny body inside it. On a piano alongside was a picture of Piaf, looking not much different from the frail little forty-seven-year-old child lying there.

It was a moment I did not wish to prolong. After one more quick last glance, I spoke briefly to a woman I took to be a relative, and hurried back into the warm afternoon. As I left, I saw that the crowd was building up even more.

Now people were being shoved and even knocked down in their rush to get into line; women lost their shoes and tempers. The boulevard was closed to auto traffic, and the great crowd was estimated to have grown into an incredible 100,000.

It had not been my intention to go to the funeral the next forenoon. But the magic of Piaf seized me, and at 10 A.M. I yielded and told a cabdriver to take me to the famous cemetery in the eastern working section of Ménilmontant. I was afraid I would be late. And I was. And the cabdriver took me to the wrong end of the cemetery.

There was nothing to do but walk to the other end of the cemetery. I stumbled among the graves and gravestones, swearing at the cabdriver, hoping to reach the rumbling noises from the people that I could hear somewhere in the distance. I saw other people also hurrying through the graveyard, some carrying sacks or bags of lunch.

I was perspiring and getting angrier now at the cabdriver, but at last I came near Piaf's burial plot. And like a mirage, there were limousines of the famous: Marlene Dietrich, Michele Morgan, Tino Rossi, Gilbert Becaud, and other stars. There were the Foreign Legion men looking so smart. Marlene of course was in deepest mourning, looking down and not up at any time, holding her lip with her finger. I did just what the others did. I hopped over the gravestones to get a better look at the famous mourners.

I made note of who Edith Piaf's neighbors were in the famous cemetery: Oscar Wilde, Balzac, Chopin, and Sarah Bernhardt.

I had arrived just as the burial service was over. Marlene's limousine was just crunching up the drive, departing, as were the others. Left behind were cars and cars of flowers and mourners, who remained to eat their lunches among the gravestones and talk kindly of their little sparrow Edith.

As I rushed out of the graveyard to try to find a phone, leaving those thousands behind, I thought to myself that for a child from the streets, Edith Piaf had probably done better than any woman of her time.

She had ten times as many lovers as most women, she had money, jewelry, talent, fame, top billing, top headlines when she was sick, she literally had everything, and I think that her cloak of the tragedienne was partly a put-on and that inwardly she was laughing a little at us for not realizing that she was having a good time and enjoying her "tragedies."

Daddy O

IT was easy to see how Jackie Kennedy had fallen, if not actually in love with him and his millions, then at least into sincere affection for him (and them). Because the Aristotle Onassis that I have seen and known (only slightly, I wish to emphasize) is a round gray Greek teddy bear of the kind that women love to pet while telling them how cute they are. When I have seen him at El Morocco, in a gray suit (although nearly everybody else was in something decently dark), and when he has puffed a chunky and expensive cigar, blowing the expensive smoke in my face, I have thought to myself that this is a millionaire you could like even if he didn't have a shipping line, an airline, or a Jackie Kennedy to his name.

"Are you loose?" he asked me when I came near the table. It was around midnight in December, 1972—the thirteenth, I think—and when I confessed I was, he asked me to join them, signaled for a chair for me, and asked me what I was drinking.

"Scotch on the rocks." I was still standing, waiting for the chair and the drink.

The Golden Greek looked up at me from his sitting position. "How are you, Professor?" he inquired.

"Professor?" I said.

"I call you Professor Wilson," he said.

I haven't figured it out until this moment, but I suspect that to him, a man wearing horn rims and a rather glum workmanlike expression in a glamorous supper club at midnight might give the impression of being professorial.

When my chair arrived, I sat between him and Johnny Meyer, his aide and nocturnal companion, who knew Onassis when the world knew Johnny Meyer better than it knew Onassis. This was away back in the 1940's, when Johnny Meyer was Howard Hughes' aide and Onassis literally had hardly a scow to his name. Or at least only three or four or half a dozen.

"Don't tell him anything, Ari, he'll put it in the paper," Johnny Meyer cautioned his boss, but this was all badinage, for Johnny had put an arm around me before and in fact had summoned me to the table. Johnny loves people around him.

"You know Jim Farley," Johnny said, nodding toward James Farley, Jr., at the next table with a beautiful girl, "who passed away about an hour ago?"

"You're referring to the famous banker?" I said, joining in.

"Banker? He couldn't finance me for a new Buick," scoffed Johnny.

"Not couldn't. *Wouldn't!*" I said.

Ari and Johnny and Jim were kind enough to laugh (Mr. Farley was indeed a bank president), and now I was within the select circle. The banter turned to Johnny Meyer's watchful eye covering the stairway down which came various beauties from the ladies' room. Johnny was making such exclamatory remarks about the bouncy qualities of the descending damosels that Daddy O became unhappy with his own seat.

"I want a ringside seat!" he announced. They exchanged chairs.

Jackie O was not there to say him nay. Onassis is an incurable insomniac who customarily goes out with Meyer when Jackie wishes to stay home and read or watch TV.

"Now *I* watch!" he said. And he looked glum. "Now is nothing!"

It was true that the downward parade of beauties ceased when he got in a seat where he could have observed them. He grumbled good-humoredly about that. We got into a discussion about traveling, touched off by Johnny Meyer's remark that they were supposed to have flown to London that night for Paul Getty's eightieth birthday party, but "Ari called me at six o'clock that we weren't going."

Ari didn't want to talk about why they didn't go and asked me not to print that they'd canceled plans to go. Johnny mentioned that a recent trip had been frighteningly turbulent.

Naturally, I wondered if the decision not to go had to do with Jackie Onassis. It was a question you simply could not ask even indirectly. I also knew that Jackie reads the columns or has friends who reads them, and that she sometimes learns of his innocent nighttime fun hunting through the newspapers.

"What plans do you have for Christmas and the first of the year?" I asked.

"I may be on the other side," Onassis said. "I've been here four times this year . . . three or four weeks at a time . . . maybe about three months altogether. Johnny, how many trips you made this year to the other side?"

"It would have been thirteen if we'd gone to London tonight . . . last year, nineteen," Johnny said.

Onassis looked at me and shook his head. "Too many," he said. Johnny laughed. "Look who's talking!"

Onassis seemed to me to be restless and also lonesome. "I thought my daughter Christina would be with me tonight," he said, "but she didn't feel like it."

In their darktime wandering, he said, they sometimes go to the busy Greek restaurants and nightclubs where men dance with men and where celebrities like Anthony Quinn are inspired to leap up and recite poetry, including some that they have written.

"We quit going to ———," Johnny said, naming a famous nighttime celebrity haunt. "They haven't swept out in months."

I mentioned a curious incident concerning Onassis. Dorothy Lamour told me she was in St. Patrick's Cathedral searching for St. Anthony's statue and couldn't find it beneath the scaffolding erected there to protect the holy figures from the blasting by contractors building the new Olympic Airways Tower across the street. James A. Farley, Sr., and several priests were in a group meeting there, shaking their heads, she said.

"Of course Mr. Onassis has no legal responsibility for the

blasting, but if Jackie Onassis knew it, being a good Catholic, she would make a nice contribution," one of the churchmen had said, according to Dorothy Lamour.

Onassis smiled and nodded but seemed to be unaware of the situation. He has always been happy to see Jackie forced into spending money (even though it's probably his to begin with). At the end of the fourth anniversary "surprise" party that Jackie gave him, he mentioned to Johnny Meyer, "Make sure Jackie picks up the tab."

Onassis' dependence on Johnny Meyer has always fascinated me. Meyer, half a year younger than Onassis, cornered the wheat market during the Depression, when he was the youngest member of the Chicago Board of Trade. He had a Rolls-Royce and a Duesenberg and lived in a triplex apartment—while others were selling apples in the street. In those days he hung out at the Chez Paree in Chicago (Tony Martin was playing the drums). In New York the place to go was the Central Park Casino, where you would probably see "the late Mayor," "The Night Mayor," Jimmy Walker.

He catapulted himself into the employ of Howard Hughes when the lanky Texan was making a movie with Jane Russell and got into the headlines as Hughes' "party giver and check signer" during the U.S. Senate's investigation of government spending for a Hughes flying boat. Hughes made fools of the investigators. "Pick-up-the-tab Johnny" landed on his feet. His reputation as a party giver and host with lots of lively phone numbers remained intact. A hatcheck girl at El Morocco accused Johnny of being father of her child, but he submitted to blood tests and was found innocent. Johnny made money in some oil investments on his own and left Hughes. Next stop: Onassis.

"Don't forget to make that call tomorrow," Johnny warned Onassis that night. "It's a sit-down dinner." Onassis nodded obediently.

My chat with them in El Morocco had been pleasant but unproductive—a columnist must always think of what news he's accumulating while he's on the town—and I finished my drink and prepared to leave. Onassis remarked to me in a gentle way that if I printed things about him, "we can't enjoy your company," a strong but friendly hint that I'd better not report this evening's activities, which, I thought, were most innocent, anyway.

It was Onassis' custom to lunch almost every day at 21 with

business associates and then to leave in his chauffeured Cadillac. One day as I was exchanging a few words with him when he was leaving, another very wealthy fellow named Maurice Uchitel, who is fond of Rolls-Royces, came out of the restaurant. Seeing Onassis departing by Cadillac, Uchitel said with a sad sigh, "Look at that! A Cadillac! He can't afford a Rolls. If the man's a little short, he can always call me. That's what friends are for."

Onassis' son Alexandros, twenty-four, died on Tuesday, January 23, 1973, after his new amphibian plane crashed as it was taking off from Athens airport. Onassis, who was in New York when he learned of the accident and flew there immediately with Jackie, declared later in a press conference that the boy's brain was destroyed and his features completely destroyed—and he decided not to try to keep him alive for a few more days.

"We weren't killing him. We were just letting him die," Onassis said. The Associated Press reported that his voice dragged, it was difficult to hear him, there were pouches under his eyes, and he had cried all night and left the house to wander about.

Ten days later, after his return to New York, I had the empty honor of telling him something else that was tragic, in a way.

I had received an advance copy of the issue of *Screw* magazine with the headline JACKIE ONASSIS NAKED and a headline inside, JACKIE ONASSIS, WORLD'S RICHEST PUSSY. Alongside were pictures of Jackie, one frontal, showing her breasts and pubis clearly, another a rear view showing her derriere.

Bad as that was, the combined text and caption was worse. Jackie was described as "the most successful whore in history" and "a top-dollar hooker."

The paper would be on the stands the following week. Knowing Johnny Meyer liked to be informed of events concerning Onassis ahead of time, even though they might be disastrous, I located him, described this story and picure setup, and waited for his reaction.

"You're kiddin'!" he said. "I'm seeing Ari at seven at the King Cole Room at the St. Regis. Could you bring the thing over? No interviews, though, nothing like that."

"OK. I wouldn't touch this thing anyhow. I just thought you'd want to see it."

"What's the name of the magazine? *Screw*? I never heard of it," he said.

This surprised me as *Screw* was already well known to the

country. Maybe Johnny Meyer was out of the country more than he knew. As this was Friday, February 2, 1973, and Onassis was in mourning, I wished to be considerate of him. As I started out to meet him, I took along a copy of the New York *Post* so I could conceal the pieces from *Screw* inside it in case there should be anybody near observing his reading.

"I talked to Ari and told him you were coming . . . he'll be here in a minute," Johnny told me. He was at the end of the bar, one of his favorite locations. He was nervous when Ari didn't arrive and made two calls to daughter Christina's upstairs suite. Each time Ari was "on the way down." I began to feel that Ari really wasn't coming down.

Suddenly we got the word that he really was on the way.

"You sit over there with Ari," Johnny said, pointing to a back table. "I'll sit over here with Christina. I don't want her to know what you're talking about. You've got it with you, haven't you?"

"Right here in my pocket."

He came in alone, Christina having remained in her suite, a small, sad, quiet man of great power, and walked directly to the back of the bar and to the small table where I was already seated. I had not seen him since the death of Alexandros and I extended my hand and expressed my sorrow. Johnny Meyer had ordered a drink for Onassis—a Jack Daniels sour mash—but Onassis waved it away.

"I had some upstairs," he said.

It was a difficult thing for me to do—doubly difficult because of his grief over his son—but he had asked for it. I pulled the sheets of *Screw* magazine from my pocket and inserted them in the New York *Post* spread out open before me.

"I think this is outrageous," I said, pointing out the headlines.

"I see," he said. His eyes wandered over the page with the two pictures of his nude wife, but he didn't linger on them. He'd doubtless already seen them in European publications. I had expected more anger and outrage from him. Now I saw that he was tired and that he seemed old and slumped. His eyes were heavy, and his movements were slow. His voice betrayed weariness. He was down, down, down, and I could almost feel his suffering.

"How much more grief do I have to take?" he asked me.

How different he was from that night at El Morocco when he'd called me "Professor." I probably shouldn't have done it, but I pointed out a disgusting caption under a rearview picture of Jackie.

"What one can do?" Onassis suddenly asked, looking up at me.

"Very little, I suppose."

"We've got nine hundred lawyers . . . we could probably get an injunction to stop it from getting on the stands. We've got the weekend," Johnny Meyer said.

"Harry Truman had a saying," I reminded them. "Never get in a pissing contest with a skunk."

Onassis shook his head, as if agreeing. "Yes, maybe we could stop publication for now. But in three months. . . ."

They would then publish it anyway and with bigger circulation because of the buildup. He repeated his question of before: "What one can do?" He added, "Sometimes, in doubt, do nothing, and silence is golden."

Sitting alongside him, I felt that I was more visibly upset about the labeling of Jackie than he was. His anger was contained. He simmered rather than exploded. It now became clear to me that he had suffered so much notoriety of various kinds since his marriage to Jackie that this was taken as just one more example, and how could he fight it?

"It is a kind of balancing," he said, quietly and philosophically.

"Balancing?" I didn't understand that at all.

"I think I am a liberal, and they thought they were liberal," he said. He didn't specify, but as he continued, I saw that he referred to the Kennedys and their group of which Jackie was a part.

"They are liberal, and the liberal viewpoint is freedom to say anything about anybody. And now it balances, it swings back, and the liberals, or anybody else, can say anything they want to about you. Like this paper!" And he jerked his thumb toward *Screw*.

He was informed on the law, I could see; he knew that under recent interpretations, a figure in public life has little protection, unless it can be established that there's malice.

"There is a Greek expression for the balancing," he said, and then quickly he removed his wife, Jackie, from any connection with the liberalism which, he had just complained, bit back at the liberals who had fostered it.

"She is too young, she is only forty," he said.

It was another age group that he was talking about, perhaps those in their sixties, or near seventies: those nearer his age.

I was impressed that he could be thinking of basic analytic philosophies at a time when his wife had been called a whore and concluded that he was a man of intelligence and judgment. One much less thoughtful, myself for example, might have hunted a gun and tried to blow the head off the author of such accusations. Onassis did not bother even to look over the sheets again but repeated his first comment: "What one can do?"

Then he calmly folded up the papers, the tear sheets with the charges against Jackie.

"I can have these?" he said.

"They're yours. I brought them for you. And I'm sorry."

"Thank you." He got to his feet heavily and, after shaking my hand, walked away from the table, hesitating a moment to talk to Johnny Meyer, who now faced him stomach to stomach. Johnny is just short of six feet. Ari is five or six inches shorter. Standing there talking to Johnny, in his somber suit and dark shoes, with gray hair and a gray, sad face, I thought he appeared to be a very sad billionaire. I wished I could read his thoughts. Many a time he must have wondered just what he was doing in the United States. Was this the land where he really wanted to be? Was this the life he wanted to lead, constantly being spied upon as the husband of the widow of President John F. Kennedy . . . always watched to see if he was still wooing Maria Callas and maybe meeting her somewhere? Didn't he often wish he was back in Greece not so famous and not so rich?

But as he said himself, "What one can do?"

Of all the rumors that a columnist deals with, it is the most recurrent: "Jackie and Onassis are splitting up. . . . They don't live together. . . . They haven't seen each other for months. . . . He's back with Maria Callas. . . ."

The people who tell you these things are usually well placed in the Onassis-and-Jackie world and have reason to know what they're talking about. The last time I remember hearing this from what had to be considered an excellent source was in October, 1972.

It was almost as though Jackie and Onassis had heard it, too.

Because when I began my newest investigation of this old rumor, I happened upon the news, as it was then, that Jackie was going to give Ari the celebrated "surprise" fourth anniversary party at El Morocco. In the next year they were together more than they'd been previously during their marriage. I ran into my informants who defended the original rumor of them splitting; They claimed it had been true, but Jackie had arranged this party to throw everybody off! ("What one can do?" as Onassis had said.)

Their frequent lack of togetherness contributed to the rumors that they might be splitting. And Onassis himself was never very romantic in his statements about the marriage. Even on the night of the surprise party which cost probably about $3,000 for sixty-two guests, Onassis did not make any pretty and loving speech. I managed to ask him well toward the end of the evening if he was really surprised.

"When you're married four years," he said, "what surprises you?"

A fine thing to say to a bride who'd plotted this little party and let it get slightly out of hand so that the bridegroom had found out about it! Nevertheless, those who know about such things declared that Jackie had scored quite a social coup in getting Mrs. Joseph P. Kennedy, her former mother-in-law, to attend her gilded soiree in the Champagne Room, along with Pierre Salinger, President Kennedy's press secretary, who went so far as to sit at the piano and pound out his version of "Sometimes I Feel Like a Motherless Child." The song was just a random selection from Pierre Salinger's repertoire and was not intended to reflect on any of the guests or the mood of the evening.

I was a witness to the party but not a guest. Jackie had expected to have a small, intimate group, but when she and her helper, Nancy Tuckerman, began phoning invitations, it grew and grew.

When I began looking around on the second floor of El Morocco that night, Johnny Meyer urged me to go right on into the party, but I did not consider this a proper invitation. I therefore waited watchfully downstairs. About 1 A.M. the octogenarian Rose Kennedy decided to leave, and it was Ari Onassis personally who took her by the arm and escorted her down the famous well-lighted stairway.

About a dozen photographers were still waiting.

Seeing them and their cameras and recoiling from some of the flashes, Mrs. Kennedy said, "Those lights blind me!" Onassis took her by the arm and escorted her from the club by another exit where there were no cameramen.

All in all, it was a working evening for Onassis; it was, to be blunt, a chore. First, Jackie and her sister, Lee Radziwill, the princess, were late. It could have been due to Jackie's gold belt from India, weighted down with assorted gems, that she wore on her black overblouse with a long white skirt. The guests had been asked to be there at eight-thirty, but it was nearer nine when Onassis and the sisters arrived to be confronted with a traffic jam which they and the party had caused.

Fretting about the delay, Onassis chose to hop from his limousine, even though it hadn't reached the curb, and proceed inside alone. Jackie and her sister waited, ladylike, till the car got to the curb. To some guests, it appeared that Onassis and Jackie had arrived separately.

The guests included some of the greatest celebrities. But some didn't know the others and they mingled and made little jokes about the lateness of the host and hostess and sort of introduced themselves. When Jackie and her sister swept in and took the private elevator to the second floor, Jackie then began introducing Ari to some personal friends that he'd barely heard about before. He took it like a champion; after all, it was *his* party.

There was a Kennedy flavor to it even though it was for the Golden Greek. Stephen Smith and his wife, Jean, sister of John F. Kennedy, were prominent in the group, and when banker George Moore proposed a toast to "the bride and groom," Stephen Smith in a frivolous mood sang out, "Who are the bride and groom?"

Everybody who heard that thought it was pretty good, and the party loosened up.

Everything was chicly understated—except, of course, the caviar, vodka, champagne and contrefilet with truffle sauce. But there was nothing as vulgar as an anniversary cake to be seen, nor was there any open mention of Ari's giving Jackie an anniversary gift or vice versa (although there was whispered speculation about that subject at some of the tables).

I was still sitting in the main room when the Onassises closed up the party upstairs and came downstairs and took the corner table where they usually sit, a few feet from the table where I happened to be. While they were having some more wine, they happily discovered that their friend Joan Fontaine was there in a champagney mood with Shipwreck Kelly and were being, as we say in my profession, "cuddly." Joan told me and them, "We're announcing our engagement for the third time."

Onassis, who is very fond of dancing, took a turn around with one of the other women party guests who'd also come to the main room, but he did not dance with Jackie. When they departed, they were bowed out of the club by the very handsome and erect white-tied Angelo, the maître d' of El Morocco for many years. Naturally, they were not presented with a check, nor did Onassis have to dig into his wallet for a credit card. All that had been arranged ahead of time by Jackie's staff. When I made a modest inquiry about the size of the check a couple of days later, one of the club executives told me, "We are still counting."

But the $3,000 figure that I obtained elsewhere did not seem at all exorbitant.

On leaving El Morocco, Jackie succeeded in taking her husband to her country place in New Jersey where he occasionally goes on holidays and weekends with her. Characteristically, he was back on the late beat Sunday night, in Manhattan, investigating the action with Johnny Meyer at P. J. Clarke's and the Hippopotamus. There are some dedicated night-owls (of whom Onassis is one) who just cannot go to bed until they have looked into the "action places" to find what's happening. Usually, nothing is, but they must be satisfied that nothing is, before they can give up and go home. Considerably later, after Onassis seemingly had outlasted even Johnny Meyer, we saw him walking along the street alone, without a topcoat, smoking a cigar. It made me nervous, thinking what could happen to a billionaire if muggers went to work on him.

I discovered that although he seems to be walking along alone, he usually isn't alone. His limousine is creeping along somewhere behind him, and it's chauffeured by a muscular Greek employee named Georgio. Onassis was almost mugged once in New York. While on one of his late strolls, he saw two men closing in on him. Just then a car from the Holmes Protective Agency shot up the street. It had a rotating light such as is on some police cars. The would-be muggers saw that, took it for a police car, and ran, leaving Onassis wondering why he was suddenly all alone. After that experience, he arranged for Georgio to be always near.

You must admire Jackie Onassis. When historians look back, they will find few if any women who have married so well and picked such interesting and successful husbands. What Presidential widow has left her widow's weeds behind to marry a billionaire? What Presidential widow, in fact, has decided to marry again? But surely that was her right, and in this day of a recognition of sex urges, when loneliness is also understood, it was not disapproved of except by the most prudish people.

Jackie had great luck with the husbands she married—but when you come to think of it, she didn't take any huge gambles.

First she married a Kennedy, which wasn't any big risk to her financially or prestigiously, since he was already a U.S. Senator, and any good-looking young Senator with Joseph P. Kennedy for a father certainly had a future.

Well, you can't blame a girl for trying to marry well, can you?

Going back to history again, was there anybody of the feminine sex who was married to a President and then to a King of the Sea? Jackie went from power, which she never greatly exercised, to money, which enabled her to go shopping. Had she been more ambitious, Jackie might have become one who pulled the strings backstage that guided the fate of statesmen and princes of finance. But at least until her mid-forties, she never demonstrated this wish. Therefore, Cleopatra will be regarded by the encyclopedists as slightly more important than Jacqueline Onassis—although the circulation managers of the fan magazines will never agree.

It will be a long time before the truth of Jackie's relationship with John F. Kennedy is told. But Joseph P. Kennedy's rumored offer of $1,000,000 or more to her, to cool off their marital difficulties when he was on the verge of getting to be President in the late 1950's and early '60's, was so well circulated that *Time* magazine printed it after JFK's inauguration.

And yet Jackie was never a sexpot.

In the age of sex's triumph over all, Jackie was regarded by many men as not "having enough meat on her." She wasn't one to excite even a sex maniac—and it was all her own fault, owing to her passion for being skinny. Attractive as she was facially, chicly as she was dressed, she inspired more than one man to comment sadly, "I don't know what Onassis sees on her"—yes, on her—because on her there wasn't much but skin and bones and ribs.

"I remember Jackie since she was ten or twelve years old in Newport, the daughter of Black Jack Bouvier," says one of the older socialites of that day.

"She was just a skinny little kid with no great physical attributes," he remembers. "Pretty, and very active, but no great figure. No breasts, no ass and no legs. . . ."

Jack Kennedy at the same time was equally unnoticed and undistinguished in the Newport group. Jack was "one of the Kennedy kids." That referred to the sons and daughters of Joseph P. Kennedy whose eldest son, Joseph Kennedy, was the pride and the hope for greatness. There appeared to be nothing but second place in prospect for Jack. Jack and the other "Kennedy boys," including Bobby and Teddy, used to frequent the right places in Newport and then New York, but nobody (except possibly they) sensed that they would one day be part of the Presidential sweepstakes.

As for Jacqueline Lee Bouvier, where was she going to go—a skinny little kid with no tits, no ass, and no legs?

Give this little girl a hand—let's hear it for the girl who capitalized very well on what she didn't have. It's something for the body molders and body builders to think over. What girl of her age with great legs, great tits, and great ass has gone as far as Jackie went without them?

Jackie proved a girl doesn't need tits and ass and legs.

In September, 1973, after Richard Burton and Elizabeth Taylor split, rumors emanating from Rome said that Aristotle Onassis had been seen with Elizabeth. This seemed preposterous to most people, but not to everybody. There was one person who remembered Elizabeth saying she quite understood Jackie marrying him. . . . "he's got great charm, he's fascinating—and he's sexy."

"The Gweat Dietwich"

"WHAT did you think of Marlene?" I inquired of an acquaintance of mine, known to be fair and honest, who had observed Miss Dietrich around the time of her seventy-first birthday when she was doing TV and continuing her one-woman shows on tour despite her status as a senior citizen.

I had expected a mild acceptance of her temperament.

"I'll tell you what I think of her!" he answered willingly. "She's devoid of graciousness; she's rude to everybody. She's hard of hearing. She's got an old lady's stoop. She insults nearly everybody who gets near her. She's a complainer; she's impossible to satisfy. I think she behaves like an idiot." He paused. Then; "She gets more mileage on less talent than anyone I know."

I was so surprised that I asked, "What in particular did you object to?"

"The objections," he answered, "are never yours, they're hers. She objects to everything. She's an impossible woman."

"They say," I suggested, "she's a perfectionist."

"That's right," he agreed. "You can never do anything that's perfect; only she can. She," he added, "is an aging bitch."

There are two sides to Dietrich, as there are to all stars, and even Marlene's own cheering section will admit that her demands and complaints are often outrageous. Her harshest critics, those who don't care for her as a performer, will grant that she is the slickest show woman left and that her act, which has been called "the world's greatest con job," is unequaled in its precision and its professionalism. "She is the last of the great ladies," declared producer Alexander H. Cohen, who first presented her to New York audiences and then produced her TV special. "When she is gone, there will be nobody left of those glamor girls who went to gold bathrooms. When I get so mad at her I want to kill her, I try to remember that."

The "Dietrich legend" of having the world's most beautiful legs and of being difficult and unapproachable have made her an enormous box-office attraction, perhaps the biggest. She got a record 40 percent of the gross receipts and a $25,000-a-week guarantee when she appeared at the Lunt-Fontanne Theater in New York in 1967. For six weeks, she took away around $250,000, which Cohen says is a modern record. On Broadway, they don't care if you're difficult; it's the box-office numbers that count.

Marlene's "legend" has been partly constructed by Marlene herself. She has been trying to make a mystery of her age since she was pushing fifty and certainly has not discouraged debate about it. There are facts, however, that she doesn't mention.

Once I discovered through contacts in medical circles that she was severely burned about the bosom by the explosion of a kitchen gadget while she was indulging in one of her favorite pastimes, cooking. I called her private number to ask her about it, since the damage to an actress' bosom could be serious. A

German voice which insisted that it belonged to Miss Dietrich's maid answered and wouldn't discuss it. On a later call, the voice that was supposed to belong to the maid grew angry and admitted that it was the voice of Miss Dietrich and demanded to know why in hell I was bothering her. A plastic surgeon had repaired her so beautifully that nobody could detect it.

"Do you know the secret of her famous figure?" a woman recently said to me. "She has a body stocking molded to every vein in her body. It cost her five thousand dollars. She wears it under those net gowns, and when you think you're seeing Dietrich, you're seeing that body stocking. Her plastic surgeon knows that his name must never appear in connection with her."

Almost everything that Dietrich does is carefully calculated; most of it is planned to enrich the Dietrich legend. As an admirer of her professionalism and knowing of her importance as a personality, I have been following her for many years.

Back in 1960, after covering the wedding of Princess Margaret and Tony Armstrong-Jones in London and the Cannes Film Festival (at the time Prince Aly Khan was killed at the wheel of his car in Paris), I went to Hamburg, Germany, to catch Marlene's concert at the Opera House.

It was "the kraut's return to krautland," somebody—probably her friend Ernest Hemingway—said. Burt Bacharach, then almost unknown outside music circles, was her accompanist.

As Marlene concluded the concert to a tremendous standing ovation, my wife and I saw her take two bows and started pushing our way through the crowd to the backstage area and Marlene's dressing room. We had come a long way and wished to say hello.

It took us fifteen to twenty minutes, for the crowd was greater than I had anticipated. When we got to the darkened backstage area, it was a half hour after midnight.

Suddenly I saw Marlene running clickety-clack across the backstage wearing only her beautiful legs and a three-quarter-length blond mink jacket.

"What's she running from—a fire?" I wondered.

Burt Bacharach loomed up, smiling and shaking hands. "She's still taking bows," he explained. "They won't go out there unless she comes out for one more bow. That's seven curtain calls *so far*."

Marlene came running back from the last bow.

"They von't go home," she said. "And I thought it was a cold town."

Settling down in her dressing room later, she admitted being overwhelmed by her *wunderbar* success in the fatherland she'd given up to become an American citizen and then asked with a sly smile if I'd noticed that she'd inserted a little Israeli melody into the program without raising any objection here in this area that had been notorious for its concentration camps in World War II.

At this time, Marlene was not yet sixty, and her shaking, shimmery singing style and deep bows in her skin-colored net gown had a suggestion of secret naughtiness that the Germans of Hamburg loved.

"That long fur piece you wore . . . was that white fox?" I asked her.

"No, that's swan's feather cape." She chided me for not recognizing it. "I thought the Germans might ruin it with rotten eggs if I wore mink." She was laughing about the fears that she'd had when she came back to Germany that had now proved so unfounded.

With her German accent which gets thicker from time to time, Marlene has been an appropriate target for spoofing, and she has been done most devastatingly by Carol Channing on TV, as well as in Carol's one-woman shows. Carol also has beautiful legs. She made the most of them in the Dietrich sketch, showing them all the way up to the pelvis, encased of course in silk stockings.

When Carol shimmered out in a diaphanous Blue Angel negligee, acting sexier than a Forty-second Street hooker, you would hear Dietrich asking in an injured voice, "Vouldn't you teenk dere'd be more applause for Marlene Dietwich?"

An eloquent guttural growl that was an exaggeration of Dietrich embellished the impersonation. *"Gott in Himmel!"* Dietrich would explode at the mention of Brigitte Bardot. And when she heard the name Sophia Loren, she would loudly and wetly expectorate, "PTTT!"

But Carol's high point of the spoof was when she had Marlene get her long beautiful legs and shoes caught in the rungs of the chair she was sitting on. Marlene would be tugging madly to get her legs free, while spitting, growling, and cursing, with her accent growing fiercer and wetter. It was a brilliant satirization. And, according to Carol, Marlene didn't object.

"Of course I dwon't objwect, dwarling," Carol claimed that Marlene said.

"I did it in Las Vegas," Carol later informed me. "Lucille Ball told me I shouldn't satirize a great legend like Marlene.

"The next month, on TV, Lucille satirized not only Marlene, but also *Hello, Dolly!*—and me."

Marlene waited until she was sixty-five to play Broadway, and she gave her greatest performance both onstage and offstage—especially off. For about ten years, she'd hesitated, and the skeptics among us said, "She'll never play New York. She's afraid of the critics. They'll murder her."

"Marlene's OK in Vegas where the audiences just listen to her on the way to the crap tables, but she'll never make it in New York," we said.

And we thought Alex Cohen was conning us when he announced he'd signed her. She'd pull out, we were sure. Cohen, it turned out, had had his troubles getting her. She kept saying no. He believes that was calculated to get him to offer her more money. She also wanted to be sure she could get Burt Bacharach to be her conductor and accompanist. When she actually arrived in New York late in September, 1967, to prepare for the opening of her show, it called for a press conference where one reporter asked her, "Have you ever thought of retiring?" and she answered, "No, have you?"

She was very bossy at the conference, held at L'Étoile restaurant (no longer in existence), and reprimanded some reporters who had somehow got behind her.

"Don't creep around my back . . . my back isn't interesting to anybody," she snapped at them. She would be wearing a $30,000 gown by Jean Louis. . . . bugle beads lined in 14-karat gold, the gown covered with gold and diamonds, she said. For the press, she was wearing a biege dress and a dark brown helmet, both by Balenciaga.

"Would you describe your hat?" somebody asked.

"That's your business, you do it," she said.

"What will you do in your show?"

"Come and see it and find out."

One reporter was ungallant enough to return to his typewriter and recount a famous anecdote. Dietrich had allegedly complained to a photographer about some recent pictures.

"Those pictures you took of me in *Garden of Allah* were so gorgeous," she complained. "Why aren't these pictures as good?"

"Well, you see," answered the photographer, "now I'm eight years older."

All this built into a major opening, glamorized by the presence of two stars who have since died, Anita Louise and Tallulah Bankhead. "Marlene's my protégée," Tallulah proclaimed. "I introduced her at the Las Vegas Sands in 1955"—twelve years before! Olivia de Havilland and Joan Fontaine, the battling sisters who had feuded and then made up again, were in the dressy crowd which Marlene proceeded to hypnotize. She was no less the enchantress in New York than she was in Las Vegas.

I was less mesmerized by her husky, throaty, brooding singing than by her figure, her agility, and her well-disciplined stage acrobatics so carefully timed as to make one remember that she was German and a perfectionist. Marlene extracted roar after roar of applause from the on-its-feet audience. I, for one, was almost overcome by the waves of flowers that were thrown at her feet by fans, who, it turned out, were to be seen there every night hurling bouquets at her dainty slippers. The Dietrich cultists who pitch the flowers are another story which I will get at a few paragraphs from here.

Marlene had little to fear from the critics, whom we had believed would be unfriendly. Vincent Canby in the New York *Times* wrote of her "magic" that "spellbinds" audiences. Douglas Watt in the *Daily News* said, "The curtain calls go on and on," and Hobe Morrison in *Variety* reported that there were many younger, prettier singers around with better voices but that "she can sing rings around them." He added, "She is a sensational hit."

There was one critic who did not adopt the reverent tone of the others: Martin Gottfried of WPAT.

Pointing out that audiences were paying $10 a ticket, he commented that "it isn't the hottest bargain in town.

"What Miss Dietrich lacks in vocal ability she does not make up in personality," he said. "She is not a performer, on the stage she is rather boring, spacing her unmusical and characterless songs with uninteresting and characterless stories. The manufactured legends are just show business gimmickry. Miss Dietrich is pretty silly, too. You can tell yourself for only so long isn't it amazing that she is seven hundred years old. OK, Dietrich is in pretty good shape for a lady her age; but she hardly looks like a young woman, and for that matter she hardly comes through as a woman at all."

That was the worst review she got and the only bad critique anybody remembered.

On opening night, Alexander Cohen invited the celebrities and a few hundred other first-nighters to a black-tie party across town at the Rainbow Room, in the RCA-NBC Building. Some of Marlene's most intimate well-wishers crowded backstage to her dressing room. Those who were not stifled by the flowers and remained were to witness one more remarkable demonstration of the Dietrich prearranged showmanship.

A couple of uniformed policemen held her in their arms protectively as they opened the door to the sidewalk when she was leaving.

Out there was such a surge of yelling humanity that the police saw no way to get her to her waiting limousine but to hoist her into the air above the heads of the mob. They held her aloft until they got to the car and then they deposited her on its roof.

Standing and then sitting on the roof of the car with her legs crossed, Marlene threw picture cards of herself at her fans. By coincidence, there were photographers there who took pictures of her atop the car.

Managing with the help of the police to get down into the car, Marlene waved good night as the limousine inched through the mob that had overrun the sidewalks and filled the street. Arriving at the RCA Building and riding the sixty-five floors to the Rainbow Room, Marlene pulled off one of the smartest press stunts since a midget sat on J. P. Morgan's lap at a Washington hearing several decades before.

A special table was waiting for her. So were several more photographers.

Seeing the photographers, who were only responsible for making her rich, Marlene pretended to be scared of them. She ran from them and crawled under a table, curling herself up into a ball. Of course some of them got pictures of her looking like a cocoon—it was a much better news photo than one of her sitting on the roof of the limousine, which was very good, too.

One man at the party attracted very little attention but should have attracted more. I first heard of him more than twenty-five years before. The handsome bachelor producer of a radio show told me he had employed Marlene on a program and asked to take her home the night after. She accepted, and he envisaged himself charming her and perhaps even making her a conquest.

The door to her apartment was opened by a man, who took both their coats and hung them in a closet while Marlene went to get into something comfortable.

"Would you like something to drink while you're waiting?" the man asked the producer who thought to himself, "How cozy. A butler and everything. This lady knows how to live!"

When Marlene returned in something comfortable, she remembered to introduce the radio producer to the drink server, her husband, Rudolf Sieber.

On the night of her New York opening, Marlene had been married to him forty-three years. He was at the party virtually incognito. At least it appeared so, because when Marlene greeted the guests at one table, she simply shook hands with him, without announcing that this was her husband, without giving him a kiss. To those who didn't know, this was just some extra man at the first-night celebration.

Discovering that he was there, I got a few words with him.

"Were you surprised at Marlene crawling under the table?" I asked.

"No," he smiled, and added, "Oh, Marlene has many little tricks."

An understatement! One of the tricks was being hoisted onto the roof of the limousine at the stage door night after night after night. The security men or police came to regard it as a regular assignment and were paid for their efforts. The limousine was parked there each night waiting for her, and the pounding it took from the crowd clambering to get at her made it a shambles in six weeks. This rooftop appearance was prearranged just as meticulously as her act onstage. It paid off, because word got around that Dietrich was pulling better street crowds even than Richard Burton had done when he was playing *Hamlet* and Elizabeth Taylor was dropping around to pick him up. It helped sell tickets.

The throwing of the flowers by strange people running up and down the aisles—the same people night after night—was just as contrived.

I began to notice this when she had her second New York opening at the Mark Hellinger Theater on October 3, 1968. One of the men throwing flowers onstage grazed me with one of his pitches, and I took note of his face, which was a portrait of ecstasy. A minute later I saw the same man hurling bouquets from the other aisle. In my mind this took him out of the amateur class and made him a professional. I was more convinced of this later when I saw him bringing her more bouquets—perhaps the same ones?—backstage. I endeavored to interrogate Alex Cohen about this phenomenon, but he tried to evade me with a joke. "No, no," he said, "Marlene is a stickler for fresh flowers and won't let me use the same flowers twice. I tried, but you know how adamant she can get."

Nevertheless, I learned from stagehands and others that when Marlene's appearing, there's a "flower room" kept aside for the floral tributes. It's sort of a "flower bunk" where these Dietrich addicts, these cultists, can go and snatch up a bouquet to hurl at her onstage. The identity of these people is a mystery, but the same faces keep appearing; even in Europe one sees some of the same faces one has seen in America. They are probably not paid in money, but in charm and smiles and murmurs of appreciation just as Judy Garland said thanks to her worshipers who overran the stage with evangelical energy.

Amazingly, the cultists who fling the flowers are rehearsed even as Dietrich's musicians are rehearsed. They are sternly rebuked if they do not drop the flowers on a specific spot. The flowers must not be too far away for Dietrich to take notice of them. For a while, one of the flower pitchers also pitched beads. This was an even greater precision job because Dietrich wanted to put on the beads and make a joke. In that body stocking, she could not maneuver too much, and the beads had to hit the target.

This required an extraspecial type of rehearsal by the thrower who actually practiced by tossing the beads at a bent quarter placed on the stage to mark the spot where the beads were to land.

Flowers are one of her weaknesses—flowers, champagne, and caviar. But her strength is her perversity.

Alex Cohen figured out that Dietrich, besides being a tremendous showman, is a great female if you can just remember that when she says no, she means yes and when she insults you, she's paying you a compliment. A difficult thing to remember in times of stress, perhaps, but Cohen has also engaged such stars as Lauren Bacall, Peter Ustinov, Maurice Chevalier, and Katharine Hepburn, who likewise knew about the joys of perversity.

Enjoying the praise and the excitement about her first Broadway appearance, on that night when she'd crawled under the table, Marlene relaxed slightly with Cohen and sighed, "Well, we've done it. But don't you ever try to get me into television."

Inasmuch as nobody had mentioned trying to get her into television, Cohen deduced that, since she'd said she didn't want it, she wanted it.

A few weeks later when he asked her on the phone whether she would be interested in doing TV, she hung up on him.

Now he *knew* she was anxious to do TV.

It was a little similar to her arrival in New York to promote the TV special in December, 1972. Cohen sent two limousines to the airport along with a couple of emissaries. One limousine was for her luggage. However, her luggage filled both limousines, and she took a cab. She also ignored the emissaries and complained about their trying to stifle her with attention. Cohen had canvassed floral experts to arrange the best possible shower of flowers for her at her hotel.

He had also been generous with champagne and caviar. He felt he had done handsomely by her, and he trusted that she would be appreciative.

There was a Prussian growl on the phone instead.

No word of thanks came from her lips. "Whoever sold you dose roses should be shot. Dey all died!"

"I had come to realize," says Alex, "that Marlene can only say thanks by making a complaint. Another woman would gush over me, but Marlene squawks and never even says thanks. That's what makes her fascinating and also makes her Marlene."

For the promotion of the TV special, Cohen and CBS staged a press conference, starring Marlene, where she appeared to be angry at everybody and allegedly insulted some of the chief opinion molders of the town. It was at this press conference, in the Louis XVI suite at the Waldorf, that a cockroach tried to upstage Marlene but without success.

Columnists are supposed to be above press conferences. They are thought to have private tête-à-têtes with people who give them. I went to this one with shame in my soul. To me a press conference has always been something no more important than an ad for a TV show, and I vowed I wouldn't cheapen myself again by going to something so trivial blown up so big. I arrived a few minutes late and found that Marlene's revelations and opinions and growling and grumbling were being taken down seriously by probably 100 "media" people. I had been wrong. This was a titanic journalistic occasion.

There was the Blue Angel up in front, with a mike in her hand, speaking such a guttural German English that I at first thought she was doing an impersonation of Carol Channing doing an impersonation of Marlene Dietrich.

Suffering a heavy cold and taking antibiotics, she was not at her most charming. There seemed to be a lot of questions referring to her age without actually mentioning it. "How does one survive so long?" somebody asked her.

"I vunder!" she said.

"You're a legend in your own time?" a woman reporter said in what may have been a catty remark.

"I'm not so sure of that, I think that's newspaper talk," Marlene said cautiously.

"What about your beauty regimen?" Again it was a woman reporter, one of those who for years have hoped to get Marlene to discuss face-lifts she has known. Marlene put her aside neatly.

"That's a whole story by itself," she said. "I don't pay much attention to myself. I very rarely look at myself unless I have to."

The ladies of the press smiled over that one, and one even went, "Ho, ho!" Marlene was striding up and down in front of the press crowd, bending over, trying to hear the questions, asking that some of them be repeated to her.

Did she live with her family?

"No, no, I don't live with the family now, no. I have a daughter with four sons. I have a husband who lives in California. No, my daughter's not still performing. It was sad, but she gave that up. Are any of my daughter's sons married? Oh, no!" Marlene shuddered at that, and a woman reporter next to me translated the shudder.

"That would very soon make her a great-grandmother!"

Bob Williams, TV columnist of the New York *Post*, cleverly trying to get at her age by asking her how old she said she was, was greeted with a shrug and a sigh: "Here come de oldest qvestion!

"I am not as old as de newspapers thwink I am," she lisped, trying to leave them with the impression that she wasn't the seventy to seventy-one that they said she was.

It was at approximately this moment that Bob Williams called out for everybody to hear, "Good God, a cockroach in this place!"

He was sitting in about the middle of the group, and he spotted the cockroach on a vacant chair next to him. He was unable to believe that a cockroach would affront Conrad Hilton by daring to come into his very flagship hotel, the Waldorf-Astoria, especially during a Marlene Dietrich press conference.

If Marlene heard the Williams flash about the cockroach, she ignored it. I thought the press conference was unproductive except for Marlene's tendency to deprecate the TV medium which she was now going into and for her flattering remarks about Burt Bacharach, whom she hoped she would work with again some time.

"Ven he gets around to it . . . I am vaiting . . . he's not only a great composer . . . he's a vunderful guy, a great personality, and I miss him. . . ."

"Greater than Gershwin?"

"I think I said that first!"

How did they get together the first time?

"I was vurking at the time with Peter Matz. Noel Coward came to New York on the way to play Las Vegas, and he needed an accompanist. I sent him Peter Matz.

"So ven my time come to play Las Vegas, and Peter Matz was inwolved, I needed an accompanist. Peter Matz said, 'If I can catch a guy on his way to California at the airport, he will be good for you.' "

"What year was that?"

"Fifty-seven . . . fifty-eight. . . ."

"When you got him at the airport?"

Marlene's pride flashed a warning note. "When Peter Matz got him at the airport!"

Marlene is alleged by some singers to know very little about singing, but she said one thing at the press conference that some people would say disputes that. Asked about her feeling for songs, she said, "First, I look for the meaning . . . the meaning first . . . then the melody . . . it's the words, not the melody, that mean the most."

I remembered overhearing a fan telling Marlene in Las Vegas once that she sang "One More for the Road" better than Frank Sinatra sang it.

With a straight face, she said of course she did.

After the conference, Marlene talked to several reporters who went up to her individually. One of them asked her about her passport. "Some papers printed you are a French citizen," one reporter said.

"Den dey don't do their homework!" she scolded. "I have been an American since 1938," she said. She seemed to brush off most questions as though they irritated her, and her manner of discounting television, which she was now going to appear on, troubled her TV sponsors. Alex Cohen later asked her what she was angry about.

"Who vas angry? Vy should I be angry?" she said.

Probably it was her calculated pose to get more publicity than she'd have received if she'd been sweet.

"Madame" may not have been angry, but she angered several of the women, who thought she was just plain bitchy. Columnist Radie Harris of the Hollywood *Reporter* wrote that Marlene told one reporter, "You American press ask such stupid questions," and said it "with all the graciousness of an adder." Angela Taylor in the New York *Times* said that although Marlene was to sing "I Wish You Love" on the TV special, she hadn't been very loving. She'd fulminated against TV, advertising agencies, and the press. "The glamorous grandmother" had for some reason been in a rage, and her opening remark to Miss Taylor in an interview following the press conference was: "I don't need you. I hate newspapers. If you're good, you don't need publicity." It went on like that for much of the interview.

Then she softened, became the solicitous hostess, asked would she have a drink, a Coke, tea—and gave her a farewell kiss.

The usually tender-tempered Radie Harris said that Marlene had "such an unsmiling, arrogant manner that there should have been a sign next to her saying 'Achtung!' "

Marlene pictured TV as a monster: "I only had two days to rehearse and had to stand until 2:30 A.M. repeating a song trying to remember where I had stood before or if my coat was in the same place. Who needs it? It's only good for people who are old and sick!"

She wasn't doing it for money, she said, and since she was allegedly getting a quarter of a million, this caused skeptical comments. She didn't like any movies. *Blue Angel* . . . well, "dat was a choke.

"You make a film . . . there are so many people inwolved . . . too many fingers in the pie," scoffing as she strode about in the mannish black Chanel pants suit with the white handkerchief in the pocket. "We need people . . . new ideas. . . . I wanted Orson Welles, but he's always somewhere else. . . ."

"Is there anything you want to do?"

"I've never wanted to do anything . . . I'm always being pushed into it by somebody else. I'm not *ambitious* at all. . . ."

"Have you ever faced a hostile audience?"

"NO! Thank God, NO!" A laugh and a toss of her head.

Did she watch TV and old pictures?

"I don't, God, no, I have better things to do than that!"

The TV programmers?

"I think they're phony. They always tell me that's what the people want."

Bob Williams wrote next day that CBS was "embarrassed" by her actions. It was pointed out that she'd had nine days of rehearsal by their way of figuring days instead of two. I have pointed out that I thought the press conference was absurd to start with, and I didn't join in it in a cooperative mood. In fairness to Marlene, I believe she felt the same way. She didn't want to do it but went through with it in a pout. I asked her one question in the final moments after the breakup, "What do you think of the sex trend in pictures?" She rather icily told me she wouldn't discuss it. Suspecting she was angry at me for printing a few days before that she was seventy but looked thirty-eight (she had complained to Alex Cohen, who told me that), I thought "To hell with you, Blue Angel," and walked away and out of the hotel.

Radie Harris hung around and got madder.

"I decry her built-in hostilities," Radie said, "especially to the media that have been so good and rewarding to her over so many years. It is reprehensible that she bites the hand that feeds her."

But the proof of the programs is in the ratings—and Marlene's special was not a smash. She wasn't nominated for any awards. It appeared unlikely that she'd do TV again. There were some critics who thought the nostalgia worthwhile. But she lost her biggest and best booster in America when Alex Cohen canceled their friendship. He had courted the press carefully over the years, and here was Marlene saying, "Jesus, where did you get these idiots? They must be the dumbest people in America."

It was just three nights after her special when I saw Cohen at an Ethel Merman birthday party at the Pub Theatrical—attended, incidentally, by Sir Noel Coward, making his last appearance in public before he died a couple of months later.

"I have no time for her whatever," Cohen told me, angrily.

Referring to her as "Her Highness," Cohen said he could not

defend her remarks about the press. Her derogatory remarks about the TV show, in advance of its being shown, had cost him some important sales in Europe, he said.

"Over the six years when she did two one-woman performances in New York and went on tour, I showed up in every city to be of help," he said. "The way she treated me was no way to treat a friend." He had thought of trying to bring her back to New York for a third one-woman show. But she had lost this with her caustic remarks at the press conference.

"She's too much trouble," he said. Known as a man of tact, he had told her frankly of his feelings about her, and he had no doubt that their palship was finished for all time.

Marlene had been a big money earner capable of making a million a year. There was little doubt that she would find another American producer.

It was doubtful that she would leave any large estate because she was a spender, sending six-page cables, phoning across the Atlantic as though it were a local call. Besides maintaining a New York apartment, she usually resided in an expensive hotel in London or Paris.

"Ageless" is one of the handy adjectives always applied to her, and I found it amusing that just in recent years she didn't want to concede reaching seventy, back in the late 1940's she didn't want to reach fifty.

It happened that when the *Information Please Almanac* of 1947 came out, I noticed that it said Marlene was born in Berlin on December 27, 1902, which would have made her forty-five. A couple of years later while I was thumbing through the *Information Please Almanac* of 1949, I found Marlene had become two years younger—she'd been born not in 1902, but in 1904. Marlene was still going on forty-five—but very slowly. Marlene or some friends had convinced some editors that there'd been a mistake. Just a quarter of a century later, I consulted another yearbook: the 1973 *World Almanac*. And what had happened to Marlene now? What birthdate do you suppose they gave to Marlene? The year 1901!

Marlene has a gentle Florence Nightingale touch that is sweet. She is always ladling out chicken soup to the stricken. I saw her helping Sir Noel up and down steps because he was in fragile health and she knew it. "He's such an old man," she said sadly. Sir Noel was born in 1899, and he may have been joking, but he liked to say that Marlene was two years older than he was, which would have had her born about 1897. *"Gott in Himmel!"* Who could ever believe that?

Carol Lynley Speaks Right Out

🏹 AN interview is always an adventure, and you always hope it will be provocative and produce some surprises.

Over thirty years, I have averaged an interview a day which comes to over 10,000. My subjects have ranged from Winston Churchill to Greta Garbo, Howard Hughes, Harry Truman, Einstein, Picasso, Hemingway, Lupe Velez, dictators Naguib of Egypt and Batista of Cuba, Humphrey Bogart, Gypsy Rose Lee (many times), Elvis Presley, Tiny Tim, and Lassie (two—no, three!—generations).

On the sleety afternoon of December 12, 1972, I was at my desk on Broadway discussing the whiskey shortage caused by a drivers' strike with my friend Tom Buchanan, a Washington public relations man.

At three fifteen, my secretary Julie Allen looked up from a phone call, and said, "It's Bobby Zarem. Are you supposed to be some place?"

Owing to a change in a couple of appointments, we'd both become confused over the schedule. Bobby Zarem, a show business publicist, said to me, "I'm waiting here at Wally's with Carol Lynley."

"Oh, Christ," I said, and with a "So long" to Tom Buchanan, and a "Wally's is on Forty-ninth Street, isn't it?" to my secretary, I started to meet Carol Lynley. I reflected as I hurried down Broadway that I had never been so badly prepared to interview Carol Lynley; never had I been so badly prepared to interview anybody. Generally I have "an angle" in mind, have looked up recent clippings on the subject's activities, and consulted my own files to see what we discussed last time. I'd done none of that about Carol Lynley and didn't even know what she was doing now to cause me to interview her. Oh, well, she would tell me soon enough!

Plunging into the midafternoon gloom of the almost-empty restaurant, I found Carol and Bobby Zarem at a back table. After apologizing for my tardiness during my hearty hellos and hand-shakes with them, I sat, decided I'd have the same thing Carol was drinking (dry white wine), and proceeded cleverly, I hoped, to find what the hell this interview was going to be about.

"Last time I saw you," I said, "I was in. . . ." I would have said London.

"At the 21 Club here! I remember it well. I was having lunch with Oliver Reed, and this friend of mine from Los Angeles sent over a note. Oliver was being verbal that day." Carol laughed. "Oliver tore it in a hundred pieces and sent word back that next time he'd punch him in the eye."

I remembered now. I was disappointed in myself for not remembering it earlier. "I never found out who sent you the note," I said.

"Oh"—Carol shrugged, and I noticed in the semidarkness that she shrugged very attractively—"it was from Del Coleman" (a well-known figure in the social life of Palm Springs, Beverly Hills, and Las Vegas). "It was nothing. Oliver was being very super-Victorian that day and also very tight."

You see, I was still sparring conversationally to see what I was going to interview Carol Lynley, this sweet, innocent-looking blonde, about. "The time before that," I said, "was at the Dorchester in London, and we had a Sunday breakfast or brunch, and you were with. . . ."

"My agent Hugh French!" she remembered. "He took me there for quail's eggs. They were very gamy, like grouse. It's an acquired taste. Oliver Reed? Yes, he's out of my life now. I used to live with him once. He went to Bulgaria, for a film, I hope."

Ten minutes had passed, and still nobody had mentioned what she and I were doing here this particular afternoon. I didn't have the courage to blurt out my curiosity. Carol mentioned in answer to a couple of questions that she had supported herself since she was ten as a model and actress, was now thirty, was "with" a well-known and important figure in motion pictures, whom I must not mention by name, and had once been married for a short time to a man whose name she despised.

"He was a terrible human being, I got ripped off by the guy at a young age, I had to pay him twenty-five thousand dollars," she said. "He's just a shit, and you can quote me."

That word from those pretty lips startled me but didn't shock me. It was a common word now from even innocent-looking young girls.

"And now," I ventured, "now that you're here for this. . . ." I had decided to take the leap. I had to find out why I was here.

"The premiere tonight," she said. Oh, of course, now I knew. It was the premiere of the shipwreck picture *The Poseidon Adventure* at the new National Theater at Forty-fourth and Broadway, a most gala black-tie affair to which I of course had tickets.

"Isn't that," I said, which was a mistake, "the picture Red Buttons is in?"

Very coolly, Carol Lynley stated that it was.

I didn't detect the true frigidity. "How did you get along with Red?" I asked.

"How did I get along with him?" Carol said. "I hate him. He's a terrible human being!"

Press agent Bobby Zarem nervously spoke up. "Oh, I don't think you want to say that."

"I *do* want to say that!" Carol's voice was clear and succinct. "I do dislike him thoroughly. I had to put up with him during the picture, but I don't now."

I hurriedly began taking all this down in pencil in my notebook, for this was the material from which good interviews are made.

"He and everything he stands for," she said. "He steals scenes; he steps on lines. He would do the things any cheap nightclub comic would do, but it wouldn't work with me. He would pretend to be my friend but would try to unsettle me. When we were about to do a scene he would say, 'Gee, Carol, I hope you can do this one, you can do it, baby, don't be nervous.' I don't like him, and he knows it. He is not very good; he is not a funny man."

I'd never heard this or any real criticism of Red, and I said this to Carol. Bobby Zarem stared disconsolately into his Bloody Mary. It is a press agent's function to keep a client from saying the wrong thing, but Carol Lynley was clearly her own boss on this interview.

"Red is basically a master of ceremonies, and he's a great MC," Carol conceded, "but sitting around on a movie set, he's a cunt."

"A cunt?" I'm afraid I lost my aplomb. I'd never heard a man called that before, but then maybe I hadn't been around in the right places.

"That's what he is, a cunt!" she blazed up. "He has one of the worst reputations in show business, and he lived up to it."

"Let me get all these compliments down before you forget them." I was madly taking down her words.

She wasn't smiling. "I have to say it," she said. "I will never work with him again. He's of the school that goes for the jugular and gets ahead by hurting people, by doing in the other guy. He's a cunt. Why don't you print that?"

"I doubt that I could," I said. "Besides, I like Red."

"Red gets on better with men," Carol said. "It's when he regards you as a superior opponent, as he did me, that he tries to do you in. It's distracting every day to put up with this onslaught from somebody who fears you're better than he is.

"But," Carol continued, "I don't think Red can stop it. It's his coming up from the Catskills and vaudeville and burlesque. I think *he* thinks it's normal behavior."

"Does he know how you feel?"

"Oh"—she laughed—"he knows. I told him every day. He was really shitty to me. But he would cover up. On our tour"—promoting the picture—"he leaped up and was kissing me and hugging me and calling me darling. It was for the benefit of the press—and for the benefit of him. It was such a schlocky thing and he's such a schlocky guy."

"Schlocky?"

"Schlocky—cheap," Carol explained. "But the best word for him is he's a cunt."

"I'm an amateur etymologist," I said, "and I don't comprehend you calling a man a cunt."

"A cunt"—and now Carol was delineating it to me carefully—"is not only feminine. It's feline, it's a situation of bitchiness, and it can be applied to a man. I think it's a wonderful description."

"It is," I agreed, "but to a man?"

Carol was patient. "Almost all my scenes in the shipwreck are with him. He plays a person who urges me on to try to survive. His character is really subservient to mine, and that's why he tries to do me in. Besides, he used to be shitty to me in front of my daughter. She said, 'Mama, why is he like that to you?' He said everything shitty to me that a man could say. Red also gets himself into situations where you think he's going to die of an overdose of cuteness."

It occurred to Carol that she should make it clear that she was not some kind of troublemaker and she told me she got along well with Ernest Borgnine . . . and with Shelley Winters . . . well. . . .

(To me, Carol merely said that Shelley "wasn't that easy to get along with, but I got along with her." But I was to be informed later that she was much more explicit to Roger Ebert of the Chicago Sun-Times in an interview before those she gave in New York. He reported that Carol told him, "There was no vanity in this movie. No makeup, no hair arrangements, because our hair was sopping wet all the time, because of the shipwreck we were supposed to be in. Shelley Winters really looked awful. She says she puts on weight for her roles, but she's that way to begin with. Shelley can drive others to almost punch her in the nose. She can be so selfish. I make it a point never to get into fights, it's so destructive. I defended Shelley a lot to everyone who hated her.

("Yes," continued Carol to Roger Ebert, as he reported it, "I was the one who defended her. Then she went on television and forgot my name. She had her secretary call me and tell me how funny it was. I said I didn't think it was funny . . . at my expense. I told her secretary I was going to punch Shelley in the nose. I just love the idea of leaping at her and putting my arms around her neck!")

In our own interview, I got around to asking Carol if she thought that living with a man out of marriage was all right morally.

"*Morally? Morals!*" She almost screamed, in derision at me bringing it up. "I haven't thought about *morals* in a long time. Gosh, that whole thing has opened up. Morals—that's almost 1950ish. People are free now to do what they want. Morality! I had a Catholic upbringing, but I don't believe in do's and don'ts. Marriage, I think, is out of date. I'm not against marriage but I'm not for it for myself. I'm crazy about Ernie Borgnine, by the way. Ernie got married again, you know; Ernie couldn't get along with Shelley Winters. But I defended Shelley (against all those that hated her) . . ."

I had now been with Carol Lynley about an hour, which is

about the average length of an interview, and I was surprised at the material I'd obtained despite my poor preparation. Actually, I hadn't obtained it; it had gushed at me from Carol's lips.

"I guess I'll see you at the premiere tonight," I said. "Who'll you be with?"

"With my agent, Peter Witt. I'll be wearing a very old 1930's bias-cut satin dress that I brought in. With a short little jacket that's very full here." She held her hands to her bosom.

"I guess Red'll be there," I said.

"Of course! Overdoing his cuteness. He'll rush up and kiss me and hug me, and I'll hug him back. What'm I going to do? Call him a cunt? That's destructive, and I'm not destructive!"

As a longtime acquaintance of Red's, I wanted to tell Red all the nice things I'd been hearing about him from Carol, and I went to the premiere with more than my usual interest in such events. We happened to sit in the same row, and as he climbed over me getting to his seat, I told him, "Wait'll you hear what I've got to tell you!"

As I saw the tender scenes between Red and Carol on the screen, when they were trying to survive the shipwreck, especially when Red was comforting Carol whose brother had been drowned, I was amazed at their acting proficiency. If they really disliked each other so much. . . . "That's craft," Carol had said.

We went over to the Allied Chemical Building to the Act I restaurant to a post-premiere party, and there I found Red Buttons.

Carol Lynley was there. First off, she had refused to pose for a picture with Red when asked to do so by a photographer.

I had staked out a table at the front window sixteen floors up overlooking Times Square which can be especially beautiful on a wintry night with the clouds and the mists close enough you could almost touch them if the windows were open. Shelley Winters, sitting at another choice table, was laughing and commanding me to come over, as she called for champagne. But there was Red Buttons.

"Hi, Oil," he said, his third hello to me that evening.

"Hi, you cunt," I replied.

"What was that?" He definitely bristled.

"Just repeating Carol Lynley's favorite name for you," I answered. "She says Red Buttons is a cunt."

Red bit his lips. "How do you spell that? With a *k?*"

I tried to apologize. "Red, that's what Carol called you today when I interviewed her." I looked in my notebook. "No, she spells cunt with a *c*. She said you are a cunt, with a small *c*."

"Oh, *that* kind of cunt!" Red shrugged. "No comment!"

"What's the story?"

"Off the record?" he said.

"Sure," I said, lying in my teeth.

"OK, now I got a call today from a radio broadcaster. He said, 'I did an interview today with "The Psycho." ' I said, 'Who's the Psycho?' And he mentioned the lady you're talking about. But that's all I know about it, and I don't want to be brought into any feud because I didn't have any!"

The broadcaster was Earle Doud over at WOR, and he told me of his session with Carol Lynley. His program was laid in a mythical banana country, and he often had his guest interviewees participate with him in a light sketch he or some of his staff had written. When Carol came on his show to plug herself and the picture, he suggested she participate in a sketch of that kind.

She refused in such strong language that he claimed that he blushed through his beard.

Red Buttons went through the Carol Lynley horror story for a year. Finally one reporter published what was supposed to be the inside story. Carol was in love with him, and he rejected her!

The Straights and the Gays

IN this "sex-oriented" Age of Indecent Exposure when the people of show business not only bared all but bared all frequently and repeatedly, I found that it was the stage—the legitimate theater—that was increasingly the nest of what we used to call illicit sex. In the Era of Genitals, one had to wonder just what was illicit anymore. Nevertheless, whatever it was, there was much of it there, in the Shubert, the Booth, the Music Box, the Morosco, the Winter Garden, the Broadway—fine, beautiful old theaters, every one. Once you heard lovely, flowery language spoken there, but now you might hear such terms as "balls naked" or "cock naked." Much of the sex that was practiced (and malpracticed) there was "straight," but probably much more was classified as "gay." The gays have always contended that one reason they're called gays is that they simply have a lot more gaiety, a lot more funsy, than the straights. But to get to the point, straight to the point about the straights, there are a lot of straights that aren't.

It was a flouncy world there in the West Forties off Broadway. One celebrated actor boasted of entertaining in the nude and saw nothing strange about it when somebody dropped into his dressing room and found him naked. He would, in the case of a stranger, put on something.

There was a rekindling of a famous European love affair when two lovers were reunited in each other's arms—two British leading men. Journalism hadn't progressed to the point where I could report that they were a "romance." They were, but they were discreet. They never had dinner or supper together in public. It wasn't an until-death-do-us part. They'd had other affairs in between, but being back together on Broadway was just "very sweet," as everybody said.

The easy acceptance of homosexuality as part of swinging show business was doubtless influenced by the British. British comedian Billy Baxter maintained humorously while starring at the Waldorf Empire Room that the British were ahead of the Americans.

"I left England because homosexuality had become legal," he said. "The way things were going, I was afraid it was going to become compulsory."

Closet fags were coming out of the closet. Gay activists were parading, making speeches, getting photographed. One British actor, blithe, airy, amusing, and outgoing, used to sweep into Sardi's and kiss Vincent Sardi, Jr., lustfully on the lips.

"Oooh, you devil, you taste luscious," he'd coo and wiggle.

And though he pretended to be kidding, those who knew him were aware he meant it, because he'd been brought to stardom by an older homosexual who financed him, encouraged him and loved him in his own way. This particular gay let the gay movement down, however, by marrying a female model and having a family.

"Very queer of me," he often said.

The bolder ones wanted to kiss in public, and hold hands, and dance together. One fairly well-known Broadway playwright waved furiously at friends when he marched in the Gay Activists' parade. A producer who found him very girlish said he was difficult to handle: always crying, stamping his foot, pouting, getting too sick to come to rehearsal, and sending a note over by his boyfriend. "But he's damned good," the producer said. He finally had one too many girlish tantrums and left the show. The producer looked around for a replacement, and such was the situation on Broadway at the time he placed the show in the hands of another homosexual.

"The beds are full of 'em," somebody said.

Broadway was amused rather than shocked. We'd known for years about an internationally famous glamor girl who fooled most of the world, but not us. "She bats both ways," they said of this sex object. We smiled about a celebrated producer considered to be a transvestite, who wore masculine attire in the summer and dresses and lingerie in the winter, when he relaxed in Florida. Half the year he was Eddie, the other half he was Edith, and it was his—I mean her—conviction that girls had more fun.

A slick, sophisticated publication called *After Dark*—"magazine of entertainment"—flourished by printing well-done articles and photographs of nude males for enjoyment of other males. It produced a calendar of nude males as *Esquire* and *Playboy* had brought out nude girl calendars. It advertised a collection of nude male pictures which it titled "Outofdrawers," explaining that the pictures were "the best in or out of their or our drawers. Limited edition, $12.95."

"FAMOUS NUDE OR DRAPED STUDIES" were offered in an ad topped by a picture of Errol Flynn boasting that it also showed Vince Edwards, Burt Lancaster, Joe Namath, Peter Fonda, Elvis Presley, and Mr. Nude America, '72. Editor in chief William Como told me he was not publishing a homosexual magazine. "We are trend setters, and gays are generally trend setters, too," he said. When the magazine presented some theater awards at a flashy party at Casino Russe, there were many caftans worn—some by women, some by men.

Homosexuality was something I was beginning to have to deal with, the same as I had to deal with—when covering "burlesk"— an uncovered pudenda. I couldn't ignore either one. However, as a male reporter, I would never have had the courage to ask an actor whether he was homosexual. But Cindy Adams, columnist and radio interviewer, came right out with it talking to Jim Bailey, a sensation in the nightclub world for his "impressions" of Judy Garland, Barbra Streisand, and Phyllis Diller.

Jim's startling resemblance to Judy Garland and Barbra Streisand was due to his own devotion to his unusual commitment, his precise mimicry of their voices and mannerisms, and his willingness to sit for an hour or two while a makeup artist converted his fine-featured face into a girl's.

"Jim wasn't making it until he found this gimmick," his mother candidly told me when he was starring at the Waldorf.

One of the other performers walked over to Bailey as he was waiting to do Judy and said, "Good luck, Jim."

Bailey, tense in his Garland hairdo, skirt, and hose on beautiful feminine-looking legs, replied: "Jim's in there. I'm Judy."

Cindy's breakthrough interview began with Cindy asking, "When you began to dress in drag, were you worried that your manhood might be impugned?"

"Sure, I was scared to death. . . ."

"But what would make a man want to dress up in women's clothes and be a female impersonator because that's what you are, right?"

"Wrong," Jim Bailey said. "I'm an impressionist. An impersonator is someone who dresses up in women's clothing for the purpose of doing women in general. I'm a special, specific woman. I'm a Judy Garland or a Streisand. *I am them.* It takes me two hours to get in the clothes and in the mood, and I literally become them. If you ask me a question, then I'll answer like them when I'm in that mood. It's as though I were possessed."

He explained that he "needed a gimmick."

He'd been singing with only medium success.

"I didn't know what gimmick. Phyllis Diller is a great friend of mine. I said, 'Phyllis, when I'm at parties, I always do you. I laugh like you and throw lines like you. I'd like to put you in my act.' She said, 'Sure, but how?' And I didn't know. I lay awake for six months trying to figure it out. And then I realized I'd have to go the whole way, and then I decided. I will go the whole way, and that's how it started."

Cindy Adams broached the subject cautiously. "When I watched you opening night at the Waldorf, I was sitting with some Japanese friends. Now I know you're going with a girl, Lucie Arnaz, for the last seven months, and I know you're all the good things a nice guy is supposed to be. Nevertheless, these Japanese friends turned and asked me a question which meant 'Homosexual?' They said to me in Japanese, *'Dosayal?'* "

"Well, Cindy," replied Jim, "I guess everybody does want to ask that at some point or other. I mean, I'm sure that people wonder about it. I knew that the day I started the act. I knew that people would go behind my back and ask. It's very strange, but when I first recognized the fact that I could be asked if I were a homosexual, my first reaction was: 'Look, if I really were, do you really think I'd say, "Yes I am?" ' At first I thought, 'Wow, this is really going to upset me. It's going to make me angry, and I'm going to get really mad.' And now it doesn't bother me. It really doesn't upset me any more because I am what I am. I'm doing what I'm doing. The people around me know better. And all I know is the only person I really have to answer to is me. Who I am and what I am is a human being, and just because I'm doing what I'm doing, it has no reflection on what I am when I'm offstage."

(After the interview, Bailey told Cindy it was one of the best he'd ever done, and he appreciated being asked honest questions in a straightforward manner.)

I then put the question to Bailey myself. "No, I am not homosexual," he said, "but I do become evasive when people ask me because I think they're invading my personal life. A lot of women interviewers become insulted because I have the nerve to come out on the stage as a girl and look better than they do, and then I come back as a man and completely masculine. They say, *'How dare he?'* There's an envy there because I come out looking pretty good—and they may have ugly legs."

The walls kept tumbling down on all phases of sex and it was show business that was hammering at them and making them tumble. After Gay Liberationists and lesbians came out of their closets, it was a natural progression that the folk singer Joan Baez should speak out bravely for bisexuals.

I'm constantly amazed by the stories that get into print, and this one shocked me. I wasn't shocked by the disclosures, but at the willingness of Joan Baez to discuss all this for publication.

"He's a bi" or "She's a bi" were expressions we'd heard for years about certain stars whom I generally found hard to understand. And we usually thought of a bisexual as being one who dressed as a girl or woman—usually dressed extremely well, too, with taste and elegance, and was considered beautiful in the eyes of men and women, too. Yes, there were several who were well known and two or three who were famous. But it was on Friday, March 9, 1973, that Joan Baez's interview given to the *Daily Californian,* the student newspaper of the University of California at Berkeley, appeared in the world press and opened it up to general discussion.

"Double your pleasure, double your fun!" was the usual comment from observers. A male columnist told me this wasn't going to lead him into any liaisons with gays. "I'm having enough trouble keeping my wife and girlfriend satisfied," he said.

"One of the nicest whatever you want to call it—loves of my life—was a woman," Miss Baez said. "It was something that happened when I was twenty-one and not since then. I'm more male-oriented now."

Miss Baez was thirty-two at the time of the interview, mother of a three-year-old son and separated from her husband. After the interview in the student newspaper, the wire services hunted her up to see if she'd been correctly quoted. She said she had been, but she wasn't sure "if the term 'bisexual' is the right one.

"Being bisexual, you're very much looked down upon by the uppity members of gay lib," she said. "The exclusivism around being totally gay is one of the most self-righteous I've ever run into.

"If you swing both ways, you really swing," she said. "I just figure, you know, double your pleasure."

One of the headlines was SHE BROUGHT A NEW KIND OF LOVE TO HER.

Miss Baez's charge that the gay libs were being snobbish with their exclusivity with gay libs and shutting out girls from their erotic pleasures, even though some of the girls were lesbians who were broad-minded, naturally stirred up animosity among the gay libs. To me, as a veteran journalist, the striking thing was that a student newspaper reporter could find the courage to ask Joan Baez such a personal question to start with. That she would admit the experience was just as surprising. Here again was proof that show business was really swinging.

The Gay Liberationists made a rather daring move to establish the right of gays to dance with gays, and lesbians to dance with lesbians, by plotting a surprise invasion of the Rainbow Grill on April 4, 1973. They tipped me off well in advance, and I was there as a witness. Previously, I had written that the Grill management had intended to eject two men dancing together but had discovered on a closer look that one was a man and one was a woman—they were just dressed similarly.

"They can't keep us from dancing together—it's not illegal anymore," a gay named Jim Glaser, a men's wear buyer, told me by phone. "We're going in there and dance—and let them try to throw us out. We'll call the police!"

As I walked to the RCA Building (the Rainbow Grill's on the sixty-fifth floor adjoining the Rainbow Room), I wondered whether I had the ethical right to tell manager Tony May, a friend of mine, what was supposed to happen that night.

Suppose he didn't know that the gays had found an official document that seemed to establish that they couldn't be halted from dancing together? Wouldn't I be sort of a rat for letting him embarrass himself in the newspapers?

While I was thinking about this, I saw a little group of young people assembling in the ground-floor lobby of the building. The gays had told me they would be a party of eight: four males, four females. They would enter in couples, go on the dance floor as couples—and then switch partners, gays with gays, lesbians with lesbians. That was their strategy.

"This must be them!" I thought.

I needn't have worried about informing manager Tony May of the plot. I found him at a rear table, frowning and conferring nervously with his maître d', Bigi, who was all for chasing the invaders out by force. Somebody else had already leaked the word to Tony May. He was ready for them. They had made a reservation under a fictitious name of "Dr. Cohen." They had come in only for cocktails (not dinner), although it was now past nine o'clock. As I sat at the back table with Tony May, they came into the room together and took a ringside table. They didn't look like people who would turn out at nine o'clock to hear the leading attraction there, singer Caroline Daye. A good detective would probably have figured out that there was something afoot.

"I'm not going to try to stop them," Tony May suddenly told me.

"I think I could stop them legally. But I am not going to give them the satisfaction," he said. "Bigi," he said to the maître d', "be sure to tell all the waiters, don't give them any trouble."

"I thought we were going to kick them out!" Bigi said, dejectedly. "We can't run them out? That's a shame!"

"That's what they want me to do . . . they just want publicity," Tony May said. "I don't know what I'll do in the future. I'll do what is best for the establishment, keeping in mind the interests of the majority of the clientele we have. But for tonight, I'm not stopping them!"

They of course didn't know of the Grill's decision. They waited, a little nervously, for Caroline Daye to finish her singing, so they could take to the dance floor. They didn't pay much attention to her. One of the gays sat with his back to her, though he could have swung his chair around and faced her.

"They couldn't be less interested in her," Tony May said with a scowl. "They're making that perfectly obvious."

They were talking while she was singing, although she was only a few feet away. One of the gays, tall and red-bearded, chattered away, ignoring her completely. Then one of the lesbians, whom I subsequently identified as Bonnie Gray, of Women's Lib, began giggling noticeably while Caroline Daye sang, with great feeling, an Irving Berlin torch song, "I Don't Want Him, You Can Have Him."

The giggling so close at hand nettled Caroline Daye, who spoke sharply about it to the audience. "Something happened to tickle this lady's fancy," she said, severely, with an angry glance at the table.

"She's from Women's Lib!" sang out one of the gays.

"Does that make her laugh?" Caroline Daye snapped.

"It's a song about male domination and the Women's Libbers think it's funny," the gay retorted.

"Well, there are two sides to every story," Caroline Daye said, trying with difficulty to retain her poise. It was an unusual predicament for her. Usually, women tended to melt or dissolve completely upon hearing these songs of the heart, and here was a woman who was moved to laughter or anger instead.

Fortunately for Miss Daye, she was about to finish, and then it was announced that Sy Oliver's orchestra would play for dancing.

Up they leaped, all eight of them, emptying their table, as they took to the floor, man with girl, man with girl, man with girl, man with girl. They didn't dance very well, and they were out of step. After about a minute of the first number, they suddenly switched partners, men with men, women with women.

There were a couple of dozen other people dancing, and when they saw men dancing with men, especially a tall red-bearded man with a short, thin, spectacularly checked-suited man, they were surprised. "What the hell's going on here?" one of the other dancers said, but he didn't complain to anybody. As it sunk in, and he saw two other men dancing together, he smiled and shrugged.

Tony May wasn't smiling. He suddenly got up and hurried to speak to a captain in the opposite part of the room.

"I was afraid nobody'd told him not to interfere," Tony said.

The men were holding each other rather close, and they were just short of dancing cheek to cheek. The little man in the checked suit switched to another man who was rather plump, and he had difficulty making his arms reach all the way around his partner. The girls were dancing belly to belly, too, and one, in a white-trouser outfit, was smiling into the eyes of a girl with skirt above the knees and beads to her waist.

"It revives the old question, 'Who leads?' " Tony May said.

The gays and lesbians were looking over their shoulders at the captains and waiters, expecting that there'd be a move to eject them. But as nobody made a move, they relaxed. I went to their table, to which two couples had returned, introduced myself, and told them that the management wasn't going to interfere.

"Come and meet the manager," I said.

That's exactly what they wanted. They were anxious for an argument about their rights.

Tony May greeted them courteously though not exactly warmly.

"Same-sex dancing, as we call it, is quite legal," a gay named Lew Todd, who was one of the spokesmen, spoke up. "We have the papers right here."

Seizing one of the documents in his hand, Tony May said, "Let's go to the bar where the light's better." After peering carefully at it, he said, "This is proposed. This hasn't passed yet." It appeared to be a proposed councilmanic resolution.

"Not that one, this one," Lew Todd said. "Dancing is not a sexual act," he went on. "Father-and-daughter dancing would be illegal. . . ."

He handed Tony May and me a Xeroxed copy of a notice from the Department of Consumer Affairs then headed by Bess Myerson. It was a little confusing. A regulation against homosexuals and lesbians being permitted to gather on the premises of catering establishments had been omitted from the latest issuance of regulations. The notice said that the bracketed material had been omitted. The material was still in the notice—but it was in brackets. Thus negatively, the gays and lesbians had the right to dance together—rather, they were not prohibited from dancing. That, at least, was the conclusion of the invading group.

"I wouldn't call that conclusive," Tony May said. "Anyway . . . how about a drink?"

Though they had mostly dropped their warlike attitude, Lew Todd hadn't.

"This is a confrontation," he told Tony May. "I prefer to dance with a man to dancing with a woman. I challenge you to have me thrown out."

Tony smiled. "I'm not going to," he said. "I'm probably ruining his whole night," he said to me.

"The last place we went to, they called the police and threw us out," Lew Todd said. "Go ahead, I challenge you. We'll make a case."

When Tony again laughed it off, things got friendlier, and we sat discussing this rather revolutionary and landmark nightclub occurrence. They had gone dancing once before, to Barney Google's, in the Eighties. And there, one of the lesbians said, "They threw us out bodily; but the next day we came back with the police, and they agreed we were within our rights."

Recalling the scene with great satisfaction, she said, "We were physically dragged off the dance floor. When we returned and won out, we declared the place liberated!"

Then they got into what you could call an "intelligent discussion" of the problem, with everybody calm.

"We want to be free to hold hands in public or dance close together, and there's no place you can do that except in the Village," one of the homosexuals said. "If ten percent of the population is gay—that's what Kinsey said, and it's probably more now—is it right that ten percent of the people be left out of everything? In New York City, that's eight hundred thousand people!"

"But there are gay bars. Why don't you go to those places?" Tony May asked. "You'd be more comfortable. I could lose a lot of business if you came here often."

"We prefer the gay bars," one said. "The drinks are cheaper.

But, you know, practically all the gay bars are owned by the the the syndicate . . . the Mafia."

Ginny Vida, an editor of children's textbooks, and a vice-president of the Gay Activists Alliance, was complimentary about Tony May's acceptance of her group. "I congratulate the Rainbow Grill on the way it handled this tonight," she said.

"Are any of you here with your lovers tonight?" I asked.

"No, none of us are paired off that way," a lesbian said.

"But you do prefer dancing with a girl to a man?" I asked her.

"Yes." She nodded, smiling. "It feels wonderful. Try it some time with the same sex. You'll like it!"

"Well, you didn't get thrown out of here," I said to Lew Todd. "Nothing really happened. Would you call this a strategic success?"

"Definitely yes. When they hear about this, other club owners will take heed . . . if they want to keep their cabaret licenses!"

And I suppose it was historic and precedent-setting. Various owners told me privately that they would eject any that they found objectionable. If the 21 Club and the Waldorf could turn away men for not wearing neckties, couldn't any restaurant also close the door on homosexuals? This was different—it got into liberalism, civil rights, and such. I never heard of anybody trying to stop them after the Rainbow Grill incident. Nor did I hear of the gays and the lesbians trying to flaunt their abnormalities in places where they weren't wanted.

Everything was smoothed out except Caroline Daye's feelings. She was still seething about having her song giggled at by a Woman's Libber. "I was shocked, I didn't expect such discourtesy," she told me. "That girl was more discourteous than any man."

"Don't you understand—your song was subjugating the woman's role to the man's? You were subordinating her place in society—she was in the position of catering to a man, bringing him his slippers . . . all of that?" The Women's Libber added, "Can you see our point?"

"But Irving Berlin wrote that song for *Miss Liberty* back in 1949!"

"Irving Berlin lived in another time!" the lesbian said.

To demonstrate their sincerity, the invader party posed willingly for pictures showing them dancing together and consented to the use of their names, but not their addresses. There had hardly been a raised voice. The staff of the Rainbow Grill did not approve of Tony May's tolerant attitude toward them, and he probably didn't approve, either. The most unsympathetic one was the dinner-jacketed maître d' and guardian of the door, Bigi.

"Just as long as none of those fellows ask to dance with me!" he grumbled.

Whither the Hell Are We Drifting?

WHILE I have no credentials establishing me as a prophet, I predict that the sexuality scene in Show Business is going to get worse.

Or "better," you'd probably say if you're a Dirty Old Man or a Horny Old Woman.

The Genitilia Generation started a passion fire that may never be put out. Let the middle-aged puritans prattle their sheer nonsense that there will be a return to innocent, nonsexual home-and-hearthside entertainment. But the kids who have grown up using the word "fuck" as easily as they say "toilet," who have never been told that you don't say "balls," "ballsy," or "prick" at the dinner table, are not going to settle for the nostalgic home-and-hearthside fare unless there's a lot of sexin' in the haymow, the cellar, the pantry, or at least in the garage or the maid's room (with the maid).

You don't hide your sexin' anymore. It's some people's hobby, some people's entertainment, more satisfying than television, better (in many ways) than the Late, Late Show. It's very cheap (especially when indulged in at home). Some sexperts claim that it gets better with practice. But the main thing is that nobody's shy about discussing it today and you're not supposed to be surprised if your spinster aunt says, "I could have been married several times, but I don't give a very good blow job."

Interviewing director Robert Wise who made $10,000,000 from

his nonsexy masterpiece *The Sound of Music*, I asked him whether it was possible today to make a film without sex in it.

"It would be very difficult," he said. "The young people would find it unbelievable. And to think that it isn't very long since we had to have even married people sleeping in double beds!"

A movie without sex would be like a candy bar without nuts in it. Apparently there lies ahead of us—unless the Supreme Court scares off the filmmakers—a wealth of candid, hard-core sex pictures which will not be thought of as pornographic by the Genitilia Generation. That'll be the only kind of pictures they've seen and those pictures will be normal to them. Moreover, since they'll not have seen soft-core or simulated sex-films, they'll become enraged if anything like that shows up. They will not know that a great battle went on about penetration and nonpenetration of the vagina and other areas, and that the penetrationists won the fight. Therefore they will consider a nonpenetrationist copulater a phony who is accepting money under false pretenses, not realizing that he was doing the best he could under existing conditions.

Will the Genitilia Generation create a new set of stars who are sexual athletes?

Will the young movie fans demand that their heroes do a genuine job of fornicating—the real thing—and no faking? Will they demand that the leading lady perform her fellatio so realistically that you can watch her gulping and be sure it's a genuine gulp?

Now this is not as absurd as it may appear to be at first. Just as motion picture "talkies" retired a number of famous stars who couldn't talk and indeed were tongue-tied before the camera, the next "sexies" may bring unemployment to many of today's stars who can't sex. Make way for the beautiful girl who fornicates her way to stardom. We've long heard of the starlet who "slept" her way to the top, and now it's not only true but it's legitimate.

The young people agree with me. *Cue* magazine (not be to confused with *Screw* magazine) printed an article by a youthful-looking columnist, William Wolf, headlined, "Films' New Sexual Freedom May Be Today's Kicks: It's Also Tomorrow's Opportunity."

How is it tomorrow's opportunity? It's a break for the boy or girl who can sex and keep sexing and doesn't mind sexing and can make it believable. They could replace the stars who can't sex, just as those who could talk replaced those who couldn't talk when sound films came in.

Maybe Katharine Hepburn, Bette Davis, or John Wayne won't want to fornicate in front of the camera. Off with their heads! Let's get somebody that can and send Hepburn, Davis, and the Duke to pasture. Who'll we get to replace the Duke in the sexies? It can't be just anybody. A Don Rickles, Zero Mostel, or Godfrey Cambridge, for example, wouldn't do. Too fat and flabby for the boudoir beat. But wait! Marlon Brando was a little fleshy when he did *Last Tango in Paris*, and nobody objected, except Maria Schneider, his leading lady, who said in some interviews that he was too fat to interest her once they went off camera.

Cue's William Wolf said that eventually the X-films of today are going to seem old-fashioned, that the public will be disappointed if there aren't closeups "of assorted sex practices," that filmmakers will reach for "maximum emotional involvement and deeper, more personal exploration of human beings . . . in the quest for new shocks."

"Get in there and go, man!" in other words.

So now the John Waynes are going to have to fornicate in front of the camera! "What we now seem about to reach is a movie world's leading performers having to bow to an industry's changing reality. Those refusing to go along will not be working, at least not in certain films."

Bette Davis and Katharine Hepburn will get the word from Casting: "Sorry, nothing today. We're looking for fornicators."

"This situation will make new demands on cast members in terms of their bodies, and in some cases, their stamina," William Wolf says. "The upheaval could prove similar to the trauma that occurred in the changeover from silents to talkies."

In other words, what they want on the male side, is studs who can stay in the saddle, and girls who can go easy riding with them without any embarrassment. Sex athletes will be required for the sexies. William Wolf agrees with me that we are not going back to purity. "Once mores begin to change, there can be some retarding of trends, but no stopping them. I can offer no useful advice to those who shun sexual explicitness, other than to suggest that they choose carefully. What I'm predicting is that the choices will become narrower and narrower for those who cannot or do not wish to swing with the radically altered times."

The man is right! Well after the Supreme Court ruling, there came to America *La Grand Boufe*, the most stomach-turning and repulsive film I've ever seen. It showed Marcello Mastroianni and three other gifted actors slowly gluttonizing themselves to death, with sex as one of the intermittent courses. They died off from overeating and their bodies were deposited in the deep freeze by their survivors. An added artistic touch was one of the performers being sprayed with human excrement when a bidet exploded. It could hardly be called a tasty picture. The direction we're going now, and will continue to go for some years, is only down.

This Was My Life

DURING late August, 1971, there came to my very messed-up desk in my Broadway hideaway an invitation to Ethiopia to celebrate their New Year's there with Emperor Haile Selassie.

Frankly, it was not that the emperor was so anxious to have me there. He could hardly have remembered we'd met once long before. I was invited indirectly by the producers of a TV film about Ethiopia's Olympics athletes. In show business it often turns out that some royal invitation has a commercial inspiration. I was anxious to return to Addis Ababa, however. I wanted to go back and determine whether you could still look out your hotel window and see cows crossing the main street.

I accepted immediately and looked forward to the trip although it would be very long.

Although I didn't know or even suspect it, there were mysterious forces working against me to prevent me from making that trip. It was almost like witchcraft.

It was perhaps two days later when the witchcraft started. I was asked by phone from Los Angeles to go on the *Hollywood Squares* TV show at the same time I was scheduled to be in Ethiopia.

"I'll be living it up with Haile Selassie in the palace at Addis Ababa that night," I said, and I added my regret—and the regrets were genuine, because *Hollywood Squares* was fun to do, and prestigious, and you got paid for it. No, I was going to be with the emperor. Sorry.

The mysterious forces didn't take no for an answer. The mysterious forces were Ralph Edwards and his staff of *This Is Your Life*—and my Beautiful Wife, the B.W., who was the principal witch in the witchcraft.

Without my knowledge, of course, they had already decided that I was to be surprised on *This Is Your Life* the week of September 13. Everything was fine until I had decided to accept the invitation to Ethiopia. Now they had to get me to change my ideas about going to Addis Ababa, and they also had to conspire with my wife by phone, from L.A. to N.Y. to obtain all the multitudinous details of my life story, my school, my family, my early days in the newspaper business. There were literally scores of calls from Hollywood to my New York apartment taken by my wife. All had to be made, of course, while I was not at home or at least not within hearing.

"You wouldn't change your mind?" one of the calls from *Hollywood Squares* asked me. I should explain that the *Hollywood Squares* people of course were part of the conspiracy. "You said New Year's in Ethiopia. We're talking about September."

"Their New Year's is the same date in September as your show, I guess they've got a different calendar," I said.

"Well, Happy New Year's," the booker for *Hollywood Squares* said in Hollywood.

All the time that *Hollywood Squares* was trying to get me on the program—as a setup to surprising me right in their audience, of making me the fall guy that night for *This Is Your Life*—Ralph Edwards' crew was biting its collective nails because not once did it give up as far as I can find out.

Deeply involved in this conspiracy were the Marty Allens—the rotund long-haired comedian and his wife, Lorraine, or Frenchy, who are our close friends. Marty and Frenchy had been instrumental in getting me booked on previous *Hollywood Squares* programs.

And so one day in the beginning of it all came a call from Frenchy.

"I've got good news for you," she announced. "The *Hollywood Squares* wants you for *two* nights. They're taping an extra show, and they would like to have you for Tuesday, September 14, and

Wednesday, September 15. Marty will be on Tuesday night. The two of you will have a lot of fun together."

"But our trip to Ethiopia . . . we could never do it," I pointed out.

"Yes, but this is two nights and this is an enormous audience. And they'll plug your book. . . ."

I was beginning to crack. The dirty dastards were getting at my weak spots, although I of course knew nothing about their ulterior motives. I thought they were just trying to get me on the *Squares* show.

"Well, let me think it over," I said.

Of course my Beautiful Wife knew all of every step of this double-crossing of Wilson that was going on right under my own roof and was participating in it. But she could not enter into it openly. She had to pretend ignorance of every development as I reported it to her. She could hardly take sides, for if she as much as hinted that she didn't want to go to Ethiopia, after all, she would be under suspicion and would be asked why. I might figure out what was going on.

However, they shouldn't have had any fears.

For I was just plain naïve and stupid.

Professional cynic that I'm alleged to be, I never scented out any trickery at all. Ralph Edwards is determined never to put on the air anybody who suspects or knows he's getting the treatment, and he had momentary worries that gossip chaser Wilson might spoil his evening. But I was an easy victim.

"What do you think, Earl?" Frenchy phoned again from Hollywood.

"Oh, all right," I groaned. I phoned the TV producer of the show in Addis Ababa and told him I wouldn't be going. I phoned Alitalia, which had arranged to fly my wife along to Addis Ababa (inasmuch as wives weren't invited on the trip to Ethiopia), that she wouldn't be going. So now, I was going to Los Angeles for two *Hollywood Squares* shows: Tuesday, September 14, and Wednesday, September 15.

The Tuesday guest appearance was a phony, but I didn't know it yet.

Now the witchcrafters had to continue the conspiracy right up to the last minute when they socked me with the book.

The Edwards show is finely timed and coordinated owing to the secrecy and surprise element. True, I was supposed to be on the

Tuesday show. Marty Allen's wife, Frenchy, phoned and suggested that we arrive in Los Angeles Monday night to have plenty of time to make the show Tuesday—the phony show that I didn't know yet was going to trap me. Because it's vital to have the surprisee in town in plenty of time, they wanted me there a day ahead . . . but of course they couldn't explain that to me either.

"But I can't go Monday, I got a lot of work to do here," I said. "We'll go out Tuesday morning. . . ."

"But if the weather's bad," Frenchy muttered.

Hollywood Squares was taped in the early evening, and I felt that with the time difference, there'd be ample time to get there.

"The weather won't be that bad," I said.

My wife also thought that we should go Monday. Now after weeks of conspiring with the Edwards secret dealers, she was beginning to get nervous. Naturally, I knew nothing about that. I was just caustic, maybe nasty.

"For some reason," I said, "you two are determined to get me to go out Monday. What the hell is it?"

When I said, "For some reason," they knew they were getting into dangerous territory. Actually, I didn't suspect anything. I was just being stubborn.

"But if the weather's bad, you leave them stranded for a guest," my wife said.

"Guess there are about a thousand others who'd be glad to do it," I said.

And so Tuesday morning arrived—and it was pouring rain. I can't remember a more dismal September morn. I looked out over the terrace of my apartment into the sky full of skyscrapers in my backyard and decided there would surely be flying trouble that day.

Riding to the airport, noticing that there seemed to be no ceiling, I had to concede (to myself only) that we might not make it to Los Angeles. My wife, who must have been in great suspense after all that planning, didn't even bawl me out. She also nicely held in her suspense.

I was thinking of missing *Hollywood Squares.*

She was thinking of me missing *This Is Your Life* after so much kindly preparation by Ralph Edwards. What would he do if I blew it?

Suddenly, however, the sun was shining. We took off.

In midafternoon we arrived in sunny smoggy Los Angeles, four and a half hours before I was due in Burbank, to do what I thought was a guest appearance on *Hollywood Squares,* but was actually to walk into a trap for Ralph Edwards.

While we usually go to the Beverly Hills Hotel, we were staying on this visit at the Marty Allens' handsome home in Beverly Hills. The excitement over the weather had of course passed now, and I was so relaxed that I went into their pool for a few minutes and stretched out, getting some sun.

Now that their zero hour was approaching, now that they had come this far, my wife and Frenchy were full of suspense but dared not show any part of it. They were being very casual as though there was nothing in store for that evening beyond my taping of *Hollywood Squares.*

Frenchy was so casual, in fact, that when she served me a light snack before I started out for my program, she was barefoot.

A couple from *Hollywood Squares* picked me up in a car about 5 P.M.

"Don't be too serious," Frenchy called to me. "Have fun with the questions. If you know the answers, fine, but if you don't, just pretend you do."

I rode off to *Hollywood Squares.* As I left, I learned later, another car arrived and took my wife and Frenchy off to the Edwards studio where they were to help explain my life after I'd been trapped. They had their dress-up dresses in bags already packed. At the Edwards studio they would meet my son Earl, Jr., and his wife, Susan, who had secretly flown into L.A. from New York and who was going to rehearse my wife in some of the questions Edwards wanted to ask her. The precision of the Edwards program is extraordinary.

They're an affable crowd at *Hollywood Squares,* and since I'd been on the show before, they gave me a cordial but not overwarm welcome.

"Oh, you're back?" That sort of thing.

Had it been overwarm, I might have been suspicious. They knew I was going to be Ralph's sucker, and they probably all wondered whether I knew.

They knew because there were three other panelists waiting in the wings to take over for me, Ralph Edwards, and Marty Allen after the trap was sprung on me and I was taken over to Edwards' studio for *This Is Your Life.*

That was the way it was to be done. Marty Allen, Ralph Edwards, and I were to be special guest panelists, and at the beginning Ralph was going to hit me with the book and carry me over to his own program, and then the substitutes would run in and take over for us.

But none of this dirty double-crossing ever occurred to me as I went to my dressing room, combed my hair, and walked out to chat with Peter Marshall, Charlie Weaver, Paul Lynde, Virginia Graham, Jan Murray, and the late Wally Cox.

"You know Ralph Edwards?" somebody said.

"What are you doing here, Ralph?" I asked shaking hands with him.

"Oh, are you on the panel, too?" he said. "I hope to get a good plug for my own program."

"How's it doing?" I asked.

"Great. But you can always use a good plug like the one I hope to get tonight."

It strikes me as incredible now that upon seeing Ralph Edwards, I did not get a flash from my brain: "He is going to trap somebody here tonight. Who is it? Could it be me?"

Yet such an obvious suspicion did not occur to me. I recalled that we'd seen each other when he trapped Carol Channing in Sardi's in New York, we chatted a moment, and I started off to talk to Paul Lynde.

"See you on the panel," Ralph Edwards said.

"I think I'm sitting somewhere next to Marty Allen," I said.

The reason that I didn't get suspicious, I've concluded since, is that I was worrying about the questions I would get on the program. When you're not a regular, you don't get many questions, and therefore each question becomes important, to you anyway. So there I was, worrying about my questions, without a thought about why Ralph Edwards was there.

And so we were on the air!

Usually they tucked me upstairs somewhere, but now I was downstairs somewhere. I was on the left, Ralph Edwards was beside me, and Marty Allen was on the right.

Peter Marshall was always kind in his introductions of the guests, but I thought the things he said tonight about me were rather perfunctory. And it seemed to me that he was doing an unnecessarily long buildup of Ralph Edwards. All right, all right, Ralph Edwards was a fine man and all that, but wasn't he being a little verbose about a guy who was there to get a plug for his program?

And still it didn't hit me. Then Ralph sitting beside me started acknowledging his introduction, and I was really surprised that he, too, was making a speech.

"This guy is really hamming it up," I was thinking. "What license has he got to make a big lecture about being a guest on this program? Jeez!" My mind was wandering. I was wishing they'd get at the questions and hoping that they'd give me one I could field.

But Ralph Edwards was going on. Would the man never stop? Then I heard Ralph say, "I've done just about every one on this show."

I had a fiendish inclination to break in to his speech and say, "Hah, hah, Ralph, you've never done me!" Oh, I wanted to say it so the man would let us get on with the questions. Owing to my normal taciturnity, I didn't say it, thank God, for one second later, I heard Ralph Edwards saying:

"I'm here to surprise somebody—an Ohio farm boy who became a columnist, Earl Wilson, this is your life!"

And, sitting there on the panel, he swung around and thrust the big "This Is Your Life" book at me, dumbfounding me completely.

My mouth flew open, and I said, "You're kidding, you're kidding, aren't you?"

I still didn't believe it. I believe that I uttered an obscenity that was muffled or bleeped from the tape. People claim that my lips positively formed the sentence, intended good-humoredly, "You son of a bitch!"

When Ralph and Marty Allen grabbed me and hauled me off the panel to the laughter of the audience and the hooting of the other panelists, even then I didn't quite believe it was true that I was the sucker. Somehow it didn't immediately get through to me, and I hear that this happens to other subjects also.

Somewhat dazedly, I rode over to Ralph's studio . . . and everybody was there.

My wife . . . Frenchy . . . my son and his wife . . . executive editor Paul Sann of the New York *Post* . . . my sister, Mrs. Peter Overman, from San Diego . . . publisher Ford Owens of the Van Wert, Ohio, *Times,* who was one of the first editors ever to pay me as much as $5 for writing for his paper, and some high school classmates from Rockford, including Mrs. Janice Brands who's still a close friend.

All these fine people had made the trip to this program for me, and I was swallowing hard and hoping I could do them justice. There was not much I could do but listen.

There was a party at the Hollywood Knickerbocker later, and I discussed my surprise with Ralph Edwards.

He was not surprised that I was surprised.

The subjects are nearly always effectively tricked. Once Toots Shor went along with Ralph on the idea that they were surprising his great friend the late Quentin Reynolds. When they got to the studio, they switched, and it was Toots who was the surprisee, with Quentin leading the tricking that trapped Toots.

I did *Hollywood Squares* the next night. Paul Lynde said to me, "When Ralph Edwards said 'Ohio farm boy,' I suddenly thought to myself, 'They've been saying it's Earl, but could it be me? I'm from Ohio!'"

Marty Allen said, "I kept thinking: Could it be a trick and was it me they're really after?"

I was the only one who wasn't suspicious, and some of my fellow craftsmen went so far as to say: "Some newspaperman. Couldn't even find that out!"

I wonder how are things in Ethiopia.